WEALTH, POVERTY AND POLITICS

REVISED AND ENLARGED EDITION

THOMAS SOWELL

BASIC BOOKS
New York

Copyright © 2016 by Thomas Sowell
Published in the United States by Basic Books,
an imprint of Perseus Books, a division of PBG Publishing, LLC,
a subsidiary of Hachette Book Group, Inc.

Books published by Basic Books are available at special discounts for bulk
purchases in the United States by corporations, institutions, and other
organizations. For more information, please contact the
Special Markets Department at the Perseus Books Group,
2300 Chestnut Street, Suite 200, Philadelphia, PA 19103,
or call (800) 810-4145, ext. 5000, or e-mail
special.markets@perseusbooks.com.

Library of Congress Control Number: 2016937086

A CIP catalog record for this book is available from the Library of Congress.

ISBN: 978-0-465-09676-3 (hardcover)
ISBN: 978-0-465-09677-0 (e-book)

10 9 8 7 6 5 4 3 2

CONTENTS

PREFACE

Facts are stubborn things; and whatever may be our wishes, our inclinations, or the dictates of our passions, they cannot alter the state of facts and evidence...

John Adams

Both the first edition of this book and this revised and enlarged edition differ fundamentally from most other discussions of economic differences between nations and within nations. The many policy proposals for ending poverty, or reducing income "gaps," "disparities" or "inequities," which abound in other discussions of economic inequalities, will not be found here.

The humanitarian goals of these many policy proposals are important. But, precisely because those goals are so important, it is crucial that these proposals be based on an understanding of the actual facts about the causes and consequences of economic inequalities. This book seeks to clarify some of those causes and consequences. If this seems like a modest task, it is a task whose neglect has led to many plausible-sounding policies that turned out to be not only ineffective but painfully counterproductive and in some cases catastrophic. It is especially painful when policies to help the poor misfire and leave the poor worse off, since they have less margin with which to absorb the consequences of other people's errors.

Many who are shocked and puzzled by large economic and other disparities between individuals, groups or nations have been driven to seek some single, key factor— whether genetics, exploitation or whatever— to explain why some are so prosperous and others so poor. The implicit assumption seems to be that people would not differ so much in their outcomes without some major differentiating factor, whether caused by genes or by human interventions that favor some at the expense of others. But where there are endeavors with great disparities in outcomes, that does not necessarily imply equally great disparities among the people engaged in that endeavor.

In many endeavors, there are multiple prerequisites for success, so that people with nine-tenths of those prerequisites need not be successful nine-tenths as often, but may in fact turn out to be utter failures. Because many economic and other endeavors require multiple factors, those individuals, groups or nations with most of those factors, but not all, can be poverty-stricken and backwards for generations or even centuries— and then suddenly surge to the forefront of human achievements, after they acquire whatever remaining factor or factors might be required. Examples such as eighteenth century Scotland and nineteenth century Japan will be examined in the chapters that follow.

Conversely, a nation in the forefront of human achievements for centuries can lose just one of the prerequisites of success and fall far behind the economic and technological progress of many other nations that formerly lagged behind it. China, as we shall see, was an example of such a retrogression, which it is currently in the process of reversing again, as China's economic and technological levels are rising rapidly.

This is not a book written to celebrate, or to demonize, any particular racial or ethnic group, or any nation or civilization. It is an attempt to understand the effects of various factors that influence the economic fates of human beings in general. Rather than try to discuss such things in the abstract, hard facts about particular flesh-and-blood peoples are examined. Some of these facts may be inspiring and others appalling, but in neither case do these facts or factors provide a basis for grading or ranking whole peoples.

Even as we avoid attempting to grade or rank the intrinsic merits of whole peoples, caught in a web of surrounding geographic, historic and other circumstances they did not choose, and equipped with a culture they did not choose, inherited from ancestors they did not choose, we cannot go to the other extreme and pretend that all their achievements are equally valuable, or even approximately comparable. On the contrary, one of the things we can at least hope to accomplish is to gain some insights into which kinds of factors have promoted human achievements and progress, and which have led to suffering and ruin.

It so happens that the illustrations here involving Russians, for example, show various negative factors, but these illustrations cannot pretend to be a grading or ranking of Russians, which would require also considering many internationally recognized Russian achievements over the centuries in literature, music and other fields, as well as great courageous stands against tyrannies that have arisen in their country, such as the monumentally heroic example of Aleksandr Solzhenitsyn in our own times. But that would be a very different, and vastly larger, book. The task undertaken here is more limited, and much more within the limits of human understanding and the human life span.

One of the key implicit assumptions of our time is that many economic and social outcomes would tend to be either even or random, if left to the natural course of events, so that the strikingly uneven and non-random outcomes so often observed in the real world imply either some adverse human intervention or else some genetic differences in the people whose outcomes are so different.

Assumptions that remain implicit can escape scrutiny, even by people who build a whole structure of beliefs and imperatives on the foundation of such assumptions. With a decline of belief in genetic determinism, the implicit assumption of evenness or randomness of outcomes in the absence of human interventions has been enough to turn a search for causation into a search for blame. Declarations of blame may be in the raucous voices of street corner demagogues or in the hushed tones of learned judges in august judicial chambers. In many contexts, this has reduced explanatory options to "blaming the victim" or blaming presumed victimizers.

As a result, even among some academic scholars the search for truth has too often been narrowed to searching for blame or to "taking sides." One small but revealing sign of this "taking sides" is blocking the release of data to people on "the other side," who might use that data against "our side"— whether the particular issue is affirmative action, global warming or whatever. More generally, taking sides can all too easily mean treating social issues involving the fate of millions of fellow human beings as if they were just intramural contests among intellectuals or politicians.

Yet, in the absence of the implicit assumption of evenness or randomness, a search for causation turns up many factors that are far from even or random, including geographic, demographic, cultural and political factors with great influence on outcomes, even if none of these factors may be enough to determine outcomes by itself. This book examines such factors, not exclusively, but in addition to other factors, including some for which human beings can be blamed, such as conquests and enslavement— but with no presumption that those things which arouse our moral indignation have more causal weight than those things which we see as simply matters of fact. This does not imply moral neutrality, but simply a recognition that morality and causation are different things, and that the great importance of each is a reason to avoid confusing one with the other.

In addition to the problems of implicit assumptions which escape scrutiny precisely because they are implicit, much confusion and mischief can result from words which have so many different meanings that they can spawn mutually contradictory beliefs, imperatives and policies. "Equality," "freedom" and "justice" are among the words which have played that role, though each of these concepts can be defined more precisely in ways that bring out their enormous importance in specific contexts.

Yet that very importance has led to these words being used in very different senses for very different purposes by politicians, ideologues and others. It is in these inconsistent and even mutually contradictory senses that many concepts deserve the warning of philosopher Charles Sanders Peirce against cherishing "some vague shadow of an idea, too meaningless to be positively false."[1]

Such chameleon-like words are very convenient for politicians and ideologues, and for that very reason require special scrutiny by others who do not wish to be trapped by words. Even statistics that may be accurate in themselves can be extremely misleading, if the words that say what the statistics are measuring are incorrect. This applies to much that is said about the "top ten percent," the "top one percent," and other income categories, as we shall see, all too often.

Wealth, Poverty and Politics is not a book about language or philosophy, however. It is a book about facts. But facts do not speak for themselves. They speak for or against competing beliefs or competing theories. If the study of facts cannot always be definitive, it can at least be clarifying. And there are few issues more in need of clarification than issues involving wealth, poverty and politics.

Thomas Sowell
The Hoover Institution
Stanford University

Chapter 1

I S S U E S

*The wealth of nations depends upon
an infinite variety of causes.*

Alexander Hamilton

It may be both understandable and commendable that people living in the most prosperous nations today are often shocked by the far lower standards of living in Third World countries, or by how the less fortunate people in their own society live. But, if our purpose is to understand the causes of such things, we cannot proceed as if what we happen to be used to around us is something that can be assumed to happen so naturally or automatically that the issue can be posed as to why other nations "fail" when they do not have the same high standards of living, as suggested by the title of a well-known contemporary study.* The subtitle of another well-known contemporary study includes "the origins of inequality,"** as if economic equality is so natural, automatic or common that its *absence* is what needs explaining.

Despite how widespread such implicit assumptions may be in much that is said today, it is questionable whether such assumptions can survive even a modest survey of history. Even in a country long recognized as one of the most prosperous on earth, the United States of America, at the beginning of the twentieth century only ten

---

* Daron Acemoglu and James A. Robinson, *Why Nations Fail: The Origins of Power, Prosperity, and Poverty* (New York: Crown Business, 2012).
** Angus Deaton, *The Great Escape: Health, Wealth, and the Origins of Inequality* (Princeton: Princeton University Press, 2013).

1

percent of American homes had flush toilets and only 3 percent had electric lights.[1] There is nothing automatic about prosperity. Standards of living that we take for granted today have been achieved only within a very minute fraction of the history of the human race, and are by no means the norm among most of the people in the world today. Standards of living far below what we would consider to be poverty have been the norm for untold thousands of years. It is not the origins of poverty which need to be explained, since the human species began in poverty. What requires explaining are the things that created and sustained higher standards of living.

Equality of economic outcomes has been even rarer than prosperity. How does one explain the *origins* of something like inequality, which has been ubiquitous as far back as recorded history goes?

The ancient Greeks had geometry, philosophy, architecture and literature at a time when Britain was a land of illiterate tribal peoples, living at a primitive level. Athens had the Acropolis— whose ruins are still impressive today, thousands of years later— at a time when there was not a single building in all of Britain. The ancient Greeks had Plato, Aristotle, Euclid and other landmark figures who helped lay the intellectual foundations of Western civilization, at a time when there was not a single Briton whose name had entered the pages of history.

Scholars have estimated that there were parts of Europe in ancient times that were living at a level that Greece had transcended thousands of years earlier.[2] There were other complex civilizations in the ancient world— in Egypt, India and China, for example— at a time when peoples in various parts of Europe and elsewhere were just beginning to learn the rudiments of agriculture.[3]

Vast disparities in wealth, and in wealth-creating capacity, have been common for millennia. But while large economic inequalities have persisted throughout the recorded history of the human race, the particular *pattern* of those inequalities has changed drastically over the centuries.

While Greeks were far more advanced than Britons in ancient times, Britons were far more advanced than Greeks in the nineteenth century, when Britain led the world into the industrial age. Britain alone produced more than 40 percent of the major inventions, discoveries and innovations in the world, from the mid-eighteenth century to the first quarter of the nineteenth century.[4] Its technological preeminence was matched by its preeminence as a conquering nation. A twentieth century Italian scholar asked, "How, in the first place, did a peripheral island rise from primitive squalor to world domination?"[5] At its peak, the British Empire included one-fourth of the land area of the world and one-fourth of all the people on earth.

Such historic changes in the roles of particular peoples and nations have occurred in other places and other times. The Chinese were for centuries more advanced than any of the Europeans, including among their discoveries and inventions the compass, printing, paper, rudders and the porcelain plates that the West called "chinaware" or simply "china." Cast iron was produced in China a thousand years before it was produced in Europe.[6] A Chinese admiral made a voyage of discovery longer than Columbus' voyage, generations before Columbus' voyage, and in ships larger and more advanced than Columbus' ships.[7] But the relative positions of China and Europe also reversed over the centuries. Various other peoples, living in various other parts of the world, have had their own eras of leadership in particular fields or in advances across many specialties.

Agriculture, the most life-changing advance in the evolution of human societies, came to Europe from the Middle East in ancient times. Agriculture made cities possible, while hunter-gatherers required far too much land to provide themselves with food for them to settle permanently in such compact and densely populated communities. Moreover, for centuries cities around the world have produced a wholly disproportionate share of all the advances in the arts, sciences and technology, compared to the achievements of a similar number of people scattered in the hinterlands.[8]

Because Greeks were located nearer to the Middle East than the peoples of Northern Europe or Western Europe, agriculture spread to the Greeks earlier and they could become urbanized earlier— by centuries— and advanced in many ways far beyond those peoples elsewhere who had not yet received the many benefits made possible by urban living. The accident of geographic location could not create genius, but it made possible a setting in which many people could develop their own mental potential far beyond what was possible among bands of hunter-gatherers roaming over vast territory, preoccupied with the pressing need to search for food. Geography does not predetermine what people will choose to do, but it can limit or expand the number and kind of options available.

Geography is just one of the influences behind vast economic differences among peoples and places. Moreover, these differences are not simply differences in standards of living, important as such differences are. Different geographic settings also expand or restrict the development of people's own mental potential into what economists call their human capital by presenting different peoples with access to a wider or narrower cultural universe. These geographic settings differ not only horizontally— as between Europe, Asia and Africa, for example— but also vertically, as between peoples living on the plains versus peoples living up in the mountains. As one geographic study put it:

> Mountain regions discourage the budding of genius because they are areas of isolation, confinement, remote from the great currents of men and ideas that move along the river valleys.[9]

Many mountain regions around the world— whether the Appalachian Mountains in the United States, the Rif Mountains of Morocco, the Pindus Mountains of Greece, the Himalayas in Asia or other mountains elsewhere— show very similar patterns of poverty and backwardness. As distinguished French historian Fernand Braudel put it, "Mountain life persistently lagged behind the plain."[10] This was especially so during the millennia before the transportation and communications revolutions of the past two centuries, which belatedly brought more of the progress of the outside world to isolated mountain villages. What these technological revolutions could not bring to the mountains, however, were the previous centuries of cultural development that other people had in more favorable environments. Peoples living in mountains could try to catch up, but of course the rest of the world would not be standing still while they were doing so.

Mountains are just one geographic feature, and geography is just one influence on human development. But whether considering geography or culture, *isolation* is a recurring factor in poverty and backwardness around the world, whether that is physical isolation or cultural isolation, for any number of particular reasons that will be explored in the chapters ahead.

Whatever the reasons for economic disparities among peoples and nations, such disparities have been as common in modern times as in ancient times. In the twenty-first century, Switzerland, Denmark and Germany have each had more than three times the per capita Gross Domestic Product (GDP) of Albania, Serbia or Ukraine, and Norway has had more than five times the per capita GDP of these Eastern European countries.[11] Such economic disparities are not peculiar to Europe. In Asia as well, Japan has more than three times the per capita GDP of China and more than nine times the per capita GDP of India.[12] Sub-Saharan Africa has less than one-tenth the per capita GDP of the countries of the Euro zone.[13]

Within nations, as well as between nations, income disparities abound, whether between classes, races or other subdivisions of the human species. Reactions to these economic disparities have ranged from resignation to revolution. Because many people regard these disparities in their own country as strange, if not sinister, it is necessary to note that such internal disparities are not peculiar to any particular time or place. Therefore explanations of economic differences cannot be confined to factors peculiar to a particular time or place, such as the era of modern capitalism or the industrial revolution,[14] much less to factors that are politically convenient or emotionally satisfying.

Factors which raise morally momentous issues, such as conquest and enslavement, cannot automatically be assumed to be equally momentous as *causal* explanations of current economic disparities. They may be or they may not, in particular cases. Peoples or nations may be rich or poor because (1) they *produced* more or produced less than others or (2) they seized more of what others had produced or had what they produced seized from them. What anyone might prefer to believe at a given place or time has nothing to do with what the hard facts are.

There is no question that the Spaniards' conquests in the Western Hemisphere, for example, not only brutalized the conquered peoples and destroyed viable civilizations, but also drained vast amounts of existing wealth in gold and silver from the Western Hemisphere to Spain— 200 tons of gold and more than 18,000 tons of silver[15]— the result of the looting of existing treasures from the indigenous peoples and the forced labor of that same population in gold and silver mines. Nor was Spain unique in such behavior. But the question here, however, is: To what extent can transfers of wealth explain economic differences between peoples and nations in the world today?

Spain is today one of the poorer countries in Western Europe, surpassed economically by countries like Switzerland and Norway, which have never had such empires. The vast wealth that poured into Spain in its "golden age" could have been invested in its economy or in its people. But it was not. It was spent. Spaniards themselves spoke of gold as pouring down on Spain like rain on a roof, flowing on away immediately.[16] Nor has it been uncommon in history for a vast amount of human suffering— whether by conquered or enslaved people— to produce nothing more than a transient enrichment of a ruling elite.

The monumental moral depredations of Spain in the Western Hemisphere had very little causal effect on the long-run prosperity of the Spanish economy. As late as 1900, more than half the people in Spain were still illiterate,[17] while most blacks in the United States were literate, despite having been free for less than 50 years.[18] A century later, in 2000, the real per capita income in Spain was slightly lower than the real per capita income of black Americans.[19] Descendants of other great conquerors, such as the founders of the Ottoman Empire or the hordes of Genghis Khan, have likewise failed to appear among the most prosperous nations of the world today.

Conversely, some groups expelled from the land of their birth, and forced to leave behind the bulk of the material assets they had accumulated over a lifetime, or over generations— surely a great injustice— nevertheless rose to prosperity again after arriving destitute in their new lands. These groups range from the Jews expelled from Spain in 1492 to the Gujaratis expelled from Uganda in the 1970s, while the Cubans who voluntarily fled their homeland after Communists took over in 1958, and the Vietnamese who fled their homeland after the Communists took over there in the 1970s, had a very similar rebound from poverty to prosperity in new countries. Morally important issues are not necessarily decisive as causal factors.

Moral questions and causal questions are both important. But confusing one with the other, or imagining that they can simply be combined into one politically or ideologically attractive package, is not a very promising approach to an explanation of economic differences.

Economic disparities among nations are just part of the story of economic inequalities. Large economic disparities within nations also need to be addressed. When considering economic differences among the people of a given country, there is a tendency to see these differences as issues about what is called "income distribution."[20] But real income— that is, money income adjusted for inflation— consists of the goods and services produced in the nation. To look at this output solely from the viewpoint of those receiving money for having produced those goods and services risks needless misconceptions, and serious social problems growing out of misconceptions.

The standard of living of a nation depends more on its output per capita than on the money received as income for producing that output. Otherwise, the government could make us all rich, simply by printing more money. By focusing on what is called "income distribution," many people proceed as if the government can rearrange these flows of money, so as to have incomes become more "fair"— however defined— disregarding what the repercussions of such a policy might be on the more fundamental process of producing goods and services, on which a country's standard of living depends. But in the vision presented in the media, and often even in academia, it is as if output or wealth just exist *somehow*, and the really interesting question is how it is distributed.

Sometimes this preoccupation with the receipt of incomes, to the neglect of attention to the production of the output behind that receipt of incomes, can lead to attempts to explain the receipt of very large incomes by "greed"— as if an insatiable desire for vast amounts of money will somehow cause others to pay those vast amounts to buy one's goods or services.

Among the many possible causes of differences in income and wealth, whether among peoples, regions or nations, one of the most obvious is often ignored. As economist Henry Hazlitt put it:

> The real problem of poverty is not a problem of "distribution" but of production. The poor are poor not because something is being withheld from them but because, for whatever reason, they are not producing enough.[21]

What seemed obvious to Henry Hazlitt was not obvious to many others, who have had alternative visions, with alternative agendas based on those visions. The difference between seeing economic disparities as due to differences in the *production* of wealth and seeing those disparities as due to the *transfer* of wealth from some people to other people is fundamental. History shows that either cause of economic disparities can prevail at particular times and places.

When exploring the influences of geographic, cultural and other factors affecting the production of wealth, a sharp distinction must be made between influence and determinism. Geographic determinism would have particular favorable natural settings more or less directly create economic prosperity and social advancement, whether by providing richer natural resources or by having a climate more conducive to working, for example.

It was easy enough for critics to show that this was by no means always the case, nor necessarily true in most cases, since there are poverty-stricken countries like Venezuela and Nigeria with rich natural resources and prosperous countries like Japan and Switzerland with meager natural resources. While certain kinds of climates may have been highly correlated with more advanced societies, as an early twentieth century geographer sought to show[22] a very different ranking of nations, by the same criteria, would have existed a thousand, or two thousand years earlier, when China was much more advanced than Japan, while Japan eventually became more economically and technologically advanced than China, thousands of years later— without any evidence that the climate had changed much in either country.

The explanatory over-reach of geographic explanations led not only to a dismissal of geographic determinism, but also to a downgrading of geography as a major influence in other senses. Yet not all early twentieth century geographers were guilty of reckless over-reach. Distinguished geographer Ellen Churchill Semple wrote in 1911: "The whole science of anthropo-geography is as yet too young for hard-and-fast rules, and its subject matter too complex for formulas."[23] Despite the failure of geographic determinism, geography can *influence* economic outcomes in other, very different ways, as we shall see. Moreover, this influence is not necessarily due to particular geographic features— such as climate or natural resources— considered in isolation, but is often due to *interactions* among particular geographic features with other geographic features, as well as interactions with other, *non*-geographic factors such as cultural, demographic, political or other influences.

Even such a simple and undisputed geographic fact as places located nearer the poles having lower temperatures, on average, than places located nearer the equator, does not always hold up when interactions with other geographic factors are taken into account. Thus London, which is hundreds of miles farther north than Boston, has average winter temperatures warmer than those in Boston, and very similar to winter temperatures in some American cities hundreds of miles *south* of Boston.[24] The average December daily high temperature in London is the same as the average December daily high temperature in Washington, D.C., which is more than 850 miles farther south than London.[25] Latitude matters, but so too does the varying warmth of different ocean currents,* and the interaction of the two can create very different outcomes from what either would produce by itself.

When particular geographic factors interact with other, *non-geographic* factors as well, the outcomes can likewise be very different from what they would be if considering particular geographic, cultural, demographic or political factors in isolation. That is why *influence* is not the same as *determinism*. Since many, if not most, economic outcomes depend on more than one factor, the likelihood of all the factors coming together in such a way as to produce equal levels of prosperity and progress among peoples and nations around the world seems very remote. Radically different geographic settings are just one of the factors making equal economic outcomes unlikely.

Cultures are among the other factors that differ greatly among peoples and nations, as well as among individuals and groups within a given nation. Like critics of geographic influences, critics of cultural influences have likewise sometimes resorted to an oversimplified picture of those influences to criticize. For example, an attempt to discredit the influence of cultural factors in economic outcomes by a well-known study— *Why Nations Fail*— rejected the idea that the culture inherited from England explained why former colonies of England like the United States, Canada and Australia were prosperous:

> Canada and the United States were English colonies, but so were Sierra Leone and Nigeria. The variation in prosperity within former English colonies is as great as that in the entire world. The English legacy is not the reason for the success of North America.[26]

---

* The Gulf Stream, originating in the subtropical waters of the Gulf of Mexico, flows northeastward through the Atlantic Ocean past the British Isles, creating milder winters in Western Europe than at the same latitudes in Eastern Europe, Asia or North America.

While it is true that all these countries are former colonies of England, and thus might be described as having been influenced by the culture of England, it is also true that the people who founded Canada and the United States were Englishmen, descendants of people steeped in the culture of England as it unfolded over the centuries— while people in Sierra Leone and Nigeria were descendants of people steeped in the very different cultures of a region of sub-Saharan Africa for many centuries, and exposed superficially to the culture of England for less than one century, during which their own indigenous cultures were by no means extinguished in the historically brief period when they were part of the British Empire. French historian Fernand Braudel referred to "the late and ephemeral colonization of Black Africa by the European powers in the nineteenth century."[27] This was hardly enough to culturally turn Africans into Europeans.

Many former English colonies populated by non-English peoples continued to observe some aspect of the culture of England after becoming independent— lawyers wearing wigs in court, for example— but these outward observances of English traditions did not prevent these former colonies from having a fundamentally very different cultural legacy from that of England, and correspondingly very different economic and political experiences going forward after independence. The attempt to discredit the influence of culture, by lumping together former colonies of Englishmen and former colonies of Africans ruled by Englishmen, only shows that virtually any belief, about almost anything, can be shown to be wrong if stated in a sufficiently simple-minded way.

Believers in genetic determinism likewise seek to discredit cultural factors, which compete with their own view that it is innate, genetic differences in intelligence which explain differences in economic disparities among races, nations and civilizations. But genetic determinism, based on undeniable contemporary differences in per capita incomes among nations and corresponding differences in mental test scores,[28] cannot explain equally undeniable radical changes in which particular races, nations or civilizations have been far ahead and which have been far behind in different periods of history— the Chinese and the Europeans being just one example of historic role reversals out of many.

Nations which went from being poor and backward to reaching the front ranks of human achievement in a century— Scotland, for example, beginning in the eighteenth century and Japan, beginning in the nineteenth century— have changed faster than genetic makeup seems likely to change, and in fact with no indication of any genetic changes at all, though there are many indications of cultural changes in both these cases. Researchers may be frustrated by the fact that the origins of particular cultures are often lost in the mists of time, though their contemporary manifestations are visible. Culture also does not lend itself to quantification, as a genetic determinist has complained,[29] and therefore cannot produce statistical analyses, such as that showing a high correlation between nations' IQ scores and their per capita incomes.[30] Such correlations may lend an air of scientific precision, but so did earlier correlations between climate and prosperity by a geographic determinist.[31]

Both sets of correlations are from data taken in an extremely thin slice of time, compared to the many millennia of human history, during which various peoples' and nations' relative achievements have changed greatly. Moreover, as statisticians have often pointed out, correlation is not causation— and, as was said years ago: "It is better to be roughly right than precisely wrong."[32]

Whether considering cultural, geographic, political or other factors, *interactions* of these various factors are part of the reason why understanding influences is very different from claiming determinism.

PART I:

GEOGRAPHIC FACTORS

The world has never
been a level playing field,
and everything costs.

David S. Landes

We all know that different tribes, races, nations and civilizations originated in different parts of the world. What we may not all know is how different the geographic settings have been in which each segment of the human species evolved its own way of life, or how recently— as history is measured— these different segments have become aware of the great variety of other segments, during what has been a recent, minute fraction of the many thousands of years that humans have existed. Even after knowledge of adjacent peoples began to spread to those beyond them, to a wider range of knowledge of others, and longer distance contact with them, it has nevertheless been only since the last years of the fifteenth century A.D. that each hemisphere has learned of the existence of the other half of the planet.

The settings in which different peoples evolved their different cultures, economies and histories may seem on the surface to be roughly similar, since all inhabited continents have rivers, mountains and plains, for example. But a closer examination of geographic settings shows how radically different some of those rivers, mountains and plains are from other rivers, mountains and plains in other regions of the world— and how different have been the opportunities they have provided for economic prosperity and, even more important, human development. *Geography is not egalitarian.* The disparities in geographic settings, and in the phenomena which arise from those settings, are at least as striking as the economic disparities that many people find so surprising.

The international concentration of tornadoes, for example, is more extreme than the international concentration of wealth. Far more tornadoes occur in the middle of the United States than in any other country, or in all of the other countries of the world combined.[1] The annual hours of sunshine in Athens are nearly double the annual hours of sunshine in London, and in Alexandria the annual hours of sunshine are more than double the annual hours of sunshine in London.[2] Earthquakes are as common around the rim of the

Pacific— in both Asia and the Western Hemisphere— as they are rare around the rim of the Atlantic.[3]

Gross disparities are common in nature: There are some insects that live only one day,[4] while turtles, like people, often live more than half a century, and some live more than a century,[5] while some redwood trees have lived for thousands of years.[6]

Sometimes we may legitimately speak in generalities about such geographic regions as the tropics or mountains or deserts. But, when we consider the respective environments in which different peoples and cultures have evolved, we need to be very specific about the characteristics of those particular geographic environments. The Appalachian Mountains are not the Alps or the Andes, and the Zaire River is not economically the equal of the Mississippi or the Yangtze, even though it has more water than either, because the Zaire has so many cascades and waterfalls that it cannot provide the same long-range transportation that these other rivers provide.

Rivers can also vary greatly in their usefulness to human beings, due to interactions with climate, since rainfall and melting snow determine how much water a river receives, and sunlight determines how much water is evaporated. About 80 percent of the precipitation falling on Africa is lost to evaporation,[7] and it is common for the abundant summer sunshine around the Mediterranean to evaporate *more* water than the rainfall brings during the summer in that region of the world.[8] Another effect of climates on rivers is that freezing weather anywhere can stop a river from flowing at all, reducing its economic value to zero until it thaws. This happens often, and for months at a time, in some regions of the world— and never in some other regions, with many variations in between.

Mountains are another geographic factor with major impacts on the lives of people living in those mountains, as well as very different impacts on the lives of people living on the lands below. Mountains are the homes of roughly 10 to 12 percent of the world's population,[9] which may seem small, but the total population living in mountains around the world is much larger than the population of the United

States, and of all but two other nations, China and India. But these mountain populations have produced no such scientific, economic or technological advances as those of the United States, or even of countries with much smaller populations, such as Italy or France. The geographic constrictions of mountain life have left many mountain peoples both poor and backward. Yet despite many patterns common among mountain peoples on different continents, there are exceptions in some mountains whose particular topography offers more favorable prospects for economic and social advancement.

Islands, deserts and other geographic settings in some regions of the world likewise differ from islands, deserts and other geographic settings in other regions, and so likewise present very different prospects for human advancement. But while these and other geographic factors are important *influences*, there is no geographic *determinism*. There are not only prosperous nations with meager natural resources, and poor countries with rich natural resources, some of the poorer countries have been so richly endowed by nature as to provoke a whole literature claiming that there is a "curse of natural resources."[10]

Interactions of various geographic factors with each other, and with *non*-geographic factors, including changing levels of human knowledge over time, make outcomes very different from what they would be if determined solely by a given geographic factor or even by geographic factors as a whole.

The same geographic feature can play very different roles in different periods of history, depending on interactions between particular geographic features with changing human knowledge and technologies. Oceans, for example were once major barriers to communication and transportation, before the knowledge of science and the technology of navigation reached a level where sailors could safely cross an ocean— after which oceans vastly expanded the cultural universe of peoples in distant lands, who could now regularly communicate with each other and interact economically across vast distances. Like many other advances, this increased the economic disparities between those better able to take advantage of these advances, such as people living in port cities versus people living in the hinterlands or the mountains.

What geographic and other interactions mean more generally is that the possible combinations and permutations of factors affecting economic and social development are far more numerous than an enumeration of individual factors would suggest. In turn this means that the probability that all of these combinations and permutations would work out in such a way as to produce even approximately equal economic outcomes around the world is remote. Changing human knowledge over time, and varying knowledge from place to place at a given time, mean that there has been nothing resembling equal opportunities to become equally productive among the tribal, racial or national groups that developed for thousands of years in different parts of the world, and evolved their respective cultures in different geographic settings with different opportunities and constraints.

The very land that people stand on is not the same in different places. Highly fertile soils that scientists call Mollisols are neither evenly nor randomly distributed around the world. Such soils are found almost exclusively in the temperate zones of the Northern and Southern Hemispheres, and are scattered very unevenly there, but are virtually non-existent in the tropics or in the arctic.[11]

This was especially important during the ages when agriculture was the most prevalent and most important of human economic activities— which is to say, for many thousands of years, except for some more fortunate regions within the most recent centuries. The economies and cultures that evolved during those millennia did so within very different economic limits in different geographic settings.

The economic effects of geographic differences are both direct, affecting standards of living, and indirect, affecting the development of peoples themselves, depending on whether a given geographic setting facilitates or impedes their communication and interactions with the rest of the human race. No society has had a monopoly on the discoveries and inventions that have advanced human beings, so for a given set of people— whether a class, a race or a nation— to be in touch with what other peoples around the world are doing has been a major advantage, and to be isolated a major disadvantage.

A larger cultural universe is important not simply because of the products, technologies and knowledge that are transferred back and forth— important as these are— but also, and perhaps more important, because people seeing repeatedly how things have been done differently by others in different places can break through the normal human inertia that keeps people doing the same things in the same familiar ways, for generations or even centuries, as happens in many geographically isolated societies.

When the Spaniards conquered the isolated Canary Islands in the fifteenth century, they took over people of a Caucasian race, living much as people had lived in the Stone Age.[12] Similarly when the British discovered the isolated Australian aborigines in the eighteenth century.[13] In other isolated settings as well, whether in distant mountain villages or deep in tropical jungles, peoples have been found living as others had lived in earlier centuries or millennia.[14]

Deserts are another geographic factor isolating peoples. The largest of the world's deserts by far is the Sahara Desert, which is a negative factor for the peoples of North Africa but a devastating handicap for the peoples to the south, black Africans in tropical, sub-Saharan Africa. This incomparably vast desert— slightly larger than the 48 contiguous states of the United States[15]— has been for centuries the largest single factor isolating the peoples of sub-Saharan Africa from the rest of the world. The dearth of good harbors in tropical Africa[16] also limited contacts with overseas cultures. As Fernand Braudel put it, "external influence filtered only very slowly, drop by drop, into the vast African continent South of the Sahara."[17]

Despite geographic influences, there can be no geographic *determinism* because, where peoples are in touch with other peoples, even an unchanging geographic setting interacts with changing human knowledge and differing human cultures that have different values and aspirations, producing very different economic and other outcomes at different times and places. Most of what are natural resources for us today were not natural resources for the cave man, who had not yet acquired the knowledge of how these things could be used for his own purposes. There have been vast deposits of petroleum in the Middle East from time immemorial. But it was only after science and technology had advanced to a level which created industrial nations elsewhere that the Middle East's oil became a valuable asset, profoundly changing life in both the Middle East and the industrial countries.

Individual geographic influences cannot be considered in isolation, since their *interactions* crucially affect outcomes. The relationship between rainfall and soil is just one example of these interactions. Not only does the amount of rainfall vary greatly from one place to another, so does the ability of the soil to hold the water that rains down on it. This crucial ability to hold water is much less in the limestone soils of the Balkans than in the loess soils of northern China. Since climate and soil affect how well different crops can be grown in different places, that has virtually precluded equal prosperity in all regions of the world during the millennia when agriculture was the most important economic activity around the world, and the basis for the urban development of societies and peoples in different parts of the world.

As with many other things, the ability of the soil to hold water is a benefit only within some given range of variation. Back in Roman times, the very flat lands of northwestern Europe, located in an area of plentiful rainfall, resulted in many swamps and swampy places, which were major impediments to agriculture. Only after centuries of development of drainage techniques did much of this land get drained and become fertile.[18] Fertility is not always something inherent and immutable in a given soil. The development of drainage and irrigation techniques, or of plows that can be harnessed to horses or oxen to plow heavy soils, greatly affects their fertility. It was the *interaction* of the soil, rainfall and changing human knowledge and technology over time that made the soils of northwestern Europe *become* fertile.

Europe was by no means the only place where the fertility of the soil changed over the centuries or millennia. Roughly two thousand years ago, the Loess Plateau in north-central China was an important agricultural region, supplying grain, lumber and livestock to the country as a whole. But today travelers in that same region can go for miles "without seeing more than a few scattered trees or some small, widely dispersed shrubs" in "a seemingly endless panorama of barren yellow hills, gullies, and ravines."[19] Such effects of deforestation have not been limited to China. Similar consequences of accelerated erosion after massive removals of trees have continued into the modern era in many other lands around the world, though the United States has had a net gain of forest land.[20] Such processes were common around the ancient Mediterranean lands[21] and have continued there into more recent centuries:

> Although incomplete and imperfect, the evidence for massive deforestation and soil erosion in the mountains of the Mediterranean between 1800 and 1950 is compelling. The timing and pace differed from place to place. The costs of landscape change varied according to local geology and economies. In places it worked to the advantage of lowland and coastal peoples, although more often it did not. Nowhere did it work to the advantage of mountain people. Soil, fuel, timber, even pasture grew more scarce or distant, and hard lives became harder.[22]

More generally, what all this means is that a given region of the world cannot be automatically assumed to be the same geographic environment over very long spans of time.

Because of the effect of sunlight in evaporating water, even places with the same annual rainfall, and the same absorption of that rain water by the land, can nevertheless have very different amounts of water in the soil to nourish crops. Because lands bordering the Mediterranean Sea receive so much more sunlight than in England, the evaporation of water is greater in the Mediterranean. As a noted geographic treatise pointed out: "An annual rainfall of 23 inches, which maintains the fresh vegetation of southern England with its mild moist summers, is inadequate at Jerusalem or Palermo for garden or vineyard, which then require irrigation to maintain growth."[23]

Not only have equal economic outcomes been rare to non-existent, the particular patterns of inequality in one era have often differed greatly from the particular patterns of inequality in another era. The vast superiority of ancient Greek society to that in ancient Britain reflected Greece's geographic advantage in being located near the Middle East, where agriculture developed in ancient times and spread into nearby southeastern Europe, centuries before it spread to all of Europe and beyond. Without agriculture, it is difficult, if not virtually impossible, to have densely populated urban societies, as distinguished from societies of wandering hunters and gatherers, or shepherds— all of whom require vast amounts of land on which to roam, in order to get enough food to sustain a given number of people.

To the present day, cities have remained the sources of much, if not most, of the advancements in civilization. Far more of these advances, and especially of landmark scientific and technological achievements, have occurred among the populations of cities than among a similar number of people living in other settings.[24]

Peoples without the geographic prerequisites for cities have long lagged behind peoples in settings that facilitated urbanization. Cities developed relatively late in the existence of the human species over scores of millennia— and so did most of the advances in what we today recognize as civilization. By making cities possible, agriculture made possible the great industrial, medical and other advances that flourished in urban environments.

Modern advances in transportation and communications can break through the isolation of many peoples, just as other technological advances can mitigate, or sometimes even eliminate, the current handicaps of various other kinds of geographic impediments to economic and social development. But what these historically recent advances cannot do is retroactively erase the effects of thousands of years of different cultural development that took place where there were serious geographic restrictions, as compared to places inhabited by peoples with millennia of experiences enriched by wider exposures to the achievements and ideas of other peoples around the world.

How we define the concept of environment is crucial. One distinguished geographer's definition was, "Environment is the total physical setting amid which people live."[25] But another geographer said, "environment means something more than local geographic conditions," and called for a "larger conception of environment,"[26] pointing out how the past experiences of forebears "have left their mark on the present race in the form of inherited aptitudes and traditional customs acquired in those remote ancestral habitats."[27] Whether an environment is described geographically or socioeconomically, the most fundamental distinction is between defining environment as what is *around* a given people or defining environment to include also what is *within* those people.

We cannot understand what is happening today without understanding past conditions that shaped both the physical and mental worlds of people living today, which are a legacy of the past, for better or worse. As one cultural historian put it, "men are not blank tablets upon which the environment inscribes a culture which can readily be erased to make way for a new inscription."[28] As another noted historian put it: "We do not live in the past, but the past in us."[29]

Chapter 2

WATERWAYS

*The fundamental reality of any civilization
must be its geographical cradle.*

Fernand Braudel

Waterways play many vital roles— as sources of drinking water for humans and animals, as sources of food such as fish and other aquatic creatures, as sources of irrigation for crops and as arteries of transportation for cargoes and people. In all these roles, waterways differ from one another, in ways that can make them more valuable or less valuable to humans. Put differently, they contribute to economic and other inequalities.

Waterways obviously differ in kind— from rivers to lakes, harbors and seas— and each kind in turn has its own internal differences, in navigability for example. Rivers flowing gently across wide level plains, as in Western Europe, are far more usable, for both commerce and the transportation of people, than rivers plunging down from great heights through rapids, cascades and waterfalls, as in much of sub-Saharan Africa. Indeed, the same stream of water can differ at different places along its route to the sea:

> A torrent that issues from its source in the mountains is not the river which reaches the sea. On its long journey from highland to lowland it receives now the milky waters of a glacier-fed stream, now a muddy tributary from agricultural lands, now the clear waters from a limestone plateau, while all the time its racing current bears a burden of soil torn from its own banks.[1]

Although the most indispensable role of waterways has been that of providing drinking water for humans and animals, without which they cannot survive, one of the most important roles of waterways for economic development has been their role as transportation arteries. The crucial fact about the role of waterways as transportation arteries for cargo and people is the vast difference in cost between land transport and water transport, which was even greater in the millennia before the advent of motorized land transport, less than two centuries ago.

In 1830, for example, it cost more than 30 dollars to move a ton of cargo 300 miles on land but only 10 dollars to ship it 3,000 miles across the Atlantic Ocean.[2] One consequence of such huge transportation cost differentials was that people living in the city of Tiflis in the Caucasus, 340 miles from the Baku oil fields by land, bought oil imported from the United States, 8,000 miles away by water.[3] Similarly in mid-nineteenth century America, before the transcontinental railroad was built, San Francisco could be reached both faster and cheaper across the Pacific Ocean from a port in China than it could be reached over land from the banks of the Missouri River.[4]

Given the vast amounts of food, fuel and other necessities of life that must be transported into cities, and the vast amounts of a city's output that must be transported out to sell, there is no mystery why so many cities around the world have been located on navigable waterways, especially before the transportation revolutions within the past 200 years that produced motorized transport on land. These cities include some located at the terminus of great rivers that empty into the open seas (New York, London, Shanghai, Rotterdam), some located beside huge lakes or inland seas (Geneva, Chicago, Odessa, Detroit) and some located on great harbors emptying into the open seas (Sydney, San Francisco, Tokyo, Rio de Janeiro). Great inland cities like Paris have often been served by multiple rivers. As French historian Fernand Braudel put it: "Without the Seine, Oise, Marne and Yonne, Paris would have had nothing to eat, drink or keep warm by."[5]

Even after the creation of motorized land transport, the differential cost of land transport and water transport did not disappear. In twentieth century Africa, the estimated cost of shipping an automobile by land from Djibouti to Addis Ababa (342 miles) was the same as the cost of shipping it by water from Detroit to Djibouti (7,386 miles).[6]

Looked at differently, where there has been a lack of navigable waterways, accessibility to the outside world has often been severely limited, shrinking the cultural universe drastically— and with it shrinking the opportunities of peoples to connect with other peoples and cultures far away. In some cases, a dearth of waterways and the presence of geographic barriers meant that people living only 10 or 20 miles from each other often had very little contact. This was especially so in places lacking horses, camels or other beasts of burden, during the many centuries before modern transportation and communications developed.

One of the remarkable facts about the continent of Africa is that, although Africa is more than twice the size of Europe, the African coastline is shorter than the European coastline.[7] This is possible only because the European coastline twists and turns, creating many harbors where ships can dock, sheltered from the rough waters of the open seas. Moreover, the coastline of Europe is increased by the many islands and peninsulas that make up more than one-third of that continent's total land area.

By contrast, the African coastline is smooth, with few substantial indentations, few good natural harbors, and fewer islands and peninsulas— which make up only 2 percent of Africa's land area. The ratio of Europe's coastline to its area is four times that of Africa.[8] Moreover, the coastal waters around sub-Saharan Africa are often too shallow for ocean-going ships to dock.[9] In such places, large ocean-going ships must anchor offshore, and have their cargoes unloaded onto smaller vessels that can operate in shallow waters. But this time-consuming process, and the greater amount of labor and equipment required, has been more costly— often prohibitively costly. For centuries, seaborne commerce between Europe and Asia sailed around Africa, and seldom stopped.

Even in those few places where large ships can enter Africa on deep rivers, tropical Africa's coasts have narrow coastal plains that often end abruptly against escarpments.[10] One important consequence of this shape of the land is that, even in places where ships can enter the continent on African rivers, they can seldom get very far inland before being confronted with cascades and waterfalls. For the same reason, boats coming from the vast interior of the continent are seldom able to continue out to the open sea, as boats— and even large ships— can do in various places on the Eurasian landmass or in parts of the Western Hemisphere.

By contrast with Africa, China has had a huge network of navigable waterways, described as "unique in the world," formed by the Yangtze River and its tributaries, as well as an indented coastline, full of harbors.[11] What was also unique were the centuries during which China was the most advanced nation in the world, on into what were called the Middle Ages in Europe.

RIVERS

It was not just in harbors, but also in rivers, that China's waterways have contrasted with those in Africa. Africa is a relatively dry continent, with many of its rivers not deep enough to carry the large ships with heavy loads that are carried on the rivers of China, Western Europe or the United States. Even the Nile was unable to carry the largest ships in the days of the Roman Empire,[12] much less the even larger ships of today.

The *average* depth of a river is not as important as its *minimum* depth on the route of a given vessel's journey, which is what determines how far a boat or ship of a given size and weight can go. The same word— "navigable"— may be applied to many very different waterways, but with very different meanings in specific, concrete circumstances. Although we may legitimately speak, in general terms, of the conditions of waterways or other geographic features of a particular country, it is always with the caveat that those conditions do not necessarily prevail uniformly throughout that country or throughout particular regions within that country. Geographic equality seldom prevails at either a local, national or international level.

Even in North America, with its many long and large rivers, there have been in the dryer western plains of the United States waterways "navigable only in rare, short periods, and only for canoes or very shallow flatboats."[13] In the eastern United States as well, the Mohawk River, which was navigable for birch canoes that carried furs for commerce in the early days of the country, turned out to be inadequate for carrying the heavy guns used in the War of 1812.[14] The Cumberland River was beset with reefs, sand bars and snags, and sometimes had long interruptions of navigation, due to changing depths of its water in different seasons.[15]

Man-made interventions on American rivers, as on rivers in other parts of the world, have taken various forms, including building locks and dams or dredging, but these interventions have been by no means equally provided, because some communities, regions or states have been more able to pay for such things and some circumstances justified the expense while others did not. In the mountains of Kentucky, even in the early twentieth century, there were few bridges for vehicles, though foot bridges were more common.[16] Therefore it was often necessary for travelers to ford rivers,[17] something that Thomas Jefferson had complained about in Virginia, more than a century earlier.[18]

Waterways, like other geographic features were, in millennia past, more or less facts of life to which human beings had to adjust as best they could. Yet, with the growth and development of human knowledge, many of these geographic features could be altered to varying degrees and at varying costs— which were not necessarily equal in all parts of the world, nor equally affordable to peoples with widely varying wealth.

In some places canals could be built, connecting rivers, and in other places— such as Suez or Panama— canals could be built connecting seas or oceans, with major economic and military impacts. Harbors could be dredged. On land, mountains could be drilled into, to provide tunnels for railroads and, later, automobile traffic. And of course eventually airplanes could soar over the most formidable mountain barriers that had dominated the economic and social life of peoples since time immemorial. But, like the geographic features they affected, these man-made factors were seldom even approximately equal in their consequences for different peoples in different parts of the world. Nor were the inequalities of one era the same in their consequences in later eras, as growing human knowledge led to new changes, which inevitably affected the existing natural and man-made environments.

Although Canada's St. Lawrence Seaway is navigable by ocean-going ships, all the way into the Great Lakes, that does not mean that it is navigable by *all* ocean-going ships. When major, man-made improvements were made to the St. Lawrence Seaway in 1959, and for many years thereafter, it was navigable by most of the ocean-going ships in the world at that time but, as ocean-going ships grew larger and larger over the years, today it is no longer navigable by most ocean-going ships, though it is still navigable by many.[19]

The Zambezi River in Africa has highly variable depths from place to place and from rainy season to dry season. In some times and places the Zambezi is barely navigable by boats requiring just 3 feet of water, though at other times and places the water level is 20 feet deeper.[20] Some rivers in Angola can support boats requiring no more than 8 feet of water.[21] During the dry season, even a major West African river like the Niger can carry barges weighing no more than 12 tons in some places.[22] But, in China, ships weighing 10,000 tons have been able to go hundreds of miles up the Yangtze River, and smaller vessels another thousand miles beyond that.[23]

Rivers in tropical Africa are seldom continuously navigable for any such distances, even when these rivers have ample water. In terms of the contours of the land, sub-Saharan Africa has been characterized as "cursed with a mesa form which converts nearly every river into a plunging torrent on its approach to the sea."[24] Most of tropical Africa is more than 1,000 feet above sea level and much of it is more than 2,000 feet above sea level. Thus the Zaire River begins at an altitude of 4,700 feet and so must come down that vertical distance before flowing out into the Atlantic Ocean, creating rapids, cascades and waterfalls on the way. Although the Zaire has more water than the Mississippi, the Yangtze or the Rhine, that does not make it the equivalent of these and other major commercial waterways elsewhere, because the Zaire's many plunges interrupt its navigability, though it may carry extensive inland traffic for various distances on level stretches. This pattern is common among the rivers of sub-Saharan Africa.

Another pattern that is common in parts of tropical Africa is a wide fluctuation in the water level of its rivers, due to highly varying rainfall amounts in different seasons. Unlike Western Europe, where the rain falls more or less evenly throughout the year,[25] except on the Iberian peninsula, rainfall patterns in parts of sub-Saharan Africa include long periods when there is no rain at all, followed by torrential downpours during rainy seasons.[26] Because of such seasonal rainfall patterns, the Niger River's chief tributary, the Benue River, has in places been navigable only two months of the year. This has led to a hectic shipping pattern:

> If they let the craft stay up the Benue a day too long, the vessels will be stuck on sandbanks for ten months! Yet if through caution or misinformation they withdraw the fleet too soon, much valuable merchandise is left behind and can only be evacuated by land at much greater cost. . . The first boats to go in are the commercial canoes, then follow the larger craft, and finally, when there is sufficient water at Lokoja, the largest power-craft and their barges sail up the river as fast as possible. Towards the end of the short season, the large craft have to come out first because of the fall in the level of the water; the medium-sized craft follow, and the small canoes may continue for some time evacuating small quantities of produce.[27]

Statistics on how many miles of navigable rivers there are in Africa, or anywhere else, can be very misleading when these are not *continuous* miles that a vessel of a given size and weight can travel before encountering water too shallow to support it, or encountering cascades or waterfalls that stop all vessels. Sometimes a canoe can go ashore and be emptied of its cargo before reaching a waterfall, with both the canoe and the cargo then being carried around the waterfall, so that the reloaded canoe can proceed on another level stretch of water. However, this is both a time-consuming— and therefore expensive— process, and one that limits the size of both the canoe and its cargo. The net result is that only a cargo that is very valuable in proportion to its size and weight is economically feasible to transport for any considerable distance in such places.

By contrast, in other parts of the world, where rivers are continuously navigable for hundreds of miles across level plains, as in various places on the Eurasian landmass or in the Western Hemisphere, bulky cargoes with relatively low value in proportion to their size and weight— wood, coal or wheat, for example— may be economically viable to transport long distances by water.

Even within the same continent, Western Europe's rivers have been very different from the rivers in Eastern Europe or Southern Europe, as well as radically different from the rivers of sub-Saharan Africa. A broad coastal plain, where the land nowhere reaches 1,000 feet above sea level, means that Western Europe has had slow-flowing rivers, which were especially valuable in the long ages before power boats could readily go against the flow of swift-moving currents. Western Europe's rivers often lead out into the open seas, providing access to seaports around the world. But most rivers in Eastern Europe and Southern Europe are quite different, in ways that affect both economic activity and the size of the cultural universe available to the peoples living in the regions through which these rivers flow. Because the warming effect of the Gulf Stream on the climate of Western Europe is lessened the farther east one goes, the waterways of Eastern Europe are frozen more often, and longer, in the winters.

Even when the rivers of Eastern Europe are flowing, often they are flowing into lakes or inland seas, rather than out into the open seas that connect with the rest of the world. The waters of the Danube, the Don and the Dnieper flow into the Black Sea, for example, and the waters of the Volga flow into the Caspian Sea. But most of the water in Russian rivers flows into the Arctic Ocean, which is hardly as accessible to the rest of the world as are the Atlantic or the Pacific. These differences in waterways are among the many reasons why Eastern Europe has lagged economically behind Western Europe for centuries.

The rivers of Southern Europe have contributed even less to the economic development of that region. Partly this is because there are fewer major rivers in this region than in Western Europe or Eastern Europe, and partly because the climate in the lands of Mediterranean Europe is one with torrential downpours in winter and very little rain in the summer, when rivers almost dry up[28] under the relentless Mediterranean sunshine in that season. Similar climates in other parts of the world, such as coastal California or southwestern Australia, have been referred to as "Mediterranean" climates.[29] However, even within the Mediterranean region itself, there are variations— with the summer being drier in the eastern Mediterranean, and drier in the southern lands than in the north.

Going from west to east, the rainfall in Rome from June through September is less than the rainfall in Barcelona during those same summer months, and the summer rainfall in Athens is less than one-third the summer rainfall in Rome.[30] Going from south to north, the summer rainfall patterns in the Mediterranean become more similar to those in the rest of Europe, and that obviously affects the rivers. Milan, in northern Italy, has more than twice as much rainfall from June through September as Rome[31]— a fact that is even more consequential for the agricultural countrysides near these cities than in the cities themselves. Given these rainfall patterns, the Po River in northern Italy is exceptional among rivers in the Mediterranean region in having an ample volume of water throughout the year, since the Po receives water from both summer rains and from melting snows in the mountains. It is also exceptional in terms of the length over which it is navigable, as it flows gently through level plains.[32]

Not surprisingly, the Po River valley, extending from Turin to Venice, has long been one of the more prosperous regions in Italy. Northern Italy in general has for centuries been more prosperous, more educated and more technologically advanced than southern Italy. Most of the great, internationally recognized cultural achievements of Italy— from Galileo, Michelangelo and Leonardo da Vinci, for example— have come from the north. Location, as well as waterways, contributed to the advantages of northern Italy, since the northern part of the country has been in closer touch with the cultures of Western Europe.

Topography also affects rivers. In Spain, even some rivers that flow year round have had only "short navigable stretches," due to the contours of the land.[33] In the mountainous Balkans, rivers often flow too steeply to be navigable, except for some that are locally navigable by small boats and rafts.[34] In places where rainfall is very scarce, dew can become a significant source of water, as in the Mediterranean highlands.[35] Exceptionally sharp differences in temperature between day and night mean that the water absorption capacity of the air during the day can greatly exceed its capacity at night, causing heavy dew to form overnight, providing enough water to enable some vegetation to survive where it could not survive if it were solely dependent on rainfall.

In the Western Hemisphere, the United States has had huge geographic advantages in its waterways, as in other ways— "a well-indented coastline punctuated by superb harbors," in the words of distinguished economic historian David S. Landes,[36] and large rivers, of which the Mississippi is the most prominent. In contrast to the plunging waters of many African rivers— more than thirty cataracts, falling a total of nearly a thousand feet in a distance of 150 miles on the Zaire River[37]— the river bed of the Mississippi slopes downward at a rate of about 4 inches per mile.[38]

Although the Nile is the longest river in the world, the Mississippi pours many times as much water into the Gulf of Mexico as the Nile pours into the Mediterranean.[39] Water is what rivers are all about, and the Mississippi has far more of it than the Nile, even though the smaller amount of water in the Nile is stretched out over a longer distance.

Africa's rivers may be more picturesque, with their cascades and waterfalls, but they provide nothing like the transportation and communications scope of rivers that flow more gently across level plains in various other parts of the world.

In contrast to the limited ability of the Nile to carry large ships, the Hudson River and the harbors at San Francisco and San Diego are all deep enough for aircraft carriers to dock right up against the land. The Great Lakes are a vast system of connected waterways, of which Lake Michigan alone is larger than the nation of Israel, and Lake Superior is larger than Lake Michigan. These lakes are also deep enough to handle many ocean-going ships, as they have been since 1959, when man-made improvements to the St. Lawrence River allowed such ships to extend their journeys from the Atlantic Ocean all the way to Chicago and other midwestern cities located on the shores of the Great Lakes.

As a noted geographer put it:

> No other equally large area of the earth is so generously equipped by nature for the production and distribution of the articles of commerce as southern Canada and that part of the United States lying east of the Rocky Mountains. The simple build of the North American continent, consisting of a broad central trough between distant mountain ranges, and characterized by gentle slopes to the Atlantic Ocean and the Gulf of Mexico, has generated great and small rivers with easy going currents, that everywhere opened up the land to explorer, trader and settler.[40]

Neither with waterways nor with other geographic features can a given geographic setting be assumed to be unchanging over time, nor changing equally in different parts of the world at the same time. Many rivers, for example, were for millennia one-way arteries of traffic. In many places during that long era, logs for example could be floated down a river, even when the only way for people in charge of those logs to return home was by land.

Sometimes, however, when people traveled by boat and where a prevailing wind blew in the opposite direction from the river's current, it could be possible to raise sails and take the boat back upriver, if the current was not too strong. Similarly when the river flow was sufficiently slow and gentle that one could row a small vessel against the current. In Kentucky, for example, flatboats equipped with oars could go upstream on some rivers.[41] But a more common situation, for many centuries, was one in which there was only one-way traffic on rivers. In ancient times, traffic on the Tigris and Euphrates rivers was exclusively downstream,[42] as was to continue to be the case for many other rivers around the world for many centuries thereafter.

The decisive change for river traffic came with the invention of the steamboat in the early nineteenth century. It changed the Mississippi River from a one-way artery of traffic to one in which, after 1815, a steamboat could go back upriver from New Orleans to Louisville.[43] This technological advance essentially doubled the transportation capacity of many rivers, by allowing personal travel and commercial traffic in both directions. But this revolutionary development came first to places that could afford steamboats and where the value of river traffic justified the expense. As late as the early twentieth century, most of the traffic on rivers in eastern Siberia was still downstream traffic.[44] Here, as in many other contexts, outcomes depended upon *interactions* of various geographic and non-geographic factors— in this case, river currents, wind currents, changing technology and differing economic circumstances.

These interactions of waterways with other geographic and non-geographic factors were also important, even aside from technological changes. South America's Amazon River, for example, is by far the most physically impressive of the world's rivers, in terms of its volume of water— by far the largest of any river in the world— its navigability* and its length, which is nearly the same as that of the Nile, while the Amazon empties dozens of times more water into the Atlantic than the Nile empties into the Mediterranean. The Amazon also empties several times as much water as the Mississippi empties

---

* "If the Amazon flowed through North America, an ocean freighter could sail from Boston to Denver," Jonathan B. Tourtellot, "The Amazon: Sailing A Jungle Sea," *Great Rivers of the World*, edited by Margaret Sedeen (Washington: National Geographic Society, 1984), p. 299.

into the Gulf of Mexico.[45] Indeed, one-fifth of all the fresh water that enters all the oceans of the world comes from the Amazon River as it empties into the Atlantic.[46]

Nevertheless, the region through which the Amazon flows, with its jungles and poor quality soils, has had no such economic development as would make the Amazon at all comparable, as an artery of commerce, to the Mississippi, the Rhine, the Danube or other rivers that, put together, do not have as much water as the Amazon has. Conversely, a very modest-sized river like the Thames, less than 10 percent as long as the Amazon, has played a major economic role as the shipping outlet for a region of thriving industry and commerce in England.* In Russia, the Yenisey and the Lena rivers each have more than twice as much water as the Volga, but it is the Volga that carries more shipping tonnage than any other Russian river, because it flows through regions containing most of the nation's population and most of its industry and farmland.

What these differences between waterways, and within a given kind of waterway, mean for their human consequences is that the possible combinations and permutations of the factors that make them useful to humans are so numerous as to make equal values of waterways to human beings located in different parts of the world very unlikely, quite aside from the fact that waterways are more available in some regions of the world than in others, and are virtually non-existent in deserts.

OCEANS

Rivers are not the only waterways whose economic roles can change over time, with changing human knowledge and technology. Oceans are perhaps an even more striking example. Oceans were once

---

* As far back as the eighteenth century, the Thames was said to have a "forest of masts," with more than 13,000 ships there in 1798. Fernand Braudel, *The Structures of Everyday Life: The Limits of the Possible*, translated by Siân Reynolds (New York: Harper & Row, 1981), p. 548.

major barriers to communication and transportation. The Mediterranean Sea was for centuries a more inviting waterway than the Atlantic Ocean, for travel and trade, before there were later advances in knowledge, because of the greater ease of navigating around the Mediterranean:

> The long summer of cloudless days and starry nights, of steady winds and fogless atmosphere provided a favorable season for sailing, when the strong diurnal breezes favored the out-going and home-coming ships, and the countless promontories and mountainous islands, visible in the lucid air, furnished points to steer by before the invention of the compass.[47]

Although sailors could not see all the way across from one shore of the Mediterranean to the opposite shore, they could usually see from one island to another, and thus could make their way past many familiar landmarks on their way from shore to shore. But this was obviously not a process that could be used in most places to get across the vast Atlantic Ocean or the even more vast Pacific.

Oceans changed from being transportation barriers to being transportation avenues only after humans learned how to navigate where there were no landmarks to follow, but simply water to be seen in all directions, all the way out to the horizon. Navigation on the oceans became possible only after science, mathematics and technology had developed sufficiently to overcome this fundamental handicap. This was done first through various ways of navigating by using the position of the sun in the sky during the day and the positions of stars at night, providing as it were, "landmarks" in the sky by which to determine directions on the ocean. Eventually, and decisively, navigating the oceans became far less complicated and more reliable with the development of the magnetic compass, which could be used more readily, and even when clouds obscured the sky. This ability to cross oceans, not simply as a few bold explorers did but as a routine matter of commerce, vastly expanded the cultural universe of peoples in distant lands.

Seaports around the gentle waters of the Mediterranean were for centuries more busy than seaports on the more turbulent Atlantic coast of Europe,* before Europeans discovered the Western Hemisphere. This discovery changed the main direction of Europe's international trade, however.

Because different kinds of ships were required to handle the very different rough waters of the Atlantic, the leading commercial and naval powers of the Mediterranean were eclipsed by the leading commercial and naval powers of the Atlantic, who had ships better adapted for the new transatlantic commerce. Where Italians had been leaders in such things as ship design and navigation when Europe's international trade centered in the Mediterranean, the Portuguese, the Dutch and the Flemish took the lead in seafaring technologies and skills when Europe's international trade faced the very different challenges of crossing the Atlantic.[48] The seas had not changed, but their economic and other significance had, with the advance of knowledge and technology.

Despite the crucial importance of agriculture as a source of a dependable food supply for a concentrated and sedentary population, fishing has been another source, and one available in regions where agriculture has not been sufficiently productive to sustain human life by itself. This has been especially important in very cold climates, but communities of fishermen have also been common in the Amazon jungles of South America and in sub-Saharan Africa.[49] In tropical lands where the fertility of the soil is often poor, agriculture may not be sufficiently productive to support the population by itself. Fishing villages represent a step upward from a hunter-gathering society toward a sedentary life, even though these villages may not represent the same degree of population concentration as cities fed by agriculture.

In other climates as well, fishing can be a major economic activity. It was said at one time that Amsterdam was built on herring,[50] and

---

* It is understandable that Europeans, used to the Atlantic Ocean, named the new ocean they discovered in the Western Hemisphere the Pacific Ocean. The Atlantic was far from being pacific.

fishing has also been important to the economy of Japan, among other places. Commercial fishing can supply a market reaching far beyond the local area, as in New England, where a name like Cape Cod provides a clue to its history.[51] In some of the lands around the Mediterranean, the soil yields so little in agriculture that many peoples have had to piece together a livelihood by combining the products of both the land and the sea, as others in that region have by combining agriculture with shepherding animals.[52]

Fishing opportunities, however, are no more evenly distributed around the world than other opportunities. A long continental shelf reaching out into the Atlantic Ocean creates an underwater environment where fish and other marine life can flourish.[53] But the land is shaped differently around and under the Mediterranean Sea, which lacks the shallow shelves of the Atlantic.[54]

As a result, while there has long been fishing in the Mediterranean, it has not been comparable to the rich fishing regions that attract commercial fishing vessels great distances out into the Atlantic waters near Newfoundland and Iceland, or into the North Sea fishing regions.[55] The net result in the early twentieth century was that an Italian fisherman's earnings averaged about one-fourth the earnings of a French fisherman and one-eighth those of an English fisherman. Nor was this due to differences in the price of fish, which was no higher in France or England than in Italy.[56] It was just that far more fish could be caught in a given time in the North Atlantic than in the Mediterranean.

Chapter 3

LANDS

> *The land on which we live has always shaped us. It has shaped the wars, the power, politics, and social development of the peoples that now inhabit nearly every part of the earth.*

> *Tim Marshall*

Land has many aspects. The simple fact of the shape of the land determines how water will flow. This has major implications for the creation and characteristics of streams, rivers and lakes, which in turn have implications for the fate of people living in a given region.

Another way the lay of the land can have important effects is by whether it spreads from east to west, like the great Eurasian landmass, or from north to south like the continents in the Western Hemisphere, stretching from North America to South America. The east-west orientation of the Eurasian landmass means that most of Europe and Asia are at similar latitudes in the temperate zone, so that similar crops and natural vegetation can grow in both places, and similar animals have natural habitats in both places. This in turn means that agricultural knowledge, as well as knowledge of animal husbandry and knowledge of both vegetation and meats, can transfer between Europe and Asia. In short, this ability to interchange knowledge that is applicable in both places means that, for centuries, Europe and Asia have had a larger cultural universe than places separated by similar distances in a north-south direction, which create greater climatic differences. Knowledge of agriculture in Canada may not be as applicable in tropical Panama.

In the Western Hemisphere, the peoples of the temperate zones of North America and South America can have similar climates, but they have been separated from each other by the vast area of the tropics between them— and the tropics have very different flora and fauna from that in either of the two temperate zones. Therefore knowledge would not pass as readily and continuously through the tropics, where such knowledge would have more limited applicability, if any applicability at all, given the different flora and fauna in the tropics. In short, north-south distances entail climate differences, more so than east-west distances do, making knowledge transfers less likely and less applicable, because knowledge of nature is less applicable in different climate settings.

Spaghetti could originate in China and yet become a favorite food in Italy, because its natural ingredients can be grown in both places, as a result of the east-west spread of the Eurasian landmass, which produces somewhat similar climates. But the Iroquois of North America were not likely to learn of any food used by the Incas of South America, not only because of transportation limitations in pre-Columbus times, but also because the north-south spread of the lands in the Western Hemisphere means that there is a large tropical region between the temperate zones of North America and South America.

Unlike spaghetti— which went thousands of miles from China to Italy— the potato, which grew in the Andean highlands of South America, never reached even the Mexican highlands in North America.[1]

Differences in the physical and chemical composition of the soil are another factor that is crucial for agriculture, as is climate. Special features of the land, such as mountains, deserts and rift valleys, can fragment a population and isolate the fragments from each other. The mountains of the Balkans have helped make "Balkanization" a synonym for the fragmentation of peoples. But this was not unique to the Balkans. As was said of the Scottish highlands in times past:

Upon the development of Scotland the great hills exercised a controlling influence. By their very existence they tended to produce two different kinds of society in the country, one of the hills and the other of the plains; and by impeding communication, they tended to break the population up into self-sufficing units, great or small.[2]

It was much the same story in the mountainous regions of Kentucky, of which a geographic study noted, "the Kentucky Mountains, in common with many other areas of similar topography, have served to isolate the inhabitants and retard development and progress"[3]— this "continued isolation" resulting in "a distinct group of people possessing the speech, customs and manner of life of a bygone day,"[4] with "the agricultural economy of colonial days, almost unmodified."[5] Such fragmentation and isolation of the fragments have also been the fate of much of sub-Saharan Africa where rift valleys, limited navigability of waterways and a dearth of animals for transportation led to results similar to those of mountain communities in many countries around the world.

Mountains

Mountains affect both the lives of people living in those mountains and the lives of people living on the land below— and it affects these two sets of people very differently.

As already noted, about 10 to 12 percent of the world's population lives in mountains, about half in Asia, and about 90 percent live no higher in the mountains than 2,500 meters or 8,200 feet. Population density in mountains is usually relatively low.[6] Certain common patterns have appeared in the lives of people living in various mountain communities around the world. The most common of these patterns have included poverty, isolation and backwardness.[7] As a noted geographer put it, human advancement "slackens its pace" in the foothills and "comes to a halt" in the mountains.[8] Nor is it hard to see why. The very nature of mountains long denied many of the people living there many of the things that promote prosperity and connection with the general progress in the rest of the world.

Fertile land can seldom be found in abundance on mountainsides, where soil is readily washed away by rain, though some of this soil collects down in mountain valleys, while the rest of it is washed away down into the lowlands. People tend to gather in the flat areas of land in the valleys amid the mountains, since this is where crops can be grown most readily. But mountain valleys are often isolated from each other, with "the population being as scattered as the flat lands they occupy," as was said of mountain communities in the Southern mountains in the United States,[9] though the same pattern has existed elsewhere around the world. The amount of usable soil in each valley tends to limit the number of people who can be fed there, so that small villages have often been the norm. These villages may be isolated from each other, as well as being isolated from the outside world beyond the mountains, even when these villages are not far from each other as the crow flies, but are not very accessible across rugged mountain terrain.[10]

These historic handicaps were especially severe during the millennia before modern transportation and communications technologies were created. However, these technological advances have almost invariably originated outside the mountains themselves, and the extent to which they have been adopted in the mountains has varied with local geographic and economic conditions. Moreover, even where these advances have been adopted extensively, that cannot readily undo all the cultural effects of previous centuries of cultural isolation.

Navigable waterways are often lacking in mountain terrain, where the steepness of the land can make for rapids, cascades and waterfalls. So this means of transportation and communication has often been denied to people in many mountain communities, such as in the Balkans.[11] Land transportation is also likely to be difficult, especially where the rugged terrain is inhospitable to wheeled vehicles, so that travel on foot is the only feasible way to get around in many places. Historian Fernand Braudel pointed out that "in 1881 the wheeled vehicle was still unknown in Morocco."[12] As another scholar said of people in the Rif Mountains of Morocco, "The Rifians are great walkers and they have to be."[13] In other mountain communities around the world, transport options have been so limited that travelers and tourists have had to employ mountain people as human carriers, substituting for pack animals or wheeled vehicles to carry their equipment and supplies.[14]

Although such patterns may be general, there are also exceptions. Parts of the Himalayas and the Andes, for example, have fertile and well-watered land.[15] The Alps have numerous mountain passes[16] broad enough to accommodate much commercial traffic and, in ancient times, Hannibal's army with its elephants. The Alps include passes whose elevation is low enough to avoid being closed by heavy snowfall most of the year, as the passes at higher elevations in the Caucasus Mountains are.[17] In short, various mountains around the world have different geographic layouts that determine to what extent there are level valleys with large enough areas of fertile land to support sizeable communities and mountain passes numerous enough, level enough and broad enough to provide ready access to other mountain communities and to the outside world.[18] Even mountains in the same country and the same region can differ in ways that make a difference to human beings. For example:

> The mouth of the Shenandoah Valley was broad, and it and the larger Valley of Virginia of which it was a part contained gently rolling, fertile land that contrasted sharply with the rough topography of the Alleghenies.[19]

In the millennia before modern transport arose, the particular topography of particular mountains affected the size of the communities that could be fed in particular valleys, their accessibility to each other and to the outside world— which is to say, the size of their cultural universe— their opportunities for commercial relations and the degree to which these communities were militarily defensible. Even after the rise of such modern developments as railroads, automobiles and electricity, the geographic layout of particular mountains determined to what extent these and other modern features were economically viable in those mountains.

Building roads— not to mention water systems, sewage systems, or electric power systems— can be extremely expensive where isolated and thinly populated mountain communities mean very high costs per capita for creating such infrastructure. In Italy's Apennines Mountains, as late as 1860, there were no roads whatever in 91 out of 123 Lucanian villages.[20] Even in the twentieth century, there were places in the Pindus Mountains of Greece more accessible to mules and to people on foot than to wheeled vehicles, and one village acquired electricity as late as 1956.[21]

In 1922, the Kentucky mountains had "a trifle over one mile of road for every square mile of area," and the quality of these roads was as meager as their quantity. These mountain roads were narrow and "in places hardly wide enough for a single wagon, and in few places wide enough so that two vehicles can pass."[22] The roadbeds were not capable of supporting vehicles with loads, except during the summer and early fall, when they were likely to be drier, but even then the difficulties were such that it was not uncommon to see two teams of horses pulling a small wagon[23]— obviously a very expensive form of transportation. Railroads brought more knowledge of the outside world into the Kentucky mountains, but railroad construction did not begin until 1856 and nearly all the railroads existing there in the 1920s had been constructed since 1885.[24]

A study of mountains around the Mediterranean in the late twentieth century noted, "Only a few roads penetrate the Pindus today, and most of those are of recent construction. The great majority are unpaved."[25] Substandard infrastructure remains common in mountains around the world, even in the twenty-first century.[26] However, modern transportation and communications technologies are making inroads into the isolation of many mountain communities,[27] though with great differences among different regions of the world. Switzerland, for example, has more than 20 times as many miles of roads per capita as in Ethiopia.[28] Differences in man-made infrastructure are as great as other environmental inequalities.

Distinguished American scholar Edward C. Banfield's classic account of an Italian mountain village where he lived in 1954 and 1955, *The Moral Basis of a Backward Society*, noted that there was only one telephone in town. In this community of 3,400 people, to which he gave the pseudonym "Montegrano," there were five automobiles for hire but no one owned a private car. Most of the people were poor farmers and laborers. One-third of the men and two-thirds of the women could neither read nor write, and some peasants had never gone beyond the next village, just four miles away.[29] When they traveled, they seldom used a cart, much less a car, to transport the belongings they took with them. As Professor Banfield noted:

> When the farm people of Montegrano travel, it is on foot leading a donkey to the sides of which large baskets are fixed . . .The range of travel, then, is limited to nearby towns. Many people have never travelled beyond these neighboring towns and some women have never left Montegrano.[30]

It was not only infrastructure and technological advances that reached mountain communities belatedly. So did cultures prevailing on the lands below. Although Islam has for centuries been the prevailing religion and culture of the Middle East and North Africa, a different religion and culture continued to prevail in the neighboring mountainous regions of Armenia and Abyssinia. And though people in the Rif Mountains of Morocco eventually adopted Islam, this was centuries after the people on the land below had already become Muslims.[31]

In language as well, Gaelic continued to survive in the Scottish highlands, long after the Scottish lowlanders were speaking English, and the Vlach language survived in the Pindus Mountains of Greece, centuries after people on the land below were speaking Greek.[32] Language differences have added to the sources of isolation and fragmentation of mountain people, especially when the languages or dialects spoken in the mountains were unknown in most of the outside world. Moreover, where mountain villages were isolated from each other for centuries, they often developed languages that were different from each other, as well as different from the language of the world beyond the mountains. A multiplicity of languages and dialects has been common in isolated mountain communities around the world.[33] Of the more than one thousand languages in New Guinea, more than 70 percent originate in the mountainous regions, which cover only one-third of the island.[34]

Law and order are yet another part of the social infrastructure that has been harder to establish and maintain in many mountain regions. Even mountainous regions nominally under the control of a nation or empire have not always or in all places been effectively under such control. Examples include the mountains of Montenegro under the Ottoman Empire, the Rif Mountains under Moroccan sultans, and the uplands of India under the Mughal rulers.[35] Both the Scottish highlands and the highlands of colonial Ceylon remained independent for many years after their respective nearby lowlands were conquered and incorporated into another cultural universe. In centuries past, it was common in many mountain regions around the world for highland peoples to raid and plunder peoples living in the lowlands.[36]

Poverty in many mountain communities long exceeded anything known as poverty in most other settings. As Professor Banfield said of the Italian mountain village in which he lived in 1954 and 1955:

> Most people in Montegrano are desperately poor. Many have nothing to eat but bread, and not enough of that. Even the well-to-do are poor by American standards. Such a town cannot support a newspaper or the kinds of activity which a newspaper would report.[37]

Such poverty and desolation in the mountains were not unique to this Italian village. A twentieth century Oxford scholar in Greece said, "I have met a Greek, brought up in this century in a mountain village, who had never seen an olive (or a fish or an orange) until he was 12 years old."[38] An early twentieth century geographer likewise referred to the "barren highlands of Central Asia where nature dispensed her gifts with a miserly hand."[39]

In various mountains in countries around the Mediterranean, it was long common in the past for peasants to rarely eat meat, and even cheese was largely confined to a few fortunately situated villages.[40] Bread was the common food for peasants in all three meals of the day. In earlier times, women made clothes for their families, and mountain people with animals brought those animals inside in cold weather. As a well-known history of Western civilization put it: "Only the most prosperous had wooden dividers separating the human from animal quarters."[41] A traveler through the Bulgarian mountains in 1574 said that he preferred to sleep outdoors, under a tree, rather than in mountain peasants' huts, where animals and people lived together "in such filth that we could not bear the stench."[42]

These broad generalizations do not, of course, apply to every mountain community everywhere. But the general pattern has been all too common in all too many mountains and highlands around the world, especially in centuries past. Even in prosperous America, in the early twentieth century, a sample of farmers in North Carolina showed that those located on the coastal plains earned three to five times the income of farmers in mountain counties.[43] A twentieth century study of a village in the Himalayas found that 20 percent of newborn babies died before they were a year old.[44]

An Appalachian county in Kentucky was called a "pauper county" in the 1890s, and was still in 2010 one of the poorest counties in the United States.[45] The life expectancy of men in that county in 2010 was less than the life expectancy of men in Fairfax County, Virginia, *by more than a decade*. Women's life expectancy in that same Kentucky county had actually declined slightly over a period of 20 years. The population of this county, incidentally, was 98.5 percent white.[46] Both foreigners and blacks have long been rare in the Kentucky mountains.[47]

Even in the early twenty-first century, most of the mountain peoples in the world still practiced subsistence agriculture,[48] as distinguished from raising crops to sell. The negative economic consequences of mountain life have been accompanied by broader negative human consequences. In many mountain communities around the world, especially in times past, the struggle for existence caused children to have to work at an early age, curtailing their education,[49] and thus isolating them from even second-hand knowledge of the wider world beyond the mountains. Illiteracy was common among people in mountain communities around the Mediterranean, on into the nineteenth and early twentieth centuries.[50]

Few people from the lands below moved up into the mountains to live, especially in times past, and those mountain people who moved down to the lower elevations encountered a different world, one which they often found difficult to adjust to, and a world in which they were often not accepted, except perhaps as sojourners for seasonal work. This pattern persisted for centuries. In medieval times, the Adriatic port of Dubrovnik "traded and maintained good relations with the people of the hinterland"— the Vlach shepherds from the mountains— but they "were not allowed to winter on the territory of the Republic nor to remain within the city."[51] Such negative reactions to mountain people in the lowlands were not peculiar to medieval Europe. Similar negative reactions to mountain peoples were common in nineteenth century France and Morocco, and in modern Nepal, India and Thailand.[52]

There was much the same resistant attitude toward mountain folk in twentieth century America, as shown by press reactions when large numbers of mountain people moved into urban communities. Such resistance was exemplified by the reactions of the *Chicago Tribune*, as noted in a scholarly study of migrations from the mountains:

> The "hillbillies" were described as a degenerate population "with the lowest standard of living and moral code (if any). . . and the most savage tactics when drunk, which is most of the time." National publicity followed, with stories in *Time, Look,* and *Harper's,* the latter under the headline "The Hillbillies Invade Chicago." That article's subhead gave away the racial slippage: "The city's toughest integration problem has nothing to do with Negroes. . . . It involves a small army of white Protestant, Early American migrants from the South— who are usually proud, poor, primitive, and fast with a knife." The message was clear and intentional: these people are "worse than the colored."[53]

The parallels with blacks go beyond the responses of others. A 1932 study of white children from small communities in the Blue Ridge Mountains found that these white children not only had IQ scores slightly lower than the national average of 85 for black children, but also had IQ *patterns* similar to those of black children— such as doing their worst on abstract questions and having IQs closer to the U.S. national average of 100 in their early years, with a widening gap as they grew older.[54] Such similarities were especially striking because blacks were far more rare in Southern mountain communities than in the South as a whole,[55] making genetic interactions far less likely.

Another study of mountain children, in East Tennessee schools in 1930, found similar patterns. These children had a median IQ of 82 on one test and 78 on another. On the test where they did better, their median IQ was 95 at age six and declined to 74 by age sixteen.* A decade later, after social, economic and educational improvements in these East Tennessee communities, the median IQ in the same schools rose to 87.6.[56]

Among those young people from the mountains in the early twentieth century who sought higher education at Berea College in Kentucky, only half returned to their home communities, usually those students who failed to graduate.[57] The tendency of more able or ambitious young people to move down from the mountains, while the less able or less ambitious remained, or moved farther up into the mountains, was expressed by a local paradoxical saying that "cream sinks and the skim milk rises" in the mountains.[58] In Spain, there was a similar Catalan saying— "always go down, never go up."[59] This pattern of an out-migration of young people from mountain communities has been a common pattern, whether in the United States or in India or in other places around the world.[60]

---

* IQ scores compare test performances *relative* to other people of the same age in the national population, since IQ stands for "intelligence quotient"— and the quotient is the mental age divided by the chronological age, and then multiplied by 100.

There have also long been seasonal migrants from the mountains, whether the mountainous regions of Spain, Nepal, South America or South Africa,[61] among other places. Remittances from both seasonal and longer term migrants have played a significant role in supporting families remaining behind in the mountains.[62] Longer lasting migrations have included many mountain men who became mercenaries in various armies[63]— the Swiss and Scottish highlanders in Europe and the Gurkhas and Montagnards in Asia, for example. Rifs from North Africa were part of General Francisco Franco's army that won the Spanish civil war in the 1930s. It has been estimated that, at a given time, there were 50,000 to 60,000 Swiss men serving in foreign armies and, over the centuries, perhaps as many as a million Swiss soldiers died fighting in other countries' wars.[64]

Mountain people have also been prominent among people who migrated permanently to other countries. An early twentieth century study noted: "Even the stay-at-home French lose emigrants from their mountain districts."[65] Most of the overseas emigrants from Southern Europe to Australia in the era before the Second World War came from geographically less fortunate areas such as the rugged hills or mountains, the steep coastlines or islands of the region, rather than from the urban areas or the plains.[66] Emigrants from such isolated areas were often illiterate and spoke local dialects, rather than the official language of their respective countries,[67] much less English. They often also lacked many of the job skills possessed by people in the more fortunate regions of the countries from which they came. It was much the same story among emigrants from Scotland to Australia and the United States in the nineteenth century. In both countries, the Scottish lowlanders spoke English and had many skills, while the Scottish highlanders spoke Gaelic and had few skills.[68]

Despite the largely negative influence of mountains on those who live in them, mountains are often a boon to those on the lands below. As moisture-laden winds collide with mountain slopes, these winds are forced upward, where the colder air reduces their moisture-carrying capacity, leading to rain and snow. It is not uncommon for rainfall on the windward side of a mountain range to be several times as much as the rainfall on the other side, in what is called the "rain shadow" of the mountains. The nature and size of the crops that can be grown on the windward and leeward lands varies accordingly.

As rain water flows down the mountainsides, creating trickles of water that join together to form streams, these streams in turn join together to create rivers. Thus water collected from a wide area of mountain territory is concentrated and delivered as rivers with many uses to people on the land below. All the major rivers of the world have their beginnings in mountains.[69] Where precipitation in the mountains takes the form of snow, the water is not released all at once, but much of it is released later and gradually, when this snow melts during warmer weather. This means that rivers are not solely dependent on the immediate rainfall to keep flowing, because melting snows from the mountains provide water to sustain the rivers during dry periods.

As with many other things, we can see its importance by seeing what happens in its absence. Although tropical Africa has Mount Kilimanjaro, it has no major mountain ranges comparable to those found in Asia, Europe or the Western Hemisphere. Therefore, during the dry season in sub-Saharan Africa, rivers and streams shrink drastically, as a result of a dearth of melting snows in the mountains to keep these waterways supplied with water. Meanwhile, the Sierra Nevada Mountains in Spain and the Taurus Mountains in Turkey each supply the water that makes a flourishing irrigated agriculture possible in the lowlands,[70] where rainfall alone would not be sufficient during the Mediterranean summer, when the sun evaporates more water than falls as rain in that region of the world.[71]

The falling waters in steep terrain that keep many mountain and highland streams and rivers from being navigable also provide opportunities to build hydroelectric dams. But the electricity generated has been another boon primarily for people living on the lands below, who live more closely together, reducing the cost per capita of transmission lines. Even before the development of electricity generation, the power of falling water was used directly to drive machinery in various factories, much as the power of moving air currents has been used in Holland to turn windmills that drive machinery there.

Not only have all major rivers originated in the mountains, so have many of the world's food staples, such as potatoes, wheat, corn, and beans.[72] In more recent times, after both law and order and modern technology have spread into various mountain regions, some have become popular tourist resorts for people from the lowlands. Many handicraft products, made by mountain people with time on their hands in winters, have long been popular both with tourists and with people elsewhere who import many hand-made articles from mountain communities in Switzerland, Tibet and many other places around the world.[73] These popular handicrafts have been another reason why mountains have been a boon to those who do not live in them. For the mountain people themselves, the sale of these handicrafts supplement what have often been meager incomes.

Natural Resources

Natural resources are often thought of as things originating in the earth, such as petroleum, gold, iron ore and the like. But, although these things are natural, they are not resources unless and until human beings learn how to find them, process them and use them. Since human knowledge is an integral part of what is or is not a natural resource, the total amount of natural resources is neither fixed nor necessarily declining over time, even after they are being used on a massive scale.

In some purely physical sense, there is of course a declining amount of all those things currently known and used as natural resources. But the fact that there is a physical limit to everything on the planet has often led to the *non-sequitur* that we are nearing that limit. This fallacy has been at the heart of innumerable alarms over the years that we were "running out" of oil, coal, iron ore or some other natural resource— claims that have proved false, time and again, going back at least as far as the nineteenth century. Yet the world's known reserves of petroleum at the end of the twentieth century were more than ten times what they were in the middle of that century,[74] when there were dire warnings that we were running out. A best-selling book in 1960 warned that the domestic oil reserves of the United States were enough to last only 13 years. But, at the end of those 13 years, those reserves were larger than they had been when this dire warning was issued.[75]

Nevertheless, in the next decade the President of the United States issued an even more dire warning:

> Above all, Carter stressed, the energy shortage was permanent. It was, he told the country, "the greatest challenge our country will face during our lifetimes," and "it is likely to get progressively worse." The president spoke with certainty. "We could," he told the country, "use up all the proven reserves of oil in the entire world by the end of the next decade."[76]

Despite such alarming statements, there was such a glut of oil on the world markets in the early twenty-first century that its price plunged to a fraction of what it had been in earlier years. Petroleum reserves indeed have a finite limit, but in no way does this indicate that we are nearing that limit. It has been much the same story with the known reserves of other natural resources. The world's known reserves of iron ore also increased severalfold during the twentieth century, even while the processing of iron ore into steel was increasing dramatically around the world. For economic reasons, it seldom pays to find more than a minute fraction of a natural resource at any given time, even if there is enough in the ground to last for centuries or millennia.[77] Iron ore has been used for thousands of years to make iron and steel, and yet it is doubtful if the amount of iron ore reserves known in ancient times was even ten percent of the iron ore reserves known today.

The "known reserves" of a natural resource depend on the cost of knowing. Oil exploration, for example, is extremely expensive. Just one initial exploration at a site in the Gulf of Mexico cost $80 million and another $120 million for exploratory drilling, to see if there were indications of enough oil at that location to make it financially advisable to proceed further.[78] At such costs, it may not pay to have more than enough specifically verified oil reserves in the world to last more than a dozen or so years, but that does not mean that we are going to run out of oil at the end of that time. As existing reserves are used, it pays to continuously keep finding more. Even an existing pool of oil is not likely to be completely drained, and much— if not most— of the oil may be left in the ground, or under the sea, as the costs of extraction rise after the most easily extracted oil is taken out. Meanwhile, new uses are being discovered for other materials found in nature that *become* natural resources with the growth of human knowledge.

It was a world-changing event in the history of the human race when the land that people stood on became a natural resource they could use to deliberately generate food through agriculture. This happened at some time within the last 5 percent of the existence of human beings, when people moved beyond gathering their food from the spontaneous produce of nature, or fishing, hunting or herding animals, and began to plant the foods they wanted. Virtually everything that we today recognize as civilization dates from the beginning of agriculture, and with it the beginning of cities.

Exactly how agriculture itself arose is one of those questions whose answer is lost in the mists of ancient times. But how agriculture came to the Western world is known. It came from the Middle East, thousands of years ago, and apparently originated somewhere between the Tigris and Euphrates rivers, in what is today Iraq. This was a geographic setting in which agriculture could not only exist but thrive, at the existing level of knowledge at that time.

The first farmers seem unlikely to have known from the outset that crops use up nutrients in the soil, which have to be replenished if the soil is to continue to yield crops of the same magnitude. But, in the land between the Tigris and Euphrates rivers, farmers did not have to know that. Annual floods washed new nutrients down over the lands, as annual floods would also do on the lands along the Nile, where another great ancient civilization arose, in Egypt.

In Asia, agriculture began on the Indian subcontinent, in the valley of the Indus River, in what is today Pakistan. Despite the arid climate, melting snows from the vast Himalayan mountain range provided the annual flooding which fertilized the land for agriculture. Here too, some of the earliest cities were built, and some of the earliest civilizations developed. It was much the same story as regards the beginning of agriculture and civilization in China:

> Agriculture seems to have started in North China in the region of the great bend of the Yellow River. . . In fact, this center of early Chinese civilization resembled in some ways the homes of other ancient civilizations— the flood plains of the Nile in Egypt, the Tigris and Euphrates in Mesopotamia, and the Indus in modern Pakistan.[79]

Elsewhere, the earliest farmers had to move on after farming a given land a number of years and seeing the successive annual crops grow successively smaller as the nutrients in the soil were used up, threatening the food supply on which human survival depended. Some peoples simply waited for nature to restore the fertility of the soil after they moved on, seeking other lands to farm. Some other peoples burned the vegetation before moving on, thereby providing the new nutrients that would gradually restore fertility as these nutrients were absorbed into the soil. But between the Tigris and Euphrates rivers, and along the Nile, annual floods could keep the land fertile, long before human beings figured out what was happening. But most other places in the world did not have this windfall gain.

Here again, we see a profound geographic inequality affecting the fates of different peoples very differently. That inequality of fertility in the land has continued on to the present day. As already noted, the most fertile soils are neither evenly nor randomly distributed around the world. A huge swath of these unusually fertile soils spreads across the vast Eurasian landmass, beginning in Eastern Europe and extending into northeastern China. In the Western Hemisphere, there is a large concentration of these rich soils in the American upper midwestern and plains states, extending into parts of Canada. In the temperate zone of South America there is another concentration of such soils across Uruguay and in east-central Argentina.[80] But the natural processes by which such soils are generated or sustained tend not to be found in the tropics or the arctic, where soil fertility is seldom comparable.

The crop yields per acre in tropical Africa are a fraction of the crop yields in China or the United States.[81] Among the many deficiencies of the soil in sub-Saharan Africa is that the topsoil is often shallow, allowing little space for plant roots to reach deep into the ground for nutrients and water.[82] Moreover, the dryness of much of Africa inhibits the use of fertilizers to supply the nutrients missing in the soil. Fertilizers used without adequate water can inhibit, rather than enhance, the growth of crops.

Even in places where there are wetlands in central Africa, these wetlands have not been as often cultivated as wetlands in temperate climates, because dangerous tropical diseases like malaria and river blindness flourish in tropical Africa's wetlands.[83] Here again, it is the *interactions* of different geographic features— in this case, climate, soil and disease— that can make outcomes very different from what they might seem from a comparison of individual gross features such as wetlands that occur in different regions of the world.

Differences in rainfall patterns also interact with the soil to make agriculture more successful in some regions of the world than in others. The rainfall pattern in parts of sub-Saharan Africa— long dry spells followed by torrential downpours— is a major handicap for growing crops, in part because the land is baked hard and dry before the massive downpours wash away part of the topsoil. This whole pattern contrasts sharply with the interaction of climate and soil in Western Europe or in the eastern and central parts of the United States, where rain falls more of less evenly throughout the year, largely on fertile soils.

Chapter 4

CLIMATE, ANIMALS AND DISEASES

Important as waterways and lands can be as influences on economic disparities among individuals, groups and nations, there are other geographic factors which can be just as important in particular circumstances. These factors include climate, animals and diseases.

CLIMATE

We may speak of climate in general terms as if it were a fixed factor, though much hard evidence shows that it is not. Fossils of marine creatures in the Sahara Desert clearly indicate that it was not always a desert. So do the fossils of tropical or sub-tropical animals and plants in places too cold for them to live today. Everything depends on the time frame of our discussions, and how much variation in climatic conditions took place in what is for us a long period of time, though centuries or even millennia are small fractions of the time that the earth has existed.

Temperatures

Waters are among the many influences on climate. Large bodies of water modify temperature on adjacent lands. Because water does not heat up as fast as land, coastal regions tend not to be as hot in the summer as the center of a continent. Conversely, because water does not lose its warmth as fast as land, coastal regions tend not to be as cold in winter as the center of a continent. Although we may think of oceans as vast inert bodies of water, whose visible movements consist of waves and tides, there are in fact large currents moving within oceans, some of these currents being thousands of feet deep, dozens of miles wide and extending thousands of miles across the ocean's surface. These currents can transfer heat from one region of the world to another, modifying climates.

As noted in Chapter 1, the interaction between latitude and the varying warmth of ocean currents makes winter temperatures in London warmer than in some American cities hundreds of miles farther south than London. An even more striking result of these interactions is that Russia's northern port of Murmansk, located inside the Arctic circle, is free of ice in winter,[1] due to the residual warmth of the Gulf Stream, thousands of miles from its source, while Russian rivers hundreds of miles farther south than Murmansk are frozen solid.

Just as the Gulf Stream transfers heat from the warmer southern latitudes to colder northern latitudes, so other ocean currents bring vast amounts of cold water down from northern latitudes to the west coast of the United States, giving San Francisco the lowest average summer temperature of any major city in the country.* Daily high temperatures in San Francisco in July and August average in the 60s or low 70s. Meanwhile, in an inland California city like Sacramento, less than a hundred miles northeast of San Francisco, daily high temperatures average in the 90s during those same months, with summer temperatures of 100 or more on particular days not being unusual.

Other interactions involving other geographic factors elsewhere likewise make temperatures very different from what they would be if determined by latitude alone or by any other factor alone. The highest temperature ever recorded in Asia, Africa, North America or South America has in each case been recorded *outside* the tropics.[2] Even though the heat of sunlight is greatest in the tropics, nevertheless the

---

* Humorist Mark Twain said that the coldest winter he could remember was a summer in San Francisco.

sun shines more hours per day during the summer in the temperate zones than in the tropics,[3] allowing a longer daily buildup of heat and fewer hours in which to cool down overnight. At the equator, the sun shines about 12 hours a day the year round but, during the summer, the sun shines longer hours in the temperate zone— reaching 15 hours a day in June at a latitude 40 degrees north or south of the equator, roughly the latitude of Philadelphia, Madrid or Beijing.[4]

The longer hours of sunshine during the summer in the temperate zones offset to a greater or lesser extent the reduced heat of the sunlight in places outside the tropics. Most record temperatures on the inhabited continents have been set somewhere between the 30th and 40th degrees of latitude. Here, as in other contexts, it is the *interactions* of factors that produce particular outcomes. Thus European cities in the temperate zone, such as Athens and Seville, have had higher record temperatures than many cities located in the tropics, including some cities located virtually on the Equator, such as Singapore.[5]

Clouds are another interaction with sunlight, because clouds intercept sunlight and reflect it back into outer space. At any given time, clouds cover approximately half of the earth.[6] But the many cloudless summer days along the Mediterranean coast of Africa have produced higher temperature records in cities located in the temperate zone there— such as Algiers, Tripoli and Alexandria— than in many cities in tropical Africa, even cities very near the equator, such as Nairobi or Libreville.[7] In the Western Hemisphere as well, cities with cloudless desert skies, such as Las Vegas and Phoenix, have reached temperatures higher than cities in the tropics, which often have many clouds and much rain. The highest temperature recorded anywhere in the world has been recorded in Death Valley, California, a desert in the temperate zone.[8]

Altitude also affects heat, so that the highest temperatures recorded in the city of Cuzco, located in tropical latitudes in the Andes Mountains of South America, are much lower than the highest summer temperatures recorded in cities like New York or Paris in the temperate zone.[9] Mountain ranges can also affect the climate of nearby regions, by blocking either warm or cold air from reaching those regions. In southeastern Europe, for example, winter temperatures in Sarajevo may be nearly 50 degrees colder than temperatures on the Dalmatian coast, little more than a hundred miles away, because the Balkan mountains block off the warm air of the Mediterranean from reaching far inland.[10] In Asia, the Himalayas block warm air from reaching Central Asia and block cold air from reaching India.[11]

While we may legitimately speak in general terms about tropical climates, temperate climates or arctic climates, more specific questions about climates in specific places, such as particular cities or their agricultural hinterlands, must take into account the *interactions* of particular combinations of factors peculiar to those particular locations. More generally, interactions within and between geographic, cultural, political and other factors are necessary to understand many economic and social outcomes.

Climate Zones

Economic historian David S. Landes was one of many scholars to note a striking pattern of economic disparities between broad climate zones: "On a map of the world in terms of product or income per head, the rich countries lie in the temperate zones, particularly in the northern hemisphere; the poor countries, in the tropics and semitropics."[12]

Some have tried to explain the fact that countries in the temperate zones are generally far more advanced economically and technologically than countries in the tropics by the energy-draining heat in the tropics, or by the many debilitating diseases that flourish there,[13] diseases whose microorganisms are killed off by cold winters in the temperate zones. We have also seen that the most fertile soils are virtually non-existent in the tropics. Nevertheless, many people from outside the tropics have gone to live in the tropics and prospered there, often far more so than the indigenous populations. The overseas Chinese minority in Southeast Asia and the Lebanese minority in West Africa are striking examples.

The British who settled in Australia are perhaps an even more striking example, since they became the majority population of the country, and about 40 percent of Australia is in the tropics. People of Japanese, Chinese and European ancestry are a major part of the population of tropical Hawaii, and are prospering there.

Ordinarily, it might be expected that people indigenous to a given geographic setting would be better able to make the most of that setting's opportunities, and better able to cope with its disadvantages, than people from a very different setting. Yet the evidence seems to suggest the opposite. But, as we have seen in other contexts, geographic environments affect people not only by the direct economic benefits or handicaps of those environments but also by the extent to which those environments facilitate or restrict the development of the knowledge, skills, experiences, habits and values— the human capital— of the people themselves.

If the geographic settings of the temperate zones foster the kind of human capital that promotes prosperity in whatever climate people live, then it is not so surprising that peoples transplanted from temperate to tropical climates prosper more in those climates than the peoples indigenous to the tropics. As a noted geographer observed, particular cultures may thrive "in regions where they could never have originated."[14]

What cultural consequences of life in the temperate zones might be valuable in other regions that were unlikely to produce such cultures? The most striking social difference between living in the temperate zones and living in the tropics is not simply the difference in average temperatures, despite another noted geographer who once built a whole theory of economic and social progress on temperature differences in different parts of the world that affected people's abilities to work.[15] Instead, the life-threatening challenge that dominated the temperate zones of the world for millennia was growing enough food during the limited spring and summer months to last through the cold winter months. It was an inescapable necessity, for sheer physical survival, to begin planting and harvesting at whatever times of the year were dictated by the local climate. In many places, that meant beginning the arduous tasks of preparing the land for planting early in the spring but, in parts of the Mediterranean lands with their peculiar rainfall patterns, it meant planting in the autumn.[16]

In any event, this meant that peoples living where seasons changed drastically during the course of a year had to develop a sense of urgency about time, and the self-discipline to fit one's life and efforts to seasonal requirements. Such qualities were not nearly so necessary in places where food could be grown year round, in addition to the availability of much food spontaneously supplied by nature in many tropical lands, or simply requiring hunting on land or fishing in waters.

The other inescapable necessity of the temperate zones, where seasons are so different from each other, was systematically saving food to store for the winter. This required not only the self-discipline of saving, but also the conversion of perishable foods like milk and fruit into storable foods like cheese and jam. Here again, this was not such a pressing necessity in the tropics. Moreover, tropical foods such as bananas and pineapples were not as storable in a hot climate as wheat or potatoes were in a cooler climate.

Modern economic and technological conditions have so freed us from having to consider such things that it is easy to overlook how imperative those things were for physical survival in the millennia before humans were able to transport vast amounts of food over great distances or to store many kinds of food in commercially dried, canned or frozen forms.

Much has been made of the fact that the Incas created a larger and more sophisticated civilization in the tropics than most societies indigenous to places elsewhere in the tropics during the same era. However, the climate in which the Inca civilization developed was not typical of either the tropics or the temperate zones. Not only does the highest daily high temperature for any month average 73 degrees in Cuzco, the former capital of the Incas, the lowest daily high temperature for any month averages 68 degrees. But despite very little change in daily high temperatures during the course of a year, there is a rainy season and a dry season, with variations in precipitation ranging from a monthly average of 5 millimeters in June to 163 millimeters in January. In addition, overnight temperatures range down to freezing levels in winter.[17]

Because of differences in rainfall and differences in overnight temperatures in different times of the year, there were different seasons when particular crops could be grown, even though agriculture in general was a year-round activity for the Inca population in the Andes Mountains. In short, while the climate in which the Inca Empire arose was not typical of either the tropics or the temperate zone, its highly variable growing seasons for different crops[18] did present the same inescapable challenge faced by inhabitants of the temperate zones— namely, the self-discipline of conforming one's life and work to a time frame dictated by the seasonally changing conditions in agriculture.

With the high altitudes of the Andes Mountains offsetting the heat of tropical sunshine, the empire of the Incas was tropical only in the narrowest sense of being located between particular lines on a map.

ANIMALS

The geography of the vast temperate zones of the Western Hemisphere is in many ways much like the geography of Western Europe, especially in the generous supply of rivers and harbors in the United States, as well as its vast level plains and, in New England, rich fishing regions offshore in the Atlantic. Yet the indigenous cultures of the Western Hemisphere were very different from the cultures of

Western Europe. This might seem to suggest that geography has had little or no influence on the economic fate of peoples. However, we need to recall yet again that it is the *interactions* of various geographic factors that are crucial to economic and social outcomes. What was totally lacking throughout the Western Hemisphere when the Europeans arrived were horses, oxen or other heavy-duty draft animals and heavy-duty beasts of burden.

Transportation

During the millennia before motorized vehicles were invented, horses were crucial to everything from transportation to farming to warfare in Europe. Among the many things which originated in Asia that became part of European culture— including paper, bells, printing, gunpowder, the compass, rudders, spaghetti, chess, playing cards and so-called Arabic numerals*— most traveled across the Eurasian landmass primarily by horse.[19] Without horses or oxen, the evolution of the whole European economy and society would have had to be radically different. And, without such heavy-duty draft animals or heavy-duty beasts of burden as existed in Europe (or the camels, water buffalo or elephants elsewhere), the economies and societies throughout the Western Hemisphere were in fact radically different from those in Europe.

The economic and cultural repercussions reached further: Nowhere in the Western Hemisphere were there wheeled vehicles. Although the wheel has often been regarded as a landmark in the technological progress of the human race, for most of the history of the human species the value of wheeled vehicles depended greatly on the availability of draft animals to pull such vehicles. In the Western Hemisphere, the Mayans created wheels but they were used on children's toys.[20] The issue is not the intellectual capacity to invent

---

* These numerals, which eventually replaced Roman numerals, were called "Arabic numerals" because Europeans first saw them in use among Arabs, but these numerals originated in India.

the wheel but the economic value of wheels in the absence of animals to pull vehicles, during the millennia before motorized transport.

The lack of heavy-duty draft animals or heavy-duty beasts of burden on land even affected what was economically feasible in water transportation. At the time of the arrival of Europeans in the Western Hemisphere, nowhere in North America or South America were there boats as large as the ships of Europeans, much less the even larger and more advanced ships that the Chinese had developed earlier. The economic viability of large ships depends on the availability of means of efficiently collecting large enough cargoes on land— both from the immediate ports and from the hinterlands— to fill such ships before a voyage, and an ability to efficiently disperse large cargoes at the destination port and into its hinterlands.

A complete absence of animals capable of carrying out such tasks limits the size of vessels that are economically viable. Waterborne commerce in the Western Hemisphere, as of the time of the arrival of Europeans, was conducted in smaller vessels, such as canoes. What this meant was that the indigenous populations of North America and South America had both a smaller economic universe and a smaller cultural universe than that of many peoples in Europe, Asia or North Africa. Not only could exotic goods travel thousands of miles across the Eurasian landmass, they could also travel thousands of miles across water in large ships. Much knowledge from the Middle East and North Africa also found its way into Europe, including the agricultural and architectural advances that the North African Moors brought with them when they invaded and conquered Spain.

The limitations of both land and water transport in the Western Hemisphere before the arrival of Europeans meant severe limitations on cultural diffusions, whether of languages, agricultural methods, animal domestication practices or political systems. Both the distances and the pace of cultural diffusion in the Western Hemisphere were far more limited in the Western Hemisphere than in the Eurasian and North African lands of the Eastern Hemisphere. For example:

The wheels invented in Mesoamerica as parts of toys never met the llamas domesticated in the Andes, to generate wheeled transport for the New World. From east to west in the Old World, the Macedonian Empire and the Roman Empire both spanned 3,000 miles, the Mongol Empire 6,000 miles. But the empires and states of Mesoamerica had no political relations with, and apparently never even heard of, the chiefdoms of the eastern United States 700 miles to the north or the empires and states of the Andes 1,200 miles to the south.[21]

By contrast, horse-drawn wheeled vehicles existed simultaneously in both France and China, located 8,000 miles apart.[22] Meanwhile, such crops as corn and beans took thousands of years to travel from Mexico to the eastern United States.[23] More generally, according to Professor Jared Diamond of UCLA, "there was no diffusion of domestic animals, writing, or political entities, and limited or slow diffusion of crops and technology, between the New World centers of Mesoamerica, the eastern United States, and the Andes and Amazonia."[24] In short, cultural universes were not nearly as extensive in the Western Hemisphere as in the Eastern Hemisphere, prior to the arrival of the Europeans.

When the British first confronted the Iroquois on the east coast of North America, the mental and material resources at the disposal of these two races were by no means confined to what they had each developed themselves. The British had been able to navigate across the Atlantic, in the first place, by using the compass invented in China, doing mathematical calculations with a numbering system from India, steering with rudders invented in China, writing on paper invented in China, using letters created by the Romans, and ultimately prevailing in combat using gunpowder, also invented in China. The Iroquois had no comparably wide cultural universe.

The cultural universe matters, and animals have been among the reasons for large disparities in the size of the cultural universe in different geographic settings. The relative cultural handicaps of the indigenous peoples of the Western Hemisphere were not unique. Similar handicaps, among others, restricted the cultural universe of the peoples of sub-Saharan Africa, and still more so the cultural universe of the aboriginal population of Australia.

Animals— whether draft animals, beasts of burden, farm animals or herd animals— were no more evenly or randomly distributed around the world than other factors in economic and social development. Dromedaries and camels, for example, were concentrated in desert lands, from the Sahara in North Africa to the Gobi Desert in Asia— dromedaries in the hot deserts and camels proper in the cooler deserts and highlands.[25] Indispensable in deserts, because of their ability to travel long distances between sources of drinking water, dromedaries and camels were rare to non-existent elsewhere.

Horses were key to the conquests of the great mounted warriors of Central Asia, such as those led by Genghis Khan and other empire builders such as the Ottomans, who penetrated into the Middle East and then extended their conquests up into Southeastern Europe. Other mounted warriors from Asia swept westward into Eastern Europe, forcing a chain reaction of westward movements of Slavs and others, often driving existing populations westward before them or driving them up into mountains from their homes on the plains. Yet horses were rare within China and even rarer in India and sub-Saharan Africa,[26] as well as totally non-existent in Australia before the Europeans arrived there in the late eighteenth century.

The arrival of Europeans in the Western Hemisphere radically changed the animal population in the New World, and with it the economic life of that half of the world. "The most important for economic life were mules, which gradually became indispensable as carriers" in much of South America, according to historian Fernand Braudel. There were half a million mules in Peru alone in 1776, and perhaps as many as two million in the hemisphere altogether. Nowhere else in the world was there a comparable concentration of mules, relative to the human population, except in Europe. Horses and oxen also proliferated throughout the Western Hemisphere after the Europeans arrived.[27] The *gauchos* of Argentina became famous for their horsemanship and the plains Indians in the United States became mounted hunters and warriors by mastering this new mode of travel. But such an animal revolution was prevented in tropical Africa, because of the tsetse fly and, in Australia, because suitable animals were simply non-existent.

Isolation

A common handicap of lagging groups around the world has been *isolation*, whether in mountain villages, on islands remote from the nearest mainland, or living where deserts obstruct access to the rest of the world. A dearth of animals also contributes to the isolation of peoples living in the same environment, often physically not very far from each other.

In addition to having impediments to communication with the outside world, the peoples of sub-Saharan Africa have had major impediments to communication with each other. The dearth of navigable waterways was just one of those impediments. The presence of rift valleys and jungles also fragmented many of the indigenous peoples. The dearth of beasts of burden, due to the tsetse fly that flourishes in much of tropical Africa, and carries a disease deadly to animals, adds to the impediments to local transportation and communication. The colorful African custom of people carrying bundles on their heads is a painful sign of a grim reality where there are few beasts of burden such as horses or camels, which can carry much more freight, much more efficiently.

Another of the cultural factors fragmenting peoples in tropical Africa has been a multiplicity of languages, out of all proportion to the size of the population. Although the population of Africa is about 50 percent larger than the population of Europe, Africans have about nine times as many languages as Europeans. Africans have about 90 percent as many languages as Asians, who outnumber them nearly four to one.[28] Extreme linguistic diversity is not only a sign of social isolation and a resulting cultural fragmentation, it contributes to the barriers separating African peoples from each other, as well as from the outside world.

Isolation has not been absolute, either in the Western Hemisphere or in sub-Saharan Africa, but cultural universes have not been at all comparable in size to those in much of Europe, Asia or North Africa. An even more severe isolation, in an even more geographically unpromising environment, was the fate of the aboriginal population of Australia before the Europeans arrived there in the eighteenth century.

Beasts of burden were even more completely lacking in Australia than in sub-Saharan Africa, or in the Western Hemisphere before the Europeans arrived. Such animals were totally non-existent in Australia when the British arrived, just as they were non-existent in most of the Western Hemisphere when Europeans arrived there in the fifteenth century, though there were at least llamas in the Andes, where they were used as pack animals.[29] However, llamas were not large enough to be ridden like horses. Also lacking in Australia were farm animals like cows, goats or sheep.

Australia had other severe geographic handicaps. In the ages before modern transportation, this vast island continent was isolated in the Southern Hemisphere, far from the mainland of Asia and even more distant from other inhabited continents. Much of the soil of Australia was of low fertility,[30] and much of the interior was a desert. Rainfall was even less reliable in the interior of Australia than in sub-Saharan Africa, with its long months without rain, followed by torrential downpours. In the vast interior desert of Australia, there were *years* without rain, followed by summer downpours.[31] This was not an environment favoring either agriculture or spontaneous vegetation, except along a coastal fringe.

Back in times when it was common to speak more frankly about different levels of achievements by different peoples, a scholarly study of world geography said that blacks in Africa, "taken as a whole, occupy a higher economic and cultural rank than the black races of Australia and Melanesia."[32] When the Europeans arrived in Australia in the eighteenth century, they found the aborigines lacking iron, even though iron was used by indigenous peoples in sub-Saharan Africa more than a thousand years earlier— and even though Australia had some of the world's largest iron ore deposits. Again, the role of geography has not been simply as a direct supplier of natural wealth, but also and more importantly as a facilitator or impediment to a larger cultural universe, from which to gain the knowledge to turn natural resources into wealth.

The Australian aborigines likewise lacked a knowledge of animal husbandry and many kinds of agriculture known to the peoples of sub-Saharan Africa, among other peoples in geographic settings with the physical prerequisites for acquiring or developing such knowledge. But even during the era of genetic determinism in the early twentieth century, not everyone attributed the lags of the Australian aborigines to genes.

The aborigines' lack of knowledge of things known to others, according to a geographic treatise published in 1911, "must be attributed to their insularity," such as was also the case among "the native Canary Islanders"[33]— who were Caucasian.[34] The fundamental problem of the Australian aborigines was seen as the geography of Australia. When the Europeans arrived, "Australia presented the unique spectacle of a whole continent with its population still held in the vise of nature"[35] and was "the classic ground of retardation,"[36] according to the same treatise. Another geographer, writing in 1924, mentioned "Australia, where primitive man is at his lowest," but added that a people subjected to such "environments could scarcely be expected to develop greatly."[37]

Australia's isolation applied to animals as well as human beings. None of the animals of Asia— the next nearest continent— was present in Australia when the British arrived in the eighteenth century.[38] Animals that were common in other parts of the world, such as bears, monkeys, hoofed animals and the various kinds of cats— from house cats to lions and tigers— were also non-existent in Australia,[39] like the cattle, sheep and goats already noted.

Nor were such Australian animals as kangaroos or koalas indigenous elsewhere. Most of the trees in Australia were of the Eucalyptus family, which is indigenous nowhere else. Many kinds of plants, birds and freshwater fish* were also unique to Australia. To a remarkable extent, Australia was for millennia its own separate world biologically.

The isolation of the island continent's flora and fauna gives some idea of the isolation of its human beings.[40] Multiple evidences point toward an isolated land and an isolated people. There was similar evidence of prolonged isolation in the Canary Islands, where there were hundreds of plants unique to those islands,[41] and a backwardness similar to that of the Australian aborigines, though the two groups are racially different and located many thousands of miles apart.

In Australia, as in the Western Hemisphere, the arrival of Europeans led to the transplanting of European animals— and, even more important, the transplanting of European knowledge, gathered from vastly larger geographic regions, forming a far larger cultural universe than that available to the indigenous population of Australia.

Europeans largely avoided the huge interior desert of Australia and settled primarily around the coastal fringes of the continent, often concentrated in cities that could be supplied with food from advanced agricultural practices developed elsewhere, and from domesticated animals brought from Europe— cities that would not have been viable for hunter-gatherers such as the aborigines. As for the aborigines' native intelligence, Charles Darwin observed them during his historic voyage around the world in the early nineteenth century, and concluded, "they appeared far from being such utterly degraded beings as they have usually been represented." He said that they had "wonderful sagacity" in tracking animals or men, and some of the remarks attributed to them "manifested considerable acuteness."[42]

The low fertility of much Australian soil, except along the coastal fringes, was compensated by the presence of rich natural resources, including not only iron ore but also titanium ore, of which Australia became the world's leading exporter.[43] But what were natural resources for the Europeans were not natural resources for the Australian

---

* Saltwater fish in the ocean were of course not confined to any given continent.

aborigines, lacking exposure to the scientific knowledge developed over the centuries in a cultural universe extending across the vast Eurasian landmass and including the Middle East and North Africa.

DISEASES

Diseases are not mere incidental aspects of life. The influenza pandemic of 1918–1919 is estimated to have taken more lives than the contemporary First World War, the most devastating and lethal war in all of history at that point. Diseases have also affected the course of history.

Europeans knew of the existence of Africa thousands of years before they learned of the existence of the Western Hemisphere. Yet European empires were established in the Western Hemisphere hundreds of years before the "scramble for Africa" began in the late nineteenth century and led to European colonial empires that extended throughout the continent. Diseases had much to do with the differing fates of these different regions of the world. Microorganisms that most of the humans involved knew nothing about at the time were, in effect, on the side of the Europeans during their conquests in the Western Hemisphere. But microorganisms were on the side of the indigenous peoples in tropical Africa.

The much larger cultural universe of the Europeans, compared to that of the various peoples of the Western Hemisphere, meant a much larger disease universe as well. Diseases endemic in Asia repeatedly made their way to Europe, along with the goods traded across thousands of miles on the Eurasian landmass, and by seaborne trade as well. This international commerce transmitted diseases from Asia, creating epidemics in Europe that, from time to time, wiped out significant fractions of the European population— from a third to a half of the population in parts of Europe during the bubonic plague of the fourteenth century.[44] But the survivors of these devastating incursions of diseases from Asia developed biological resistance to those diseases, in addition to having biological resistance to diseases originating in Europe.

When European and indigenous races confronted each other in the Western Hemisphere, whether in battle or in peace, the microorganisms that neither of them knew about decimated the indigenous peoples, while the Europeans were not nearly as vulnerable to the diseases of the Western Hemisphere, though syphilis began to spread in Europe after the return of the first European sailors from the Western Hemisphere.[45]

Once European diseases took root in the indigenous populations of the Western Hemisphere, these diseases spread through whole native societies, to people who had no direct contact with Europeans. When Pizarro's army was marching toward the capital of the Incas, people who had never seen a European were dying of European diseases inside that capital.[46] It was said of a kindly Spanish priest, who went among the native peoples of the Western Hemisphere in friendship, as a missionary, that he was probably responsible for more deaths among them than even the most brutal conquistador.[47] It was not uncommon, in parts of the Western Hemisphere, for half or more of a given tribe of indigenous people to be wiped out by European diseases to which they had no biological resistance.

In sub-Saharan Africa, the tropical diseases were so deadly to outsiders that, at one time, the average life expectancy of a white man in tropical Africa was said to be less than one year. No part of Europe is in the tropics, and Europeans' exposure to other peoples was largely in the temperate zones, so most Europeans had little opportunity to develop biological resistance to tropical diseases. Only after medical science advanced to the point where it could cope with deadly tropical diseases— by either curing them or preventing them by public health measures— was it feasible for Europeans to establish empires in tropical, sub-Saharan Africa. The swiftness with which these conquests were accomplished suggests that the human defenders in tropical Africa were not nearly as formidable as the unseen microorganisms that had held European conquerors at bay for centuries. Yet again, a given environment does not determine a fixed outcome, because of its interactions with changing human knowledge— in this case, medical knowledge.

Among the peoples of tropical Africa, diseases contributed to their isolation from each other, because of the devastating effects of diseases carried by the tsetse fly on animals that might otherwise have become beasts of burden or useful draft animals that could have helped connect different peoples, and could have played useful roles in agriculture.

North and south of the tropics, the situation was very different in Africa. Europeans began settling in what is now the Republic of South Africa— the great majority of which is in the temperate zone of the Southern Hemisphere— in the middle of the seventeenth century. In ancient times, the Romans incorporated much of North Africa, in the temperate zone of the Northern Hemisphere, within their empire. There being no decisive disease barrier between Europeans and North Africans around the Mediterranean, conquests went each way in different periods of history. The North African Moors invaded and conquered Spain during what were the Middle Ages in Europe, and retained control of Spain for centuries, leaving behind both physical and cultural remains of the society they created during their reign.

It was not only in the Western Hemisphere that the larger disease universe of the Europeans proved deadly to peoples they encountered. Writing of his observations during his round-the-world voyage, Charles Darwin said:

> Wherever the European has trod, death seems to pursue the aboriginal. We may look to the wide extent of the Americas, Polynesia, the Cape of Good Hope, and Australia, and we find the same result.[48]

Darwin quoted other observers in various parts of the world, who likewise reported that the arrival of Europeans brought deadly diseases to the native population, even when the Europeans themselves showed no sign of these diseases. In other words, the

Europeans were carriers of the disease microorganisms, but their own biological resistance protected themselves. This was not unique to Europeans, however. Darwin pointed out that some Polynesians had a similar effect on people in the East Indies. It was said that the same phenomenon could also be seen among animals, that according to another observer, "sheep, which have been imported from vessels, although themselves in a healthy condition, if placed in the same fold with others, frequently produce sickness in the flock."[49]

Diseases are no more evenly distributed around the world than other geographic factors. Malaria is a tropical disease but it has been a sufficient danger in countries outside the tropics to cause many peoples in temperate zones to locate their homes up on hillsides, even when they work during the day on farms in the lands below, where there are mosquitoes that may be carrying the disease. But usually these mosquitoes are not as prevalent during the daylight hours as they are in the evening.

At one time, malaria was prevalent in the Great Lakes regions of both Canada and the United States, as well as in various other parts of the United States. With the passage of time, however, various defensive measures and preventive measures had malaria in retreat, persisting longest in the South, where the Mississippi River system and various Atlantic and Gulf Coast rivers "meander sluggishly through level coastal plains on the slow route to the sea."[50] Since malaria-carrying mosquitoes breed in stagnant or sluggish waters, the same geographic features that make rivers navigable also made them sources of malaria in the South, longer than in much of the rest of the country.

LOCATION

Location is a significant geographic factor, even aside from the particular characteristics of a particular location itself. For the ancient Greeks to be located near where agriculture developed in the Middle

East gave them historic opportunities that they used to make historic intellectual contributions to Western civilization and to the world:

> Greece stands for the very foundation of Western thought and sensibility. It stands for science and mathematics, for skepticism and observation as opposed to a world ruled by supranational forces. Greece is the birthplace of philosophical inquiry that still shapes modern thinking— from Plato's rationalism to Aristotle's empiricism. The first recorded works of the Western literary tradition are the epic poems of Homer and Hesiod. Aeschylus invented drama, Sophocles gave us tragedy, Aristophanes was the father of comedy. Herodotus and Thucydides set the model for the study of history. Pericles stands for the art of oratory, and the Athens of his time was the fount of democracy.[51]

For the islands of Japan to be located where China was readily accessible across water meant that the Japanese had access to a civilization that for centuries was in the forefront of human advances— and thus Japan could, for example, adapt Chinese writing to make their own language a written language. This meant that the Japanese had an opportunity to become literate, centuries before other peoples in Asia or elsewhere who were not located near a more advanced civilization. Nor did small, isolated communities have the same incentives for developing writing themselves as larger, more widespread societies with numerous commercial and other interactions taking place at distances too great for verbal communication alone.

The advantages of coastal peoples over inland peoples, or the advantages of peoples on the plains over peoples living in mountains, are advantages conferred by the simple fact of location, and are advantages common around the world. During the era of mass immigration from Europe to the United States, Polish immigrants from Russia or from Austria— Poland itself having been dismembered and absorbed into these empires— were almost always unskilled workers, but those relatively few Polish immigrants who did have specialized work skills as weavers, tailors or cabinet makers were predominantly from Prussia,[52] where they acquired such skills from being located in a German culture.

During the era of European colonialism, location near Western institutions like schools gave those segments of the conquered people in such locations major advantages over their compatriots in the hinterlands. Other locational differences created other locational windfall gains or windfall losses. In colonial Ceylon, for example, British missionaries set up schools in more favored portions of the island nation, while the British authorities assigned American missionaries to the less favored northern tip of the island, where the Tamil minority was concentrated. But, because the American missionary schools concentrated more in science and mathematics, the Tamils became more proficient in these fields and better represented in occupations requiring such training. A study found that members of the Tamil minority received a majority of the *A*'s on university entry exams.[53]

In Nigeria, the Ibos lived in the poorly endowed southern part of the country, and had once been slaves, but they seized upon opportunities provided by Western missionary schools in their region, while the peoples of the Muslim north rejected schools run by Christian missionaries. The Ibos rose to such professional, administrative and business occupations as were open to Africans under British rule, far more so than the peoples in northern Nigeria— and Ibos dominated such occupations, even in northern Nigeria.

The location of the United States, insulated by two oceans from the wars that ravaged Europe and Asia, enabled the American people to develop their own way of life in relative peace, using the culture that had developed in Europe without having to suffer the devastating, and sometimes incessant, wars that their European ancestors and contemporaries had to endure. By contrast, Mediterranean islands like Sicily and Malta were located in the path of contending nations and empires that, for centuries, fought each other over, and on, the territory of these islands, leaving behind a legacy of destruction, conquest and both culturally and genetically altered populations. Similarly situated small islands met a similar fate in various other regions of the world.[54]

Britain is an island even closer to the nearest continent than various islands in the Mediterranean but, in addition to being a much larger island, and therefore much harder to conquer, Britain has not been located in the crossfire between contending empires. Moreover, the rough waters of the English Channel have been more of an obstacle to conquering invaders than the calm waters of the Mediterranean. Nothing provides absolute protection, of course. After all, Britain was invaded and conquered by the Romans in ancient times and by the Normans nearly a thousand years later. But, after eventually becoming a unified and advanced nation in the wake of the Norman conquest of 1066, Britain has not been invaded in nearly another thousand years since then. What the English Channel has also done during that time has been to make it unnecessary for Britain to maintain a large standing army, like those of nations on the continent of Europe, sparing the British both the expense and the political dangers of large standing armies.*

Location has mattered, not only for Britain as a whole, but also for its internal constituents. Being located near enough to continental Europe to have ready access to the trade and technology of its European neighbors allowed the British to gain the benefits of those continental nations that were for centuries more advanced than the British. These advantages were most beneficial to England, the closest part of Britain to the European coast. These advantages passed, with a lag, to other parts of the British Isles— Wales, Scotland and Ireland— as did the further advantages when England began to surpass its continental neighbors and lead the world into the industrial revolution.

---

* "This peculiar felicity of situation has, in a great degree, contributed to preserve the liberty which that country to this day enjoys, in spite of the prevalent venality and corruption. If, on the contrary, Britain had been situated on the continent, and had been compelled as she would have been, by that situation, to make her military establishments at home coextensive with those of the other great powers of Europe, she, like them, would in all probability be, at this day, a victim to the absolute power of a single man." Alexander Hamilton, "Consequences of Wars Between States," Alexander Hamilton, James Madison and John Jay, *The Federalist*, Number 8, edited by Benjamin Fletcher Wright (Cambridge, Massachusetts: Harvard University Press, 1961), p. 123.

The fate of whole races, nations and civilizations can depend on whether they happen to be located in the right place at the right time or in the wrong place at the wrong time. Moreover, what was the right place or the wrong place has varied greatly over the centuries.

PART II:

CULTURAL FACTORS

If we learn anything from the history of economic development, it is that culture makes almost all the difference. Witness the enterprise of expatriate minorities— the Chinese in East and Southeast Asia, Indians in East Africa, Lebanese in West Africa, Jews and Calvinists throughout much of Europe, and on and on. Yet culture, in the sense of the inner values and attitudes that guide a population, frightens scholars.

David S. Landes

Geography is an influence but not predestination. Much of the influence of geography on income and wealth derives from its effects on the size of the cultural universe available to different peoples in different physical settings. An enumeration of places with rich concentrations of natural resources, such as oil in Saudi Arabia or gold in South Africa, would be a very poor guide to places with high incomes per capita. As *The Economist* magazine said of Nigeria, it is "rich in oil reserves but otherwise desperately poor."[1]

Without the cultural prerequisites for developing natural resources into real wealth, the raw physical resources themselves are of little or no value. The natural resources we use today were even more abundant in the era of the cave man, but the people of that prehistoric era were culturally not yet able to use most of those resources.

Even physical capital is of little or no use without the cultural prerequisites to operate it, maintain it, repair and replace it as it wears out. Conversely, the mass destruction of physical capital, as in Western Europe during World War II, was followed by an economic recovery in a relatively few years after the war was over. That recovery has often been credited to aid from the United States under the Marshall Plan. But subsequent efforts to promote similar economic development in the Third World with transfers of both financial capital and physical capital to the governments of those countries, over a long period of decades, have failed repeatedly to produce anything comparable.

The difference is that the cultural prerequisites— the human capital— which produced the physical capital in Western Europe before the war survived the war and could produce it again. But that particular human capital, which developed over the centuries in Western Europe, did not exist on the same scale in the Third World, and could not be created overnight, or even over several decades, in societies with a very different set of cultures. Third World countries were not being asked to re-create their own societies after some calamity. They were essentially being asked to create a *Western* economy without the centuries of the particular cultural evolution that led up to those economies in the West.

Geography is not the only limitation on the size of the cultural universe available to a given population. Language is another. Quite aside from whatever qualitative criteria linguistic scholars might apply to a given language— such as its consistency, precision or subtlety— the sheer *quantitative* dimension, the number of people who speak that language, can determine its economic and social value to the people to whom it is their native tongue. Since language is a means of communication, how many people a given language can communicate with is one major measure of its value to those who speak it. If the number of people around the world who speak Czech is a fraction of the number of people who speak German, then even various Czech scientists, philosophers, novelists, and other writers may choose to write in German to reach a wider audience. For the same reason, books published in other languages are more likely to be translated into English or German than to be translated into Czech or Catalan.

What this means is that even if Czechs and Germans were the same in everything else— which is seldom the case between any two groups— a substantial difference in the size of their respective populations would create a difference in the size of their respective cultural universes, and therefore in the range of economic and other opportunities open to them. This was even more of a factor in centuries past, when literacy was not nearly as widespread, so that the size of the reading public often differed, even among populations of similar size, so that there was little incentive for anyone to publish as much in one language as in another, much less translate writings from other languages into the languages of relatively small literate populations.

In earlier centuries, it was also common for many pockets of different languages and dialects to persist, before improved mass communications arose to homogenize the language and culture across broader regions within a given country. In times past, isolated mountain or highland villages, for example, often spoke different languages and dialects from those of the surrounding population on the lands below, and sometimes different from one village to another. Moreover, many of these languages and dialects had no written versions. The same was true in isolated pockets of indigenous peoples displaced by invading populations, as in North America, South America, Australia and New Zealand, for example. Here the leaders of these displaced indigenes, as well as outsiders sympathetic to their plight, have often urged the preservation, or even resurrection, of their native languages and cultures, even though such linguistic isolation would be a major handicap inhibiting their progress in the world around them, after the world of their ancestors, in which indigenous cultures evolved, was now irretrievably lost.

Cultures also differ in their respective time horizons. Even within a given culture, different age groups often have different time horizons. Paradoxically, the young who have decades of life ahead of them are often more focused on the immediate present, while the old whose years ahead may be few often think of the long-run consequences for their children and grandchildren or the fate of society as a whole. Given that different societies have different mixtures of old and young— with societies often differing in median age by two decades or more— those societies with a large proportion of young males especially may be more volatile in their reactions to passing events and less mindful of the longer term consequences of precipitous actions. Even when leaders of these societies are of mature years, the political weight of the more volatile youth can influence policies focused on the immediate present.

Time is important in other ways, and these ways likewise differ from one culture to another. As already noted in Chapter 4, there was an urgency attached to conforming one's activities to the requirements of the season of the year in temperate zones, during the millennia when agriculture was the largest and most important economic activity. Time has also acquired increasing importance in a different sense. In more recent times, the rise of commercial and industrial societies has made punctuality essential to coordinating many activities requiring simultaneous interactions in factories and offices.

Here, as in other things, some cultures have made punctuality more of a priority than other cultures have. Germans and Japanese, for example, have tended to be more strictly punctual than the peoples of Latin America, perhaps reflecting different levels and/or longer traditions of industrialization and commercialization. But habits, however formed, have consequences, long after the conditions in which those habits were formed have changed.

Great conquering peoples, whose elites have been able to live off wealth extracted from the conquered and the plundered, have been able to disdain commerce, industry and labor as the occupations of those they have subordinated, while celebrating the military traditions and the leisurely and luxurious lifestyle of their elites, made possible by those conquests. But, long after the era of their military glory has passed, the cultural attitudes formed among the elites of that era can remain and, diffused beyond the elite, serve as a cultural impediment to the economic advancement of a society long exempted from a necessity to develop the human capital of its own people.

Spain was a classic example during its "golden age" in the sixteenth century, when gold and silver poured in— literally by the ton— from its conquered lands in the Western Hemisphere. Spain's earlier, centuries-long military campaigns to drive out the Moors, who had conquered and ruled them, was a valuable prelude and preparation for Spanish military conquests that gave them the world's largest empire in the century that followed the reconquest of their own land. But, as a noted historian pointed out, "The Spaniards had acquired their national unity and built a huge Empire by being soldiers and crusaders, not by being merchants and craftsmen."[2] A contemporary Venetian ambassador said of sixteenth century Spain, "I do not think that there is another country less provided with skilled workers than Spain." Its technology lagged, even at the height of its military glory, and Spain was also backward in the sciences, compared to contemporary European nations.[3]

Nevertheless, the vast wealth pouring into Spain, especially from the Western Hemisphere, allowed the Spanish elite to live in luxury and leisure, enjoying the products of other countries, purchased with the windfall gain of gold and silver. At one point, Spain's imports were nearly twice as large as its exports, with the difference being covered by payments in gold and silver. One of the consequences was that, not long after ships arrived from the Western Hemisphere laden with these precious metals, gold and silver would be in short supply in Spain.[4]

It was a source of pride, however, that "all the world" served Spain, while Spain "serves nobody,"[5] as a proud Spaniard of that era put it. But what this meant economically was that other countries developed the human capital that produced what Spain consumed, without Spain's having to develop its own human capital, even among its "inactive, though prosperous, aristocracy."[6] Even the maritime trade that brought products from other parts of Europe to Spain was largely in the hands of foreigners, and European businessmen flocked to Spain to carry out economic functions there.[7] The historic social consequence was that the Spanish culture's disdain for commerce, industry and skilled labor would be a lasting economic handicap bequeathed to its descendants, not only in Spain itself but also in Latin America. This cultural legacy would last long past the time when Spain could simply live on the gold and silver extracted from the Western Hemisphere.

Other kinds of windfall gains can likewise relieve other societies, or particular groups within a given society, from the pressures to develop their own human capital to the fullest. The vast, rich and readily accessible petroleum deposits in the Middle East have allowed a fabulously wealthy elite to live a life of great luxury and leisure, as in sixteenth century Spain, and in this case to import not only industrialists and technicians from Western nations to develop and operate the Middle East's petroleum industry, but also to import large numbers of workers from various parts of Asia to serve in a variety of lower-level occupations. Thus neither the elites nor the masses have had to develop their human capital to the fullest, so that the Gross Domestic Product per capita in various oil-rich nations of the Middle East is often lower than in other countries with far less valuable natural resources.

Conversely, as already noted, the peoples of the temperate zones have had no choice but to develop their human capital to cope with the inescapable fact that they cannot grow enough food in the winter to survive, while people in the tropics have had no winter to cope with. British historian Arnold Toynbee formulated the thesis that "challenge and response" is a key to progress— that people who are forced by circumstances to develop the skills and/or discipline to cope with surrounding circumstances have tended to create the most advances. Even with Toynbee's caveat that some challenges can be too overwhelming to produce much progress,[8] the idea that large windfall gains can inhibit long-term progress, by reducing the need to develop human capital, is an idea that can be worth keeping in mind when trying to assess the economic effects of culture.

Chapter 5

CULTURE AND ECONOMICS

*Civilization and culture both refer to the overall way of
life of a people, and a civilization is a culture writ large.*

Samuel P. Huntington

When we try to explain differences in economic and other
achievements between nations, races or civilizations, some
argue that these differences are due to innate genetic differences in
mental potential[1] and others argue that differences are due to the
environments in which people live. Both seem to assume that all the
causes of differences in achievements fall into just two categories,
heredity and environment. In fact, these terms are often simply
defined that way, so that whatever is not hereditary is called
environmental. But does this mean that, for those who reject genetic
determinism, a group's position in American society is determined by
factors peculiar to American society, for which American society can
therefore be praised or blamed, as the case may be?

A vast amount of evidence from around the world suggests
otherwise.

GROUP DIFFERENCES

There are many groups with a particular culture of their own, who
take that culture with them wherever they go, in culturally very
different kinds of societies. Germans, for example, have for centuries

had both a very specific set of skills and a very specific way of life, whether they lived in Germany, Brazil, Russia, Australia or the United States. Cultures include not only customs, values and attitudes, but also skills and talents that more directly affect economic outcomes, and which economists call human capital. Distinguished historian Arnold Toynbee likewise saw the importance of human capital, though that term had not yet been coined when he said, in 1915, that "the world's only true wealth" was "the skill and nobility and genius of human beings."[2] Tangible material wealth is only a conversion of pre-existing physical material into a form that is more valued by human beings. The ability to do so is the real wealth.

Among the skills in which Germans have excelled has been the building of pianos. The first pianos in colonial America were built by Germans, who also led the way in building pianos in Australia, France, Russia and England.[3] The world's leading optical firms designing camera lenses in the first half of the twentieth century were German, including Zeiss, Schneider and Voigtländer— and the leading optical firm in the United States was created by two German immigrants named Bausch and Lomb.

Germans have likewise excelled in military skills, literally for millennia. There were German generals in the Roman legions, as well as German generals in czarist Russia[4] and in South America.[5] The United States had German generals in the Revolutionary War of 1776, and American armies fighting in Europe in both World War I and World War II were commanded by generals of German ancestry— Pershing* and Eisenhower, respectively. Other top commanders of American military forces in World War II who were of German ancestry included Admiral Chester Nimitz, who commanded the Pacific fleet, and General Carl Spaatz, whose bombers reduced much of Germany to rubble. During the Middle Ages, the Teutonic Knights conquered Prussia, which became the

---

* This was the anglicized version of a family name that was in earlier generations "Pfoerschin." Virginia Brainard Kunz, *The Germans in America* (Minneapolis: Lerner Publications, 1966), p. 54.

heartland of German military prowess for centuries to come. In both World Wars, the armies of Germany inflicted far more casualties on opposing forces than the Germans sustained themselves.[6]

Social patterns among Germans likewise appeared not only in Germany but also in other countries around the world, in cultural environments that differed radically from one another. More was involved than differences in skills, important as such differences have been. Behind such skills are cultural *values* that give a priority to the acquisition of those skills— and new skills as the old ones become obsolete over time, making the mastering of new skills imperative. In short, the heredity-versus-environment dichotomy does not exhaust the causes of different productivity in different groups. The external environment, whether geographic or social, can be an influence but not predestination. Different groups living in the same external environment can have very different productivity if their internal cultural values produce very different priorities as to what they *want* to do, and at what sacrifices of other things.

An emphasis on education was a cultural pattern found in Germany itself, where kindergartens originated and where research universities were developed that were later imitated in the United States. Nineteenth century Germany was one of the first European nations to have free and compulsory education, as well as more teachers per capita than in many other European countries, and with a higher proportion of the national output being devoted to education.[7]

This emphasis on education was also part of the culture of Germans living in other countries, including countries where the culture of the majority population had no such commitment to education. The great majority of Germans living in nineteenth century Russia, for example, were literate at a time when the great majority of Russians were illiterate.[8] In German farming communities pioneering in the wilderness in nineteenth century Brazil, schools appeared in the first clearings in the woods,[9] while most native-born Brazilians remained illiterate on into the early twentieth century.[10] In the Austrian Empire in 1900, the illiteracy rate among German males over the age of ten was 5 percent, while among other males of the same ages illiteracy was 45 percent among those who were Polish, 67 percent among Serbo-Croatians and 71 percent among Romanians in the same empire.[11]

When Czernowitz University was established in nineteenth century Romania, it had more German students than Romanian students, and most of its professors were German.[12] In Estonia, a university established in 1802 by the czarist government of the Russian Empire likewise had a majority of Germans among its students and faculty for most of the nineteenth century.[13] In the city of Riga in adjoining Latvia, most of the education was conducted in the German language, even though Germans were a minority of the city's population.[14]

Germans are just one of the groups who have taken their own particular culture with them when they immigrated to other societies, so that the general *environments* of those various other societies were not the controlling factor in these groups' economic or other outcomes in those societies. How we define "environment" is crucial. It is not simply a matter of semantic preferences. If we define environment as simply the surrounding circumstances, then we are left unable to account for different cultural groups having very different outcomes in the same environment, creating among other things disparities in income and wealth.

To account for radical differences in income and wealth among groups living in the same society, environment can be defined as what is going on *around* a group, while culture means what is going on *within* each group. If we choose instead to define environment as all non-genetic factors, then the various cultures of different groups in a given society are included in the environment of that society. But what we cannot do is go back and forth between different conceptions of what environment means— not if we expect to reach consistent or rational conclusions.

Many other groups besides Germans have had their own respective cultures, which they take with them into very different settings around the world. These would include the overseas Chinese in various Southeast Asian countries and in the Western Hemisphere;[15] the Lebanese in West Africa, Australia, and North and South America;[16] Jews in Europe, the Middle East, the Western Hemisphere and Australia;[17] and the various peoples of India on every inhabited continent.[18]

Given the cultural differences that these groups take with them wherever they go, there is no reason whatever to expect them to have the same incomes or wealth, either compared to each other or compared to the existing majority populations of the countries to which they immigrate. Nor do the empirical data show any such equality. That this is a matter of culture, rather than a matter of initial wealth upon arriving in a given country, is shown by how many groups have arrived in various countries far poorer than the existing population of the host country and have nevertheless eventually risen above the economic level of those who were there before them.

The history of the overseas Chinese in the countries of Southeast Asia— as well as in the United States— is a classic example of immigrants whose first wave arrived with little more than the clothes on their backs and a willingness to work as hard as it took for them to get ahead. Often, in centuries past, these poverty-stricken emigrants from China had little or no education and knew little of the language or customs of the countries they went to.

Seldom did the laws or practices of the Southeast Asian countries in which the Chinese settled offer them equal rights with either members of the colonial ruling race or with the indigenous population. In colonial Malaya, for example, the British provided schools for the children of the Malays but the Chinese had to provide their own.[19] In nineteenth century America, a long and painfully tragic story can be summarized by saying that the Chinese were treated even worse than in Southeast Asia.[20] In Peru, guards were posted on an island where Chinese contract laborers were assigned the task of shovelling bird manure into sacks for export as fertilizer, working under stifling heat and stench. The guards were not there to prevent escape from the island, but to prevent the ultimate escape of suicide.[21]

The desperate situation of the Chinese in various other countries in the nineteenth century also led to high rates of suicide among them. These suicides sometimes began in the Portuguese port of Macao on the coast of China,[22] where many Chinese had been lured or trapped into holding pens for the semi-slave trade of indentured laborers to be shipped to other countries around the world— including hundreds of thousands to the Western Hemisphere. Despite being mostly young men in the prime of life, a majority of those sent to Cuba died under the brutal working conditions there before completing the eight years of their labor contracts.[23] In nineteenth century Cuba, there were years when more than a hundred Chinese committed suicide,[24] but thousands more were simply worked to death.

Although most Chinese immigrants to the United States in the nineteenth century did not come through the Macao indentured labor trade, circumstances in the United States were sufficiently dire that the suicide rate of the Chinese in San Francisco, as late as the mid-twentieth century, was almost three times the national average.[25]

Over the years and generations, the Chinese in the United States have become prosperous, overcoming many obstacles, of which those created by others have not been the only ones. The initial poverty and lack of education of Chinese immigrants to nineteenth century America was another problem they had to overcome, and did. Such struggles were not new to the Chinese who came to America. Of all the Chinese immigrants who arrived in America before the First World War, most came from Kwangtung province in China,[26] where "the bitter struggle for existence" in that over-crowded province had made them "industrious."[27] Since U.S. laws had severe restrictions against admissions of immigrants from China until 1965, these immigrants from Kwangtung (now Guangdong) and their descendants continued to be the majority of Chinese Americans during that era.

Poverty has also been a problem for hundreds of thousands of new Chinese immigrants arriving in the United States as late as the twenty-first century, whether legally or illegally, from Fujian province in China. Like other immigrants in other times and places, the Chinese from Fujian have not scattered randomly across the United States but have concentrated in their own communities, located in this case in Brooklyn, New York. These Fujianese have been described as "really poor, as in four-people-to-a-single-room, all-rice-diet, soda-can-collecting poor." They have "crammed themselves into dorm-like quarters, working brutally long hours waiting tables, washing dishes, and cleaning hotel rooms— and sending their Chinese-speaking children to the city's elite public schools and on to various universities."[28] Like numerous other places from which resolute and hard-working people have come, Fujian province has been a geographically harsh environment— "mountainous and infertile."[29]

It has been suggested facetiously that the first word of English these Fujianese learn is "Harvard" and the second word is "Stuyvesant," one of New York's elite and highly selective public high schools. While most of the students admitted to the city's elite public high schools come from middle class or higher-income neighborhoods, a significant number come from lower-income neighborhoods where the Fujianese live. Fujianese parents often get their children tutored, in order that they can do well on tests for admission to elite public high schools, as gateways to good colleges and a better life.[30]

Jews have been classic examples of a very similar pattern, and nowhere more so than in the United States, where most arrived *en masse* from Eastern Europe in the late nineteenth century, among the poorest of the immigrant groups, settling in grossly overcrowded, squalid and unsanitary tenements on New York's Lower East Side. Their men usually began working as lowly peddlers on the streets, while their women and children worked at home in "sweatshop" conditions, with sewing machines whirring for long hours in the tenements, doing piecework on garments.[31]

Despite the Jews' long tradition of reverence for learning, and the spectacular proliferation of world-class Jewish intellectuals in the nineteenth and twentieth centuries, the initial rise of Eastern European Jews in America was *not* through education. Although most Jews who arrived in the United States in the early twentieth century were literate in *some* language, that did not mean that they were literate in English. As a detailed study of these immigrants pointed out, their literacy in Yiddish or Hebrew might serve as "an index of participation in Jewish culture" but it was not "a language tool widely applicable within the context of economic adjustment" in the United States.[32]

A 1911 study showed that two-thirds of the children of Polish Jews were behind the grade level they were supposed to be in, according to age.[33] During the First World War, so many American soldiers of Polish and Russian ancestry— most of them Jews— scored so low on the U.S. Army's mental tests that testing pioneer Carl Brigham (creator of the Scholastic Aptitude Test) declared that the Army test results tended to "disprove the popular belief that the Jew is highly intelligent."[34] Years later, after more Jews in America acquired more knowledge of English and their mental test scores rose above the national average,[35] Brigham recanted his earlier conclusions. He pointed out, belatedly, that many of the Jewish soldiers tested in the First World War came from homes where English was not the language spoken. He characterized his earlier conclusions as— in his own words— "without foundation."[36]

Although it was not through education that Jews first rose in American society, nevertheless after having risen in business— whether to a modest or a greater extent— the Jewish immigrants then pushed their children on to educational achievements, which set the stage for their rise in the professions as physicians, attorneys and the like.

It should also be noted that, neither in the medical nor the legal profession did Jews find all the doors of opportunity open to them. Jewish doctors and lawyers could go into private practice, whether in Jewish or Gentile communities, but they were kept out of many hospitals and leading law firms. In the academic world, there were quota limits on how many Jewish students would be admitted to various colleges and universities, and Jewish professors were a rarity until after the Second World War. Nevertheless, when the barriers began coming down over the years, the Jewish population had a backlog of fully qualified people ready to enter those institutions, and even become disproportionately represented in them.

Lebanese immigrants have had a history in some ways very similar to that of the Jews. Like Jewish immigrants from Eastern Europe who settled in the United States, the earliest Lebanese immigrants to Australia, Brazil, Mexico and West Africa were not very educated, and their initial economic rise came from success in business, typically beginning at the lowest level, as peddlers.

Lebanese immigrants to Brazil in the early twentieth century had a 29 percent illiteracy rate.[37] Most of the Lebanese who first settled in Mexico during the same era had not even completed elementary school. Illiterate Lebanese immigrants in Mexico would often keep letters that they received from Lebanon for months, until they could find someone who could read these letters to them and then write their replies for them.[38] Most of the earliest Lebanese immigrants to Australia were illiterate.[39] So were most of the early Lebanese immigrants to West Africa.[40] In the African nation of Sierra Leone, the Creoles looked down on the Lebanese immigrants because they were uneducated and poor. But the Lebanese did not remain that way long— and then the Creoles' contempt turned to resentment and hostility, when the Lebanese became successful in business.[41]

Like other immigrants in other countries around the world, the Lebanese did not emigrate from random locations in their homeland nor settle randomly in the nations to which they moved.

The vast majority of the early Lebanese immigrants who arrived in Sierra Leone after the First World War came not from cities like Beirut but from villages where they had been peasants or similarly low level workers.[42] In short, they came from very narrowly specific geographic locations within Lebanon and settled in very narrowly specific locations in Sierra Leone— the Shi'ite Muslims in one area, the Orthodox Christians concentrated in a different location, the Maronite Christians from one part of Lebanon in another location and the Maronites from another part of Lebanon in still a different location.[43] People's behavior is no more random than geographic features, despite how often intellectuals and others regard non-random outcomes as strange, if not suspicious.

Whether in West Africa, North America, South America or Australia, Lebanese immigrants typically began as peddlers,[44] sometimes following in the footsteps of Jewish peddlers, as in Brazil,[45] where successful peddlers moved up to other work, often as owners of small shops, with newer immigrants from the same or other groups replacing them as peddlers. Even such huge and well-known enterprises today as Macy's, Bloomingdale's and Levi Strauss among the Jews, and Haggar and Farah among the Lebanese, began at the level of the lowly peddler. Here, as among other groups that rose from poverty to prosperity, dogged perseverance over the years and generations was the key.

In the United States, where large-scale immigration from Lebanon began in the late nineteenth century, most of the early immigrants— including women and children— began as itinerant peddlers, with Lebanese peddler networks spreading literally across the country.[46] After a Lebanese peddler became financially able to settle down with his own store, it was usually a family enterprise, open 16 to 18 hours a day, with children stocking the shelves and making deliveries, and with wives sometimes relieving their husbands in the store, in addition to their other tasks in the home. Home was often next door to the store or upstairs.[47]

This pattern was very similar to that among Lebanese in Sierra Leone,[48] as well as among the Chinese in Southeast Asia or Jews in the United States. Milton Friedman was raised in living quarters over his family's store, a pattern that he described as common among the immigrants to America in that era.[49] Lebanese children were inducted into the family business and its requirements at an early age:

School-age children, when not in school, were at their parents' elbows, waiting on customers, making change, stocking shelves, and imbibing the shrewdness of operating an independent business on meagre resources. They were inculcated with the parents' work and thrift ethics and the lesson that family unity and self-denial was essential to the family's goals.[50]

In country after country, successive generations of Lebanese moved up, step by step. Commerce was the occupation of most of the early Lebanese immigrants, whether in Argentina,[51] Australia,[52] Sierra Leone,[53] various Caribbean islands,[54] or the United States,[55] among other places. But Lebanese success in business later allowed them to give their children more education, including education at colleges and universities. This too happened in a number of countries in which the Lebanese settled,[56] and increasing numbers of new immigrants from Lebanon in later years also arrived already well-educated.

With the Lebanese, as with the overseas Chinese and the Jews, what mattered was not that they first arrived in various countries as immigrants with very little education, but that they came from a culture which valued education highly— so that, once they became financially able to do so, they saw to it that their children acquired higher education, and thus could expand their horizons from commerce to the professions such as medicine, law and science, as many did.

The patterns of upward mobility seen among the overseas Chinese, the Jews and the Lebanese are of course not the only patterns of upward mobility. Many Cubans who had been professional and business people in their homeland, before Fidel Castro seized control and imposed Communism in Cuba, fled to the United States, where they were concentrated in nearby Florida. Unable to take much of their physical wealth with them to America, and usually unable to resume the same professions they had back in Cuba, since their Cuban educational or occupational credentials carried no weight in the United States, these refugees found themselves suddenly at the bottom, economically. As one account put it, "they crammed into small apartments and became dishwashers, janitors, and tomato pickers."[57]

For the overwhelming majority, the story of their success was one of arduous toil, swallowed pride, and sacrifice for their children. Former executives parked cars; judges washed dishes; doctors delivered newspapers. Women who had never held jobs before worked as seamstresses, hotel maids, or shrimp sorters at warehouses by the Miami River— work so painful they called it *la Siberia*. As one émigré put it, "I was determined that my children would be middle class even if I had to have two jobs— which I did for fourteen years."[58]

Yet these Cuban refugees who found themselves at the bottom, when their exodus began in 1959, had children who, by 1990, earned more than $50,000 a year twice as frequently as white Americans. Forty years after these Cuban refugees arrived in the United States, the total revenue of Cuban American businesses was greater than the total revenue of the entire nation of Cuba.[59] Similarly, as late as 1994, the 57 million overseas Chinese produced as much wealth as the one billion people in China.[60]

Yet again, all this takes us back to the question: What do we mean by "environment"? If we mean simply the immediate surroundings, then it is hard to see why other groups, living in the same immediate surroundings as the Fujian Chinese in New York— and on the whole living at higher economic levels— do not get their children into the city's elite public high schools as often as the Fujianese do. Nor is it obvious why native-born white Americans do not have high incomes as often as Cuban Americans do.

If instead we see "environment" as including the cultural values that led the Fujianese to make extraordinary sacrifices for the education of their children, or Cuban American refugees to make similarly extraordinary efforts to lift their families up from the bottom, then this situation is less puzzling because it is obvious that not all groups have these same cultural imperatives. But while this makes the problem of understanding the success of these extraordinary groups less puzzling, it also makes the task of trying to get other groups to do the same far more daunting.

Nor does heredity, in the sense of genetics, provide a convincing explanation of group differences when, for example, various ethnic groups in the Habsburg empire with illiteracy rates several times that among the Germans eventually became predominantly literate in later times. If their descendants proved capable of mastering literacy, there is no reason to doubt that previous generations also had the innate ability to do so. But, while compulsory education could force later generations to become literate, *cultural* heredity— which is passed on from one generation to the next, just like genetic heredity— would still favor ethnic groups whose inherited values would determine how much time, effort and dedication would go into their education.

INTERNATIONAL DIFFERENCES

For different nations around the world to all have even approximately similar incomes or wealth, despite their great differences in geography, culture, history, political systems, religious beliefs and the demographic makeups of their respective populations, would require virtually a miracle. Nevertheless, the status quo is by no means predestination, and the histories of particular very poor and very backward nations of the past that have moved to the forefront of human achievement and prosperity show what can be done. The dramatic rise of Scotland in the eighteenth century, Japan in the nineteenth century, and Singapore, Hong Kong and South Korea in the twentieth century all show what can be done— and, to some extent, how.

None of these heartening examples of dramatic economic rises was due to the international transfers of wealth known as "foreign aid." Nor were these economic rises due to "nation-building" by outsiders, whether foreign governments or various experts supplied by international agencies such as the World Bank or the International Monetary Fund. Despite the many attempts to blame the poverty of some nations on exploitation by other nations or by foreign investors, it would be hard to find many nations that rose from poverty to prosperity by ridding themselves of colonial overlords— however desirable that might be on other grounds— or by confiscating the property of foreign investors. Indeed, impressive lists of the failures, or even counterproductive consequences, of such approaches can be, and have been, compiled.[61]

Still less often can nations be found that rose from poverty to prosperity by expelling, or by driving out through oppression or mob violence, various minorities widely described as "exploiters" or "parasites"— such as the Jews in Eastern Europe, the Chettiars in Burma, the Asians in East Africa, or others in various other parts of the world and in different periods of history.

Often the nations that drove out such groups were worse off economically after they were gone, and the nations that welcomed them were better off. Spain, for example, after driving out its Moorish conquerors in 1492, then drove out the Jews that same year. Later— after entering its "golden age" of worldwide empire in the sixteenth century— Spain drove out the Moriscos in 1609. The expelled Jews contributed to the economies of the Islamic world and helped make Holland a major economic power. After the Moriscos—Christianized Moors— were forced out, Spain's agriculture suffered because their replacements were unable to maintain the country's intricate irrigation system or other aspects of agriculture.[62] In addition, a bishop who had favored their expulsion nevertheless asked: "Who will make our shoes now?"[63]

The United States benefitted from the arrival of millions of Jews from Europe, who eventually rose to provide disproportionate numbers of people in many professions, including world-class scientists who were disproportionately represented among those who created the first nuclear bomb, on which America's international position as a superpower rested.

The descendants of great conquering nations and peoples often have little to show economically from the historic feats of their ancestors, whether the hordes of Genghis Khan, the Spanish conquistadors, the Ottoman Turks or others. Some conquests have left behind prosperous progeny among the descendants of the conquerors but these were usually conquests by nations that were already prosperous, such as the British who conquered and settled Australia and most of North America, displacing the indigenous populations in both places. The even larger conquests of Spain in the Western Hemisphere usually led to nations in Latin America that have seldom been as prosperous as the former British colonies in North America or Australia, even when the Latin American countries have had fertile soil and rich natural resources.

If there is any common thread in these widely varying outcomes, it seems to be human capital— and the cultural values behind the acquisition of human capital. This can be seen by comparisons of nations and by comparisons of groups within given nations. When Charles Darwin stopped in Australia during his historic voyage around the world in the early nineteenth century, he compared the development of the area around Sydney harbor with what he had seen in South America: "Here, in a less promising country, scores of years have done many more times more than an equal number of centuries have effected in South America."[64]

Argentina, for example, has been described as "among the world's most richly endowed countries" with "extraordinarily fertile" land, in which the roots of some plants go down 15 feet in soil unencumbered by rocks.[65] Unlike some other Latin American countries, Argentina's population is predominantly of European ancestry. Yet Barbados, whose population is predominantly of sub-Saharan African ancestry— that is, this population originated in a region of the world much poorer than Europe— has a 40 percent higher Gross Domestic Product per capita than that of Argentina.[66]

Although the Barbadians arrived in the Western Hemisphere as slaves and the Spaniards arrived as conquerors, the Barbadians absorbed the British culture, in which they lived longer than the peoples of sub-Saharan Africa from which they came, and the British culture was very different from the culture of Spain, as regards the values attached to work, education, and entrepreneurship, among other cultural factors that the British promoted and the Spaniards often disdained. Cultural differences among groups within Argentina reinforce the conclusion that the inherited culture from Spain was no more economically productive in the Western Hemisphere than it was in Western Europe, where Spain has long been one of the poorer countries.

Immigrants to Argentina from various other parts of Europe than Spain have been much more economically successful than the native Argentines, even when these immigrants were initially very poor on arrival. This was especially true of immigrants from Italy, who were the largest number of immigrants to Argentina in the nineteenth and early twentieth centuries. Italian immigrants were 40 percent of all immigrants to Argentina as early as 1864 and remained nearly 40 percent half a century later, in 1914.[67]

Two of the most striking ways in which Italians in Argentina differed from the Argentines was in the Italians' willingness to take on the hardest work, and to save, even out of low incomes. Seasonal migrants from Italy were in great demand as agricultural laborers, and have been credited with contributing to the vast expansion of agriculture in nineteenth century Argentina.[68] In addition to Italian agricultural laborers who were called *golondrinas* or swallows, because they came and went with the seasons, there were other Italian farm workers who remained as permanent residents. These latter Italians often began as peons and then saved over the years until they could become sharecroppers and then eventually landowners.[69]

Despite the unusual fertility of Argentine land, the country imported wheat, until foreign farmers— notably Italians, but also including Germans from Russia, among others— arrived and transformed Argentina into one of the world's great wheat-exporting nations.[70] But the fact that the land was always capable of growing wheat meant nothing before Argentina acquired people who were prepared to do what was necessary to be successful wheat farmers. Yet again, geography is not predestination.

In the cities, as in the farmlands, Argentines were outperformed by immigrants. As of 1914, foreigners— who were about 30 percent of the Argentine population— owned 72 percent of the commercial businesses in Argentina, and 82 percent in Buenos Aires.[71] Italian entrepreneurs in Buenos Aires predominated in the production of alcoholic beverages— except beer, where the Germans were pre-eminent,[72] as they were also pre-eminent among the leading beer brewers in the United States and also created China's famous Tsingtao beer, as well as being prominent producers of beer in Australia.

Argentines were not noted for saving, and were in fact called "the spendthrift of the world."[73] In 1887, the Banco de la Provincia de Buenos Aires had twice as many depositors who were citizens of Italy as there were who were citizens of Argentina.[74] During that era, most of the Italian immigrants were laborers but, at the same time, most of Argentina's masons, seamen, tradespeople, architects, importers, engineers and restaurant and hotel owners were also Italian.[75]

This role of Italians in supplying skilled workers, and others with much human capital, to other countries was not unique to Argentina,* nor were Italians the only group to play that role in Argentina. In 1895, about three-fifths of Argentina's industrial workers and about four-fifths of the owners of industrial enterprises were foreigners.[76] As late as the 1920's, it was said of Argentina that "if you want a shoe soled, a lock or kettle mended, a bookcase made, a book bound or a pamphlet printed, a roll of film developed or a camera repaired, you will go to an immigrant or the son of an immigrant."[77] In the middle of the twentieth century, more than three-fourths of all Argentine generals, admirals, and bishops were either immigrants or (mostly) the sons of immigrants.[78]

The Argentine government itself recognized differences between immigrants from different countries in Europe, and sought to attract people from outside the Spanish culture prevailing in Argentina. They

---

* "Emigration from Italy was responsible for the spread into northern Europe, the countries of Islam, and even the Indies, of a skilled labour force of artisans, artists, merchants, and artillerymen. . . Italian inventors, artists, masons, and merchants travelled along every road in Europe." Fernand Braudel, *The Mediterranean and the Mediterranean World in the Age of Philip II*, translated by Siân Reynolds (New York: Harper & Row, 1972), Vol. I, p. 416.

deliberately sought at first to attract immigrants from Britain, Germany and Scandinavia, but without much success, so they then welcomed immigrants from Italy and Spain— preferably *northern* Italians and *Basques* from Spain, people with very different cultures from those in southern Italy or in the rest of Spain— Basques, for example, being noted for being "thrifty and hard workers."[79] The Argentine government's representatives in Europe also recruited Germans from Russia.[80] Volga Germans, many of whom had grown wheat in Russia, settled in what then became Argentina's wheat belt.[81]

While people from outside the prevailing Spanish culture of Argentina dominated much of that country's economy, Argentines dominated its political institutions. In the early twentieth century, Argentina was one of the world's most prosperous nations— ranking above France and Germany, for example.[82] But, by the middle of the twentieth century, disastrous political policies had dropped Argentina out of the front ranks of nations economically.

Despite its rich soil and other natural advantages, including a location that spared it from being devastated by two World Wars like nations in Europe, Argentina's political culture destroyed the prosperity that the country's economy had once enjoyed. Messianic political demagoguery and class warfare rhetoric and policies, epitomized by Juan Perón and his wife Evita— patroness of "the shirtless ones"— were part of an economically counterproductive pattern that began before them and continued long after their time, nullifying both the advantages provided by nature and the human capital supplied largely by foreigners, whether immigrants or international investors and entrepreneurs. As of 2015, *The Economist* magazine reported that Argentina's economy had "barely grown for four years," was running a budget deficit and had an inflation rate of about 25 percent per year.[83]

Argentina was by no means the only country in Latin America whose economic advancement was heavily dependent on foreigners to develop its economy— especially those from countries other than the founding nations of Spain or Portugal. In the early nineteenth century, even such basic items as doors, flour, salt, sugar, furniture and shoes were imported into Brazil.[84] Much of the industry of Brazil was created by German, Italian and other immigrants, beginning in the late nineteenth century, and their descendants remained dominant in these industries even into the middle of the twentieth century.[85] Importers in São Paulo were almost invariably immigrants during the period from the late nineteenth century until the end of the Second World War.[86]

German immigrants in Brazil pioneered in clearing virgin forests to establish a flourishing agriculture. The state of São Paulo also subsidized the immigration of Italian peasants.[87] Italians and Germans helped turn São Paulo into the industrial heartland of South America.[88]

In Brazil's state of Rio Grande do Sul, Germans in the early twentieth century were the sole producers of metal furniture, trunks, stoves, paper, hats, neckties, leather, soap, glass, matches, beer, confections, and carriages, as well as the sole owners of foundries and carpentry shops.[89] Such dominance of foreigners in industry was not due to a lack of wealthy Portuguese Brazilians, but to the fact that members of the Brazilian plantation-owning elite families who pursued non-agricultural careers tended to go into the professions, rather than into commerce or industry. As of 1913, there were only two Brazilian-owned firms among the top 15 exporters in the port city of Santos.[90]

The government of Brazil, like the government of Argentina, deliberately recruited Germans in Europe[91] to be immigrants who would not be reluctant to do the hard physical labor of pioneering in the wilderness, nor were disdainful of it, like people from the Portuguese culture of Brazil and the Spanish culture of Argentina. Europeans from outside the Iberian peninsula were deliberately sought as immigrants, not only by the governments of Argentina and Brazil, but also by the governments of Chile and Paraguay, for the hard work and severe living conditions that went with pioneering in opening up virgin wildernesses in these countries.[92]

German immigrant farmers in Chile turned a virtually barren wilderness into one of the agricultural showplaces of South

America.[93] Such industrial enterprises in Chile as tanneries, saw mills, soap factories, flour mills, distilleries, shoe factories, and shipyards were also established by Germans.[94] The industrialization of Chile was so much the work of immigrants in general that they and their children still owned three-quarters of the industrial enterprises in Santiago in the middle of the twentieth century.[95] Nor was this an unusual pattern in Latin America. In the words of historian Fernand Braudel, it was immigrants who "created modern Brazil, modern Argentina, modern Chile."[96]

Seldom were these immigrants simply prosperous foreigners who brought their wealth with them. On the contrary, most of them were working-class people who rose to *become* middle class in Argentina.[97] In Brazil and Paraguay, the German farmers were usually of peasant origins and faced harrowing conditions in the early years when they began pioneering in the wilderness, where it was a struggle just to survive.[98] What immigrants brought to Latin America was human capital, whether in the form of specific skills or just a willingness to work hard and save their money— as contrasted with the Spanish and Portuguese settlers' disdain for manual labor, or for commerce and industry, or for thrift.[99] Latin American governments recognized these cultural differences at the time, despite however much the recognition of such differences may be taboo in many places today.

Not all these immigrants were from Europe. Japanese immigrants played a significant role in the economies of Brazil and Peru. Although the Japanese were only 2 to 3 percent of the population in Brazil's state of São Paulo, and owned less than 2 percent of its land, they produced nearly 30 percent of the state's agricultural output in the early 1930s— including 46 percent of the cotton, 57 percent of the silk, and 75 percent of the tea. A substantial proportion of the banana plantations were also in Japanese hands.[100]

Peru was another Latin American nation in which a small number of Japanese immigrants played a disproportionate role in the economy. Beginning in the late nineteenth and early twentieth centuries as agricultural laborers, working under conditions that led to high death rates,[101] the Japanese in Peru soon moved into urban communities, where they began working in occupations ranging from domestic servants to small business owners.[102] Eventually, the Japanese owned three-quarters of all the barbershops and 200 grocery stores in Peru's capital city, Lima. Even as agricultural laborers, the Japanese work habits made them more in demand than Peruvian workers, and the Japanese laborers were paid more.[103]

The Japanese acquired a reputation not only for hard work, but also for reliability and honesty.[104] They also took more interest than Peruvians in the education of their children.[105] The illiteracy rate in Peru was 79 percent in 1876 and, though it declined over the generations, 58 percent of the population were still illiterate in 1940. Manufacturing firms in Peru during this era were usually controlled either by foreigners or by recent immigrants.

Like other minority groups who have been more successful than members of the majority population in other times and places, the Japanese were resented in Peru. These resentments were expressed in editorial criticisms and in boycotts of Japanese-owned businesses, though these boycotts failed because the Japanese usually charged lower prices than others.[106] However, political measures against the Japanese were more effective. These included a law requiring at least 80 percent of all employees to be Peruvians,[107] and immigration from Japan was severely restricted in the mid-1930s.[108]

Disdain for commerce and industry at the higher social levels of Hispanic and Portuguese societies— whether in Europe or among their Western Hemisphere offshoots— has been paralleled by an aversion to manual labor and hard work at the lower social levels. What has been involved in such attitudes has not been simple laziness, but what a scholar writing about seventeenth-century Spain characterized as "pride in indolence," reflecting an aversion to the "stigma" associated with manual work in that culture.[109]

Centuries later, Paraguayans were bewildered by the unrelenting work of people in Japanese agricultural colonies in their country,[110] and Honduran farmers complained that it was unfair for them to have to compete with German farmers in their country, since the latter were considered to be working too hard.[111]

Latin America has by no means been unique on the world stage in not simply failing to reach the standards of productivity set by others, but in positively rejecting, resenting and restricting those who were more productive— and explaining away their own lags by blaming "exploitation" by others at home and abroad. Latin American intellectuals led the way in developing "dependency theory," blaming the lags of South Americans on North Americans and others. Eventually, the striking success of Asian countries that opened their economies to foreign trade, foreign investors and foreign technology eroded the foundations of dependency theory in Latin America. But not before whole generations had been sacrificed to this self-indulgence by Latin American intellectuals.

When considering cultural or other factors, timing must also be considered among the reasons for particular outcomes. Finally abandoning dependency theory offered the possibility for more economic progress, but the negative effects of all the years when that theory was an obstacle to economic growth were not negated. Similarly, a nation whose population remained illiterate, while literacy became widespread among other nations, will of course benefit from finally bringing literacy to its own people, but that will not put its people on a par with people in countries where literacy has been the norm for generations, or for centuries.

Timing is important in another sense. It has long been observed that a transplanted culture is less subject to change than the culture in its country of origin. Thus, many words and phrases in the French spoken in Quebec and in the Spanish spoken in Mexico have become archaic in France and Spain. Some of the counterproductive attitudes that Latin America inherited from Spain have been said to have begun to change in Spain itself, more so than in Latin America.[112]

It is hard to escape the fact that former British colonies proper— that is, countries founded by a transplanted British population— have generally done better economically than former Spanish or

Portuguese colonies. Nor can this be due to the British Empire's having made better initial choices as to places to settle, because the Spanish Empire was established first, giving Spain the first choices. Spaniards conquered lands and peoples in both North America and South America in the 16th century, before the first permanent British settlement in America was established, tenuously, at Jamestown in the 17th century.

A Latin American intellectual and public official who lamented that "there is not one developed nation in Latin America" pointed out that "we began this race with conditions equal to, or even better than, the rest of the world." These included universities established in Argentina, Chile, Mexico, Peru, Bolivia, Ecuador, Colombia and the Dominican Republic *before* Harvard was founded in 1636 as the first college in what was to become the United States. Nor were other European offshoot societies the only ones to surpass Latin America economically: "We won our independence 150 years before countries such as South Korea and Singapore, which, despite their past as colonies of empires that took advantage of them, and despite their lack of significant natural resources, today exceed, several times over, our per capita income."[113]

Chapter 6

CULTURAL DIFFUSION

> *The Saracen conquests in the seventh century brought its*
> *southern and western shores into political and cultural*
> *union with Arabia, Persia and western India, and*
> *introduced from the East new field crops like rice and*
> *cotton, new fruits like oranges and lemons, improved*
> *technique in ceramics and textiles, and oriental standards*
> *of beauty in color and design.*
>
> Ellen Churchill Semple

The benefits of a particular culture can obviously be diffused from its source to other places by the movement of people who have that culture, as with the movement of Germans, Italians and Japanese into Latin America. But particular products of a culture can also move from one place to another without a movement of people, as chess and so-called Arabic numerals spread from India to become part of the culture of Europe, without any corresponding movement of people. Yet another way for culture to spread beyond its original source is for that culture to be imposed on subordinate groups. The history of such outsiders' attempts to change the culture of others has largely been a history of failure. The centuries-long attempts of Christian Europe to force Jews to change their religion are just one example. The Czars' "Russification" program, and similar attempts in Hungary and Serbia likewise created more resentments than results.

Nevertheless cultural diffusion has taken place on a massive scale over the centuries by particular groups, races, nations and civilizations borrowing particular cultural features from others for their own benefit, by their own choices and at their own pace. Western civilization's replacement of Roman numerals by Arabic numerals, even in countries that were once part of the Roman Empire, and which retained many other features inherited from Rome, was a result of voluntary decisions made throughout Western societies, without any campaigns of persuasion by Arabs or by the people of India. Arabic numerals were simply *better*— not merely *different*, as multiculturalists might say— when it came to mathematical operations. Just writing the year of Columbus' voyage to the Western Hemisphere in Roman numerals— MCCCCXCII— shows the cumbersomeness of these numbers, and mathematicians have other objections.

The point here is that cultural borrowing has long taken place voluntarily, on a large scale, for largely practical reasons. We have already noted some of the many cultural features of Asia that spread to Europe over the centuries. A similar process of cultural diffusion occurred between different regions within Europe. Among the cultural advances that spread, over the centuries, from Western Europe to Eastern Europe were coins, castles, crossbows, paved streets, printing presses, power looms, vaccinations, railroads and automobiles.[1] When Lithuania established the University of Vilnius in the sixteenth century, most of the students came from Eastern Europe but most of the faculty came from Western Europe.[2] When Dorpat University was established in Tartu, Estonia in 1802, it was in effect a German university on the soil of the Russian Empire, with nearly half its faculty coming from Germany itself, and the remainder including domestic Baltic Germans.[3]

Not all social groups, races, nations or civilizations have been equally receptive to absorbing cultural advances from others. Even countries whose governments actively sought immigrants with cultures different from their own, such as in Latin America, were not necessarily countries whose populations then emulated those imported cultures. Often separate enclaves of more advanced groups have persisted for generations or even centuries in lagging societies, whether in Latin America, Eastern Europe or Southeast Asia. For whatever reasons, some societies have been receptive to other cultures, while other societies have been very resistant— a difference that has had major consequences for both kinds of societies.

RECEPTIVE CULTURES

In some cases, geographic or other handicaps impeding the internal progress of a people or a nation have been overcome by absorbing advances made by more fortunate peoples elsewhere, and then using and improving those advances for their own economic or other benefit.

Japan in centuries past was a classic example of a country lacking the geographic advantages of more fortunate nations that had pioneered historic advances. By contrast with ancient China's many outstanding natural harbors and extensive network of navigable rivers, along with unusually fertile land in its northern region, Japan was a much smaller country, with smaller and steeper drainage areas, making its rivers less navigable because their waters flowed more steeply and swiftly down to the sea.[4] Much of Japan is mountainous, with only a fraction of the country's land being level enough for agriculture.[5] Japan's largest level plain is only 120 miles long.[6] In addition, there is a dearth of natural resources in Japan.

Given these geographic handicaps, it is not surprising that Japan lagged for centuries behind the economic level of China, during the era of Chinese world leadership in many fields, centuries ago. One of Japan's few geographic advantages has been its accessibility to the sea, so that its coastal areas have been in communication with the outside world. Moreover, these coastal areas are a substantial proportion of the total land area of Japan, where no part of the country is more than 70 miles from the sea.[7] Among other things, this meant that the more advanced culture of China was physically accessible to Japan for more than a thousand years. More important, Japan was culturally *receptive* to aspects of the Chinese culture. In addition to adapting Chinese writing to create a written version of the Japanese language, Japan also adopted some Chinese philosophical ideas, as well as such mundane things as the cultivation of cotton and the technology for spinning and weaving it into cloth.[8]

For more than two centuries, however, the government of Japan cut the country off from much of the outside world. From 1638 to 1868, emigration from Japan was forbidden, on pain of death, and Japanese who happened to be abroad at the time of this decree were forbidden to return. According to leading scholars of East Asian history, "The Japanese, who had been technologically and institutionally abreast of the Europeans in many respects and ahead in some at the start of the seventeenth century, fell drastically behind."[9] Isolation took its toll in Japan, as it has elsewhere.

The historic shattering of Japan's barriers against the outside world came abruptly in 1853, with the intrusion of Commodore Matthew Perry's American warships into Japan. That Perry could sail into Japanese waters with impunity was one indication of Japan's weakness and backwardness at that time. The country's backwardness was further revealed by the reaction of the Japanese people to a train that Perry presented as a gift:

> At first the Japanese watched the train fearfully from a safe distance, and when the engine began to move they uttered cries of astonishment and drew in their breath.
> Before long they were inspecting it closely, stroking it, and riding on it, and they kept this up throughout the day.[10]

In the years following Commodore Perry's mission, Japanese receptivity to Western culture became extraordinary, approaching adulation. The United States was singled out for special praise and depicted as an "earthly paradise."[11] Euphoric depictions of the United States were part of a general depiction of Western peoples and nations as enviable and great.*

As an indication of the economic level of nineteenth century Japan, its per capita purchasing power in 1886 was one-fortieth of that in the United Kingdom, though by 1898 this had risen to one-sixth.[12] Japan's rise to an economic parity with the leading Western nations over the next century was achieved by a mass importation of Western technology and Western experts to begin teaching that technology in Japan, while Japanese students were sent overseas to study in Western universities. Meanwhile, inside Japan, more Japanese children were going to school. While fewer than half of Japanese children were going to school in 1886, by 1905 that had risen to 95 percent, and continued rising.[13]

By the beginning of the twentieth century, Japan's own people had advanced to the point where most foreign experts were no longer needed and were gone.[14] During the first half of the twentieth century, Japan was producing many industrial products, though much of what it produced during that era were cheaper imitations of Western products, and not of the highest quality. However, the second half of the twentieth century saw the Japanese become pace-

---

* There were later reversals of these attitudes in Japan during the early twentieth century, as fanatical nationalism arose. Those Japanese emigrants who went to the United States during the earlier, pro-American period largely remained loyal to the United States during the Second World War, despite having been discriminated against before the war and despite being interned during the war. But Japanese emigrants who went to Brazil, during the later, nationalistic and anti-Western period, remained loyal to Japan throughout the war and refused to believe the news that Japan had surrendered. That Japanese Americans were loyal to the United States, despite being discriminated against and interned, while Japanese in Brazil were loyal to Japan, despite being treated better in Brazil than Japanese in the United States and not being interned, suggests again that defining "environment" as the *surrounding* circumstances may fail to explain outcomes that depend on the culture *within* a given group. See Yasuo Wakatsuki, "Japanese Emigration to the United States, 1866–1924: A Monograph," *Perspectives in American History*, Vol. XII (1979), pp. 465–466; William Petersen, *Japanese Americans: Oppression and Success* (New York: Random House, 1971), pp. 86–87; Yukio Fujii and T. Lynn Smith, *The Acculturation of the Japanese Immigrants in Brazil* (Gainesville: University of Florida Press, 1959), pp. 49–51.

setters in both technology and quality, in fields ranging from cameras to automobiles to electronics.[15]

This evolution was especially striking in photography. However, the first Nikon camera in 1948 was an obvious imitation of a German camera called the Contax, and the first Canon camera was a copy of Germany's world-renowned Leica. But, as time went on, Japan's Nikon and Canon cameras were developed into standard-setters in their field, and their sales eclipsed the sales of the cameras they had initially imitated. Japan also produced high-speed trains that eclipsed anything produced in the United States.

Although Britain and Japan have been culturally quite different in many ways, they were nevertheless similar in being island nations that for centuries lagged behind the progress on the mainland nearest them— that is, continental Western Europe and China, respectively. Britain and Japan were also very much alike in having cultures that were receptive to absorbing the advances of other nations and, eventually, developing those advances further, surpassing their erstwhile superiors.

Within Britain, the Scots likewise absorbed much from the English, beginning with the English language, and eventually rose to surpass the English in engineering and medical science.[16] From the late eighteenth century through the first half of the nineteenth century, a disproportionate share of the leading British intellectuals, in a variety of fields, were of Scottish ancestry.

These included David Hume in philosophy, Adam Smith in economics, Joseph Black in chemistry, James Watt in engineering, Robert Burns and Sir Walter Scott in literature, James Mill and John Stuart Mill in economics and politics, and Robert Adam, who was internationally renowned for his designs of everything from palaces to book bindings.[17] As a noted historian put it, "in every branch of knowledge this once poor and ignorant people produced original and successful thinkers."[18]

During the Middle Ages, Europe as a whole learned much from the Islamic world of the Middle East and North Africa, especially in mathematics and philosophy,[19] but also in agriculture and architecture.

Militarily as well, the Islamic world was more advanced at that time. The Ottoman Empire invaded and conquered much of Southeastern Europe, while North African Moors invaded and conquered Spain. As the distinguished British magazine *The Economist* put it in 2014:

> A thousand years ago, the great cities of Baghdad, Damascus and Cairo took turns to race ahead of the Western world. Islam and innovation were twins. The various Arab caliphates were dynamic superpowers— beacons of learning, tolerance and trade. Yet today the Arabs are in a wretched state.[20]

During the centuries of the Moors' rule in Spain, Cordoba became "the centre of learning for all Spain, and the entire Western world."[21] The Western world was very receptive to cultural advances from the Islamic world, both those originating in that world and those transmitted from Asia through the Middle East. As a noted American scholar pointed out:

> Modern mathematics is based on the Arabic system of notation, and algebra was an Arab invention. During the intellectual revival of western Europe in the eleventh and twelfth centuries many Christian scholars went to Cordoba and other Muslim intellectual centers to study classical philosophy and science. At the same time, Christian merchants learned Muslim commercial practices and techniques.[22]

Anyone who doubts the cultural and technological level achieved by the Islamic world a thousand years ago need only visit the great mosque in Cordoba, built when the Moors were the ruling conquerors of Spain. As for tolerance, when in 1492 Christian Spain finally freed itself and drove out the last of its Muslim overlords, it also expelled Jews *en masse*— more of whom fled to the Islamic world than to Christian Europe, which was at that time less tolerant than Islamic North Africa and the Ottoman Empire. That world was obviously quite different from the world of today. Part of the difference reflects a difference in receptivity to other cultures in the Middle East at different periods of history.

UNRECEPTIVE CULTURES

Eventually, the Western world would overtake the Middle Eastern and North African countries, both militarily and in terms of science and technology. But now the Islamic countries were by no means as receptive to the cultural advances made in the Western countries as the West had once been when the countries of the Middle East and North Africa were ascendant— or as the Islamic world itself had once been receptive to absorbing cultural advances from other societies.

This mutual receptivity to each other's culture in the Middle Ages is now very much part of a long gone past. One revealing sign of today's lack of cultural receptivity to Western culture in the Middle East is that in today's Arab world— about 300 million people in more than 20 countries[23]— the number of books translated from other languages has been just one-fifth of the number translated by Greece alone, for a population of 11 million people.

Over a five-year period, a United Nations study showed that the number of books translated in the Arab world was less than one book for every million Arabs, while in Hungary there were 519 books translated for every million people, and in Spain 920 books per million people.[24] Put differently, Spain translates more books into Spanish annually than the Arabs have translated into Arabic in a thousand years.[25] This too was a pattern very different from the Islamic world of earlier centuries. Even the philosophy of ancient Greece once reached Western Europe in Arabic translations, which were in turn re-translated in Spain into Latin or into the vernacular languages of Western Europe.[26]

Cultural isolation can have effects very similar to the effects of geographic isolation, making it harder for individuals, groups, nations or whole civilizations to keep up with the advances of others. China's decline from world leadership in many fields was likewise marked by resistance to learning from others. Early in the fifteenth century, the government of China imposed severe restrictions on contacts with the outside world, destroying the large ships in which a Chinese admiral had made voyages of exploration covering longer distances than

Columbus' much smaller ships. Such voyages were now not only forbidden but the building of ships capable of making such voyages was banned, and records of earlier voyages to what were regarded as the lands of foreign barbarians were destroyed. A twenty-first century American scientist assessed China's position as of the time this fateful decision was made:

> Before the decision, China had a fleet of ocean-going ships bigger and more capable than any European ships. China was roughly level with Europe in scientific knowledge and far ahead in the technologies of printing, navigation, and rocketry. As a consequence of the decision, China fell disastrously behind in science and technology, and is only catching up now after six hundred years.[27]

In the eighteenth century, when King George III sent gifts to the emperor of China that included various devices showing technological advances in the West, the emperor of China replied that there was nothing China lacked. He said: "We have never set much store on strange or ingenious objects, nor do we need any more of your country's manufactures."[28] A rejection of advances from another culture could hardly have been more explicit— or more catastrophic, as China became ever more vulnerable to Western imperialism as the technological gap between the two civilizations widened.

Since no given culture is better in all things, much less for all time, a lack of receptivity to the cultural advances made by others is a self-imposed isolation that can be as damaging as isolation imposed by geography.

LANGUAGES

Language differences have long been a major factor in cultural isolation among countries around the world. It has been said that "Knowledge travels in the baggage of languages."[29] But not all languages contain the same amount or range of written knowledge. The languages of Western Europe developed written versions centuries before the languages of Eastern Europe, because Western Europe was conquered by the Romans and acquired Latin letters as a result. This centuries-long head start in literacy meant that, even after the languages of Eastern Europe developed written versions, they did not immediately acquire the same range, volume or variety of knowledge available in the languages of Western Europe at that time. There were many consequences of this.

Even though Estonians, for example, had a written language in the nineteenth century, most of what was written in that language during the first half of that century was confined to religious subjects. But the working language of educated people in Estonia was German, whether a particular individual was of German ancestry or not.[30] Nor was this situation unique to Estonia.[31] Although the Czech language had an earlier and wider literature in Bohemia, this literature had declined by the early nineteenth century and the Czech press at that time was said to be still in its infancy, with a circulation only a fraction of that of the German newspaper in Prague.[32] Elementary schools for Czech children were taught in their native language but, until 1848, there was no high school in Bohemia that taught in Czech. To advance to that level required a child to know German.[33]

For many people in Eastern Europe, becoming educated for careers in science or in various professions meant being educated in the German language. Moreover, given the prevalence of ethnic Germans in many higher occupations in parts of Eastern Europe, entering many elite occupations there often meant acquiring the German culture in general, to fit in with elite colleagues. In nineteenth century Bohemia, for example, it was said that no military officer would speak in Czech.[34] When in nineteenth century Estonia, men educated at Tartu University "identified themselves as Estonians" that was "a previously unheard of phenomenon."[35]

Many among the rising generation of educated Czechs and Latvians greatly resented having to change their language and culture, in order to advance in the world. Ethnic Germans of course had no such obstacle to overcome, so no one could claim that this situation was "fair." But the more fundamental question is whether this unfairness was something inherent in the circumstances of the time and place, or something arbitrarily inflicted on non-Germans in Eastern Europe.

While the argument could be made that Germans ruled the Habsburg Empire, and so could be accused of treating other groups unfairly, very similar patterns existed in Romania, ruled by Romanians, and in Latvia and Estonia, then parts of the Russian Empire, ruled by Russians.

The practical question was whether the presence of substantial German minorities in various parts of Eastern Europe, including both the Baltic and the Balkans, increased or decreased the opportunities of the peoples indigenous to that region. From an economic standpoint, it is clear that culturally German educational institutions were open to people who were not Germans, and so these institutions were available sources of human capital that were not equally available in the languages of the indigenous populations of Eastern Europe at that time.

Similarly, among those rural villages in Eastern Europe that were largely populated by German farmers in those days, German law was often allowed to prevail by Eastern European rulers. This allowed both Germans and non-Germans living in those villages greater freedom than in most of the rest of Eastern Europe.[36] Moreover, the presence of Germans with higher skills than those in the indigenous population benefitted the whole economy, providing higher output per capita, additional kinds of products and additional jobs, all of which benefitted the indigenous population, as well as the Germans. It was precisely the Germans farmers' greater skills and productivity which had prompted Eastern European rulers to welcome them and provide incentives for them to immigrate by letting them live under laws with which they were already familiar.

From a political perspective, however, Germans in Eastern Europe were seen by many Eastern European peoples as an alien elite dominating business and the professions, and their culture was seen as a barrier to the indigenous peoples, rather than an opportunity to advance themselves by acquiring knowledge available to them in this foreign culture that was not equally available in their own culture at that time and place. But the Latvian intelligentsia, for example, saw Latvians as a people "consigned by long oppression to lowly stations in life."[37]

The situation of the Germans in Eastern Europe was by no means unique on the world stage. Much the same combination of economic advances and social resentments was created by the presence of the overseas Chinese minority in such Southeast Asian countries as Thailand, Vietnam, the Philippines, Malaysia and Indonesia.[38] Few among the indigenous peoples of these countries sought to acquire the culture of the overseas Chinese, including their willingness to work hard for long hours— certainly not as many as resented Chinese domination in education, industry and commerce.

Much the same pattern appeared in other countries, where either a foreign minority or a different ethnic group within the same country, but with a different culture, outperformed the local majority population in educational institutions and/or in the economy. These would include, at various times and places, Armenians in the Ottoman Empire, Ibos in Nigeria, Tamils in Sri Lanka, Indians and Pakistanis in East Africa, Japanese in Peru, Indians in Fiji, Jews in Eastern Europe and Lebanese in West Africa, among others.

The political incentives in these and other countries have been to demonize whatever minority outperformed the majority population, often accusing these minorities of "taking over" whole industries, even when in fact they created industries that had not existed before. However the political mobilization of resentment turned out— and in some countries, such as Sri Lanka and Nigeria, it produced horrific civil wars— this politicizing of group differences operated against a receptivity to human capital available from more economically successful cultures.*

Often instead, politics promoted a sense of grievance against those with a more successful culture, and a sense of entitlement to some demographically based "fair share" of jobs and incomes. As an ethnic leader in India expressed it, "Are we not entitled to jobs just because we are not as qualified?"[39] An ethnic spokesman in Nigeria similarly decried "the tyranny of skills."[40]

Implicit in this focus on demographically based "fair shares" of economic benefits is an assumption that questions about sharing the wealth can be separated from questions about producing that wealth in the first place. But the damage to national economies after the expulsions of productive minorities suggests otherwise, whether it was the expulsion of the Asians from Uganda in the 1970s,[41] the expulsion of the Germans from Czechoslovakia after the Second World War,[42] the expulsion of the Moriscos from seventeenth century Spain[43] or the expulsions of Jews from France and various German cities in medieval times.[44] Similar economic damage has been done in countries where hostile policies by governments, or outright violence by mobs, led productive minorities to flee, as the Huguenots fled from France in 1685[45] or as Jews fled Eastern Europe in the late nineteenth century.[46]

Hostility to more productive minorities, who both increase the national standard of living and provide cultural examples and opportunities for members of the majority population to acquire the

---

* Sometimes, where the majority population is more advanced, and the lagging minority speaks a different language, some lament the imposition of the majority group's language. But Arnold Toynbee made the case for such intervention in 1915: "In Great Britain at the present moment the numerically small Welsh-speaking minority of school children have to learn English as well as their mother tongue, but the English majority do not learn Welsh. Here we have 'suffering' or disadvantage to one party, without injustice: the Welsh child does not learn English because it is the English-speaking majority's interest that he should do so, but because it is his own. His only quarrel is with the fact that the English population is much larger than his, and its language much more widely spoken, and it is as useless to quarrel with facts as it is to beat the sea and bind it in chains." Arnold Toynbee, *Nationality & The War* (London: J.M. Dent & Sons, Ltd., 1915), pp. 17–18.

human capital of a more advanced culture, in order to become more productive and advance themselves, might seem to be irrational. But it is quite rational, from the standpoint of the self-interest of leaders of lagging groups, to keep the groups they lead resentful of more advanced groups, and to blame those advanced groups for their own group's failure to share more fully in the economic benefits created by skills and knowledge that are not as prevalent in the lagging group's own culture.

Looked at differently, to the extent that individual members of lagging groups acquire the skills and cultures of more advanced groups, they may be absorbed into these groups or, at a minimum, feel less need of their own group leaders. However economically beneficial various aspects of the culture of more advanced groups might be to the lagging group as a whole, the absorption of that culture is a clear threat to group leaders, who see the erosion of the indigenous culture as the erosion of their own role as leaders and the piecemeal loss of their constituency.* Indeed, fear of cultural erosion, and ultimately cultural extinction, has been expressed by the leaders and the intelligentsia of many lagging groups, at various times and places around the world.[47]

An eighteenth-century Czech scholar, for example, expressed fears that the increased use of the German language among fellow Czechs meant that, the next generation "will already be German, and in fifty years more German than Czech will be spoken" in the cities of Bohemia.[48] Nor were such fears groundless. As a later historian said of that era, "Czech-speakers preponderated in Prague only among the lower classes," and though "the Czech language as such was by no means close to death," it had "retreated to the fields, the stables, and the kitchens," where it was spoken by servants and subordinates, and was at this point in history, "a badge not of nationality but of ignorance."[49] Most servants in Prague during this era were Czech,

---

* To say that leaders of lagging groups have strong incentives to advocate policies which protect their own interests, to the detriment of the groups they lead, is not to say that all group leaders make this cynical calculation. The ability of the human mind to rationalize to itself should not be under-estimated.

except for an occasional German nurse or governess. Most German households had servants and most Czech households did not.[50]

Halfway around the world, in twentieth century Sri Lanka, with its Sinhalese Buddhist majority speaking Sinhala and its Tamil Hindu minority speaking the Tamil language, the same fear was expressed that the more successful minority would culturally absorb the less successful majority over time. Sinhala language activists in 1956 warned Buddhist priests "that if they didn't do something there would be no more Buddhism and no more Sinhalese."[51] It was much the same story in Canada's province of Quebec in the 1970s, where the French-speaking majority severely restricted by law the use of English in many institutions, including private businesses. The chief architect of this policy, Cultural Development Minister Camille Laurin, declared that "French must become the common language of all Quebeckers." As elsewhere this was because of a "need for French-speaking Quebeckers to concern themselves constantly with their cultural survival, and their own inferior economic and political position"[52] in Canada.

Similar fears of cultural extinction for similar reasons have been expressed in Fiji, Pakistan, Malaysia, the Philippines and Burma.[53]

Legal restrictions on the use of non-majority languages that seem almost inexplicable in their scope and pettiness, whether in nineteenth century Bohemia or in twentieth century Quebec,[54] are at least comprehensible as part of a drive by group leaders and group intelligentsia to prevent the cultural co-opting of members of lagging groups. These group leaders and intelligentsia have been trying to stave off the assimilation and absorption of fellow group members into economically more advanced groups. Today, in America, black youngsters seeking to speak the standard English of the larger society, often as part of a more general absorption of educational and other components of the larger culture, have been accused of "acting white"— a charge that can bring anything from ridicule to ostracism to harassment or outright violence from fellow blacks.[55]

Internal attempts to prolong the longevity of a lagging group's cultural features have often been aided and abetted by outsiders who romanticize the exotic, and seek to artificially preserve lagging cultures, as if cultures were museum pieces, rather than ways of dealing with the practical challenges of life.

Even a culture that may once have been well adapted to the particular circumstances of an earlier time can become an impediment to progress under fundamentally changed conditions. This can be especially so in the case of indigenous peoples historically displaced by an invading population that has taken over much of the land and resources that made their previous environment economically viable. After that supporting environment has been irretrievably lost, preserving a culture adapted to that lost environment can be a serious disservice, whether among Maoris in New Zealand or among indigenous people living on Indian reservations in the United States, or among other displaced indigenous peoples around the world.[56]

In short, in many times and places there have been many obstacles to cultural receptivity among lagging groups. The enthusiastic embrace of aspects of a different culture by eighteenth century Scots and nineteenth century Japanese was a rare exception. So too was the spectacular rise of Scotland and Japan to the forefront of world achievements in a remarkably short time, as history is measured.

On a smaller scale, various groups within particular non-Western countries seized upon educational opportunities presented by the presence of Western educational institutions during the era of European colonialism. Like the Scots and the Japanese, these indigenous groups often came from regions with geographic handicaps, such as soil too poor for the people in the region to support their growing population. The Ibos in the southern part of Nigeria and the Tamils in the northern part of Sri Lanka were among such groups in various times and places, including Indonesia, Algeria, and the Philippines.[57]

Armed with Western education and other Western cultural advantages, the Ibos and the Tamils spread out to other regions of their respective countries, outperforming other groups in businesses, civil service and the professions, bringing benefits to the general population, and at the same time stirring resentments of their striking success. Racial and ethnic toleration has been rare to non-existent in many societies around the world. Historian Arnold J. Toynbee said in 1915, "hardly a single national society in Europe has yet become capable of national toleration"[58]— in this case, toleration toward fellow Europeans of different ethnicities. Unfortunately, intolerance has not been confined to Europeans, but has been common among peoples and nations around the world. Intolerance has been especially fierce where a minority outperforms a majority.[59]

Some have sought to depict racial differences, based on skin color differences, as uniquely poisonous sources of intergroup hostility. W.E.B. Du Bois' 1903 statement that "the problem of the Twentieth Century is the problem of the color-line"[60] has been taken as prophetic by many. But however plausible or widespread this view, the actual history of the twentieth century shows its biggest and most ghastly mass murders to have been between people with the same skin color— whether Hutus and Tutsis in Rwanda,[61] Serbs and Croatians in the Balkans,[62] Hindus and Muslims in India,[63] the Khmer Rouge and their victims in Cambodia[64] or the Nazi Holocaust against the Jews.[65]

Whether in Europe, Africa or Asia, mass murders of people of the same skin color were the rule, rather than the exception, during the twentieth century. These deaths greatly exceeded murders across the color line, even during the era of sadistic lynchings and other violence against blacks in America's Jim Crow South or violence against indigenous Africans in the white-ruled Republic of South Africa during the oppressive era of racial apartheid. Discriminatory policies and practices are easier to enforce against people who are visibly different. But, when passions rise to murderous levels, ways have been found to identify people who do not differ in complexion.

Intolerance has been rampant in many parts of the world, and it cannot be localized to a particular place or a particular reason, whether skin color, religion or some other immediate cause. Unfortunately, neither can its consequences be limited to a lack of cultural receptivity.

Chapter 7

CULTURE AND PROGRESS

One of the most overlooked aspects of excellence is how much work it takes. Fame can come easily and overnight, but excellence is almost always accompanied by a crushing workload, pursued with single-minded intensity.

Charles Murray

Economic and social progress, whether among individuals, groups or nations, depends on both tangible and intangible factors. The tangible factors would include geography and existing physical wealth as a foundation for economic growth. The key intangible is human capital, and among the varieties of human capital is what has been aptly called "the radius of trust" within which individuals and groups cooperate in economic and social endeavors. Attitudes toward work and attitudes toward progress itself are also among the intangibles. What is tangible may make a stronger visible impression but it is by no means certain that its economic effect is greater than the economic effect of intangibles included in the concept of culture.

Among the many ways that cultures differ is in the ability of individuals and groups to trust and cooperate with one another. The radius of trust differs greatly from one group, race, nation and civilization to another— and these differences can have major implications for disparities of income and wealth between nations or within nations.

TRUST AND HONESTY

While trust permits many mutually beneficial forms of cooperation, trust without *trustworthiness* is a formula for disaster. The limits of honesty in a given society limit the radius of trust in that society, and this can have an economic impact that outweighs many tangible advantages of a given society.

The Soviet Union, for example, was one of the most richly endowed nations on earth, if not *the* most richly endowed, in natural resources. It was one of the few industrial nations with such an abundance of petroleum that it was a major exporter of oil. It contained soil of legendary fertility and the world's largest level plains.[1] The Soviet Union also had the world's largest reserves of iron ore, one-fifth of all the forested land in the world, the world's second-largest deposits of manganese,[2] and one-third of the world's natural gas,[3] in addition to being for many years the world's leading producer of nickel.[4] The Soviet Union was self-sufficient in virtually all natural resources and exported substantial amounts of gold and diamonds. As of 1978, it supplied nearly half of all the industrial diamonds in the world.[5]

Yet, despite all these advantages in natural resources, and a well-educated population, the Soviet economy was far less efficient than the economies of Germany, Japan or the United States, according to a study by two of its own economists.[6] The result was that the standard of living of the Russian people was significantly lower than that in Western Europe, the United States or Japan— even though Japan is one of the world's most poorly endowed nations when it comes to natural resources.

How could a country so richly endowed by nature as the Soviet Union have a standard of living below that of so many other countries with far less in the way of natural resources? The Soviet Union was almost a tailor-made refutation of geographic determinism. The other influences at work that offset the country's many natural advantages were both cultural and political. Back in the nineteenth century, when the country was more candidly called the Russian Empire, John

Stuart Mill commented on a cultural handicap that would impede its economic development:

> The universal venality ascribed to Russian functionaries, must be an immense drag on the capabilities of economical improvement possessed so abundantly by the Russian empire: since the emoluments of public officers must depend on the success with which they can multiply vexations, for the purpose of being bought off by bribes.[7]

The cost of corruption in an economy does not consist solely, or even primarily, of the bribes paid, the money stolen or the goods pilfered. These are all internal transfers, rather than being themselves net reductions of the country's income or wealth. The main costs consist of the things that are *not* done— the businesses that are not started, the investments that are not made and the loans that are not granted, because the rate of return on such economic activities would have to be much higher to make such activities worthwhile in a very corrupt economy than in an economy in which the risks of being deprived of the fruits of one's efforts were much lower.

When the czarist government sought to modernize the Russian economy in the late nineteenth century, and invited Western business firms to set up operations in Russia, those firms hired Russian workers and eventually Russians in managerial positions, but they made it a point *not* to hire Russian accountants. Nor were accountants the only problem. A French observer in the early twentieth century referred to "the extraordinary waste— to be polite— that reigns among the Russian administrators."[8]

Popular expressions among the Russians included "as honest as a German" and "as punctual as a German,"[9] suggesting the rarity of such qualities among Russians themselves. Why and how these cultural differences came to be what they were may be lost in the mists of time, but the economic importance of such cultural qualities is plain.

Widespread corruption in Russia continued, even under the draconian punishments of the Stalinist dictatorship in the days of the Soviet Union. Despite punishments that included years in slave labor camps, the Soviet economy had whole classes of people known as *tolkachi*, whose sole purpose was to carry out illegal economic activities on behalf of Soviet economic enterprises that could otherwise find it difficult to meet the goals set for them by central planners in Moscow, within the severe limitations of what they were officially allowed to do in the government-controlled economy.[10]

The widespread corruption that existed in czarist times persisted in Russia throughout the Soviet era, as well as in Russia after the breakup of the Soviet Union. The stock of a Russian oil company was estimated to sell for about one percent of what the stock of a similar oil company in the United States would sell for, because "the market expects that Russian oil companies will be systematically looted by insiders."[11] Bribes of between $10,000 and $15,000 were required to gain admission to some well-regarded institutions of higher learning in Moscow, according to a Russian newspaper, which estimated that at least $2 billion a year were paid in such outlays by Russian students and their parents.[12]

Russia was not unique, though its great abundance of natural resources and low standard of living provides a dramatic example of how the benefits of tangible factors can be outweighed by the handicaps created by negative intangible factors. It was much the same story in Nigeria, as *The Economist* magazine reported in May, 2015:

> How does a big oil producer end up with no fuel? The irony of that predicament is not lost on citizens of the country with sub-Saharan Africa's largest oil reserves. They endure hours-long queues at petrol stations and buy on the black market. . .
>
> For a country that churns out roughly 2m barrels of oil a day, this is a scandal. The chief cause is Nigeria's inability to process its crude. Corruption and mismanagement have left its four state refineries to rot, forcing this fuel-guzzling country to import up to 80% of its needs.[13]

Latin America has likewise been seen, by many who have studied it, as a place where "the inability to trust and work with others" has been "antithetical to effective entrepreneurship."[14] In any part of the world, pervasive corruption can make the large investments needed to fully develop natural resources simply too risky for either local or foreign investors to take a chance. Where the level of dishonesty, and consequently the level of distrust, is not high enough to completely stifle economic activity, they may nevertheless be high enough to constrain economic activity in various ways.

Many businesses may be organized as family-run enterprises in societies where losses from embezzlement, pilferage or other costly internal dishonest activity by employees drawn from the general public would be prohibitively expensive otherwise. The incidence of such theft varies greatly from one country or culture to another. Losses from shoplifting and employee theft, as a percentage of sales, have been more than twice as high in India as in Germany or Taiwan.[15]

Restricting the pool from which employees, and especially higher-level employees or managers, can be drawn means restricting the amount and level of talent available. It can also mean restricting the size of the business itself to what can be run efficiently by the number of qualified family members available. Where there is an enterprise too large for all positions to be filled by family members, that can mean that more of management's time is spent inspecting and monitoring routine operations by their employees from outside, to guard against internal dishonesty, with correspondingly less time available for more complex management decisions. Sometimes it can mean that companies may engage in vertical integration* beyond the point where that would be economically worthwhile in a more honest society, where a company could rely on the punctuality, quality control and integrity of the suppliers of the materials used in its own operations.[16]

---

* "Vertical integration" is a term used by economists to describe producers who expand their operations to include things usually produced by other firms that supply the materials used in the production process. Examples would include steel mills which own their own iron ore deposits or restaurants which grow food in their own gardens or farms.

In other cultures, however, the radius of trust can be sufficiently large and reliable within particular groups to allow those particular groups to prosper, not only in prosperous countries, but even in Third World countries with unreliable and corrupt legal systems. Members of such groups as the Marwaris in India or sub-groups of the overseas Chinese in Southeast Asia have been able to engage in financial transactions with one another, without contracts or other recourse to the legal or political institutions of the larger society. That is a special advantage in countries where the formal legal system is either ineffective or corrupt, for this gives members of groups with a wide radius of trust among themselves the advantage of being able to make economic decisions faster, wider and with less risk than can other members of such societies.

A high degree of trust within particular groups can also be an advantage in more advanced economies. Hasidic Jews in New York, for example, can sell consignments of expensive jewelry for one another on the basis of verbal agreements, and share the proceeds later, on the basis of these informal understandings.[17] The Marwaris have done the same across international trading networks that they control.[18] So have sub-groups of the overseas Chinese,[19] and a similar pattern can be found among sub-groups of Lebanese immigrants in West Africa and in parts of the Western Hemisphere.[20]

While a whole society can seldom, if ever, develop as strong a sense of trust as that among Marwaris, Hasidic Jews or sub-groups of the overseas Chinese or Lebanese, nevertheless some societies have a strong enough sense of honesty and decency among their people as to enable many useful economic and other activities to take place without the heavy costs and risks that restrict such activities in other societies. Everything from the use of credit cards to the collection of taxes depends on most people being sufficiently trustworthy so that recourse to the forces of the law can be reserved for that segment of the population which lacks the elementary level of trustworthiness required for a viable society on a large scale.

While some theorists may tend to discuss people in the abstract, actual flesh-and-blood human beings differ enormously in their behavior, not just from individual to individual, but from group to group and from one culture to another. Various tests of honesty reveal very striking differences.

When a dozen wallets with money and identification in them were deliberately left in public places in various cities around the world in 2013, the number returned with the money still in them varied from eleven out of twelve in Helsinki to one out of twelve in Lisbon. Moreover, the one that was returned in Lisbon was returned by a visitor from the Netherlands; no Portuguese returned any. In Rio de Janeiro, four were returned.[21] Earlier international tests using wallets with money in them, conducted by the *Reader's Digest*, found 67 percent of these wallets returned, with the money still there, in the United States, 70 percent in Stockholm, and 100 percent returned in Oslo (Norway) and in Odense (Denmark).[22]

When a television station in Copenhagen tried to duplicate the experiment, "they literally could not even leave the wallets— people would instantly pick them up and come running after them, so they had to give up!" A Danish economist estimates that the level of honesty in Denmark saves the criminal justice system a sizeable amount annually.[23] That is aside from how much more investment is likely to be made in such an economy by both foreigners and Danes. By contrast, in Mexico 21 percent of the wallets were returned.[24] What is gained locally by those in economies with a lower level of honesty seems unlikely to equal in value the investments deterred, and the jobs not created.

Similar contrasts among nations were found in a five-year study of which United Nations diplomats paid their parking tickets in New York City, where diplomatic immunity shielded them from prosecution. Egypt, with 24 U.N. diplomats, had thousands of unpaid parking tickets during that five-year period. Meanwhile Canada, with the same number of U.N. diplomats as Egypt, had no unpaid parking tickets at all during the same five-year period. Nor did Britain, with 31 U.N. diplomats or Japan with 47 U.N. diplomats.[25]

More systematic international studies of corruption have found that most of the countries rated as most corrupt were among the poorest countries, even when they had rich natural resources.[26] Besides being a moral issue, honesty is also an economic factor whose presence or absence can be of major importance. Like other factors that affect income and wealth, it is neither evenly nor randomly distributed among nations or within nations. Sometimes a strict honesty may apply within a group while robbery of others is not only accepted but praised, as among desert marauders:

> Though robbery abroad is honorable and marauder a term with which to crown a hero, theft at home is summarily dealt with among most nomads. The property of the unlocked tent and the far-ranging herd must be safeguarded. The Tartars maintained a high standard of honesty among themselves and punished theft with death.[27]

Like other factors involved in economic activity, levels of honesty can change over time. Reporting on economic progress in Africa in 2013, *The Economist* magazine said, "our correspondent visited 23 countries" and "was not once asked for a bribe— inconceivable only ten years ago."[28]

VARIETIES OF HUMAN CAPITAL

Human capital is important, not just in helping a country recover from devastating losses of physical capital, such as after a war. It is also a major factor in economic progress in normal times. Human capital is in fact the biggest difference between ourselves and the cave man.

There is a tendency by some to equate human capital with education. No doubt education is one of the varieties of human capital. While years of education are often used as a rough proxy for human capital in general, not only is much human capital gained outside of educational institutions, some education develops little human capital when it produces few, if any, marketable skills— and some education may even produce negative human capital, in the form of attitudes, expectations and aversions that negatively impact the economy. These can include, in some cultures, an unwillingness of educated people to work with, or dirty, their hands. Depending on its content, education may sometimes create ideological aversions to working in the private sector or a refusal to do anything that does not seem to qualify as "meaningful work"— that is, work spontaneously agreeable and fulfilling in itself. But every society has work that simply must be done, despite not meeting that standard, work ranging from garbage collection to emptying bed pans in hospitals.

The industrial revolution was not created primarily by people with much formal education. It was in fact largely the work of people with practical job skills and experience, rather than a mastery of science or a systematic study of engineering. The industrial revolution was already well underway before formal study of science and engineering became widespread. Even in later times, such industrial pioneers as Thomas Edison and Henry Ford had very little formal education, the Wright brothers were high school dropouts and, in the electronic age, Bill Gates and Michael Dell were dropouts from college. In short, human capital is not synonymous with formal schooling.

Just as human capital takes other forms besides education, so there can be widespread education without equally widespread human capital. Russia in the twenty-first century has been called "a society characterized by high levels of education but low levels of human capital."[29] Among the more directly economic aspects of this is that, while Russia has about 6 percent of the world's college-educated population, it has less than one-fifth of one percent of the world's new patents and patent applications. During the years from 1995 to 2008, Germany produced about 60 times as many patents as Russia, Japan nearly 200 times as many patents and the United States about 500 times as many patents. Even the small city-state of Singapore produced more patents than Russia.[30]

None of this says that education is unimportant. But both its importance as one form of human capital and its distribution require specific scrutiny, rather than general celebration. Here, as elsewhere, few things are equal among individuals, groups or nations.

Education as a Cultural Value

The effects of differences between the way different cultures value education do not end with the effect of differences in literacy rates, even though literacy is a fundamental factor in the fate of individuals, groups and nations. Different cultures differ not only in the amount of education people seek, but also in what kinds of education they seek, and in the qualitative levels they achieve in that education. Comparisons of people from different social groups with the "same" education, measured in years of schooling, miss the other dimensions of education— and can therefore often falsely ascribe discrimination when the rewards differ among individuals from different social, racial or other groups with ostensibly the "same" education, as measured by years in school.

It is not uncommon for some culturally distinct minority to have not only more education but also qualitatively better education than the surrounding majority population, either in terms of education in intellectually more challenging specialties or in terms of higher individual achievements in their education. In 1972 most of the *A*'s on university entrance examinations in Sri Lanka went to members of the Tamil minority, rather than members of the Sinhalese majority.[31] During the days of the Ottoman Empire, Armenian students outperformed students from the Turkish majority, and even wrote better in the Ottoman Turkish language than Turkish students did.[32]

Choices of educational specialties can also differ greatly among groups with different cultures in the same society. In Malaysia, during the 1960s, when university admissions were still based on academic qualifications, there were more university students from the Chinese minority than from the Malay majority. The disparity was especially great in mathematical, scientific and technological specialties. During the 1960s, Chinese students received 1,488 Bachelor of Science degrees in Malaysia, while Malay students received just 69. In engineering, Chinese students received 408 Bachelor's degrees during the decade of the 1960s, while Malay students received just four.[33]

In Germany in the late nineteenth and early twentieth centuries, Jewish students were similarly statistically over-represented in German universities,[34] as they were in other times and places, whether in Eastern Europe, Argentina or Australia.[35] Today, in New York City's three elite and highly selective academic public high schools— Stuyvesant, Bronx Science and Brooklyn Tech— Asian students outnumber white students by more than two to one. This is in a city where Asians are only 14 percent of the city's public school population.[36]

By contrast, majority groups that are lagging economically tend also to lag educationally, both quantitatively and qualitatively. As university students they tend to specialize in easier subjects, rather than in subjects like mathematics, science or engineering. This in turn often leads to less promising careers— or to unemployment. What one study referred to as the "well-educated but underemployed" Czech young men in the nineteenth century[37] had many counterparts in other countries in the twentieth century, when the "educated unemployed" became a common expression, whether in Europe, Asia or elsewhere.[38]

People who have acquired academic degrees, without acquiring many economically meaningful skills, not only face personal disappointment and disaffection with society, but also have often become negative factors in the economy and even sources of danger, especially when they lash out at economically successful minorities and ethnically polarize the whole society they live in.

In various Eastern European countries between the two World Wars, such young members of newly educated lagging majorities provided much of the membership of anti-Semitic movements,[39] which became politically powerful, leading to discrimination and even violence against Jewish students in the universities. Not only were frustrated young graduates from majority populations— many the first generation of their families to reach higher education— among the disaffected who blamed better prepared minorities for their own lags, the intelligentsia of lagging groups have likewise promoted group identity ideology and group identity politics.

This pattern extended far beyond Eastern Europe. In many other places and times, soft-subject students and intellectuals have inflamed hostility, and sometimes violence, against many other successful groups, whether in India,[40] Hungary,[41] Nigeria,[42] Kazakhstan,[43] Romania,[44] Sri Lanka,[45] Canada,[46] or Czechoslovakia.[47] In contemporary America, many colleges and universities have whole departments devoted to promoting a sense of racial and ethnic grievances against others, while celebrating the isolation of group identities, epitomized by ethnically separate residences on campus[48] and sometimes even ethnically separate graduation ceremonies.

As in other places and times, whether in Europe, Asia or elsewhere, the intelligentsia of lagging groups have celebrated and/or fabricated past glories of these groups, in the interest of trying to retain individuals who might otherwise be tempted to rise into the larger society. When the author of the celebrated American book and television miniseries *Roots* was challenged on its accuracy by historians, his response was: "I was just trying to give my people a myth to live by."[49]

This approach was by no means unique to blacks or to the United States. An international study of ethnic groups found "cultural revivals" to be a "response" reflecting "an awareness of the danger of a fading group identity."[50] Daniel Patrick Moynihan said of his fellow Irish Americans: "The cruel part of this history is that by 1916 Irish nationalism in America had little to do with Ireland. It was a hodgepodge of fine feeling and bad history with which the immigrants filled a cultural void."[51] Preoccupation with past glories, even when they are genuine, can be an impediment to receptivity to current advances available from other cultures, as happened in the case of China and the Middle East.

The pursuit of accurate knowledge and the pursuit of ideological satisfaction are inherently conflicting goals, whether in American universities today or in universities in other times and places. A history of East Central Europe between the two World Wars characterized Romanian universities in that era as "numerically swollen, academically rather lax, and politically overheated," serving as "veritable incubators of surplus bureaucrats, politicians, and demagogues."[52] Decades later, universities in Sri Lanka likewise had "a backlog of unemployed graduates" who had specialized in the humanities and the social sciences.[53]

Despite beliefs in some quarters that education makes people more tolerant of other cultures and groups, it has been precisely individuals from newly educated groups, often lacking marketable skills, who have promoted group polarization, whether in Europe, Asia, Africa or the Western Hemisphere. A noted African scholar, for example, declared: "the educated Nigerian is the worst peddler of tribalism."[54]

It was much the same story with the nineteenth century Czech intelligentsia, including university students and school teachers, who promoted Czech cultural nationalism.[55] Among their demands were that street signs in Prague, which were in both Czech and German, be exclusively in Czech.[56] In the town of Budweis, Czech cultural nationalists demanded that there be a quota of Czech music to be played by the town orchestra.[57] There has been a similar insistent pettiness about language, in similar circumstances, in twentieth century Quebec, where laws required that not only street signs be solely in French, but also imposed legal restrictions on the use of English inside private businesses.[58] Quebec authorities even attempted to force pilots landing or taking off in Quebec to use French to communicate with air traffic controllers. Only a threatened international pilot boycott of Quebec forced the local authorities to back down on this dangerous demand that lives be risked by communication in an unfamiliar language.[59]

Even aside from ethnic issues, more years of schooling cannot automatically be equated with increased human capital. Everything depends on whether more years in schools, colleges and universities actually create economically meaningful skills, or whether academic credentials create a sense of entitlement beyond what the holders of those credentials actually produce.

This is not to say that economic benefits are the only benefits of education. But it is to say that expectations, or claims, of entitlement to higher incomes or wealth have no basis unless the specific kinds of education, and the specific qualitative level of that education, actually create sufficient additional output to cover the additional income or wealth expected.

When individuals from lagging groups— whether racial, regional or other social groups— tend to take less challenging courses, especially when these individuals are the first generation of their respective families to reach the college or university level, such individuals are unlikely to create as valuable services as people who study such obviously useful things as medicine, science or technology. In many poorer countries, especially, the "educated unemployed" are often numerous enough to be not only a major disappointment but a social and political danger.

Even many of those with academic credentials, but no economically meaningful skills, who are in fact employed are often employed in government bureaucracies, since they are unlikely to be much in demand in competitive markets, where employers are spending their own money, rather than spending the taxpayers' money. Sometimes jobs in government bureaucracies may be created in order to absorb large numbers of young people who could otherwise be frustrated and embittered enough to be politically troublesome for government officials, or even dangers to the society at large.

In poor countries especially, swollen bureaucracies and the red tape they generate are often an impediment to economic activity by other people who in fact do have the human capital to advance the economy and create much needed rises in living standards for the society at large.

Attitudes Toward Work

Attitudes toward work differ greatly among groups in the same society, as well as between one society and another— and obviously such differences can affect the production of wealth.

Many contemporaries of American antebellum Southern whites commented on the lack of a work ethic among them.[60] These included not only visitors from the North or from other countries, but even such staunch Southerners as General Robert E. Lee.[61] "Many of the whites," according to a leading Southern historian, "were disposed to let good enough alone and put off changes till the morrow."[62]

When German immigrants pioneering in America cut down trees while clearing land for farming, they laboriously dug the stumps and the roots out of the ground, so that all the land could be planted and plowed. Southerners usually either cut down the trees, or even simply girdled them and left them to die and rot, but in any case left the stumps in the ground and plowed around them.[63]

There were similar contrasts in the production of dairy products. In 1860, the South had 40 percent of the dairy cows in the United States but produced just 20 percent of the butter and only one percent of the cheese.[64] The greater success of the largely German dairy farmers of Wisconsin, compared to the poor showing of dairy production in the South, was explained by a scholar who wrote: "The close attention to duty, the habits of steady, skillful routine accepted by butter fat producers of Wisconsin as a matter of fact, are traits not yet present in southern culture."[65] This was said in 1932. The work attitudes and practices of the South persisted into at least the first half of the twentieth century.

Such differences in work habits have been common in other countries as well, such as among laborers tapping rubber trees in colonial Malaya during the 1940s:

> Many rubber estates kept records of the daily output of each tapper, and distinguished between the output of Chinese and Indian workers. The output of the Chinese was usually more than double that of the Indians, with all of them using the same simple equipment of tapping knife, latex

cup and latex bucket. There were similar or even wider differences between Chinese, Indian and Malay smallholders. . .[66]

Some groups avoid work, not necessarily out of laziness, but as a matter of principle. In times past, some European nobility or offspring of affluent classes considered work beneath them. But the British during the reign of the Tudors were not among those with this attitude:

> The younger son of the Tudor gentleman was not permitted to hang idle about the manor-house, a drain on the family income like the impoverished nobles of the Continent who were too proud to work. He was away making money in trade or in law.[67]

In Spain, for example, there were many people with some kind of noble title but little else, who dwelled in "thousands of sometimes tumbledown houses," a class "that sought to live 'nobly', not soiling its hands with dishonourable work." Among the popular sayings about such people was "on the *hidalgo*'s table is much linen but little food."[68]

At other times and places, even people with no special social status avoided certain kinds of occupations as "menial" work, thus reducing their own economic options, and sometimes their ability to acquire valuable human capital as well. In eighteenth-century England, domestics in the homes of wealthy and cultured people often acquired knowledge of food, manners, people and organization that they later put to use when they went on to become owners and operators of their own inns or other enterprises where they could use the knowledge and skills they had acquired.[69] In a later era, some black Americans from a similar background went on to become among the most successful caterers in nineteenth century Philadelphia.[70] At other times and places, poor people not handicapped by aversions to "menial" labor were able to survive and later move up, as many Italian immigrants did in Brazil, where shining shoes in Rio de Janeiro, São Paulo and Santos was an almost exclusively Italian occupation at one time.[71]

Attitudes Toward Progress

Economic outcomes are affected not only by attitudes toward work but attitudes toward progress as well. In modern industrial societies, progress is more or less taken for granted, but this was not always so, even in countries that are today modern societies. A history of the rise of Western civilization said of Europe in medieval times, "the very idea of innovation was lacking: men did what custom prescribed, cooperated in the plowing and to some extent in the harvesting, and for many generations did not dream of trying to change."[72]

Here, as in other things, Britain became an exception. Wealthy landowners in Britain were not content to be passive recipients of rents, but actively managed and promoted improvements in farming. Britain had "aristocratic landowners who were not above getting their boots muddy" managing their land, and these landowners followed a vigorous literature devoted to the efficient managing and improvement of agriculture.[73] By the late eighteenth century, England was one of the leaders in agricultural advances— making farming in Britain very different from farming in the feudal serfdom of Eastern Europe or in the small peasant farming in continental Western Europe.[74] Affluent and educated classes in Britain were also active in commerce and industry, as well as in agriculture, letters, law, and politics.[75]

By contrast, young people from newly educated indigenous peoples in newly independent countries in sub-Saharan Africa in the twentieth century often disdained the study of agriculture, even in countries where agriculture was a major part of the nation's economy. In Nigeria, more than 40 percent of the jobs for senior agricultural researchers were vacant at one time.[76] In Senegal, it was 1979— three decades after independence— before agriculture was even taught at the university level, though the country's University of Dakar had thousands of liberal arts students.[77]

In parts of the Third World, many people who have gotten an education feel that certain kinds of work are now simply beneath them. This includes working with their hands, even as an engineer, where they "recoil from the prospect of physical contact with machines,"[78] preferring a desk job instead.

The prevalence of such attitudes is another cultural handicap for any group or nation, especially those currently lagging economically. Sometimes the problem is not just an aversion to work, or to certain kinds of work, but also a lack of drive for progress. Here again, America's antebellum South was an example:

> Techniques of Southern agriculture changed slowly, or not at all. So elementary a machine as the plow was adopted only gradually and only in scattered places; as late as 1856, many small farmers in South Carolina were still using the crude colonial hoe. There was little change in the cotton gin, gin house, or baling screw between 1820 and the Civil War.[79]

The cotton gin, a crucial factor in the economy of the antebellum South, was invented by a Northerner. When it came to inventions in general, only 8 percent of the U.S. patents issued in 1851 went to residents of the Southern states, whose white population was approximately one-third of the white population of the country. Even in agriculture, the main economic activity of the region, only 9 out of 62 patents for agricultural implements went to Southerners.[80] The lesser dedication of Southerners to economic activity, and a corresponding lesser investment in their own human capital, was also reflected in lower levels of skills in the South, both among labor and management.

As a scholarly study of the South noted, "the South for a long time stood outside the tradition of business enterprise" in the United States, and the "first southerners to become captains of industry learned the technique in northern factories and counting houses," from which many did not return to the South.[81] In the antebellum era, travelers from outside the South commented on the lax way that Southern businessmen ran their businesses.[82] In the 1850s, a Northern traveler through the South said, "you become astonished at the little attention men pay to their business." Many Southern businessmen were unreliable when it came to either paying their bills or delivering goods and services when promised.[83]

Labor in the South likewise had lesser investment in human capital. As late as 1932, a study concluded:

> Compared to their brothers in highly industrialized areas, southern workingmen have yet to become skilled. In textiles the finer weaves are done in large proportion in Eastern mills. In iron and steel the more complex fabrications and higher grade moldings are the products of Pittsburgh and Gary.[84]

Because "the southern workman has remained to a large extent on the outer margin of the skilled industrial group,"[85] his apparently cheap labor "was dear in reality because of lack of skill."[86] Sometimes, during this era, "skilled workmen are imported from the North to some particularly favored center of industry in the South."[87]

Differences in habits and attitudes are differences in human capital, just as much as differences in knowledge and skills— and such differences create differences in economic outcomes. As of the Civil War era, the North produced 14 times as much textiles as the South, despite the South's virtual monopoly of growing cotton. The North also produced 15 times as much iron as the South, 25 times the merchant ship tonnage and 32 times as many firearms.[88]

Even where the South had natural resource advantages, such as iron ore and coal deposits located much closer together in Birmingham than in such other iron and steel producing centers as Pittsburgh or Gary, Indiana,[89] Southern deficiencies in human capital, in both labor and management, handicapped the development of the steel industry in Birmingham.[90] It was much the same story of rich natural resources and poor human capital in the Southern lumber industry.[91] Similarly, when the Southern textile industry began, with the advantage of being located in one of the world's leading cotton-growing areas, much of the textiles turned out in the South had to be sent to New England for dyeing, bleaching, and finishing.[92]

Fortunately, the South changed over the years, especially in the second half of the twentieth century, partly as a result of a greater influx of people from other parts of the country. However, such cultural changes are not easy to create in all societies or among all groups in a given society.

For outsiders to attempt to change a culture may be resented as well as resisted. As economic historian David S. Landes put it, "criticisms of culture cut close to the ego" and "injure identity and self-esteem."[93] Outsiders can seldom change a lagging culture, without a receptivity to cultural changes within the lagging group itself.

PART III:

SOCIAL FACTORS

In no society have all regions and all parts of the population developed equally.

Fernand Braudel

Many social factors can affect economic differences between nations and within nations. These include the size and demographic makeup of their populations, and the human capital and social mobility in their societies. Like geographic and cultural factors, none of these things is the same between nations or among all groups within nations.

While there have long been concerns, and sometimes alarms, about the size of the population, especially as regards its sustainability, the quality of the population has usually received much less attention. But median age differences alone— which can be two decades or more between nations or between different groups within the same nation— can produce large differences in human capital, based on work experience alone, quite aside from what other differences there may be in education or in particular specialized skills.

Societies also differ in their ability to use whatever human capital already exists in their respective populations. Cultural or political restrictions on the economic roles open to some segments of the population— whether due to sex, race, religion or other characteristics— are not simply losses to those particular segments of the population involved, but are also losses to the society as a whole. Yet it has been all too common, in many countries around the world, to forfeit the use of much human capital available within their own borders, rather than allow some groups to rise as far as their productivity would take them.

A society which arbitrarily restricts the education or employment of women, for example, can forfeit half the human capital potential of its own population. Other societies, through restrictions, hostility, violence or outright expulsions drive out ethnic groups with more human capital per capita than in the population at large, because those human capital differences lead to corresponding differences in income and wealth, provoking envy and resentments. The skills forfeited in this way have ranged from clock-making to nuclear physics. Irrational as this might seem, from the standpoint of the economic well-being of society as a whole, it is often quite rational from the standpoint of political leaders responding to political incentives created by large differences in skills and prosperity among different groups in the same society, and the resentments engendered by those differences.

Sharp cultural differences between different groups suggest that differences in economic and social outcomes are by no means mysterious, even aside from geographic, demographic and other influences. For example, a Russian Empire official in 1818 reported that "even the girls of the poorest families" of Jews could read, at a time when illiteracy was the norm in the population of the Russian Empire. He added that there were "at least ten books in every household" among the Jews.[1] By contrast, in Frederick Law Olmsted's travels through the antebellum South, he noted a dearth of books, even in the homes of plantation owners,[2] and, in earlier times, Thomas Jefferson complained that the area where he lived in Virginia was "without a single bookstore."[3] He ordered many books from England for his extensive library. But in eighteenth century Scotland, "Even a person of relatively modest means had his own collection of books, and what he couldn't afford he could get at the local lending library, which by 1750 virtually every town of any size enjoyed."[4]

Money differences cannot account for such differences in how people chose to spend their money. Economic determinism is no more valid than geographic determinism or genetic determinism. It would be hard to understand the social patterns of many peoples in many places around the world, without understanding their unique histories and cultures. They cannot be treated as if they were abstract people in an abstract world, despite how often some intellectual models or public policies may do so.

Sometimes these differing groups are ethnically different and sometimes they are simply groups concentrated in different regions of the country. In a country whose population consists primarily of people descended from immigrants from elsewhere in the world, as is the case of the United States or Australia, for example, intergroup differences may be due to the respective countries from which the immigrants came or due to the particular time period at which they arrived, since the agricultural, commercial or industrial development of the receiving country can change greatly over the generations and centuries.

In the United States, for example, the country itself changed greatly over time— economically, socially and technologically— as did the immigrants who arrived in the country from increasingly varied sources. The technologies that brought immigrants across first the Atlantic Ocean, and later the Pacific, also changed. The country that the Pilgrims arrived in, during the seventeenth century, was not the same as that when the Germans arrived during the eighteenth century, or the Irish and the Chinese during the nineteenth century, or the country that people from Latin America began arriving in during the late twentieth and early twenty-first centuries.

The technology that first brought most immigrants from Europe across the Atlantic was that of wind-driven ships with sails until the second half of the nineteenth century, when steam-driven ships replaced sailing ships. This changed both the economics of immigration and the geographic sources of the immigrants. Wind-driven ships took from one to three months to cross the Atlantic, depending on variations in the winds. The unpredictability of arrival times in America also meant unpredictable dates of the ships' return to Europe, making those same ships' new departure times for the next voyage from Europe also unpredictable. This in turn meant that prospective immigrants had the additional expenses of living an unpredictable amount of time in port cities, waiting for the ships that would take them across the ocean. These were serious, and sometimes ruinous, costs for the working-class people who predominated among the European immigrants to the United States.

Among the ways of coping with these costs during this era were (1) becoming an indentured servant for a specified number of years on arrival,* in exchange for someone else paying the cost of passage and/or (2) crossing the Atlantic less expensively in the vacant space of a cargo ship, since such ships usually had vacant space going from Europe to America, because Europe was shipping manufactured goods in exchange for America's raw materials, the latter having greater bulk for a given value. These factors meant that most of the immigrants to America during that era came from Western Europe. Eastern Europe and Southern Europe had less trade with America, and the emigrants originating there were poorer, so that few could afford the costs of crossing the Atlantic during the era of wind-driven ships.

The advent of steamships changed both the economics and the geography of immigration from Europe. Instead of taking an unpredictable one to three months for the voyage across the Atlantic, steamships now crossed the Atlantic in a predictable ten days, so that both their arrival and departure times were also predictable. The resulting reduction in expenses— both at sea and in ports— now put transatlantic voyages within the means of millions of people in Eastern Europe and Southern Europe, and these people now became the largest part of an increased immigration from Europe as a whole, beginning in the second half of the nineteenth century. Steamships also made voyages across the much larger Pacific Ocean economically feasible for working people, leading to significant immigration from China, and later Japan, to the Western Hemisphere. In the second half of the twentieth century, air travel would make Asia a major source of immigrants to the United States.

---

* More than half of all the people who came to early colonial America, in the colonies south of New England, were indentured servants. Most were males from the ages of 15 to 24, and the usual term of indenture was four years. Abbot Emerson Smith, *Colonists in Bondage: White Servitude and Convict Labor in America 1607–1776* (Gloucester, Massachusetts: Peter Smith, 1965), pp. 3–4; David Galenson, *White Servitude in Colonial America: An Economic Analysis* (Cambridge: Cambridge University Press, 1981), pp. 23, 25, 28, 102–103.

Among the differences between immigrants who arrived during the era of wind-driven ships and during the era of steamships was that the latter had a choice of destinations, while many of the immigrants who could only afford to travel in the vacant spaces in cargo ships during the era of wind-driven ships had to go wherever the cargo ships were going. Thus many of the early Irish immigrants landed in Boston, which was not a very promising economic or social location for people with little education or commercial or industrial skills, and people of the Catholic religion in Protestant New England, at a time of religious polarization.

Many German immigrants during that same era could land at New Orleans, but usually had sufficient money to travel up the Mississippi River to settle in places like St. Louis or Milwaukee or end up in rural areas in Wisconsin. Thus Germans could pick and choose destinations more favorable to their own circumstances, to an extent that the Irish could not.

During the era of steamships, most Jewish immigrants from Eastern Europe were very poor like the Irish before them, but now they could choose their own destinations on passenger steamships. They had skills in garment production and they landed in New York where the more prosperous German Jews were already settled and owned garment factories that would employ them. In the longer run, New York proved to be almost tailor-made for the poor Jews from Eastern Europe— a city with free public libraries and, for later generations, free elite and academically selective public high schools and even free city-financed colleges of high quality.

Yet for other groups who arrived in New York without the cultural orientations of the Jews, these treasures were of little relevance,* so these other groups with other cultures could not rise so far or so fast as the Jews. Nevertheless, it took time for all this to unfold, and even

---

* As a personal note, I was among the blacks from the South who arrived in New York in the 1930s. As a child nine years old, I had no idea what a public library was, much less that there were selective and elite high schools, and the thought of college had never crossed my mind. Fortunately, others made me aware of such things and their implications. But not everyone from a similar background had someone to make them aware of such things or their importance.

the Eastern European Jews spent many years in poverty on New York's Lower East Side. Generations later, in the early twenty-first century, another poverty-stricken group arrived, this time from Asia— immigrants from Fujian province in China— who seized upon the same educational treasures as the Jews had before them, and their offspring rose. But, in the many years in between, other groups had arrived in New York and had neither sought nor found these avenues of upward mobility.

With different peoples having come to a different America in different centuries, bringing with them different skills and cultures from different countries around the world, and with their descendants having spent different numbers of generations living on American soil, the combinations and permutations of interacting factors were too numerous to make a similarity of economic or other outcomes likely at a given time.

When the U.S. Army gave mental tests to its soldiers during the First World War, for example, soldiers of Scottish ancestry scored above the average of white draftees, while soldiers from groups that had emigrated from Poland and Russia— mostly Jews— scored below that average.[5] Did that mean that the Scots were more intelligent than the Jews? Or did it mean that a group whose peak immigration years were generations earlier than the Jews' peak immigration years, and who spoke English even before arriving in the United States from Scotland, could understand mental test questions and test instructions written in English better than people who grew up in homes where English was not usually the language spoken? With the passing years, as more American Jews grew up speaking English, their IQ test scores rose above the national average.

Other performances and achievements among different groups were likewise affected by the varying combinations and permutations of these groups' arrival times, arrival locations, phase of the country's economic and social development at their time of arrival, the complementarity or competition of other groups at the time and place of their arrival, the regions from which they left, the demographic makeup of the groups themselves, in terms of age, sex and proportions of children, the skills they brought with them and the values they cherished. To expect even approximate equality of achievement and reward among the various groups at a given time would be to defy the odds.

During the late nineteenth century, in a post-Darwin era when "the survival of the fittest" was an idea transferred from animals in nature to social groups in human societies, the striking economic and social differences between immigrants from different parts of Europe— especially between those from Western Europe and Eastern Europe— led to widespread belief in influential quarters that these socioeconomic differences between these groups were a sign of genetic inferiority in the newer arrivals from Eastern Europe and Southern Europe.[6] The heyday of genetic determinism was the early twentieth century, and the issues raised had implications reaching well beyond those raised by differences between groups originating in different regions of Europe.

Few social issues are so controversial as those revolving around the question of differences in mental capabilities among societies or among different groups within a given society. Genetic determinists have offered the simplest explanation of such differences, based on innate biological differences. But the simplest explanations are not necessarily the most accurate. As the passing years brought more evidence undermining genetic determinism, there was an erosion of support for theories of innately superior and innately inferior peoples, especially after Hitler and the Nazis took this theory to its logical conclusion with the Holocaust.

In the second half of the twentieth century, the revulsion against genetic determinism led many to go to the opposite extreme of denying or downplaying capability differences or performance differences among racial or ethnic groups. From this emerged multiculturalism, which regarded all cultures as being entitled to equal respect. Multiculturalists tend to either dismiss the idea of cultural differences in economic or other effectiveness as "stereotypes" or else blame whatever differences exist on either discrimination or socioeconomic differences that prevent the lower achieving group from having the prerequisites for reaching the same performance levels as others. This has often been carried to the point of encouraging lagging groups to proudly cling to their own culture, or even resurrect it in some cases, with little concern that these groups' economic and educational lags might be— at least in part— a result of the cultures they were being encouraged to cling to.

Chapter 8

POPULATION

One of the reasons sometimes offered for income and wealth disparities among nations is that some nations are said to be "overpopulated" and therefore living in poverty. There are other aspects of populations besides numbers that can also affect economic outcomes for individuals, groups or nations. These include age and mobility, both geographic mobility and social mobility.

POPULATION SIZE

Over the centuries, a recurrent fear has been that the number of people would grow to exceed the number for which there was adequate food. In times past, this concern has been felt from the individual family to local or national communities, and many have worried that the population of the world would grow to a size exceeding the world's capacity to provide enough food to sustain the people in it.

In geographic settings where there has been a sharply limited amount of land available on which to grow food— as on small, isolated islands, or in a very limited area of arable land in a valley isolated amid barren mountains, for example— severe limitations on the size of the population that could be fed often led to draconian practices in times past. These included killing newborn babies, especially female babies, since a girl might not grow strong enough, soon enough to produce enough food to sustain herself, and the family as a whole had little food to spare. Female infanticide at one time prevailed in various Pacific island groups and in the Nilgiri Hills in India, for example, and the resulting sex imbalance among adults led to a sharing of one wife among two or more men.[1] Among the benefits of economic progress was reaching a level of productivity where such desperate and anguished decisions as killing newborn babies no longer had to be made.

Other ways of coping with population pressures have included widespread religious celibacy among monks and nuns who made up a significant proportion of the population in Tibet and, at one time, an unusual number of priests and nuns originated in a barren plateau in France.[2] Emigration has been another response to population growth reaching locally unyielding limits on how many people could be fed and sustained. There have also been seasonal migrations of peoples from many mountains and highlands around the world, working in the lowlands of their own country or in other countries, in roles ranging from laborers and servants in Switzerland to miners in South Africa, peddlers in Morocco and professional wet nurses in Spain's aristocratic households.[3] Longer lasting migrations have included terms of military service in foreign armies, and permanent emigration to settle in other lands.

Concerns over whether the world will produce enough food to sustain the people in it go back even before Thomas R. Malthus' famous *Essay on Population* in 1798. But what Malthus did was to spell out a theory in a stark and dramatic form that made the issue indelible and historic. The Malthusian theory was based on two propositions. The first proposition, according to Malthus, was that "Population, when unchecked, increases in a geometrical ratio," while subsistence "increases only in an arithmetical ratio." The second proposition was: "By that law of our nature which makes food necessary to the life of man, the effects of these two unequal powers must be kept equal."[4]

In other words, if human beings did not restrain their own reproduction, then famine, disease and other disasters would bring population back down to what the food supply could sustain. Such concerns about the sustainability of population have waxed and waned over the centuries since Malthus wrote. But they have never completely died out. In 2014, for example, a *New York Times* writer referred to Malthus' population theory as being based on "an eminently sensible premise: that the earth's carrying capacity has a limit."[5] But to say that there is a limit— on anything— is not to say that we are nearing that limit. As we have seen with false alarms about an exhaustion of natural resources, a finite limit, as such, tells us nothing about whether or not we are nearing that limit.

However plausible the Malthusian theory might seem, it has consistently failed the test of empirical evidence, even in Malthus' own lifetime.[6] There is no consistent correlation between population size or density and real income per capita. Poverty-stricken sub-Saharan Africa has a population density that is only a fraction of that in prosperous Japan,[7] which has several times the number of people per square mile. It is possible to find some poverty-stricken countries with greater population densities than some prosperous countries. But there is no consistent relationship between population density and either wealth or poverty. Looking at what happens over time likewise gives no support to the theory that "overpopulation" causes poverty. As one of the leading economic development economists of the twentieth century pointed out:

> Between the 1890s and 1930s the sparsely populated area of Malaysia, with hamlets and fishing villages, was transformed into a country with large cities, extensive agricultural and mining operations and extensive commerce. The population rose from about one and a half to about six million; the number of Malays increased from about one to about two and a half million. The much larger population had much higher material standards and lived longer than the small population of the 1890s. Since the 1950s rapid population increase in densely-populated Hong Kong and Singapore has been accompanied by large increases in real income and wages. The population of the Western world has more than quadrupled since the middle of the eighteenth century. Real income per head is estimated to have increased by a factor of five or more.[8]

Although advocates of the "overpopulation" theory argue that rising population threatens to create more poverty, virtually no one seems able to provide examples of countries that had a higher standard of living when their population was half of what it is today.

Famines at various times and places have been taken by some as confirmation of Malthus' theory. But famines ceased in densely populated regions like Western Europe and Japan, while they continued in thinly populated regions like sub-Saharan Africa. Famines have usually been local phenomena, often caused by local crop failures or by military conflicts or other disasters that interfered with the distribution of food. Even when there is ample food available in the world at large, not all local transportation systems have been capable of moving vast amounts of food into a famine-stricken area quickly enough to avert mass starvation and the fatal diseases to which people weakened by hunger are more vulnerable.*

With the development and spread of modern transportation systems, famines have declined. However, particular places at particular times can become susceptible to famine when these places are *politically* isolated for political reasons. Two of the most devastating famines of the twentieth century occurred in the Soviet Union in the 1930s under Stalin, when millions of people died— and, decades later, in China under Mao, when tens of millions died.

Neither of these totalitarian dictators was going to admit to the outside world that there was a famine in his country, much less call on other countries for food, since that would undermine the ideology they were promoting internationally, and perhaps undermine their own regimes. Nor were the people living under these repressive regimes allowed free communication with the outside world. But the long-run capacity to produce enough food to support the people was

---

* Sixteenth century famines, though common in Mediterranean Europe, struck primarily towns because of "the slowness and prohibitive price of transport and the unreliability of the harvests." Fernand Braudel, *The Mediterranean and the Mediterranean World in the Age of Philip II*, translated by Siân Reynolds (New York: Harper & Row, 1972), Vol. I, p. 328.

not the issue. In the Soviet Union, the famine was concentrated in the Ukraine, which had been one of the great food-producing regions before the famine, and would be again after the famine.[9] In neither the Soviet Union nor in China had population exceeded the capacity of the land to feed the people, and in both places today an even larger population is being fed. In twenty-first century China, an estimated one-fourth of the population is overweight.[10]

DEMOGRAPHIC COMPOSITION

The mixture of ages within a given population varies greatly from one society to another, as well as among ethnic or other groups within a given society. The median age in Japan, Germany and Italy is over forty, while the median age in Guatemala, Nigeria and Afghanistan is under twenty.[11] Within the United States, Americans of Japanese ancestry are more than two decades older than Puerto Ricans.[12] If we measure adult work experience from age eighteen on, this means that a forty-year-old worker has more than ten times as much experience as a twenty-year-old worker. How can disparities of that magnitude in opportunities to acquire knowledge, skills and maturity not create a disparity in economic outcomes among nations and within nations?

In countries where diseases, poverty and other factors produce shorter life spans, a smaller share of the population reaches the ages where levels of individual productivity are highest and, among those that do, they remain at those levels for less time before dying.

Within a given nation, incomes vary greatly with age, and wealth even more so. Moreover, these disparities among age cohorts have increased over time, as the value of the physical strength and energy of youth counts for less when mechanical sources of power have rendered human strength less important, and more complex technology has made knowledge, experience and analytical skills more valuable. The net result is that the age at which people receive their highest incomes has shifted upward in the United States.

Back in 1951, most Americans reached their peak earnings between 35 and 44 years of age, and people in that age bracket earned 60 percent more than workers in their early twenties. By 1973 people in the same 35-to 44-year-old bracket earned more than double the income of the younger workers. Twenty years later, the peak earnings bracket had moved up to people aged 45 to 54 years, and people in that bracket earned more than three times what workers in their early twenties earned.[13]

None of this should be surprising, because people accumulate human capital as they grow older, whether in the form of specific knowledge and skills or just maturity in dealing with other people and with the responsibilities of their work. What we choose to call "labor" is no longer simply physical exertions in the production process. Many, if not most, workers are supplying not only labor but human capital, and the growing pay differential between experienced workers and entry-level workers suggests that human capital is increasingly in demand in an economy that is growing both technologically and organizationally more complex.

The way children are raised also differs greatly— and consequentially— from group to group and from one income level to another. A study found that American children in families where the parents are in professional occupations hear 2,100 words an hour, on average. Children whose parents are working class hear an average of 1,200 words an hour— and children whose family is on welfare hear 600 words an hour.[14] What this means is that, over the years, a ten-year-old child from a family on welfare will have heard not quite as many words at home as a three-year-old child whose parents are professionals.

Child-rearing practices differ by race, as well as by class. White American parents play with, talk to and listen to their children three times as often as black American parents.[15] Black parents, on average, have less than half as many books in their homes as white American parents, and that cannot be solely a matter of economics, because black parents in the highest socioeconomic quintile have slightly fewer books in their homes than white parents in the lowest socioeconomic quintile.[16] Nor are books as expensive as upscale tennis shoes or various electronic devices that are common in black ghettos.

It is painful to contemplate what this means cumulatively over the years, as poor children in general, and black children in particular, are handicapped from their earliest childhood. It is not just in the quantity of words they hear that they are handicapped. They are also handicapped in both the quantity and the quality of their parents' education. In addition, only 9 percent of American women with college degrees who gave birth in 2013 were unmarried. But 61 percent of women who were high school dropouts and gave birth that year were unmarried.[17]

It is hard to escape the conclusion reached by *The Economist* magazine: "Nothing the government can do will give the children of Cabin Creek the same life chances as the children of Bethesda." Equal opportunity, in the sense of being judged and rewarded by the same standards as others, cannot possibly mean equal chances in life for children born and raised in these very different settings— where household incomes in Bethesda are more than five times those in Cabin Creek and college degrees fourteen times as prevalent.[18] Another way of saying the same thing is that the fact that *life* is unfair is not the same as saying that a particular institution, or a particular society, is unfair. *We cannot tell where the unfairness occurred by where the statistics were collected.*

If the mix of children raised in welfare families is racially different from the mix of children raised in families with parents who are professionals, then statistics collected at a given employer's business, after these children have grown to adulthood, may well show a racial disparity between which employees are in higher occupations and which are in lower occupations, even if the employer has treated every individual the same when hiring or promoting. Even if these employees were all born into the world with identical brain cells, the prospects of one set of them were enhanced while they were growing up and the prospects of the other set were blighted. This happened years earlier, before either set of people reached the employer.

GEOGRAPHIC MOBILITY

One of the ways individuals and groups seek to raise their economic level is by moving from places where prospects seem poor to places where prospects seem more promising. These moves can be for relatively short distances, as among shepherds leading their flocks from fields where these flocks have eaten most of the vegetation to fields where there is much vegetation still available. Or the moves can be from one country to another or from one continent to another, as people from various parts of Europe immigrated to America and Australia, or people from India immigrated to Fiji, Malaysia, Africa and both North America and South America. Like other factors affecting the economic level and progress of peoples, migrations have not been even or random factors, but factors reflecting many inequalities and creating more.

Immigration has not been random, either in the particular places in the home country from which the immigrants leave or in the particular places where they settle in the country to which they relocate. Of the Italian immigrants to Australia between 1881 and 1899, 88 percent came from places containing only 10 percent of the population of Italy.[19] Nor did they settle evenly or randomly in Australia. Nearly nine-tenths of the Italian immigrants to Australia who came from the Mount Etna region of Sicily settled in the northern part of the state of Queensland, while Italian immigrants from the nearby Lipari Islands settled together hundreds of miles away, in Sydney and Melbourne.[20]

In the United States, such patterns went right down to the neighborhood level. During the era of mass immigration from Europe to America, Italian immigrants from different places in Italy lived clustered together on particular streets within Italian neighborhoods in New York, San Francisco and other American cities.[21] Similar clusters of Italians from particular places in Italy were also common in Buenos Aires and Toronto during that same era.[22]

German immigrants from particular regions of Germany— or Russia, for that matter— likewise tended to cluster together, whether in North America or South America:

> Württembergers were heavily concentrated in Philadelphia but were comparatively rare in Milwaukee. Mecklenburgers flocked to Milwaukee but not to Philadelphia. Hanoverians were common in Cincinnati and St. Louis, but relatively uncommon in Wisconsin and Michigan. Even within German enclaves, both urban and rural, distinct provincial concentrations developed. For example, in New York's *Kleindeutschland* of 1860, Bavarians dominated the Eleventh and Seventeenth wards, Prussians the Tenth, and Hessians the Thirteenth.[23]

Frankfort, Kentucky, was founded by immigrants from Frankfurt in Germany,[24] and Grand Island, Nebraska, was first settled by Schleswig-Holsteiners.[25] German farmers who had immigrated to Russia during the eighteenth century, and whose descendants then emigrated from there to the United States in the nineteenth century, did not settle in existing German American enclaves, much less among the American population at large. These German immigrants from Russia settled in their own separate communities of Volga Germans and Black Sea Germans— separate from each other, as well as from other Germans and from Americans in general.[26]

It was much the same story in South America. In nineteenth century Brazil's states of Rio Grande do Sul and Santa Catarina, "one valley might be inhabited almost entirely by Germans from one state or region and the next by Germans from another." Many Germans from Westphalia, for example, lived in Estrela, while Germans from Pomerania lived in Santa Cruz and Germans from Swabia in Panambí.[27] In Argentina, as late as 1967 a visitor found a village church where hymns were being sung "in typical Volga German style" and the service, the minister and the parishioners were such that "It was difficult to believe that I was in Latin America, that the ancestors of these people had left Germany for Russia 200 years ago."[28]

Such patterns have been common among other immigrants going to and from other countries around the world. As noted in Chapter 5, when immigration from Lebanon to Sierra Leone began after the First World War, most of the immigrants came from particular villages and settled in particular parts of Sierra Leone among people from the same villages and with the same religion. Lebanese immigrants to Colombia likewise came from particular places in the Middle East and settled in clusters together in particular places in Colombia.[29] Of all the Chinese who immigrated to the United States between the mid-nineteenth century and the First World War, most came from Toishan, just one of 98 counties in the province of Kwangtung (now Guangdong).[30] In the twenty-first century, immigrants from the province of Fujian have settled together in a particular Brooklyn neighborhood.[31]

Such non-random clusters of immigrants from many countries living in many other countries have been the rule, rather than the exception. Moreover, even after the era of mass immigration from Europe was over, if one wished to have Americans of Northern European ancestry and Americans of Southern European ancestry living randomly distributed among one another in the New York metropolitan area in the second half of the twentieth century, one would have had to move just over half of all Americans of Southern European ancestry living in the New York area.[32]

The fact that the difference between black and white neighborhoods is visible to the naked eye, in a way that these other differences are not, does not make the black-white difference unique. Moreover, *within* black communities, different kinds of people have long clustered in different places. A study of the black community in Chicago during the 1930s showed delinquency rates of more than 40 percent in some black neighborhoods and delinquency rates under 2 percent in other black neighborhoods.[33] Residential separation between different kinds of people within black communities has also been found in Harlem and in other black communities as well.[34]

In earlier centuries, people from Western Europe with urban skills often settled in the cities and towns of Eastern Europe, becoming in many cases an absolute majority of the population in these urban communities, while the indigenous Slavs were the great majority of the rural population in the surrounding countrysides. As a noted historian put it:

> Towns were largely inhabited, trade was largely carried on, by people different in ethnic origin from those of the surrounding country. In a Slav country, townsfolk might be Germans. In Roumania they were likely to be Greeks and Jews. In other parts of the Balkans they might include Macedonians.[35]

In general, people sort themselves out in all kinds of groups, within races as well as between races, and in all sorts of countries around the world. There are reasons for such non-random residential patterns within groups as well as between groups. Like other patterns in many other kinds of human activities, they are not random because people are not behaving randomly, but *purposefully*— and their purposes, circumstances, skills and values differ.

While immigration is a voluntary form of geographic mobility, other mass movements of people have been less voluntary, or not voluntary at all. The most involuntary of all geographic transfers were those of slaves, such as those of millions of Africans shipped across the Atlantic and of at least a million Europeans shipped to North Africa alone, while other Europeans were enslaved in the Ottoman Empire. Refugees have fled from famine, as in Ireland in the 1840s, from mob violence as Jews fled from Eastern Europe later in the nineteenth century or from persecution in Nazi Germany in the 1930s, and many other peoples fled from war in many other times and places around the world.

Other peoples have moved into new countries as conquerors, as has happened in many places in many eras. Turks are not the indigenous people of Turkey, nor the Malays in Malaysia or the English in

England. Often indigenous populations living in the lowlands have been forced up into the highlands or mountains by invaders, as the Vlachs were in southeastern Europe when masses of Slavs invaded the region in the Middle Ages.[36] In other geographic settings, conquerors have simply appropriated the most desirable land, leaving the conquered to find whatever land was left or to be assigned to particular, less desirable places, as happened to American Indians confined to reservations. In some cases, this led to the fragmentation of the conquered peoples, when the land where they could settle was isolated in non-contiguous patches here and there.

SOCIAL MOBILITY

Social mobility is often discussed as a matter of individual good fortune, such as that in nineteenth century Horatio Alger novels about plucky lads who overcame adversity and eventually rose to reap their just reward. But social mobility is far more important to the economic fate of nations. Put differently, a nation which creates obstacles to the use of the talents, potentialities and achievements of some segments of its own people— whether defined by race, religion, sex, caste or whatever— is needlessly depriving itself of a source of greater prosperity. Yet that is precisely what has been done in innumerable times and places, for thousands of years, in many countries around the world.

Countries with fewer, or less rigid, barriers have often benefitted from the arrival of productive individuals and groups who were stifled or persecuted in the countries from which they fled. Huguenots who fled religious persecution in seventeenth century France created the watchmaking industry in London and made Switzerland the premier watchmaking nation in the world.[37] Jewish scientists fleeing persecution in 1930s Europe played key roles in making the United States the first nuclear superpower.[38] Immigrants and their children also played major roles in creating modern industries in such Latin American countries as Argentina, Brazil and Chile.[39]

Internally, Americans who rose from obscurity, or sometimes even poverty, to create or revolutionize whole industries would include Thomas Edison, Henry Ford, the Wright Brothers, Andrew Carnegie, David Sarnoff and many others whose impacts spread across the country and, in some cases, around the world. Therefore much concern was aroused in the early twenty-first century when claims were made that social mobility had declined greatly in the United States. This concern was often expressed in terms of a setback for "social justice," but a decline in social mobility would also have implications for the economic fate of the country as a whole.

Like so many words and phrases with great emotional appeal and political impact, neither "social mobility" nor "social justice" has been unambiguously defined. A dictionary defines "mobile" as "anything that can be moved." Clearly, by this definition a car with a 500 horsepower engine is mobile, even if it is parked at a given time or even most of the time. Another car, with an engine only half as powerful, would not be said to be more mobile, even if the second car was used as a taxi and was therefore in motion a greater percentage of the time. Mobility exists *ex ante* while movement exists *ex post*.

Society *A* is more mobile than Society *Z* to the extent that individuals in Society *A* face fewer external restrictions on their upward movement. But how much upward movement actually takes place in either society depends also on the *internal* qualities of individuals— their skills, intelligence, work habits and other factors that can affect the likelihood of their rising economically.

Differences in the definition of "mobility" or "opportunity" involve far more than semantic preferences. These differences in definitions change the substance of what is being said or insinuated. To deliberately take an extreme example, even a society in which individuals are confronted with no external barriers whatever to upward mobility in its economy may nevertheless have particular individuals or groups who do not actually move upward at all, if their internal qualities are not sufficient to cause them to rise. Conversely, a society with many barriers to upward mobility may nevertheless have particular individuals or groups who move upward anyway, overcoming or circumventing those barriers.

Given the many things that go into economic productivity, and the many differences among people in their likelihood of having all those things to the same degree, there is a fundamental difference between equal *opportunity* and equal *probability* of achieving a given outcome— a difference often ignored or blurred, not only in popular discussions but even in scholarly studies. For example, Professor Angus Deaton of Princeton says:

> One way of measuring equality of opportunity is to look at the correlation between the earnings of fathers and sons. In a completely mobile society, with perfect equality of opportunity, your earnings should be unrelated to what your father earned; by contrast, in a hereditary caste society, in which jobs are handed down from one generation to the next, the correlation would be 1.[40]

The statement that there would be no correlation between the earnings of parents and their children, in a society with "perfect equality of opportunity" is in defiance of both heredity and environment. Whether what individuals inherit from their parents is genetic or cultural, it cannot be dismissed as a causal factor in their subsequent productivity or in the earnings resulting from that productivity. Much depends crucially on the meaning of the concept of *mobility*. If by "a completely mobile society" one means a society in which movement is unimpeded by external obstacles, that in no way precludes *internal* differences in productivity or earning capacity. But, if by "a completely mobile society" is meant a society in which movement takes place independently of parental origins, then the statement is true by definition— immune to confirmation or refutation in the real world, and therefore irrelevant to the real world.

In short, we cannot determine how much mobility— that is, *opportunity* to move upward— a given society has by how much upward movement actually takes place. Equal opportunity is not the same as equal probabilities of success. The distinction is fundamental, despite how often that distinction is blurred by those who equate equal "opportunity" with equal "life chances," and declare a society without equal outcomes to be a society without equal opportunity. Far more is involved than semantic preferences as to how a given society is to be characterized. Concrete efforts to advance economically lagging groups can be directed primarily at correcting society and its institutions or directed primarily at getting members of lagging groups to reorient themselves toward acquiring more human capital. It is an empirical question as to what the facts are in any particular case, and we cannot allow that question to vanish into thin air by verbal sleight of hand in the definition of words.

If native-born Americans in lower income brackets do not move up nearly as often as immigrants who arrived in those same lower income brackets— the Chinese and the Cubans, for example— then the question must be raised whether there are external barriers to mobility blocking the rise of native-born Americans— barriers which somehow exempt immigrants. That hardly seems to meet even the test of plausibility. A more realistic explanation might be that low-income immigrants bring a different set of attitudes and values than the attitudes and values of low-income Americans. A further exploration of differences between low-income immigrants and low-income native-born individuals will be made in Chapter 12, drawing upon empirical evidence from both England and the United States.

In the meantime, we need to consider those studies which simply measure social mobility by how much movement there is, up or down the economic scale. It is these kinds of studies which have led many to conclude that social mobility as an opportunity has declined in America. Even within a framework that defines mobility by the amount of movement, there are different questions that can be asked. For example, social mobility might be measured by (1) how much incomes and wealth rise within the lifetime of individuals, (2) how much incomes and wealth rise from one generation to the next, or (3) how much the relative positions of the latest generation differ from the relative positions of their respective parents.

As regards the first question, a number of studies show that the income and wealth of individuals rise substantially over their lifetimes.[41] Despite many discussions of the "top 20 percent," the "top 10 percent" or the "top one percent," as if these brackets contained given sets of people over time, hard data say otherwise. For example, among Americans twenty-five years old, only 11 percent have been part of a household whose income was in the top 20 percent. But, by age forty, 53 percent have been part of a household in that bracket— and, by age sixty, 70 percent have been in households at that income level at one time or other. Fewer people reach the top 10 percent of households but, by age sixty, 53 percent of them have been in a household in that income bracket at some point in their lives. Even the top one percent of households has been reached at some point by 11 percent of sixty-year-olds.[42] This is hardly surprising, since most people begin their careers earning entry-level salaries and then move up over the years, as they acquire more experience, skills and maturity.

When social mobility is defined in terms of how the incomes of one generation compare to the incomes of their parents, that is a fundamentally different question. Fortunately, two of the leading studies of social mobility in recent years— *Getting Ahead or Losing Ground: Economic Mobility in America* (2008) and an update of that study titled *Pursuing the American Dream: Economic Mobility Across Generations* (2012)— were both published by The Pew Charitable Trusts, which distinguish various kinds of social mobility, though some who have quoted from these studies have not. One of the things these Pew studies measure is "whether a person has more or less income, earnings, or wealth than his or her parents did at the same age."[43]

The answer? "The vast majority of Americans have higher family incomes than their parents did." Likewise, "Fifty percent of Americans have greater wealth than their parents did at the same age."[44]

A different question addressed by the Pew studies is how "a person's rank on the income, earnings, or wealth ladder compared to his or her parents' rank at the same age."[45] In other words, do the children end up in a similar or a different relative position in income among their contemporaries, compared to their parents' rankings among the contemporaries of their day? To this question, the answer from the 2012 Pew study is: "Sixty-six percent of those raised in the bottom of the wealth ladder remain on the bottom two rungs themselves, and 66 percent of those raised in the top of the wealth ladder remain on the top two rungs."[46]

This is the crucial finding on which many commentators have based their assertion that social mobility in America is now a "myth." However, these Pew studies themselves caution that their data do not include immigrants, because of a lack of "historical family and economic data,"[47] such as were used for studying families that were in America for both parents' and children's generations. This is a crucial caveat because the original 2008 Pew study itself said that its findings do *not* apply to immigrant families, for whom "the American Dream is alive and well."[48] That statement is seldom quoted by many who cite the Pew studies as proof that social mobility in America is a "myth."

Chapter 9

MENTAL CAPABILITIES

> *We are phobic about saying out loud that children differ in their ability to learn the things that schools teach. Not only do we hate to say it, we get angry with people who do. We insist that the emperor is wearing clothes, beautiful clothes, and that those who say otherwise are bad people.*
>
> *Charles Murray*

There is a vast, complex and inconclusive literature on the mental potential of different racial groups. But the practical question for anyone investigating current economic disparities between individuals or groups is not what their mental potential was at birth— or at conception, since the prenatal behavior of mothers is known to affect many things.[1] The practical question is what human capital individuals develop as they grow up and can bring with them as adults to a job or a college, or to the creation of a business or a scientific endeavor.

Such developed capabilities have obviously varied enormously, not only among racial or ethnic groups, but also among people living in major urban centers, as compared to people living in secluded mountain villages or in other isolated or otherwise unpromising locations. An empirical study of outstanding figures in the arts and sciences showed them to have been far more numerous in urban areas than among a population of the same size in other settings.[2] There have also been vast disparities between different geographic regions and between nations, as well as within nations.[3]

No one familiar with the geography of Italy can seriously believe that people born in Sicily or in the mountain village called Montegrano had just as favorable life chances as people born in the Po River valley. Nor is this a new phenomenon of modern times. As previously noted, the Greeks were far more advanced than the British thousands of years ago. In the days of the Roman Empire, Cicero warned his fellow Romans against buying British slaves, since they were so hard to teach.[4] Given the vast cultural gulf between the illiterate tribal Britons of that era and the complex and sophisticated society of ancient Rome, it is hard to imagine how things could have been otherwise. With the advantage of centuries of historical hindsight, however, we can recognize today that this disparity in human capital was not permanent— which is not to deny that it was present, and consequential, at the time.

Today, with the specter of genetic determinism hovering in the background, many are loath to admit that there are major differences in developed mental capabilities among racial or ethnic groups. Tests that show such differences are often dismissed as "culturally biased" tests and historical evidences of such differences are dismissed as "stereotypes." Racial differences in patterns of employment and promotion are treated as evidence of employer discrimination. People who present empirical evidence of differences in current mental capabilities are often denounced as racists. Such reactions are not confined to racial or ethnic "leaders" or "spokesmen," or to politicians responsive to racial or ethnic voting blocs. Many academic scholars have had similar reactions and so have some Supreme Court justices.

Yet such over-reactions are hardly necessary to escape the racial claims of genetic determinists. We know, for example, that there have been, not merely individual whites, or white families, but whole communities of whites from isolated mountain regions in America whose average IQs have been similar to, or lower than, the average IQs of black Americans.[5] Mental tests given to American soldiers during the First World War likewise showed that whites from some Southern states scored lower than blacks from some Northern states.[6] A similar pattern can be found internationally, when comparing those sub-Saharan Africans in more favored environments with Caucasians from more unfavorable environments— for example, peoples in Africa who were producing iron centuries before the Caucasians in the Canary Islands, who were in the fifteenth century living like people lived in the Stone Age, and ignorant of iron.[7]

Both the black and the white American populations during the formative years of the United States were, in socioeconomic terms, downwardly biased samples of the races they came from— that is, the populations of Britain and of sub-Saharan West Africa. The white settlers in early America have often been referred to as "a decapitated society" by scholars studying that era. For example:

> No royalty, no aristocracy, no leisure class. Practically no bishops or judges or scientists or great statesmen made the journey. With insignificant exceptions the highest ranks, the highest professions, the men of highest learning and highest crafts and skills all stayed at home.[8]

Here, yet again, there was no even or random statistical distribution of people or of skills or achievements. The founding generations of Americans were a socioeconomically downwardly biased sample of the population from which they came in England. Nor is it hard to understand why. The upper classes had little reason to abandon their prosperous and comfortable lives, and subject themselves to the ordeal of a long and dangerous voyage across the Atlantic Ocean— where many ships sank in the turbulent and stormy waters during the era of sails. Even those people who arrived safely in America were then confronted by the rigors and dangers of establishing pioneer societies in a strange new land. Later generations of emigrants from other parts of Europe likewise tended to be from the "lower walks of life" as unskilled laborers and farmers.[9]

The black population brought to America as slaves was likewise a downwardly biased sample of the peoples of sub-Saharan Africa, where the most advanced and most powerful tribes conquered and enslaved the less advanced and more vulnerable tribes, just as similar things happened on other continents. Contrary to fictionalized accounts such as *Roots*, the pervasive pattern in West Africa was that of Africans enslaving other Africans, and then selling some of their slaves to whites, who transported them to the Western Hemisphere. With both the black and the white populations of the United States— which, together, constituted almost the entire population of the country, as late as the middle of the twentieth century— being drawn disproportionately from the non-elites of Europe and Africa, the rise of the United States to the forefront of human achievement in numerous fields seems inexplicable by genetics.

While such evidence undermines genetic determinism, that does not make mental test differences irrelevant today, any more than the great achievements of the British, many centuries after the decline and fall of the Roman Empire, deny that Britons in Roman times were not functioning at the same intellectual level as Romans. Both leaders and members of lagging groups today can take only a limited amount of solace from evidence suggesting that their lags are not genetically determined. The greater the unrealized mental potential, the greater the waste, and the more urgent the need to correct whatever things are causing that waste, whether those causes are internal, external or both.

PREDICTIVE VALIDITY

Mental tests to measure developed intellectual capabilities have been caught in a crossfire of controversies, just like other mental tests that some regard as measuring innate potential. However, a distinction must be made between the *predictive validity* of a mental test and the question whether it measures "real" intelligence, however the latter might be defined. Clearly no current mental test can retroactively measure "native intelligence"— that is, mental potential years earlier, at birth, which is what the controversies over innate intelligence are ultimately all about. The predictive validity of a test, however, is a very different and straightforward statistical question about the extent to which a particular test's results correlate with later performances in schools, on a job or in some other endeavor.

Obvious as this might seem, the Supreme Court of the United States nevertheless ruled in the landmark 1971 case of *Griggs v. Duke Power Co.* that employers must "validate" tests which have a disparate impact on minority groups, when those tests are "unrelated to measuring job capability."[10]

In other words, the *plausibility* of the test's relevance to the job, as judged by third parties with neither expertise nor experience in the jobs themselves, must be the criterion, according to the Supreme Court— *not* the objectively demonstrated statistical correlation between the scores received on a test and the scorers' subsequent performances on the job. But if scores on an IQ test correlate with the quality of pilots' subsequent performances in the air, this means that the test is predictively valid, even if there is not a single question on the IQ test that has anything to do with flying a plane. Even if an IQ test does not measure "real" intelligence— however defined— if whatever it does measure is correlated with pilots' subsequent performance, then it is predictively valid for that specific purpose, whether or not it measures either current intelligence or innate mental potential.

Educational Tests

Employment tests are not the only tests under attack when they result in different racial or ethnic groups scoring at very different levels on these tests. The use of such tests to determine who will and will not be admitted to selective public high schools, such as Lowell High School in San Francisco or New York City's three highly selective academic high schools— Stuyvesant, Bronx Science and Brooklyn Tech— has also been under attack, especially by spokesmen for racial or ethnic groups who do not gain admissions as often as others. Even larger numbers of attacks have been directed at college admissions tests across the country.

With academic admissions tests, as with tests for employment and promotions, intergroup disparities have often been extreme. At one time Jewish students were so overrepresented among those who successfully passed admissions tests to Stuyvesant High School that Stuyvesant was referred to by critics as a "free prep school for Jews" and a "privileged little ivory tower."[11]

Today, it is Asian American students who predominate, not only at Stuyvesant but at Bronx Science and Brooklyn Tech as well. At all three of these highly selective schools, where admissions are based on academic tests, Asian American students are not only a majority of all students but outnumber white students by more than two to one.[12]

The issues raised by critics of academic admissions tests, whether at the high school or college level, raise questions that go to the heart of what education is about and what its role is in the larger society. The ultimate value of high performance schools and colleges is not determined by the benefits they confer on whatever individuals or groups constitute the students who pass through these institutions. The most important value of such institutions consists of the benefits conferred on society at large from the work in later life of people with high-powered intellectual skills— whether in medicine, science or other endeavors.

The ultimate value of elite high schools is not measured by how many of their graduates were admitted to Harvard or by the fact that, in some years, more graduates of Brooklyn Tech have been admitted to M.I.T. than the graduates of any other high school in the country.[13] The value of top-level institutions in general is in what their students achieve in later life that benefits vastly more other people.

The many prizes and awards accumulated over the years by students from Stuyvesant, Bronx Science and Brooklyn Tech are just symptoms of their graduates' contributions to society at large. These include many Westinghouse Science awards, Intel Science awards, Pulitzer Prizes and multiple Nobel Prizes. Seven graduates from the Bronx High School of Science alone have gone on to receive Nobel

Prizes in physics alone,[14] and graduates from Stuyvesant and Brooklyn Tech have also gone on to receive Nobel Prizes.

That a particular student goes on to become a brain surgeon is of course significant in that individual's life, but it is of far greater significance to vastly more people whose lives are saved in the course of the surgeon's career. Just one graduate of New York's selective Townsend Harris High School, Jonas Salk, made an incalculable contribution to society— and to the world— by developing a vaccine that put an end to the tragic scourge of polio.

The envy and resentment of achievements that have been painful facts of life in other times and places around the world are perhaps not surprising in an educational context. But such envy and resentment are certainly nothing to be encouraged, to the ultimate detriment of society at large, whose progress is advanced disproportionately by the achievements of people with highly developed levels of human capital.

To refer to Stuyvesant High School as a "privileged little ivory tower" may be clever, but cleverness is not wisdom. Slippery use of the word "privilege" is part of a vogue of calling achievements "privileges"— a vogue which extends far beyond educational issues, spreading a toxic confusion in many other aspects of life. A privilege exists *ex ante* and is fundamentally different from an achievement, which exists *ex post*. Students whose demonstrated academic achievements earn them admission to high-powered educational institutions are fundamentally different from students admitted on the basis of demographic "diversity" or political expediency.

Whether the elite public high schools of New York were overwhelmingly Jewish in one era or overwhelmingly Asian in a later era, their lack of demographic "diversity" seems not to have adversely affected their educational performances or their graduates' achievements in later life. And that is what such schools are there for, not to present a tableau that matches fashionable preconceptions.

Passionate advocacy of the interests of lagging minorities has seldom been followed by equally dedicated empirical investigation as to whether those minorities have actually benefitted, on net balance, from the success of those advocacies. The triumph of egalitarian principles and demographic "diversity" in the rest of New York's educational system has not resulted in an increase in the number or proportion of black or Hispanic students passing the admissions tests to get into Stuyvesant, Bronx Science and Brooklyn Tech. On the contrary, the numbers and proportions of black and Hispanic students have *declined* substantially over the years at all three institutions.[15]

Back in 1938, the proportion of blacks attending Stuyvesant High School was almost as high as the proportion of blacks in the population of New York City.[16] But 1938 was the last year when this was true. The sharpest declines occurred in the second half of the twentieth century, when the socioeconomic position of blacks was far higher than in 1938. As of 1979, blacks were 12.9 percent of the students at Stuyvesant but, in 1995, the *New York Times* reported that only 4.8 percent of the students at Stuyvesant were black.[17] As of 2012, the *New York Times* reported that blacks were now 1.2 percent of the students at Stuyvesant High School.[18] In short, over a period of 33 years, the proportion of blacks gaining admission to Stuyvesant High School fell to just under *one-tenth* of what it had been before.

None of the usual explanations of racial disparities— racism, poverty or a "legacy of slavery"— can explain this major retrogression over time. Back in 1938, both racism and poverty were worse than in later times, and the blacks of 1938 were generations closer to slavery. Clearly, something else was happening.

Such distressing and puzzling trends present a challenge to believers in either heredity or environment, where environment is defined in the usual socioeconomic terms. There is no obvious, or even plausible, genetic reason why blacks of an earlier generation should have been more able to meet demanding mental test standards to get into an elite public high school. An environmental explanation in socioeconomic terms has even worse problems, since socioeconomic conditions have clearly improved among blacks since 1938, both absolutely and relative to the general population. One of the few possibilities left is that the culture within black communities has in some respect changed for the worse over the years.

There have long been different cultures among blacks. One has been the culture of the old South, the culture which created many handicaps for white Southerners,[19] of which the low mental test scores of white soldiers from Southern states during the First World War[20] were just one symptom.

The thousands of volunteers from the North who went into the South after the Civil War to take on the formidable task of educating the children of freed slaves were led by people who operated on the premise that a major objective of that education should be displacing the Southern culture that blacks had absorbed. This premise was publicly proclaimed at the time,[21] in contrast to the opposite premise in our own times that preserving and praising the black culture is an important and positive factor in education.

A disproportionate share of the Northern educators who went South after the Civil War were from New England, and sought to replace the Southern culture among blacks with the contrasting culture of New England. Given the limited economic resources available, this was possible only in a relatively few educational institutions, but those few institutions produced a very disproportionate share of future black leaders and pioneers in a number of fields.[22]

One of those institutions was the first black public high school in the country, founded in 1870 in Washington, D.C. In 1899, when tests were given in the city's four academic public high schools— three white and one black— this black high school scored higher than two of the three white high schools.[23]

That was not an isolated fluke. As late as 1954, when Chief Justice Earl Warren declared in a Supreme Court opinion that "separate educational facilities are inherently unequal," this all-black public high school sent 80 percent of its graduates on to college— a higher percentage than that among any white public high school in the city.[24] Although the IQ of blacks has consistently averaged around 85 over the years, the average IQ at this school— called by various names over the years, including Dunbar High School after 1916— was consistently at or above 100 every year from 1938 to 1955, except for 1945, when it was 99.[25] This was in the absence of preselection by IQ tests, and with many students with IQs below 100 being admitted to Dunbar on the strength of their academic records.[26] Nor was there "diversity." This school had an all-black student body during the entire 85 years of its academic ascendancy, from 1870 to 1955.

Some of its graduates began going to elite colleges in the late nineteenth century, and the school's first graduate who went to Harvard did so in 1903. From 1892 to 1954, Amherst College admitted 34 of these graduates. Of these, 74 percent graduated from Amherst and 28 percent of these graduates were Phi Beta Kappas.[27] Nor was Amherst unique. Over the years, the school's graduates went on to become Phi Beta Kappas at Harvard, Yale, Cornell, Dartmouth, Williams, and other elite institutions.[28]

In terms of their later careers, "the first black who" pioneered in a number of fields also came from this one school. These included the first black man to graduate from Annapolis,[29] the first black enlisted man in the Army to rise to become a commissioned officer,[30] the first black woman to receive a Ph.D. from an American university,[31] the first black federal judge, the first black general, the first black Cabinet member and, among other notables, Dr. Charles Drew who achieved international recognition for his pioneering work on the use of blood plasma.[32] During World War II, when black military officers were rare, there were among Dunbar High School's graduates "many captains and lieutenants, nearly a score of majors, nine colonels and lieutenant colonels, and one brigadier general."[33]

All of this from one public high school in a black community was remarkable enough. What is relevant to the issue of culture was that this was a school which, from its beginning, had a wholly different cultural orientation from that of the ghetto culture. Seven of its first ten principals were educated in a New England environment. Four had degrees from colleges located in New England and three had degrees from Oberlin College, which was established by New Englanders in

Ohio as a deliberate project to plant New England culture in the midwest. Dunbar High School issued a handbook on behavior to its students that spelled out how one should act, not only in the school but in the world at large.[34] The values and deportment these students were taught would today be called by critics "acting white."

Nor did the difference in the way Dunbar students behaved go unnoticed in the local black community. Dunbar High School became so controversial among blacks in Washington that the late Pulitzer Prize-winning *Washington Post* columnist William Raspberry said that you could turn any social gathering of the city's middle-aged blacks into warring factions by simply saying the one word "Dunbar."[35] Resentments of Dunbar's achievements in Washington's black community were as common as resentments of the achievements of New York's elite public high schools and resentments of other achievements by other groups in other countries around the world.

The clash between proud alumni of Dunbar and other blacks antagonistic to the school became so bitter that a controversy over what to do with the original Dunbar High School building, after a more modern building was built to replace it, became literally a federal case that went up to the U.S. Circuit Court of Appeals. When the issue was first raised in Washington's City Council, a member of that Council declared, "There are people in this city who say that the school represents a symbol of an élitism among blacks that should never happen again. I say we should raze it."[36] After the Dunbar alumni lost in the courts, the original Dunbar High School building was demolished. It was one of many triumphs of the ghetto culture across the country in the second half of the twentieth century, with consequences that spread far beyond educational institutions.

Dunbar High School was begun as an academic high school for black youngsters living anywhere in Washington. But, in the wake of the *Brown v. Board of Education* decision in 1954, Washington public schools became neighborhood schools— and Dunbar, being located in a ghetto neighborhood, became a typical ghetto school. More than 80 years of quality education came to an abrupt end. In 1993, *Policy*

Review reported: "A smaller percentage of Dunbar students go to college now than did 60 years ago."[37] Sixty years earlier would have been in the depths of the Great Depression and 1993 was in the midst of a decade of prosperity. But the cultural change outweighed economic progress when it came to educational consequences. As of 2014, the *Washington Post* reported:

> Dunbar has persistent truancy issues, and fewer than one-third of the students are proficient in reading. Only six in 10 students graduate on time, and only four in 10 make it to college. [38]

The changing social climate of the 1960s and beyond included a celebration of the ghetto culture, essentially an offshoot of the dysfunctional redneck culture of the South,[39] though often regarded as something uniquely black or even African, despite much evidence to the contrary.* So pervasive did the influence of this ghetto culture become that even middle-class black youngsters felt a need to adopt attitudes, values and behavior from that ghetto culture, as a sign of racial solidarity, or a need to avoid the stigma of "acting white" and the social consequences which could follow, ranging from ridicule to ostracism to threats and outright violence.

Legendary basketball star Kareem Abdul-Jabbar described what it was like for him as a youngster growing up in this culture:

> I got all A's and was hated for it; I spoke correctly and was called a punk. I had to learn a new language simply to be able to deal with the threats. I had good manners and was a good little boy and paid for it with my hide.[40]

---

* So-called "black English" or "ebonics" has no connection with languages in Africa but very strong connections with the way English was spoken, centuries ago, in the parts of Britain from which white Southerners came. See, for example, David Hackett Fischer, *Albion's Seed: Four British Folkways in America* (New York: Oxford University Press, 1989), pp. 256–258; Frank L. Owsley, *Plain Folk of the Old South* (Baton Rouge: Louisiana State University Press, 1949), p. 92.

None of this was unique to a particular individual or a particular place. It was a growing influence among blacks across the country. A study of black youngsters in the racially mixed, affluent suburb of Shaker Heights, Ohio, found these youngsters far behind their white peers academically. Nor was the reason mysterious. Black students spent far less time studying and far more time watching television or engaging in other activities.[41] Nor was this simple laziness. There was an actual aversion to behaviors regarded as "acting white." According to the researcher who studied these black middle school students, "The 'White behavior' most often singled out for criticism was 'talking proper.'"[42] In other words, speaking standard English was seen as a racial betrayal.

"What amazed me," the researcher said, "is that these kids who come from homes of doctors and lawyers are not thinking like their parents; they don't know how their parents made it." Instead they "are looking at rappers in ghettos as their role models, they are looking at entertainers."[43] The normal incentives against short-sighted young people throwing away their education— and thus, in many cases, their chance for a decent life— are greatly reduced when schools promote them to the next grade, whether they have learned what they were supposed to have learned or not. When asked why they were not taking their school work seriously, many black students in Shaker Heights said that they knew they were going to be promoted to the next grade anyway.[44] What lay ahead of them in life after they finished school was apparently beyond their time horizon.

School teachers and administrators were not the only adults reducing the incentives for black youngsters to take school work seriously. Many black leaders and spokesmen, like leaders and spokesmen for other lagging racial or ethnic groups in various other countries, depict their group's problems as primarily or solely due to other people, and depict opposing those other groups *and their culture* as the way to advance. Moreover, many among the intelligentsia in the media and in educational institutions go along, in the spirit of helping blacks. One of the black leaders who rejected this approach was

Martin Luther King, Jr. He said, "We can't keep on blaming the white man. There are things we must do for ourselves."[45] But that has not been the prevailing view.

It is not just in elite schools that we can see educational retrogression among black youngsters. We have grown so used to seeing ghetto schools lag far behind other schools that it may be surprising for some to learn that this was not always the case. As of 1941, for example, test scores in a sample of classes in Harlem elementary schools were very similar to test scores in a sample of classes in the same grades in white schools in working-class neighborhoods on New York's Lower East Side.

In April of that year, there were some questions on which sixth grade classes in some Harlem schools did marginally better than sixth grade classes in the white schools on the Lower East Side, while on other questions these white sixth graders did marginally better than their counterparts in Harlem. The same was true of third grade classes in the two neighborhoods in May 1947. December 1941 saw all sixth grade classes in the sample of Harlem schools do marginally better than sixth grade classes in the sample of Lower East Side schools on all the questions. February 1951 saw a class in a junior high school on the Lower East Side do marginally better than the average of an all-male and an all-female junior high school in Harlem.[46]

In short, there were no serious differences in test results in these samples of Harlem schools and Lower East Side schools during those years. These were all just ordinary working-class neighborhood schools, with no real difference in educational results between those schools that were black and those that were white. Yet other data in later years showed a general nationwide pattern of black test results far below those of whites. As of 1994, for example, black 17-year-olds read at the same level as white *13-year-olds*.[47] But even these wide disparities between black and white students were exceeded by disparities between black students attending the general run of public schools and those attending some highly successful public charter schools, such as those run in a number of states by the KIPP organization and by Success Academy schools in New York. Both serve predominantly low-income black and other minority students.

The KIPP ("Knowledge Is Power Program") network schools have more than 50,000 students in public charter schools across the country. Blacks constitute 58 percent of these students and Latinos 38 percent. Most of these students— 87 percent— are from families with incomes low enough to be eligible for federal free lunch or reduced-price lunch programs. At various grade levels, children educated in KIPP schools have scored higher on reading and math tests than students in their local school districts or in their state. Graduating seniors from KIPP high schools who take the SAT have an average score of 1373[48]— the kind of score found among students admitted to the top tier of colleges.

As of 2013, according to the *New York Times*, children in the fifth grade in one of the Harlem academies in the Success Academy network of public charter schools "surpassed all other public schools in the state in math, even their counterparts in the whitest and richest suburbs." The following year, children in the Success Academy network of public charter schools as a whole scored in the top 3 percent in English and in the top 1 percent in math.[49]

These striking disparities in educational outcomes within low-income minority neighborhoods are especially striking when the public charter school is physically located in the very same building as a regular public school. In 2013, 58 percent of Success Academy students scored at or above grade level in English and 82 percent scored at or above grade level in math, while public schools located in the same buildings with them had "passing rates as low as 4 and 5 percent."[50]

Neither poverty, genes nor "a legacy of slavery" can explain the vast differences in educational outcomes between public charter school students and the regular public school students from the same neighborhood who were taking classes in the same school building. Nor is there any magic formula that can be painlessly applied to get the same educational results for the public school system as a whole.

The charter schools in the Success Academy network, and in the KIPP schools network, both feature extraordinary amounts of work by students and teachers, whether measured by hours in the day or days in the year. A regular school day in the KIPP schools is from 7:30 AM to 5:00 PM, plus additional weeks in the summer.

Hard work was also a key factor in the past success of Dunbar High School in Washington, during its years of academic ascendancy. At one point during that era, in response to a parental protest to the board of education, Dunbar teachers agreed to reduce the amount of homework "to one hour per night for each major subject."[51] That was still hours of homework on a daily basis.

Not all individuals or all cultures are prepared to invest the kind of time and effort required for educational success. Just as whites as a group tend to invest more time in their homework than blacks, and Asians more than whites, so ghetto blacks who spend the kind of time on their school work required in successful charter schools can do better than middle-class black students in Shaker Heights who invest less time in their education. Although many charter schools admit students by lottery, they are implicitly selective in that parents who enter their children in the lottery can differ from parents who do not bother. The workload at successful charter schools, and the large amount of homework, can lead less dedicated students to withdraw. The outstanding educational performances of the remaining black students in these kinds of charter schools can be seen as an indication of how much of a handicap having less interested and more disruptive students in their midst can be.

Political incentives are for government officials to supply public schools with things that are in demand from organized constituencies such as teachers' unions that want smaller classes, better facilities and job protection. Yet there is little evidence that these are the things required for good education. The school known after 1916 as Dunbar High School had already achieved academic success under other names, going back to its founding in 1870, after which it was housed successively in makeshift facilities, including a church basement, before it acquired a building of its own as the Sumner School in 1872, and then as the M Street School in 1892.[52] However, the student body at the M Street School grew to be nearly 50 percent larger than the building's capacity. Yet, under adverse physical conditions, the M Street School nevertheless achieved educational excellence.

By contrast, in the early twenty-first century, another Dunbar High School building was built, costing more than $100 million and sporting many advanced features. But its academic record has been abysmal. Political incentives are to spend money on things that create a good impression, whether or not those kinds of things create good educational results. Political incentives can also create policies to limit the disciplining of disruptive minority students, even when their disruptions create an atmosphere in which other minority students are unlikely to get an adequate education.

Individuals' values and choices have more correlation with outcomes than various tangible factors within the scope of government, not only as regards educational outcomes but other outcomes as well. Despite the prevalence of poverty in many black communities, the poverty rate among black married couples has been in single digits every year since 1994.[53] In other words, those blacks whose behavior put them outside the pattern of the spreading ghetto culture escaped poverty to a far greater extent than other blacks.

Colleges and Universities

At the college level, egalitarian and demographic "diversity" criteria have triumphed in admissions policies and practices, even at elite institutions, so the question is how this has affected the outcomes for black and Hispanic students in college and beyond. Affirmative action policies can ensure that there are more minority students on campus, but these policies cannot ensure that they will graduate, much less graduate with degrees in challenging subjects like mathematics, science and engineering.

Despite rising numbers of black students admitted to the University of California at Berkeley during the 1980s, the number of black students *graduating* actually declined.[54] Conversely, when a ban on affirmative action in admissions to the University of California system was imposed in the following decade, the number of black students declined slightly in the system as a whole, but the number of black students *graduating* increased. The number of Hispanic students who graduated also rose substantially,[55] now that minority students were being admitted to those particular campuses of the University of California system that matched their academic qualifications, rather than being mismatched with Berkeley or UCLA for the sake of demographic representation.

In the wake of the ban on affirmative action, the number of black and Hispanic students who graduated in four years rose 55 percent; those who graduated with degrees in science, technology, engineering and mathematics rose by 51 percent; and those who graduated with grade point averages of 3.5 or higher rose by 63 percent. These results confirmed what many critics of affirmative action in academia had been saying for years: Students mismatched with institutions whose standards they did not meet would either fail to graduate as often as others or would manage to graduate only by avoiding difficult subjects like science, technology, engineering, and mathematics.

A widely acclaimed attempt to say otherwise, that affirmative action in college admissions was successful— *The Shape of the River* by former college presidents William Bowen and Derek Bok— had crucial defects:

> 1. Although the study purported to show that blacks admitted under affirmative action policies with lower academic qualifications did well, the actual samples in the statistics lumped together *all* black students— those who were admitted with the same qualifications as other students and those admitted under affirmative action with lower qualifications than the other students.[56] The absence of data on the group

specifically at issue— those particular black students who were admitted with lower qualifications— makes that study the statistical equivalent of *Hamlet* without the prince of Denmark.

2. Despite Bowen's and Bok's apparently triumphant finding that black students in their sample "graduated at *higher* rates, the more selective the school that they attended,"[57] that is *not* the mismatch hypothesis being tested. The mismatch hypothesis says that the larger the *differential* in academic qualifications between black and white students at a given institution, the larger the racial differential in failure to graduate tends to be. When this hypothesis is tested at specific, individual institutions (as was done in the Thernstroms' *America in Black and White*) rather than in aggregations of institutions from different SAT levels (as in *The Shape of the River*), the mismatch hypothesis is confirmed. Both studies use combined SAT scores as the measure of academic qualifications. The data in *America in Black and White* show that the difference between the combined SAT scores of black students and other students at Harvard, for example, was 95 points—1305 points versus 1400 points— while the difference at Rice University was 271 points. Correspondingly, the racial difference in dropout rates was 2 percentage points at Harvard and 15 percentage points at Rice.[58] In the Bowen-Bok aggregations, Rice is included in an aggregation that also includes Princeton,[59] which has a much smaller racial differential in SAT scores than at Rice and a correspondingly smaller racial differential in dropout rates, namely 4 percentage points— while Harvard is omitted from this selection of schools with top SAT scores. Thus confirmations of the mismatch hypothesis

within the same category of institutions vanish from view when the focus is on comparisons of different aggregations. Statistical wonders can be performed with aggregations, but these wonders do not necessarily stand up when individual institutions are examined. Data from other studies of individual institutions show results very similar to those in *America in Black and White* and very different from those in *The Shape of the River*.[60]

3. Other researchers were denied access to the raw data from which Bowen and Bok derived their conclusions.[61]

The acclaim for the Bowen and Bok book may have had more to do with how welcome its conclusions were in many quarters, rather than the quality of its evidence or logic. What they said fit the prevailing vision, which was apparently enough to exempt their conclusions from the further requirement of fitting the relevant facts.

INNATE POTENTIAL

Developed mental capabilities are not only more readily measured but are more demonstrably important than innate mental potential. Indeed, the significance of innate potential derives largely from whatever role it might have as a source of, or limitation on, developed mental capabilities. Whether we are choosing a plumber or a surgeon, what we most want to know is that individual's skill at plumbing or surgery, not whether that skill was due to heredity or environment.

Early Twentieth Century Controversies

During the heyday of genetic determinism in the early twentieth century, it was widely assumed by genetic determinists that genetic potential put a ceiling on the mental capabilities that could be developed in some racial or ethnic groups. Because members of some groups were deemed to be intellectually capable of being no more than the proverbial "hewers of wood and drawers of water," genetic determinists supported eugenics— a term coined by Francis Galton, who advocated "the gradual extinction of an inferior race."[62] As late as 1944, Gunnar Myrdal, in his landmark study, *An American Dilemma*, reported hearing "everywhere in contemporary white America" a belief in a "biological ceiling," indicating that "the mind of the Negro race cannot be improved beyond a given level." This belief was "phrased as an excuse by the Negro's friends and as an accusation by his enemies."[63]

The eugenics movement spanned the Atlantic. Perhaps even more remarkably, it spanned the ideological spectrum, from conservatives like Winston Churchill and Neville Chamberlain to people on the left like John Maynard Keynes and leading Fabian socialists in England, while a similar sweep in the United States ranged from socialist Jack London to conservative icon Henry L. Mencken.

Many American writings by genetic determinists of that era sought to show that Eastern Europeans and Southern Europeans were innately inferior intellectually to Northern Europeans.[64] This was an era when the origins of mass immigration from Europe to America had shifted from the Northern and Western regions of Europe to its Eastern and Southern regions, provoking fears that intellectually inferior and culturally unassimilable immigrants were flooding into the United States. Belief in the innate inferiority of blacks was already so widespread and so unquestioningly believed that the literature on this subject was not comparably large.

Later empirical evidence undermined the conclusions drawn at the peak of the ascendancy of genetic determinism. Jews began to score above the national average on mental tests, for example,[65] leading to mental test pioneer Carl Brigham's recantation of his earlier views.[66] Others brought out the fact that white soldiers from several Southern states scored lower on the Army's mental tests than black soldiers from several Northern states,[67] undermining the most widely accepted racial version of genetic determinism.

Not only did such results undermine the theory of a genetic basis for black-white differences in performances on mental tests, these results were also inconsistent with the presumed innate mental superiority of Northern Europeans to Southern Europeans, since the American South was settled primarily by the supposedly superior Northern European population from Britain while the massive immigration from Eastern Europe and Southern Europe settled primarily outside the South.*

A closer examination of the performances of black soldiers on mental tests during the First World War raises questions about their cultural level at that time, just as cultural questions were raised when Carl Brigham reexamined his conclusions about white immigrants who had been raised in homes where English was not the language spoken.

For blacks who took the Army mental tests, their very low level of literacy at that time was likewise a factor to be considered, though few commentators took that into account. One sign of the effect of the low level of literacy among black soldiers taking the Army mental tests, and how that could affect the results, was that illiterate black soldiers were able to answer some of the more difficult test questions that did not require understanding the meaning of written words more often than literate black soldiers were able to answer much simpler questions that did. The Army Alpha test was administered to those soldiers who could read and the Army Beta test was administered to those who were illiterate.

In parts of the Army Alpha test used during the First World War, the modal score of literate black soldiers was *zero*— derived by

---

* The lower mental test scores of Southern whites are consistent with the fact that many, if not most, white Southerners emigrated from culturally isolated regions of Britain *before* those regions were incorporated into the mainstream culture of the country and before the spectacular rise of Scots to the forefront of achievements, after having been what historian Henry Buckle called "poor and ignorant" people. See Grady McWhiney, *Cracker Culture: Celtic Ways in the Old South* (Tuscaloosa: University of Alabama Press, 1988), pp. 55–56.

subtracting incorrect answers from correct answers, in order to neutralize the effect of guessing. These results were despite the fact that the actual intellectual substance of some of these questions involved only knowing that "yes" and "no" were opposites, as were "night" and "day," "bitter" and "sweet" and other similarly extremely easy questions— questions too simple to be missed by anyone who knew what the word "opposite" meant.

In the Army Beta test, given to soldiers who could not read, some of the questions involved looking at pictures of a pile of blocks and determining how many blocks there were, including blocks that were not visible, but whose presence had to be inferred (and counted) from the shape of the piles. Yet fewer than half of the illiterate black soldiers who took the Army's Beta test received a score of zero on such questions, which were more intellectually demanding, but did not require the ability to understand written words like "opposite" or written instructions that may have been challenging to literate black soldiers whose literacy might have been very thin during that era, when many blacks had very little education— either quantitatively or qualitatively— in inferior Southern schools.

Given the very small quantity and very low quality of education received by that generation of blacks, even those who were technically literate were unlikely to have a substantial vocabulary of written words. So it is hardly surprising that the completely illiterate black soldiers did better on substantively more challenging questions than blacks with some ability to read did on simpler questions.[68]

Later Twentieth Century Controversies

During the second half of the twentieth century, the research of Professor James R. Flynn, an American expatriate in New Zealand, brought out the fact that raw scores on IQ tests had risen in a generation or two by a standard deviation or more, in more than a dozen countries,[69] calling into question the belief that scores on these tests measured some fixed genetic endowment.

The repeated re-norming of IQ tests, in order to maintain the definitional average IQ at 100 while the number of questions answered correctly changed, had previously concealed this huge rise in raw scores on IQ tests. These rises in raw scores included the raw scores of black Americans, whose IQs had remained at about 85 over the years as the tests were renormed. But the average number of questions answered correctly on IQ tests by blacks in 2002 would have given them an average IQ of 104 by the norms used in 1947–1948, which is to say, slightly higher than the average performance of Americans in general during the earlier period.[70]

While genetic determinism encountered many empirical problems, this is not to say that genetics has no effect at all. By one of the simplest and most decisive tests— differences between the correlation of IQ test scores of fraternal twins with each other, compared to the correlation of IQ test scores between identical twins— it is clear that genetics has an effect, since the latter correlation is higher,[71] and identical twins have identical genes, while fraternal twins share only some genes, like other siblings. But because genes affect IQ differences between individuals, it does not follow that genes are the reason for differences in IQ among groups.* It was clearly not the sole factor, as shown by Jewish soldiers scoring below the national average on mental tests during the First World War but Jews scoring above the national average in later years.

Whether, or to what extent, existing gaps in IQ between groups are due to heredity is by no means a settled issue. But even with something that is generally agreed to be determined primarily by heredity, such as height, that does not mean that all existing differences in height are due to heredity, much less that heights cannot vary for other reasons besides heredity in particular cases or change over time. The average height of Britons, for example, was once greater than the average height of the French, as far back as the

---

* *"That a trait is genetically transmitted in individuals does not mean that group differences in that trait are also genetic in origin."* Richard J. Herrnstein and Charles Murray, *The Bell Curve: Intelligence and Class Structure in American Life* (New York: The Free Press, 1994), p. 298. This crucial statement, with all its words italicized in the original, has been almost universally ignored by critics.

early eighteenth century, and continuing on into the twentieth century. However, after 1967, the average height of the French equaled the average height of Britons.[72]

While the gap in height between the British and the French closed, a gap between the heights of North Koreans and South Koreans opened up after the country was partitioned following the Second World War,[73] with people in North Korea living under a draconian dictatorship that kept them poverty-stricken and ill-fed. In Holland, the average height of young males increased from 5 feet, 4 inches to about 6 feet between the middle of the nineteenth century and the early twenty-first century.[74] Here, as in other contexts, saying that a particular factor can influence outcomes— as latitude influences climate, for example— in no way says that this particular factor *determines* outcomes, when there are other factors whose interactions can make the outcomes be very different from what those outcomes would be if determined by one factor alone.

Even in the absence of these various empirical findings, the theories of genetic determinism that prevailed in the early twentieth century suffered from the very thin slice of the millennia of human history from which they generalized.

The recurring theme in discussions of American immigration laws during that era was that immigrants from Southern Europe were mentally inferior to those from Northern Europe— inferior not just in education or in various other contemporary accomplishments, but innately, genetically and permanently inferior.[75] In the past few centuries, Northern Europe has in fact outperformed Southern Europe in many ways— in its economies, and in science and technology, for example. But, in ancient times, Southern Europe outperformed Northern Europe by at least as much— and there is no indication that the genes of people in either part of Europe changed. Meanwhile, China over the centuries lost its once commanding lead over all the Europeans— and over Japan, which much later overtook China, again without any indication that genes had changed in any of these races.

Looked at another way, strongly similar economic and social patterns have been found among people in certain geographic settings, such as mountain communities in various parts of the world— which is to say, among people of different races, with no genetic connection to one another. Believers in genetic determinism will have to explain not only the coincidence of such non-genetically based similarities among these mountain peoples, scattered around the world, but also why persistently lagging groups, from Canary Islanders in the past to sub-Saharan Africans to Australian aborigines, have shared an unusually severe degree of isolation.

There have been not only individual whites, but whole communities of whites, who scored at the same average IQ level as American blacks, or lower. The national average is itself an amalgam of very different IQs among groups as well as individuals, so that comparison of any given group with the national average can suggest a uniqueness that is simply not there. During the era of mass immigration to America from Europe, immigrants from Spain, Italy, Greece, Portugal and Poland scored at or below the average IQ level of American blacks.[76] Other groups of whites with average IQs no higher than those of blacks have included white mountaineer communities in the United States, canal boat people in Britain, and the Gaelic-speaking inhabitants of the Hebrides Islands off Scotland[77]— again, culturally isolated groups.

Perhaps the strongest argument made by genetic determinists is that the most economically prosperous and technologically advanced nations and races in the world today have populations with higher average IQs than the poorer and less technologically advanced nations and races.[78]

Yet, even putting aside the fact that widespread use of IQ tests is little more than a century old, representing a very thin slice of the millennia of recorded history, the terms of the genetic generalization are similar to the gross terms used in making geographic comparisons between the temperatures of places at different latitudes. No one denies that latitude can affect temperature, but it is equally undeniable that the waters around the city of Bergen in Norway are free of ice year round, while at the same latitude in Canada the winter ice in Hudson Bay is not completely melted until early summer.[79]

In both cases— geographic and genetic— comparisons must be made between highly specific circumstances, because more than one factor is involved in the outcomes, and comparisons of different combinations of those factors are necessary to validate claims made for one particular factor. As we have already seen, those particular whites from similarly isolated settings as blacks have had similar mental test scores, when we are comparing black children in America with white isolated mountain children in America, for example. Similarly when we are comparing the general development of Canary Island Caucasians when they were invaded by the Spaniards with the general development of Australian aborigines when they were invaded by the British.

Genes may be neither necessary nor sufficient to explain most of the social patterns of disparate achievements that genetic determinists have tried to explain. However, the relative influence of heredity and environment on the intelligence of different races remains an unresolved issue. It has been neither proved nor disproved.

Even if we were to accept IQ tests as a universally valid measure of intelligence, for the sake of argument, the existing *range* of IQ scores among blacks extends far above the average IQ of whites, even though whites as a group have higher average IQs than blacks as a group. The eugenics agenda of the genetic determinists in the early twentieth century seemed to be based on an implicit assumption that there was an inherent *ceiling* on the intelligence of particular racial or ethnic groups, not simply that the *average* of their intelligence was lower at a particular time or place.

Groups with identical ranges of innate intellectual potential can still end up with different averages, if environmental circumstances cause different rates of reproduction or survival in various segments of their respective populations. In other words, environments can change the statistical average of IQs, even if the range of IQs remains unchanged. It has been suggested, for example, that the failure to reconsider "current welfare policies"— which may be promoting a higher rate of reproduction of lower classes within the black community— may be "our society's greatest injustice" to the black population. It was pointed out that three-fourths of the blacks who failed mental tests given by the armed forces at that time "come from families of four or more children."[80]

Few American professionals' families of any race have four or more children, which may be more common among unwed teenage mothers who are high school dropouts, for whom the children are their meal ticket for welfare, in a world with very few better options for them, by the time they have frittered away their educational opportunities. To have the proportion of the black population that is born to unwed teenage dropouts artificially increased by government policies is hardly a benefit to either the black population or to the society at large.

It may also be worth noting that isolation, which can have such negative economic and cultural effects, can also affect heredity as well as environment. Small and highly isolated communities, such as in mountain villages, especially in times past, could mean that, over the generations, most people living in such places could end up biologically related to one another and therefore suffer the negative biological consequences of in-breeding. That can be especially likely to become a factor where very few outsiders move into these poverty-stricken and culturally backward communities. This is a factor at least worth considering as regards the low IQs found in white mountaineer communities in the United States, canal boat communities in Britain and among the Gaelic-speaking inhabitants of the Hebrides Islands off Scotland.

Even if it could be proved that genetics has nothing to do with intelligence— and neither that nor the opposite has been proved— differences in developed mental capabilities between individuals and groups would still be of major consequence, and mental test differences could not simply be waived aside as irrelevant.

In the heated, and sometimes bitter, controversies between those who ascribe educational, economic and other differences between groups to genes and those who ascribe these differences to discrimination, a third option that is often overlooked is that different groups with different cultures do not necessarily *want* to do the same things, or are not prepared to make the same efforts and sacrifices for the same things. Two groups of whites whose contrasting levels of achievements often attracted attention in times past were those from New England and those from the South. An antebellum Southern writer in a leading regional publication of that era ascribed their differences in outcomes to differences in what they valued:

> The one content to laze away life with as little labor as possible and all the enjoyment compassable; his log hut, wool hat, homespun suit, and cornbread and bacon the limit of his desires for domicile, vesture, and food. . . The other instinct with life, activity, intelligence, never satisfied with the present well-being while anything better is beyond to tempt his longings and his wits.[81]

This was just one of many contrasts drawn between Southerners and New Englanders in that era— some of these contrasts buttressed with hard data.[82] But, whatever the degree of accuracy or inaccuracy of this particular description of Southerners and New Englanders at the time, the more general point, applicable to other groups in other times and places, is that what members of culturally different groups *want* to do, and value enough to make the efforts and the sacrifices required to do it, is a factor that cannot be either ignored or implicitly assumed to be the same in all cultures and among all peoples.

Nor can questionnaires or other forms of survey research determine people's desires, much less how much they are prepared to do in pursuit of those desires. We might all like to be millionaires, certainly if wealth were available as an inheritance, but not everyone is prepared to put aside many other competing desires and aspirations for the sake of pursuing that goal. Others might be willing to put aside many things in order to become a millionaire, and still others would regard achieving that goal as just a spur to go on to become multimillionaires or even billionaires.

Research that finds different groups having very different economic, educational or other achievements cannot legitimately regard these differences as evidence or proof of either internal deficiencies or external barriers, by implicitly assuming that all the groups are equally seeking the same achievements. Nor will polls or questionnaires on which different groups list or rank various goals the same be conclusive, because *it costs nothing* to say that you are in favor of education or upward economic mobility, and it costs much to spend years of dedication and sacrifice of other things in order to reach those goals.

When it comes to behavior, it is a different story. The black youngsters in affluent Shaker Heights who did not spend as much time on their school work as white youngsters in the same community were one example. Such intergroup differences are by no means unusual, or confined to the United States. In Australia, Chinese students spend more than twice as much time on their homework as do white students.[83] There are many other evidences of the cultural values behind such outcomes.

The backlash against genetic determinism, after its heyday in the early twentieth century, has produced social philosophies lacking even as much evidence as the genetic determinists had. Multiculturalists today decry any recognition that some peoples have superior achievements or inferior achievements at a given time and place, though it is blatantly clear that Greeks were far more advanced than Britons in ancient times and Britons were more advanced than Greeks in the nineteenth century. Today, tests that show some groups far better at some things than others, are often dismissed as biased tests. Apparently, according to that view, some groups cannot possibly be better or worse than other groups at a given time or place, or at least we cannot publicly admit it.

Such reactions, or over-reactions, to genetic determinism can be especially harmful to groups that are lagging, since it turns their attention and energies away from the many available ways in which they can improve themselves and their prospects, as other lagging groups have done before them— sometimes rising dramatically— and instead leads them into the blind alley of resentments and lashing out at others.

PART IV:

POLITICAL FACTORS

The worst political blunder in the history of civilization was probably the decision of the emperor of China in the year 1433 to stop exploring the oceans and to destroy the ships capable of exploration and the written records of their voyages. . . The decision was the result of powerful people pursuing partisan squabbles and neglecting the long-range interests of the empire. This is a disease to which governments of all kinds, including democracies, are fatally susceptible.

Freeman Dyson

In addition to the influence of such long-run or general factors as geography and culture, particular economic and other social outcomes can be influenced— or even determined— by particular individual happenstances at particular junctures in history. The decision of the fifteenth century emperor of China to isolate his country from the outside world was just one of those fateful political decisions with unforeseen repercussions that changed the course of history for a whole civilization. Such happenstances cut across such general influences as geography or culture, preventing either geographic determinism or cultural determinism.

The decision of the Spanish government to finance Columbus' voyage across the Atlantic, in search of an alternate route to India, obviously changed the course of history for the entire Western Hemisphere and, to a considerable extent, for Europe as well. Had the Japanese government not made the fateful decision to bomb Pearl Harbor, Japan today might be a very different country, without the fundamental and enduring social and institutional changes that took place during the years of American occupation after Japan's defeat in the Second World War.

Sometimes the happenstance that changes the course of history is not a conscious decision but the unpredictable outcome of a crucial military battle between closely matched armies on a chaotic battlefield, where victory could easily have gone to either side. Such was the battle of Waterloo in 1815, which the victor— the Duke of Wellington— afterwards called "a near run thing." But his victory over Napoleon determined the fate of generations yet unborn, in countries across the continent of Europe.

Had Hitler not been a fanatical anti-Semite, at a time when many of the world's leading nuclear physicists were Jewish, the United States might not have become the first nation with a nuclear bomb, as a result of the Manhattan Project, which was created in response to the initiative of Jewish physicists who had fled to America to escape mortal dangers in Europe.

Political influences on economic development go beyond particular government decisions, policies or actions. More fundamentally, the presence or absence of an effective governmental framework, within which economic activities can take place, has been a major and enduring influence on a people's prosperity or poverty. In times and places where there was no effective government on the scene, people have improvised their own, whether vigilantes in pioneer communities in the days of the American wild west, or in caravans crossing the deserts, or in many isolated mountains where formal law enforcement was seldom seen. Organizations deliberately operating outside the scope of government, such as crime syndicates on land or pirates at sea, have likewise set up and enforced their own internal rules. Clearly it has long been recognized that some framework of rules is a necessity for economic or other social activities to take place.

Where an existing governmental framework collapses, many other activities dependent on that framework are disrupted or discontinued until some kind of replacement can be pieced together. The decline and fall of the Roman Empire meant the collapse of a framework of law and order across Western Europe, within which economic, educational and other activities had flourished in relative safety and peoples were connected with other peoples, with whom they had been able to coordinate many and varied activities for their mutual benefit, across the vast expanse of the empire. Like other things, the value of an effective governmental framework may be more accurately assessed and more keenly appreciated after it is gone.

Culturally less advanced invaders from various parts of Europe proved to be capable of defeating the Romans militarily, but were not capable of running the empire, which fragmented and collapsed. The elaborate network of Roman roads which tied the far-flung empire together fell into neglect and disrepair, and travel became not only more difficult but also more dangerous, without the armed protection of imperial forces. This in turn forfeited the economic benefits of highly specialized production— both industrial and agricultural— in different parts of the empire, whose output had been transported by land or sea to widely scattered consumers during the era of Rome's rule.

Pottery, for example, was produced in the south of France in Roman times, when that pottery could be found as far north as England and as far south as Portugal.[1] But, after the end of the Roman Empire, the quantity, quality and range of distribution of pottery all declined.[2] Nor was pottery unique. As a leading geographer and historian put it, "the artifacts that survive show that the quality of their workmanship had declined sadly since the days of the Roman empire." He added:

> Pottery was coarser, metal goods less refined, and cloth unquestionably of poorer quality. Almost all such goods were made for local consumption. There was little or no long-distance trade in the goods of everyday life.[3]

Similarly, the impressive Roman aqueducts that brought water to the cities of the empire, often from great distances, fell into disrepair and disuse, though these aqueducts were built solidly enough to survive physically for thousands of years to the present day. But they no longer brought water to the cities:

> The medieval city had fewer amenities than the Roman. There was little provision for water supply and almost none for the disposal of sewage. . . Sewers were almost non-existent.[4]

Retrogressions in living standards were widespread and long-lasting. Some skills developed in Roman times atrophied and disappeared.[5] Cities were no longer as large nor as advanced as they had been in Roman times.[6] It has been estimated that a thousand years passed before Western Europe regained the standard of living it once had, back in the days of the Roman Empire.[7] The high and thick stone walls surrounding many European communities in the Middle Ages suggest something of the perils of the times. Nothing could more plainly indicate the importance of having or not having an effective national government, quite aside from questions about the wisdom or justice of its laws, decisions and policies.

Many places and times have never achieved a national government as effectively in control as the Roman Empire was at its zenith, nor a national government with similar control of even a more modest-sized area. Such places and times have seldom achieved the economic or social progress that Rome once had. At the other extreme, the Soviet Union covered an even larger area than that of the Romans, with pervasive totalitarian control of individuals and groups. Yet, despite a wealth of natural resources, the Soviet Union never achieved a standard of living equal to that of other modern nations with far fewer natural resources. The point here is simply that there must be some degree of government control, in order for economic activities to flourish, which is not to say that more government control is always better.

What scope and degree of government control of economic activities would be optimal is a complex question, with very different answers in different places and times. Even the strongest advocates of free markets recognize the need for some enforceable framework of laws to guarantee the physical safety of persons and their property as they engage in economic activities, so that investments can be made with assurance that crops can be harvested and belong to those who planted them, or even longer-run commercial or industrial investments can be made with assurance that the returns received after many years are likewise guaranteed to the investors.

Others may regard a government which restricts itself to the role of maintaining the surrounding conditions, under which specific economic decisions are made by private parties, as a government which does nothing. But what may be called "nothing" often took centuries to create, and whole peoples can retrogress for centuries when that governmental framework collapses, as in the wake of the decline and fall of the Roman Empire.

Many decisions in a society can be made either by governmental institutions, or by economic or social organizations, or by individuals or families. Each of these decision-making processes has advantages and disadvantages, depending in part on where the most accurate and relevant knowledge can be brought to bear, and be corrected by feedback based on the consequences.[8] There is no need here to try to settle the question of what is the optimal mix of political decisions in an economy. It is sufficient for present purposes that there are governmental prerequisites for a flourishing economy, and that these prerequisites cannot be taken for granted.

We are so familiar with governments at many levels— from local municipal governments to national governments to international governmental organizations like the British Empire in the past or the European Union today— that our familiarity makes it easy to take governments for granted, as things that exist more or less naturally, almost like sunshine and rain. But, in reality, formal governmental institutions such as we see all around us today emerged only in the latest stages of the scores of millennia during which human beings have existed. How national governments emerged, and the consequences of the ways they emerged, and in some cases spread to the international dimensions of empires, has implications for larger questions of wealth, poverty and politics.

Chapter 10

POLITICAL INSTITUTIONS

The State is the most precious of human possessions; and no care can be too great to be spent on enabling it to do its special work in the best way: a chief condition to that end is that it should not be set to work, for which it is not specially qualified, under the conditions of time and place.

Alfred Marshall

Political decision-making is more than just the story of particular government laws and policies at particular times and places. It is also, and more fundamentally, the story of how particular kinds of political institutions emerged in different settings and in different eras, to make decisions that have impacted economic developments, for better or worse.

The size of the area within which a given set of laws and policies apply can be considered the political universe of a given government, and its size can influence the size of the economic universe and the cultural universe, even if the political universe is not co-extensive with them. There are international trade and international migrations of people, for example, but each nation has laws regulating, promoting or impeding both. The larger the area over which the same laws and policies apply, the greater the opportunities for large-scale production, with its economies of scale that can reduce production costs per unit of output, permitting a higher standard of living for people within larger political units.

Within a larger political universe, many economic activities that once took place within the home or farm, can take place in commercial and industrial enterprises specializing in such activities and providing the same goods and services better or cheaper. For example, when Alexander Hamilton surveyed the American economy in the early days of United States, he found that most clothes worn by Americans were home-made. That may seem strange today because of today's far larger market for industrially produced clothing, at lower production costs, in part due to economies of scale, and in part due to the invention of the sewing machine in the nineteenth century, as well as far lower transportation costs, due to the invention of railroads, and later trucks, as well as technological advances in seaborne and then airborne transportation.

On the world stage, and over the millennia of recorded history, the expansion of production from the home or local village level to successively larger markets was facilitated by successively larger political units, culminating in nations and empires. The economic benefits of political expansions are not the only benefits. Dangers from nature, such as floods, or dangers of attack from other human beings, provide incentives for individuals to consolidate their efforts, in order to produce larger and stronger political units in self-defense. As geographer Ellen Churchill Semple said, more than a century ago: "A common natural danger, constantly and even regularly recurring, necessitates for its resistance a strong and sustained union, that draws men out of the barren individualism of a primitive people, and forces them without halt along the path of civilization."[1]

In addition to understanding some of the benefits of individuals coalescing into societies, and societies consolidating into progressively larger political units, we need to consider the process by which nations and empires have emerged— and the economic and social consequences of differences in the pace and completeness of that political process among different peoples in different places and times.

THE EMERGENCE OF NATIONS

There was a China many centuries before there was a Britain or France, and these European nations in turn predated the United States by centuries. But there were even longer millennia before there were any political units large enough to be considered nations by the standards of today. Moreover, the process of forming nations has by no means been irreversible. Not only was Carthage obliterated by the Romans, Poland was just one of the many nations swallowed up by larger empires, and one of the few that was later reconstituted, after the breakup of dynastic empires in Europe and the Middle East, in the wake of the First World War. And, of course, the Roman Empire itself fragmented into many local sovereignties that coalesced over the centuries into the nations of today in Western Europe and North Africa, none of which has reached a size comparable to that of the Roman Empire.

The incentives for moving beyond the ancient bands of hunter-gatherers, and forming successively larger political units over the millennia, were both political and economic. Larger governing units usually mean more powerful units protecting the society or advancing its interests in the international arena. Larger political units also offer economic benefits. Tribes or villages can seldom, if ever, produce and sell in a large enough volume to reap the full benefits of lower production costs per unit, which result from specialization and economics of scale that mass production firms and industries reap*— if they have a large enough market for a vast outpouring of their products.

Cities may be able to reap some of the benefits of specialization, when there has been a large enough local market for the resulting output, so that specialized workers are able to devote themselves, full-time, to producing one particular product or engaging in one particular process, such as printing or weaving. But cities have usually

---

* The economic effect of the division of labor was demonstrated by a writer who decided to make his own toaster from scratch by himself. It cost him $1,837.36, as compared to $6.10 for a toaster available in a supermarket. Moreover his toaster ended up producing warm bread, rather than actual toast. William Easterly, *The Tyranny of Experts: Economists, Dictators, and the Forgotten Rights of the Poor* (New York: Basic Books, 2013), pp. 247–248.

been way stations on the road to the creation of nations, though there are still a few city-states, even today, such as Singapore or Monaco.

The Pace of National Development

The economic and social benefits of larger societies do not ensure that such societies will emerge everywhere. In some places and times, the spontaneous coalescing of smaller groupings into successively larger groupings over time has lagged so far behind the pace of the same process in other contemporary societies that people living in small and vulnerable societies have often been simply conquered or enslaved by larger and more powerful societies. This process has taken place in Europe, Asia, Africa and in both North America and South America, as well as among Polynesians in the Pacific.

Among the reasons why various societies coalesce into larger political units at different paces is that some societies are more in communication and interaction with other societies, with greater frequency or over wider areas, so that their respective peoples and rulers can come to know and work with other peoples and rulers over long periods of time, slowly resolving their differences through trial and error, and gradually building up ties that create mutual benefits which all have incentives to preserve and expand.

This process, however, may be much slower, or even non-existent, in regions fragmented geographically, as in the Balkan mountains, or on small islands scattered across a vast sea, or in much of sub-Saharan Africa, with its many limitations on communication and transportation. Peoples in such isolated places have usually been unable to create nations on a scale like that of ancient China or the Roman Empire, and slow to create nations even on a scale like that of moderate-sized nations like Italy or Thailand.

The radius of trust can be a major factor in the pace and extent to which small social groupings coalesce into successively larger political units, just as it has been a factor in creating larger economic units. Small mountain communities, for example, have been especially slow to coalesce into larger governmental units. As one geographic study put it, "Political solidarity has a hard, slow birth in the mountains" because of various "forces working against political consolidation."[2]

These forces working against consolidation into larger political units include a multiplicity of languages and dialects among fragmented mountain populations,[3] impeding even simple communication. Clan, tribal and religious differences have likewise fragmented mountain populations, along with the geographic isolation of mountain communities from one another, whether with or without cultural contrasts among the different settlements. The limited economic benefits of cooperation between very poor mountain communities can also mean reduced incentives to consolidate. There is not the same reward for cooperation or consolidation as in richer places, especially richer places with contrasting skills and very different natural resources, such as make trade beneficial to all the parties involved.

Family and tribal feuds have long been common among mountain peoples around the world,[4] whether in the mountains of Taiwan or Afghanistan or in America's Appalachian Mountains. The geographic fragmentation of mountain peoples has been an obstacle to developing a wider radius of trust, or even a wider radius of toleration. Among the consequences of such social fragmentation of populations have been "minute mountain states" and "dwarf republics" in the words of Ellen Churchill Semple.[5]

Even where there are, formally speaking, large mountain nations such as Afghanistan, these are not necessarily nations whose national governments actually have effective control over all the territory they nominally govern. More than a hundred years ago, mountainous Afghanistan was described as a region with "no sense of unity" among its numerous tribes— a situation which "offers little hope of Afghanistan ever developing national cohesion."[6] Little has happened in more than a century since then that would contradict that assessment. Political consolidation has sometimes been forced upon fragmented mountain peoples by foreign conquest or by the threat of such conquest, which sometimes led to defensive alliances against that outside threat. But these temporary alliances seldom led to permanent consolidations into nationhood.

Switzerland has been a rare exception, perhaps due to the many mountain passes into the Swiss Alps[7] that kept the people in these mountains from being as isolated as peoples in many other mountains around the world, while the large valleys in the Swiss Alps presented better opportunities for large settlements, more in touch with each other and with the outside world.[8] More fundamentally, despite the Alps in the southern part of Switzerland, not all of the country is mountainous. Despite the dearth of navigable waterways in other regions of the world known for their mountains, Switzerland has such navigable waterways as Lake Geneva and Lake Lucerne, as well as navigable rivers, including the Rhine.

The empire of the Incas in the Andes Mountains of South America was another, and even more striking, exception to the small size of nations in mountainous terrain. The Inca Empire covered 906,000 square kilometers— more than 20 times the size of Switzerland and roughly the size of France and Germany put together.[9] There were long and large valleys between the mountain ranges of the Andes, those valleys in the lower elevations being suitable for agriculture.[10] This created a very different geographic setting from those in various other mountains around the world, where people are more fragmented geographically in small communities, kept small by the very limited amount of arable land in many mountain valleys and by formidable geographic obstacles to communication and transportation.[11]

Unlike other mountains lacking major navigable waterways, the Andes include Lake Titicaca, more than 100 miles long, more than 900 feet deep and with a surface area of more than 3,000 square miles[12]— larger than the combined areas of New York City, Los Angeles, Chicago, Dallas, Phoenix, Houston, and San Antonio. The peoples living around the enormous perimeter of this lake had ready communication with each other across a navigable waterway. Lake Titicaca has been called "the cradle of the Inca Empire."[13] And the empire's capital, Cuzco, was situated between two rivers.

The presence of vast numbers of llamas in some of the mountain valleys of the Andes gave the Incas small but numerous pack animals that were lacking elsewhere in the Western Hemisphere before Europeans arrived with their animals. In these settings, the Inca Empire began and later spread to other geographic settings in western South America, for a distance of 4,000 kilometers from north to south.[14]

The imperative to produce specific crops at specific times of the year, and to preserve the resulting food, which peoples in temperate zone climates felt for millennia, were in the Inca Empire challenges supplied by the peculiar climate of the region where that empire originated. The unique situation of a vast and high mountain range, located in the tropics, gave the Incas a unique climate that was quite different from the climates common in either temperate or tropical zones. The seasonality of the climate in the Andes was based on great differences in the amount of rainfall at different times of the year, even though the average daytime high temperature varied little—from the high 60s to the low 70s— throughout the year in the Inca capital of Cuzco.

This seasonality, plus the vulnerability of crops to drought and hard frosts, due to overnight temperatures that could fall to freezing levels during the winter, as well as changing weather conditions from one year to the next, created the same life-threatening challenge faced for millennia by peoples located in the temperate zones. The Incas met this challenge by creating large networks of food storage facilities, scattered throughout their far-flung empire, and by developing ways of making some perishable foods storable.[15] Thus the geographic environment of the Incas produced the same necessity for developing self-discipline, and human capital in general, that peoples in the temperate zones had to create in order to survive. Despite its location in the tropics, the Inca Empire was not tropical in any meaningful climatic sense.

Special local conditions made Switzerland and the Inca Empire exceptions to the handicaps that kept the peoples in many other mountains poor, backward and unable to create large, well-functioning political units. However, mountains are not the only geographic feature that can fragment a population and isolate the fragments from one another, impeding the formation of nation states. Other geographically isolated and fragmented regions, such as the Canary Islands and much of sub-Saharan Africa, have likewise been culturally divided, with far more different languages than among similar numbers of people living on a broad mainland and in ready communication with each other.

In the fourteenth century, the Canary Islanders were speaking languages in some of these islands that were unintelligible to people on some other islands in the same group.[16] The peoples of sub-Saharan Africa were likewise handicapped by a multiplicity of languages. In those parts of sub-Saharan Africa with less severe geographic handicaps, larger communities arose than in other parts of tropical Africa. For example, empires arose in the bend of the Niger River that were much larger than other nations in sub-Saharan Africa,[17] though not as large as some empires in some other parts of the world with more geographic advantages. In Africa, as elsewhere, the larger and more advanced societies often conquered or enslaved their smaller or less advanced neighbors.

Since power is inherently relative, the ability of small political units to survive independently has often depended on the size and power of other political units located within striking distance of them. As Fernand Braudel pointed out: "In battle, as in everyday life, there is no equality of opportunity."[18]

Sometimes what saves some small or vulnerable societies from conquest is the poverty and backwardness of some such societies. As a noted geographer put it, "natural wealth has always brought the conqueror," but the security of "unproductive highlands lies more in their failure to attract than in their power to resist conquest."[19] However, this can also mean that cultural isolation, with its attendant poverty and backwardness, can be more long-lasting among the small and vulnerable peoples who have been spared conquest.

At other times, a small country such as Switzerland may be spared because none of the larger powers around it wants any of the other rival powers to gain control of such a strategically located country—in this case because of the Alps, whose many mountain passes are of great economic and military value to other nations. Universal military training within Switzerland, and the country's rugged terrain make military conquest too costly for what might turn out to be only a temporary victory for an invader, who could expect military intervention by a rival power or powers unwilling to see them gain control of such a militarily important area as the Alps. To the major powers surrounding Switzerland, control of the Alps by the Swiss poses no such threat as control by a rival major power.

Slavery

In a world largely free of slavery today, it may be hard to realize that slavery was an almost universal institution for thousands of years. Despite widespread misconceptions in the United States today that the institution of slavery was based on race, for most of the millennia in which slavery existed around the world, it was based on whoever was vulnerable to enslavement and within striking distance.

Thus Europeans enslaved other Europeans, just as Asians enslaved other Asians and Africans enslaved other Africans, while Polynesians enslaved other Polynesians and the indigenous peoples of the Western Hemisphere enslaved other indigenous peoples of the Western Hemisphere. The very word "slave" derived from the word for Slav—not only in English, but also in other European languages, as well as in Arabic[20]— because Slavs were so widely enslaved by fellow Europeans (and others) for centuries before Africans began to be brought in chains to the Western Hemisphere.[21] In ancient Rome, the slaves included thousands of Greeks, as well as Britons, Syrians and Jews.[22] China in centuries past was "one of the largest and most comprehensive markets for the exchange of human beings in the world."[23] India has been estimated to have had more slaves than that

in the entire Western Hemisphere— including children kidnapped by
the original Thugs.[24] In some of the cities of Southeast Asia, slaves
were a majority of the population.[25]

As of the time when the United States was formed in 1776, Adam
Smith wrote in *The Wealth of Nations* (published that same year) that
Western Europe was the only part of the world where slavery had
been "abolished altogether."[26] But even Western Europeans held
many slaves in their overseas colonies.

Over the centuries, the consolidation of various regions of the
world into nations with armies and navies reduced the number of
places that could be raided for slaves without great costs and risks.
Among the places where this consolidation process lagged, whether as
a result of geographic or other fragmentation of peoples or for other
reasons, were the Balkans, the backwaters of Asia and much of sub-
Saharan Africa. Africans were not singled out by race for ownership
by Europeans, they were resorted to increasingly as other sources of
supply dried up. The slow pace of political consolidation in much of
sub-Saharan Africa left many small and vulnerable societies there,
whose people were raided and enslaved, largely by other Africans
from more geographically favored settings— coastal peoples enslaving
less advanced and less consolidated inland peoples, for example.[27]

It was from the coastal peoples of West Africa that whites purchased
slaves for shipment to the Western Hemisphere.[28] In East Africa, both
Africans and Arabs raided and enslaved the more vulnerable inland
peoples.[29] Meanwhile, the growing scope of international commerce
and the growing wealth of nations eventually made economically
feasible the transportation of vast numbers of slaves from one
continent to another, thereby creating racial differences between the
enslaved and their owners as a dominant pattern in the Western
Hemisphere. Elsewhere, such a pattern was by no means limited to
Europeans owning non-Europeans, however. There were many
examples of the reverse— that is, non-Europeans enslaving
Europeans— quite aside from vast regions of the earth where neither
the slaves nor their owners were either black or white.

Even after much of Europe was consolidated into nations with military and naval forces, unprotected coastal settlements in Europe, and European sailors at sea, remained vulnerable to slave raids by pirates from the Barbary Coast of North Africa. These pirates enslaved at least a million Europeans between 1500 and 1800. That is more than the number of African slaves transported to the United States and to the American colonies from which it was formed.[30] The Ottoman Empire also enslaved Europeans. Among other ways, it imposed a systematic levy of a certain percentage of young boys from the conquered peoples in Southeastern Europe, these boys being taken away as slaves, converted to Islam, trained and assigned civil and military duties in the empire.[31] Other European slaves were acquired by purchase. Among these were Circassian women from the Caucasus region, who were highly prized as concubines by wealthy men in the Ottoman Empire, and such positions were sufficiently prized by Circassians that mothers groomed their daughters for such roles.[32]

The economic consequences of slavery, both during its existence and in its aftermath, have been a matter of controversy among scholars. However, some of the more extravagant claims— that slavery was the basis for the prosperity of the United States, or of Western civilization in general— are clearly false. The American South, where slavery was concentrated, was for centuries the poorest and most backward region of the country, for its white population as well as for its black population. In Brazil, where slavery was concentrated in that country's northern region, this too was, and remained, the poorest region. Brazil's industrial development was concentrated in its southern region, and was largely the work of immigrants, most of whom arrived after the abolition of slavery. Similarly, it was in the era after slavery was abolished that the United States rose to become the leading industrial power in the world— and here, too, this dramatic economic rise took place primarily outside the region where slavery had been concentrated.

Perhaps the most sweeping claim for the supposed economic effects of slavery is that the profits of slavery financed Britain's industrial revolution.[33] But even if all of Britain's profits from slavery had been invested in its industry, that would have come to less than 2 percent of Britain's domestic investments during that era.[34]

Despite attempts to depict slavery as a *localized* evil, inflicted on one race by another, it was a vastly larger evil, inflicted on peoples around the world. As internationally recognized historian of slavery David Eltis put it:

> Slavery until recently was universal in two senses. Most settled societies incorporated the institution into their social structures, and few peoples in the world have not constituted a major source of slaves at one time or another.[35]

To say that American society is illegitimate today because it had slavery when it was founded would be to say that virtually every nation around the world— whether of black, white or other races— was illegitimate at that same time, which hardly seems to be what critics are trying to suggest. At some period of their history, as John Stuart Mill put it, "almost every people, now civilized, have consisted, in majority, of slaves."[36]

While societies around the world had slavery, Western civilization was the first to turn against slavery, ending it within Western societies during the nineteenth century, with Brazil being the last Western nation to abolish slavery in 1888. Many non-Western societies then had slavery stamped out within them by Western nations that took over those societies during the era of European imperialism. But elsewhere vestiges of slavery persisted on into the late twentieth century and early twenty-first century, especially in parts of the Middle East and Africa.[37]

EMPIRES

Conquests, whether ancient or modern, have led to very different kinds of political rule and social settings. Within the broader category of imperialism is what can be called *colonialism* proper— that is, the transplanting of a portion of the conqueror's population to the conquered territory, forming a colony reproducing the institutions of the conqueror's homeland for a population that essentially displaces the conquered indigenous population. The United States, Canada, Australia and New Zealand were colonies that were offshoots of British society in this sense. But the Spanish empire in the Western Hemisphere, and in the Philippines in Asia, was one in which Spaniards were usually a ruling class in a population that remained largely composed of indigenous peoples.

The culture of the conquerors tends of course to be more pervasive throughout society in colonies where the population consists predominantly of people from the conquering nation. But in the Spanish, Ottoman, Roman and other empires, a more common pattern was one in which the conquering rulers were of a race or culture different from that of the majority population that they ruled. This was also the pattern in those parts of the British Empire located in Asia and Africa. This often created an intermediate class of functionaries and subordinates drawn from the conquered people. This intermediate class learned at least the language, and often also other aspects of the conqueror's culture— thus creating or accentuating cultural fault lines within the indigenous population that persisted into later eras after conquered countries became independent.

As an extreme example of this internal social and cultural fracturing of the indigenous population, when Sri Lanka became independent in the middle of the twentieth century, its ruling elites spoke English and the nation's laws were written in English, a language which the majority of the population subject to those laws did not understand. A similar situation had existed, centuries earlier, in England itself, where the Norman conquerors spoke French, and both parliamentary proceedings and the laws of the country were written in French, which of course most of the population did not understand. King Edward III, whose reign began more than two and a half centuries after the Norman conquest of England in 1066, was perhaps the first king of England who spoke more than a few words of the English language.[38]

What many imperial conquests created or accentuated was not only a vast gulf between the rulers and the ruled, with the former often treating the latter as— in John Stuart Mill's words— "mere dirt under their feet,"[39] but also an additional social fracture among the conquered peoples that often lasted into later generations, even after imperial rule gave way to independent nationhood. This was in addition to pre-existing differences among conquered peoples who had never come together on their own to create a nation as large as the political unit created by the conqueror.

Language differences have been impediments to consolidating smaller political units into larger political units, whether nations or empires. This problem has been dealt with in different ways at various times and places. In China, one of the advantages of the written Chinese language is that it is a non-phonetic language, its symbols conveying ideas rather than using individual written words as building blocks for ideas. Therefore peoples who cannot understand each other's spoken languages or dialects can nevertheless communicate with each other in written Chinese. From a political standpoint, this can facilitate the consolidation of linguistically different peoples into a larger nation or empire.

Other consolidations of political units into larger nations or empires have been facilitated by requiring at least a leadership class in the subordinate governing units to know the language of the ruling people. The spread of Islamic empires in the Middle East and North Africa, was spearheaded by Arabs, but the vast territories they conquered over the centuries contained predominantly non-Arab populations, speaking native languages other than Arabic. But because the sacred book of the rulers— the Koran— was written in Arabic, this spread the Arabic language and literacy in general to many non-Arab peoples who sought to become Muslims, either for religious reasons or to receive the benefits of literacy or to escape the disabilities of non-Muslims in the Islamic empires.

The British Empire, as it existed in Asia and Africa, was ruled largely through Britons acting as viceroys in the respective conquered territories and over the indigenous peoples, but often with these territories and peoples being more immediately administered by local, indigenous officials under a policy of "indirect rule." This in turn meant that there was an indigenous elite who learned to speak the English language, as a prerequisite for serving under the colonial overlords from Britain. Through missionary schools, a portion of the indigenous general population also became educated in English. Because the British Empire, at its zenith, encompassed one-fourth of the land area of the earth and one-fourth of the world's population, the language of an island people living off the coast at the western end of the Eurasian landmass became the language of more than 500 million people, only a fraction of whom live in England.

Although the spread of the language of the conqueror to the conquered was one of the ways of overcoming language barriers to the consolidation of smaller political units into larger political units, this process also had other, unintended, consequences. The imposed language could also become a *lingua franca* among linguistically different groups among the conquered peoples, facilitating both economic transactions and, in some cases, eventually political cooperation in demands for independence from their conquerors. In times and places where the conquerors no longer felt like expending the blood and treasure necessary to continue maintaining control over conquered territories and peoples, these territories and peoples became independent in the form of larger nations than had existed before they were conquered.

Just as imperialism, whether ancient or modern, has combined peoples into larger governmental units than the conquered peoples ever combined into themselves, so the end of empires has often threatened the continued existence of those larger units. Thus the Roman Empire, for example, combined independent tribes in ancient Britain into Roman Britain, within a government that covered a great part of the island. But, when the Romans withdrew, four centuries later, to go defend the empire that was under attack on the continent of Europe, Britain fragmented into tribal areas again and retrogressed economically.

This pattern would be repeated, more than a thousand years later, when European imperialism in Asia and Africa collapsed after the Second World War. In Nigeria, for example, the Hausa-Fulani tribes of the north had never been combined in the same country with the Ibos, Yorubas and various other tribes in other parts of the country before the British began taking over that region of Africa in the late nineteenth century and named it Nigeria.

After the British pulled out in 1960, independent Nigeria was repeatedly racked by inter-tribal mob violence, a ghastly civil war and a series of military coups and counter-coups, these crises reflecting tribal hostilities in a country the indigenous peoples never created, but where they were thrown together under outside imperial rule. This pattern of post-independence polarization and violence was not unique to Nigeria. As the international treatise *Ethnic Groups in Conflict* by Professor Donald L. Horowitz put it: "In a large number of ex-colonial states, the independence rally gave way to the ethnic riot."[40]

Geographically, Nigeria has been one of the more fortunate regions of sub-Saharan Africa. Watered by the great Niger River and its principal tributary, the Benue, and blessed with natural resources, including iron ore and large petroleum deposits, the peoples of that region had produced iron centuries before the Christian era, and had developed their own cities and countries before the British arrived— but nothing on the scale of the Nigeria that the British created, with its tribal antagonisms that had never been resolved, but only suppressed, under British rule. According to Professor Horowitz's treatise:

> What the colonialists did that was truly profound, and far more important for ethnicity, was to change the scale of the polity by several fold. The colonies were artificial, not because their borders were indifferent to their ethnic composition, but because they were, on the average, many times larger than the political systems they displaced or encapsulated.[41]

Like Roman Britain more than a thousand years earlier, Nigeria was an artificial creation of the conquerors, and its prosperity and viability were in jeopardy, once the conquerors pulled out. Nigeria has managed to remain one country but one of the poorest and most turbulent countries in the world. That this is more a product of political factors than of either geographic handicaps or inherent deficiencies of its people is suggested by the fact that Nigerians living in England and the United States have had an impressive record of success. According to the distinguished British magazine *The Economist*, "Nigerians abroad are generally keen on education; in Britain their children achieve considerably higher marks than white British ones and those of many other immigrant groups."[42] In the United States likewise, Nigerians have done very well both educationally and economically:

> In 2010, there were some 260,000 Nigerians in the U.S., a mere 0.7 percent of the black American population. Yet in 2013, 20 to 25 percent of the 120 black students at Harvard Business School were Nigerian. As early as 1999, Nigerians were overrepresented among black students at elite American colleges and universities by a factor of about ten.[43]

Nearly one-fourth of Nigerian households in the United States have incomes of more than $100,000— a level reached by under 11 percent of black American households.[44] With all due allowance for the fact that immigrants may be different from the people left behind in their country of origin, the contrast between the way Nigerians progress under American institutions and the way they fail to make comparable progress under the institutions in their homeland is much like the way the overseas Chinese and the overseas Indians have long progressed far better outside their respective homelands. This suggests that there may well be similar reasons, that the political structures and practices in Nigeria may be a major handicap that nullifies the potential of both its people and its geographic setting. Contemporary genetic determinists have attributed Africa's post-independence problems to "low intelligence,"[45] but the record of Nigerians in Britain and the United States suggests otherwise.

In Asia, British India was a similar story on an even larger scale than Nigeria. The extremely heterogeneous peoples living on the Indian subcontinent were lumped together by their conquerors, for their conquerors' convenience— but without the indigenous peoples' having resolved their differences and coalesced voluntarily over time into this political entity. After the British pulled out in 1947, the carnage was even greater than in Nigeria. The number of people killed in the 1947 mob violence between Hindus and Muslims has been estimated in the vicinity of a million, as British India split into a predominantly Hindu India and a predominantly Muslim Pakistan.

Nevertheless, despite this split, aimed at reducing Hindu-Muslim conflict, both India and Pakistan have subsequently been racked sporadically by internal conflicts between various groups, with East Pakistan eventually breaking off to form the new nation of Bangladesh. Overseas Indians, like the overseas Chinese and like the Nigerians living in America, have long prospered in many other countries around the world, where they were free from the political and other constraints, deficiencies and conflicts of their native land. Despite the widespread poverty in India, Americans of Indian ancestry have the highest incomes of any group tracked by the U.S. Bureau of the Census.[46] (Religious groups like Mormons and Jews are not tracked). In 2012, the average family income of Indians in America was over $100,000.[47]

Other multi-ethnic, post-colonial nations that emerged after being freed by the breakup of empires have had similar internal turmoils. Whether these nations subsequently split internally, as happened with India, Yugoslavia and Czechoslovakia, or remained intact like Nigeria, Sri Lanka and the Philippines, their internal strife has taken its toll, both economically and socially.

While such historical patterns demonstrate once more the powerful negative force of isolation on economic and social development, these patterns also show why the transportation and communications revolutions of the past two centuries cannot undo all the effects of earlier centuries or millennia of isolation. Even if the transportation and communications revolutions were to become as complete in formerly isolated parts of the world as in other regions that have long had a wider cultural universe, that cannot undo the fact that peoples living in a wider cultural universe have had centuries or millennia to become acquainted with other peoples and to work out cooperative relationships with them, while those living in isolation have not.

The fact that isolated peoples have usually been poorer and more backward has often meant that they had less demand for transportation and communications advances, which therefore reached them belatedly and on a smaller scale. A life-changing advance like railroads, for example, reached parts of Eastern Europe and the Balkans only after trains had already spread rapidly across Western Europe in the first half of the nineteenth century. As late as 1860, there was not a single mile of railroad track south of the Danube and the Sava rivers.[48] We have already noted that a train was a complete mystery to people in Japan in 1853, when that country was a poor and backward nation. It was a quarter of a century later before the first railroad reached Serbia.[49] This was nearly half a century after the first railroad was built in Britain.

Meanwhile, in the United States, even the less industrialized South had a railroad hub in Atlanta, which made it a target for General William T. Sherman's army in its devastating march through Georgia during the Civil War. However, railroads remained rare in mountainous parts of the South. It was 1912 when a region of Kentucky lost its negative distinction as "the largest mountain area in the United States untouched by railroads."[50]

The economic effects of imperialism have varied too greatly to be reduced to a single pattern or formula, despite many attempts to say that the conquest and exploitation of other peoples explains the prosperity of the West and the poverty of many non-Western peoples. Portugal, which once had an empire on three continents (South America, Africa and Asia) is today one of the poorest nations in Europe. Macau, once a Portuguese possession on the coast of China, today has a per capita Gross Domestic Product more than three times that of Portugal. Spain, whose even larger empire included extensive territories in both North America and South America, as well as the Philippines in Asia, is likewise one of the poorest countries in Western Europe, with a Gross Domestic Product per capita that is less than half that of Switzerland, which never had an empire and has few natural resources. Turkey, successor to the great Ottoman Empire, has a Gross Domestic Produce per capita roughly half that of Portugal and less than one-sixth that of Switzerland.[51]

Great conquering peoples are seldom also great commercial or industrial peoples or great international investors, though Britain and the Netherlands were striking exceptions during the era of European imperialism, as Japan was also during the shorter era of its conquests in East Asia and Southeast Asia during the first half of the twentieth century. But great historic conquerors like the Spaniards, the Portuguese, the Russians, the Ottoman Turks and the Mongols under Genghis Khan and his successors tended to disdain commerce and industry themselves, and leaders in such economic activities in the lands they conquered were often members of either the indigenous conquered peoples or minorities such as the Armenians in the Ottoman Empire or Jews in Eastern Europe.

While Europeans have been the leading imperialist conquerors of the past five centuries, in the preceding centuries Europeans did not control even all of Europe. North African Moors ruled Spain for centuries during Europe's Middle Ages, and the area now known as Russia was a satellite and tributary of the great Mongol empire established by Genghis Khan. The Ottoman Empire extended up into southeastern Europe and, in the seventeenth century, its army besieged Vienna. Yet none of these great non-European conquerors left a legacy of leading economic nations, just as most great European conquerors did not. In the Western Hemisphere, Barbados— most of whose population are the descendants of African slaves— has a higher Gross Domestic Product per capita than Argentina, most of whose population are the descendants of Europeans.[52]

Having had an empire did not, of course, *preclude* nations from prosperity, such as in Britain, Belgium and Japan for example. Various British offshoot nations— Australia, New Zealand, Canada and the United States— have likewise prospered after Britons conquered and displaced the respective indigenous populations of these countries. But the prosperity of these British offshoot nations did not consist fundamentally of wealth transferred from the conquered peoples, like the vast amounts of gold and silver transferred to Spain from the peoples it conquered in the Western Hemisphere. The lands and other natural resources seized from the indigenous peoples obviously had a value, but that value was greatly exceeded by the wealth created after the land and other natural resources passed from populations that included many hunter-gatherers to more urbanized and eventually industrialized societies.

This in no way changes the *moral* principle condemning robbery, slaughter and oppression, but that only shows the need to distinguish moral principles from *causal* principles, despite how tempting the amalgamation of those two very different principles can be from a political or ideological point of view. Non-Western peoples in Third World countries— or their leaders or the intelligentsia of these countries or other countries— may prefer to explain away their economic lags by the exploitation of their countries by Western imperialists. But whether or not that is true from a *causal* perspective matters greatly in terms of what can be done to raise the standard of living of people today, while nothing can be done to change the past.

One of the most ambitious, and most politically effective, theories attributing the poverty of non-Western peoples to their exploitation by Western nations was V.I. Lenin's theory of imperialism. In his book *Imperialism, The Highest Stage of Capitalism*, Lenin presented statistics on the location of foreign investments by industrial European nations:[53]

BILLIONS OF MARKS, CIRCA 1910

	GREAT BRITAIN	FRANCE	GERMANY	TOTAL
Europe	4	23	18	45
America	37	4	10	51
Asia, Africa, and Australia	29	8	7	44
Total	70	35	35	140

The countries listed across the top of the table in capital letters are the industrial countries investing in various parts of the world. The recipients of these investments are listed along the side of the table in lower-case letters. Although Lenin's claim was that industrial nations were investing in non-industrial regions of the world, as a source of what he called "super-profits," the huge and heterogeneous categories he chose— for example "America," meaning the entire Western Hemisphere— make it impossible to know, from these statistics, whether the industrial nations' investments were being made in non-industrial areas or in other industrial areas within vast regions of the earth containing both.

Nevertheless, Lenin's theory of imperialism was accepted by many people around the world, despite an absence of any serious evidence for it, and despite the availability of much evidence to the contrary elsewhere. A country-by-country breakdown of investment statistics, rather than Lenin's gross categories like "America," shows that it was precisely the already more prosperous and industrialized countries that were the prime destinations of European capital investments. During the period covered by Lenin— the late nineteenth and early twentieth centuries— the United States was the largest single recipient of British, German, and Dutch capital.[54] As regards American investments in other countries, for much of the twentieth century, the United States invested more in Canada than in all of Africa and Asia put together.[55] Only after Japan and other Asian nations rose to prosperity in the later decades of the twentieth century did Asia become a major destination of American foreign investment. In short, prosperous nations invest far more in other prosperous nations than in Third World nations, from whom Lenin and others have claimed their prosperity derived. Usually neither the imports nor the exports from Third World countries are at all comparable to the imports or exports from other prosperous countries.

Particular individuals, such as British entrepreneur Cecil Rhodes or King Leopold of Belgium, amassed great fortunes from their respective nations' empires, as the Spanish elites derived immense wealth from Spain's empire in the Western Hemisphere. But that is very different from saying that the general populations of the imperial nations prospered from the wealth extracted from the conquered peoples or that colonial exploitation explains economic gaps today between former conquered peoples and their former conquerors. The ancient Romans were already more advanced than the ancient Britons when the Romans conquered Britain, which is why a smaller number of Roman invaders could overcome a larger number of British defenders. This was a pattern that would be repeated many times over the centuries in many parts of the world.

One way of trying to estimate the economic value of empires to the conqueror is to compare how the conqueror's economy fared with and without the empire. Japan is an especially revealing example, since it has had virtually no natural resources of its own, and invaded many countries that had the natural resources it lacked. Then, with its defeat in 1945, it was suddenly deprived of the large amount of land it had conquered in China, as well as all of Korea, Malaya, the Philippines, and the East Indies. Moreover, large numbers of Japanese troops and civilians who had been living in its empire for years were suddenly sent home to a devastated Japan. There were some economically very stringent years but, within a single generation, Japan had not only recovered economically but was one of the most prosperous nations in the world, with a higher standard of living than ever.

As for natural resources, it was cheaper to buy them than to pay for a huge military establishment to conquer other nations and seize their natural resources. In Europe, Nazi Germany had also conquered vast amounts of territory during World War II, and lost all of it when it lost the war— as well as losing part of its own territory, when maps were redrawn by the victors. Before the war, the Nazis said that Germany needed *lebensraum*— living space for its large population. Today Germany has an even larger population living in a smaller space— and having a higher standard of living than ever. The postwar collapse of Western nations' far-flung empires in Asia and Africa likewise left these European powers with higher standards of living than before, after they recovered from the devastations of the war.

Chapter 11

POLITICS AND DIVERSITY

No arbitrary obstacles should prevent people from
achieving those positions for which their talents fit them
and which their values lead them to seek.

Milton Friedman

Despite the many benefits of being able to draw upon cultural features from a variety of sources, these benefits can have costs, and those costs can vary in both economic and political terms. Cultural receptivity in a society does not imply cultural diversity in its population. Even at the height of Japan's nineteenth century enthusiasm for importing Western technology and science, Japanese government officials did not fling the gates of immigration open to Western settlers in Japan, nor change their own political or social systems to those of Western societies. Japan today remains one of the most racially and culturally homogeneous nations on earth. Similarly, during earlier centuries, when Europeans were acquiring many products, inventions and concepts from Asia, there were very few Chinese, Japanese or Indians living in London or Paris, and few Europeans living in Asian cities.

Cultural diversity may exist within a society in a number of ways. Sometimes immigrants from other societies bring different cultures with them, as has often happened in the United States, Latin America, Southeast Asia and other places. Sometimes there are numerous indigenous ethnic groups with different cultures, who have coexisted within the same society for centuries, as in India or in the Ottoman or Habsburg empires.

Sometimes the cultural differences have been regional, rather than racial or ethnic, but nevertheless substantial, as between American white Southerners, whose ancestors originated in one part of Britain, and New Englanders whose ancestors originated in a very different part of Britain, and who maintained a very different way of life in the United States. Even within the same geographic setting, people of the same race and language have often differed and clashed when they were of different religions, as in the Balkans, whose history is written across the landscape in churches converted to mosques, and mosques converted to churches, as well as in towns and cities with multiple names in different languages, marking the advances and retreats of various conquerors over the centuries. Social class differences within a given nation can also produce economic and other outcomes as diverse as differences between racial, ethnic or other groups.[1]

Acquiring the material or cultural achievements of other peoples is very different from acquiring the people themselves as immigrants from a different culture. Importing products, technologies or other particular cultural features from other countries can have very different consequences from importing people from the countries where such products, technologies or other cultural features originated. The recipient countries can selectively choose which particular items from another culture to accept, while immigrants bring with them the whole ensemble of their cultural features, whether or not the receiving nation wants them all.

Another difference between importing selected cultural features, rather than importing people, is that importing cultural features is an incremental and reversible decision, subject to feedback from on-going experience, while importing people as permanent settlers tends to be a categorical and irreversible decision, regardless of what later experience turns out to be, or what the consequences are for generations yet unborn. The whole culture of a country can be altered in unpredictable and irreversible ways after the arrival of large numbers of people unfamiliar with the unspoken but prevailing habits, norms and values that foster the kind of radius of trust that holds a society together.

Perhaps the biggest difference between importing cultural features and importing peoples with different cultures is that the former is a decision which individuals can make for themselves, while the latter is a collective governmental decision, made under political incentives.

THE ROLE OF GOVERNMENT

Government, like other institutions, has its scope and its limitations, even aside from whatever might be the scope and limitations of particular government officials. In theory, government has a monopoly of power within a given jurisdiction. In practice, it usually has the largest power controlled by any given decision-maker within its jurisdiction. What government can actually accomplish, however, is limited to what power can accomplish, which is much, but by no means all. While government can either force or forbid particular acts, that is not the same as saying that it can therefore accomplish whatever larger purpose it has in mind by doing so.

Political Power

It has been claimed that "stateways cannot change folkways,"[2] but ruthless political power holders have often suppressed folkways. For example, even in a society whose culture has been generally accepting of people with a different culture, political power holders who are not accepting can impose a brutal racism. Conversely, even in societies with bitter antagonisms among different groups, political power holders can clamp down to prevent these antagonisms from being expressed in words or deeds.

The Nazi dictatorship in Germany during the 1930s and 1940s, for example, featured a racism unmatched in its heedless ferocity, killing millions of men, women and children simply because they were Jews. Moreover, Germany's dictator, Adolf Hitler, continued to pour resources into the Holocaust, even when Germany's own armies were in retreat, and could have used those resources to defend against opposing armies that were closing in on Germany from all sides, dooming the whole Nazi regime. Yet this level of racial fanaticism had not been characteristic of German culture before Hitler, either within Germany or among Germans living in other countries around the world.

Anti-Semitism was by no means unknown in Germany before Hitler. But, to the extent that Germans differed in racial attitudes from other Europeans, they tended to be somewhat less racist, rather than more. As of the time when Hitler took power in Germany, about one-fifth of all the Jews in the country had come there as refugees from Eastern Europe, where anti-Semitism was rampant.[3] One sign of the more accepting culture of Germany was that, during the previous decade, nearly half of all marriages of Jews in Germany from 1921 to 1927 were to people who were not Jews.[4] In nineteenth century America, German immigrant communities welcomed German Jewish immigrants as members of their *Turnvereine*, singing groups, and other cultural organizations.[5] German Jews likewise participated in the cultural life of German organizations in Chile and in Czechoslovakia.[6]

As regards other racial or ethnic groups as well, Germans tended to be somewhat less racist than other Europeans or other peoples around the world. The first anti-slavery meeting in North America was held by Germans in 1688, and Germans in Brazil were likewise anti-slavery.[7] In antebellum America, enclaves of Germans in Texas, Virginia and St. Louis were also noted for being against slavery.[8] When North Carolina voted in the early nineteenth century to disenfranchise "free persons of color," the western counties voted to let these free blacks continue to have the franchise, these western counties having concentrations of Germans and Scotch-Irish voters.[9] Germans also tended to get along with the indigenous peoples of the United States and of Paraguay better than other European settlers,[10] and in Australia Germans established missions to help the aborigines.[11]

Nevertheless, stateways prevailed over folkways for 12 tragic and horrifying years in Nazi Germany. If fanatical racial policies by political leaders could so override culture in Germany, the effect of political power in other contexts would be hard to deny.

In the second half of the twentieth century, a very different situation existed in ruthless dictatorships under Marshal Tito in Yugoslavia and under Saddam Hussein in Iraq. These dictatorships kept bitterly antagonistic groups from breaking out in lethal violence against each other, as they did in the wake of the eventual ending of those dictatorships. But, whether in democratic or undemocratic nations, political decisions can either moderate or accentuate friction between social groups with different cultures. Despite the overwhelming power of government in some contexts, this is not to say that power is equally effective in achieving whatever end result is desired.

Governments can readily do things which depend on force, such as fighting wars, punishing criminals or confiscating wealth. However, power is limited in its effects not only by opposing power but also by knowledge— or, rather, by the *limits* of knowledge available to a given power holder.

Even under the ultimate power of one human being over another— slavery— for certain kinds of work, slaves were *paid*.[12] This was not due to generosity but to necessity, and was a clear indication that there are limits to what can be accomplished by power alone, even when it includes the ultimate power of life and death.* Similarly in modern totalitarian regimes, where those in power are free to do whatever they wish to whomever they wish, this seldom translates into achieving the economic goals they seek— China's "Great Leap Forward" program under Mao being a classic economic disaster in which people starved to death by the tens of millions. Mao had the power to force vast numbers of people to do whatever he ordered, but that did not mean that this would achieve the economic results he sought.

---

* In various societies around the world, slavery included not only the power to inflict pain, but even the de facto power of life and death, since the death of a slave under severe punishment was unlikely to be prosecuted.

The crucial fact is that it is far easier to concentrate power than to concentrate knowledge. Either slaveowners or totalitarian dictators can establish output norms and inflict punishment on those who fail to meet them. But norms that some people are capable of meeting and others are not— with power holders lacking the knowledge of who specifically are in each category— mean that simply punishing or even killing those who fail to meet the norms can be futile or even counterproductive, when the punishment impairs or destroys those incapable of meeting the norms. On the other hand, establishing output norms that virtually everyone can meet means forfeiting the additional output that more skilled, more capable or more insightful individuals could produce under other incentives, but which they are less likely to produce when there is no reward for doing so.

For crude tasks, such as picking cotton in the American antebellum South or harvesting sugar cane in Caribbean slave societies, setting norms with allowances for age and sex differences, can be an economically viable system, even if not as efficient as some other arrangements. But for more challenging tasks requiring judgment, initiative or insight, some kind of reward has often been necessary, even under slavery or totalitarianism, in order to get individuals to reveal their own possession of such capabilities, which a power holder seldom has the knowledge to assess otherwise. Thus slaves exercising the judgment required for processing tobacco in the antebellum South were paid, and were treated better, than slaves picking cotton.[13] Where extraordinary abilities were required, extraordinary arrangements could be made.* Some urban slaves, whether in the antebellum South or in ancient Greece and the Roman Empire, worked as employees paid by employers other than their owners, with the latter simply collecting a share of their earnings.[14]

In the Ottoman Empire, galley slaves rowing ships were among the worst treated of all slaves anywhere, but other slaves in the Ottoman Empire were assigned roles requiring complex skills and sophisticated

---

* See, for example, "Simon Gray, Riverman: A Slave Who Was Almost Free," *Mississippi Valley Historical Review*, Vol. 49, No. 3 (December 1962), pp. 472–484.

intelligence— up to and including exercising governmental responsibilities. These latter slaves could acquire both wealth and power.[15] Similar differences in the treatment of slaves existed in the days of the Roman Empire or in ancient Greece, among other places, based on whether the tasks assigned to them were easily monitored by those with the power of punishment or instead involved a level of intelligence, judgment and initiative not readily detected without recourse to rewards, in order to elicit voluntary revelations and use of special individual capabilities.

Modern totalitarian dictatorships have likewise encountered limits on what could be accomplished economically, even by unlimited power, exercised by people whose knowledge was inherently limited. Central planning authorities in the Soviet Union could assign production quotas to individual factories, but only the manager in charge of each factory's equipment and personnel, and aware of its surrounding conditions, knew what each factory was or was not capable of producing. This fundamental problem— the separation of knowledge and power— was especially acute when the issue was not simply the efficiency of given equipment and given resources under given technological conditions at a given time, but the development of *new* methods to promote economic progress. Soviet premier Leonid Brezhnev complained that Soviet enterprise managers shied away from innovation "as the devil shies away from incense."[16]

There was no way for power holders under that government-controlled economic system to know who among the enterprise managers had the potential to become the equivalent of an economic innovator who could transform a whole industry, as John D. Rockefeller, Henry Ford or Bill Gates did in a very different kind of economy, where market results— rather than government decisions— determined who would prosper and who would not.

Whatever the form of government— whether monarchy, democracy, dictatorship or whatever— it is far easier to concentrate power than to concentrate knowledge. This has both economic and political implications. As John Stuart Mill said in the nineteenth century, "even if a government were superior in intelligence and knowledge to any single individual in the nation, it must be inferior to all the individuals of the nation taken together."[17] Obvious as this might seem, its implications are far from obvious. For example, the transfer of economic decision-making from individuals in the general population to government officials, armed with expertise— their own or that of their consultants or subordinates— has often been seen as transferring those decisions to where there is more ample knowledge, when in fact this can be a transfer from where there is more knowledge scattered among the many to where there is less knowledge concentrated in a few.

The history of government economic central planning in the twentieth century, whether in democratic or undemocratic countries, is a case in point. In the early twentieth century, many people in various countries took it as more or less axiomatic that the efficiency of an economy could be much improved if more economic decisions would be transferred to governmental institutions, unbiased by individual profit motives and dedicated to the good of the general public, rather than special interests. Thus, in the United States, President Woodrow Wilson described the Federal Reserve System created during his administration as a government financial institution which "provides a currency which expands as it is needed and contracts when it is not needed" and that "the power to direct this system of credits is put into the hands of a public board of disinterested officers of the Government itself"[18] to avoid control by bankers or other special interests.

Such a view of a selective role of government in the economy was called Progressivism in early twentieth century America. In other countries, a vision of a more pervasive economic role of government was held by socialists or communists.* What socialists and communists had in common was a belief in government central

---

* Although some Scandinavian welfare states have been called "socialist," they might more accurately be called redistributionist states, using high tax rates to transfer large amounts of wealth in money and in kind, rather than states concentrating on government officials directly operating industrial, commercial and financial enterprises.

planning of the economic system as a whole, based on government ownership and control of the principal means of production in industry, agriculture, commerce and finance. Where they differed was in whether the government officials who were to wield this power should be elected by the general public, as advocated by democratic socialists, or chosen by some autocratic process, including dictatorship, as advocated by the communists.*

Although both socialist and communist governments began by replacing market economies with centrally planned economies in the twentieth century, by the end of that century most democratic socialist governments and most communist dictatorships had abandoned central planning after experiencing its results. Then, as many economic decisions were transferred from government officials to private individuals and organizations operating in markets, the rate of growth of output usually increased— dramatically in India and China. In both of these countries, this lifted millions of people out of dire poverty, as had happened in various other countries before. Despite the Marxian premise that the poor are poor because they are exploited by the rich, none of the Marxian dictatorships around the world with comprehensive central planning ever achieved as high a standard of living as was common in various market economies in Western Europe, North America or in such Asian nations as Japan and South Korea.

Despite the indispensability of government for some economic activities and its value for some other economic functions, the limitations of its ability to carry out some more sweeping economic activities under comprehensive central planning are not simply the limitations of particular individuals who wield power, but include inherent limitations on what power itself can accomplish. Further limitations can result from the nature of the incentives inherent in political institutions and processes.

---

* Other central planners included fascists, who allowed private ownership of the means of production, but with these owners subject to government dictates. In Germany, a special xenophobic form of fascism was called National Socialism, more commonly known by a contraction of this party's name in German as Nazis.

Political Incentives

Although the scope of what political institutions can accomplish has inherent limitations, what they actually do depends also on what those who direct these institutions *want* to do. That in turn depends on what kinds of incentives the institutional leaders face.

For institutions, as for individuals, self-preservation is usually a top priority. Understandable as this may be, its implications can affect the direction and consequences of government actions. For example, a government agency may be set up to perform some function that is widely agreed to be desirable, such as removing harmful substances from the water or air. The problem is that government is essentially a categorical institution operating in an incremental world.

When a government agency's mandate is to prevent harmful substances from polluting the water or air, that mandate is categorical, but the harmfulness of substances is incremental. For example, a certain amount of a polluting substance in the water or air may be very dangerous, a somewhat lower amount may still be harmful but, eventually, at extremely minute traces, that same substance may become not only harmless but even beneficial. "It is the dose that makes the poison" is the way an old saying expressed this incremental variation in the harmfulness of substances.

In these circumstances, financial considerations would inhibit private individuals or private organizations from attempting to remove the last extremely minute traces of a pollutant from their own drinking water, if they received that water from a lake that they owned or if they were attaching some device to their faucets to further purify their tap water. But a government agency making the same decision faces very different incentives and constraints.

The financial constraints may be less keenly felt by government officials when it is the taxpayers' money, rather than their own, that is being spent. Moreover, the *political* costs of leaving any detectable amount of a pollutant in the drinking water can be prohibitive. In a democratic country, political opponents of whatever administration is in office can accuse the agency of being reckless or calloused about the public's health and safety. The net result may be the expenditure of far more resources than necessary to protect the public's health and safety, when the real imperative is to minimize political dangers to the agency itself.

Similar incentives apply when an agency's mandate is to regulate human activities, rather than inanimate things such as pollutants in the water or air. A government agency set up to counter employment discrimination, for example, might begin by forbidding and taking legal action against employers who refuse to hire qualified individuals from particular racial or ethnic groups. Thus such once-common employment announcements as "No Irish Need Apply" can easily be banished, though this particular discrimination had in fact eroded away in the United States before there were anti-discrimination laws and agencies to deal with similar discrimination against other racial or ethnic groups. But, as the incidence of such discrimination declines over time, the agency is unlikely to reduce its requests for appropriations, personnel or power.

On the contrary, the definition of "discrimination" is likely to expand over time, ensuring not only the survival but the growth of the anti-discrimination agency. Thus employers who hire and promote employees solely on the basis of these employees' individual qualifications or performances— irrespective of whatever group they come from— may nevertheless find themselves accused of discrimination by the agency, if qualifications or performances differ among the groups themselves, so that objective standards have a "disparate impact" on the employment or promotion of individuals from different groups. If job applicants with a history of crime and imprisonment are considered unsuitable for some kinds of jobs, the government agency may deem the employer to be engaged in racial or ethnic discrimination if the crime rate differs among groups.

Since differences among groups in their skills and cultures have long been common around the world, there are almost inexhaustible disparities in their respective outcomes, any one of which can be deemed to be discrimination, ensuring the perpetuation of the agency.

Where government agencies administer group preferences—
"affirmative action" in American terms*— these preferences have
often been justified as temporary policies, designed to ease the
transition of lagging groups to a world where they have caught up and
such preferences will no longer be needed.[19] But, even in countries
where time limits were announced at the outset— as in Pakistan,
India and Malaysia— such programs have persisted for generations
beyond the supposed cut-off date.[20] Government agencies with a
categorical mission seldom declare their mission accomplished and
their continued existence unnecessary.

In short, when a governmental institution is given a categorical
mandate— whether to deal with pollutants, discrimination, crime,
homelessness or other problems— the incentives are not the same as
when private individuals or private organizations face an incremental
problem requiring an expenditure of their own money, as
distinguished from spending the taxpayers' money. Private individuals
and organizations have financial incentives to act incrementally,
pursuing a given activity so long as the incremental benefits exceed
the incremental costs— but not beyond that point. A government
agency, however, has incentives to pursue activities so long as those
activities produce any benefit, or even the appearance of a benefit,
since appearances matter in politics. The fact that government is
essentially a categorical institution, and political issues tend to be
discussed in categorical terms, facilitates such mismatches of
incremental benefits and incremental costs.

In a democratic country, the voting public's perceptions can trump
economic realities at election time, even if reality ultimately asserts
itself later. Voters are free to believe whatever they prefer to believe,
and political leaders have every incentive to tell the voters what they
want to hear. Economic competition in the marketplace can

---

* Similar group preferences in other countries have been called "positive
discrimination" in Britain and India, "standardization" in Sri Lanka, "sons of the
soil" preferences in Malaysia and Indonesia and "reflecting the federal character of
the country" in Nigeria.

financially punish beliefs that differ from reality, but competition for votes at election time can politically punish reality that differs from popular beliefs.

If the incremental costs of a given government program exceed its incremental benefits, or even if the net effect of the program is detrimental, that does not matter politically if the public perceives the program as beneficial. There are many incentives for false perceptions to be promoted, whether by those who run government agencies administering a particular program or by private interests who benefit from a program or policy at the expense of the public at large. When benefits are concentrated in a narrow segment of the population, while costs are diffused over the population at large, the average member of the narrow constituency can have far more incentives to promote the program or policy than the average member of the general public has to invest the time and effort required to uncover the reality behind the politically generated appearances.

Whatever damage may be done to a society's ability to create wealth by such problems inherent in political decision-making may be equaled or exceeded by the damage done by political decision-making in a culturally diverse society that leads to polarization among the peoples who constitute that society.

THE POLITICS OF POLARIZATION

Disparities in income and wealth, whether within nations or between nations, can arise from many causes. However, the presumed causes that are politically popular have tended to be those which involve the less fortunate being victims of the more fortunate. General or impersonal influences, such as geography, demography and culture have had no such political attraction as explanations, despite whatever causal weight they may have in fact.

The Politics of Resentment

It might seem as if every society, whether rich or poor, can always use greater productivity, wherever it is available. But it only *seems* that way. Politically, there is a major problem, especially in a poor country, when some racially or socially distinct group has markedly higher levels of skills or economic experience than that in the rest of the population.

From an economic perspective, this situation presents a valuable opportunity for the more productive portion of the population to supply much needed human capital to enable the economy as a whole to become more productive, creating benefits for the population at large. Moreover, the presence of people with such human capital also presents an opportunity for individuals in the rest of a society to acquire some of this human capital themselves, whether by example, by working with or observing the more productive group, or by studying to acquire such skills in educational institutions. Knowledge is one of the few things that can spread to others without those from whom it originated having any less remaining for themselves.

From a *political* perspective, however, the situation is entirely different. As noted in Chapter 6, when more productive groups freely compete in a market economy, this leads to visible disparities in economic outcomes that are resented by the less successful groups. Political leaders in many lagging countries have been keenly aware of this prospect.

A political leader of the Malays in Malaysia, for example, said candidly, "Whatever the Malays could do, the Chinese could do better and more cheaply."[21] This provided a political rationale for imposing preferential policies for the benefit of the Malays, which is to say, discrimination against the Chinese in Malaysia. This same political leader observed:

> These few Malays, for they are still only very few, have waxed rich not because of themselves but because of the policy of a Government supported by a huge majority of poor Malays. It would seem that the efforts of the poor Malays have gone to enrich a select few of their own people. The poor Malays themselves have not gained one iota. But if these few Malays are not enriched the poor Malays will not gain either.

> It is the Chinese who will continue to live in huge houses and regard the
> Malays as only fit to drive their cars. With the existence of the few rich
> Malays at least the poor Malays can say that their fate is not entirely to
> serve the rich non-Malays. From the point of view of racial ego, and this
> ego is still strong, the unseemly existence of Malay tycoons is essential.[22]

What is involved in such reactions is not simply poverty or envy, but *resentment*. If the issue was envy, then it would be hard to explain the pride that Malays have had in their own wealthy Malay sultans and Malay royalty.[23] Sultans are in a much more enviable position than most Chinese in Malaysia. The sultans are likely to be wealthier, and their wealth has come by inheritance, rather than by personal achievement. But personal achievement is much more of a threat to the egos of others than inheritance is, not only in Malaysia but elsewhere.

In the United States, for example, three heirs to the Rockefeller fortune have been elected governors of three different states, and two Roosevelts with inherited wealth have been elected President of the United States. It is the Asian immigrants of a later time, many of whom have been refugees, who in many cases arrived on American shores with little money and a few words of broken English, but who have worked their way up from the bottom to a modest prosperity, and whose children excel in school and then head off to prestigious colleges and universities, who are threats to the egos of lagging groups in America who have made nothing like the same use of their own opportunities.

Korean immigrants to the United States, for example, worked an average of 63 hours per week as storekeepers in Atlanta, with one-fifth of them working 80 hours or more.[24] In New York, Korean greengrocers have gone out to pick up their fruits and vegetables from wholesalers at 4:00 AM, enabling them to select the best of these fruits and vegetables and to save on delivery charges that other greengrocers had to pay.[25]

The children of such Asian families have shown a similar work ethic in school— and have provoked the same resentments by their superior academic achievements as adult high achievers have provoked in members of lagging groups in countries around the world. Children of Asian families have for years been beaten up by black classmates in the public schools of New York and Philadelphia[26]— with little or nothing being done by the authorities to stop it, and no editorial indignation about it from people in the media who are quick to cry "racism" at any passing remark that can be construed as critical of any of the groups currently in favor among the intelligentsia.

Like the Asian immigrants to America today, Jewish, Lebanese and Japanese immigrants have at various times in the past arrived in various countries around the world with little money, but much human capital, and prospered as a result— provoking resentments among those who were there before them, and who made no similar use of their own opportunities. There have also been examples of the same social phenomenon among groups who migrated within their own country and rose to prosperity, and who were likewise resented. The Marwaris and Bengalis in various parts of India, Armenians in the Ottoman Empire, as well as Ibos in Nigeria and Tamils in Sri Lanka are among other examples of the same social phenomenon.[27]

In many countries, the political priority of protecting majority group egos has trumped the economic or other benefits of making use of the best skills and talents available in the economy. After Nigeria became independent in 1960, a high political priority among the Hausa-Fulani peoples in northern Nigeria was to get rid of the Ibos from southern Nigeria, who had dominated professions and skilled occupations in northern Nigeria under British rule. Ibos were driven out of northern Nigeria, often to the accompaniment of lethal mob violence, even when there were not enough qualified northern Nigerians to replace the Ibos, and European expatriates had to be hired to take their place instead.[28]

In the same vein, when Romania acquired territory from the defeated Central Powers after the First World War, this territory included universities that were culturally German or culturally Hungarian. The Romanian government made it a political priority to force Germans and Hungarians out of these universities, even though most Romanians were still illiterate at that point, and so could not replace the Germans or Hungarians.[29] The expulsion of Asians from Uganda in the 1970s led to the collapse of the Ugandan economy, because there were not nearly enough qualified Ugandans to replace them in the business sector that people from the Indian subcontinent had dominated for generations.[30]

These were not isolated examples. Distinguished development economist P.T. Bauer of the London School of Economics, who studied Third World countries for years, reported a general pattern in those countries of "persecution of the most productive groups, especially minorities, and sometimes their expulsion."[31]

However much productive minority groups might benefit a national economy in a poor country, their marked success threatens the egos of the lagging majority, provoking often bitter resentments. In Bolivia, a terrorist of indigenous descent, when asked why he was engaging in terrorist activity, replied: "So that my daughter will not have to be your maid."[32] When the new nation of Czechoslovakia was created out of the dissolution of the Habsburg Empire after the First World War, one of the new Czech leaders' first political priorities was preferential treatment of Czechs which meant discrimination against Germans, setting in motion a series of major tragedies for both Czechs and Germans over the next three decades.[33]

If poverty or envy were the fundamental problem, then a more productive economy and a spreading of productive skills to those without them might seem to be the answer. But neither of these things can cure resentments at being in a galling inferior position. Nor can a transfer of economic benefits to those who are resentful, for such transfers are tangible reminders of their inferior position, and what cannot be transferred are the achievements which created the economic output in the first place.

For those seething with resentments, it is not sufficient to have a rising standard of living. From the standpoint of resenters, the priority is that those in a superior position must be brought down. In some cases, even the killing of the more fortunate is often not considered sufficient. They must be made to suffer both physical agonies and personal humiliations to bring them down to the level of those who attack them— and below. That has been a common pattern, whether the targets of violent actions have been the Chinese in the Philippines, Armenians in the Ottoman Empire, Jews in Nazi Germany or Tutsis in Rwanda, among others.

The Chinese in the Philippines are among the many productive groups whose economic success has led to violent backlashes. As an international study noted:

> In the Philippines, millions of Filipinos work for Chinese; almost no Chinese work for Filipinos. The Chinese dominate industry and commerce at every level of society. Global markets intensify this dominance: When foreign investors do business in the Philippines, they deal almost exclusively with Chinese. Apart from a handful of corrupt politicians and a few aristocratic Spanish mestizo families, all of the Philippines' billionaires are of Chinese descent. By contrast, all menial jobs in the Philippines are filled by Filipinos. All peasants are Filipinos. All domestic servants and squatters are Filipinos.[34]

The same study also noted: "Hundreds of Chinese in the Philippines are kidnapped every year, almost invariably by ethnic Filipinos. Many victims, often children, are brutally murdered, even after ransom is paid."[35]

A study of the Ottoman Empire described the mass slaughters of the Armenians by Turkish mobs in 1894, including "bayoneting the men to death, raping the women, dashing their children against the rocks."[36] In 1915 there was a death march imposed on Armenians, in which thousands perished, many of the women were stripped naked and forced to walk into the city that way.[37] This was a foretaste of the calculatingly sadistic humiliations heaped upon the Jews in Nazi concentration camps a generation later.

It was much the same pattern in Rwanda in the late twentieth century, when the Hutus slaughtered hundreds of thousands of Tutsis. Young children were often killed in front of their parents, by cutting off one arm, then the other. A United Nations official reported: "They would then gash the neck with a machete to bleed the child slowly to death but, while they were still alive, they would cut off the private parts and throw them at the faces of the terrified parents, who would then be murdered with slightly greater dispatch."[38]

Such atrocities reflect vengeful resentments that cannot be assuaged by a higher Gross Domestic Product per capita. The feelings behind ghastly acts of revenge are not simply envy, but resentments— lashing out at those whose success has inflicted a galling position of inferiority, and wounded feelings of inferiority, on those who resent.

Yet it is also a puzzling and disturbing fact that some groups who inflicted horrific atrocities on others had previously co-existed peacefully for years, or even generations, with those who eventually became targets of their rage. *The Times of India*, for example, referred to "neighbours leading long-time friends to gory deaths" during intergroup outbreaks of violence in Mumbai (Bombay) in 1992–1993.[39] In the Balkans as well, "outbursts of hatred and great violence occurred between people who had also known times of harmony or at least passive acceptance of each other."[40]

Such disturbing patterns not only raise sobering questions about how secure any apparent *detente* between racial or ethnic groups is in fact. These patterns also suggest that some catalyst may be needed to arouse the feelings behind the horrors— and of course no one can know in advance when any such catalyst may arise, even in the most tranquil settings, whether that catalyst appears in the form of a particular episode or a particular skilled and talented demagogue.

Sri Lanka, for example, was in the middle of the twentieth century rightly held up to the world as a model for good relations between a majority and a minority. Its main ethnic groups were seen by observers, both inside and outside the country, as having good— even "cordial"— relations with one another.[41] There had been no riot between the Sinhalese majority and the Tamil minority during the previous half-century. The educated and Westernized elites of both groups lived peacefully in the same Westernized residential enclaves.

Nevertheless, within a decade after Sri Lanka emerged from British rule as an independent nation in 1948, an ambitious politician named Solomon Bandaranaike, seeking the prime ministership by turning the Sinhalese majority against the more prosperous Tamil minority, set in motion group polarizations that escalated into mob violence, and then a civil war that lasted a quarter of a century, with unspeakable atrocities on both sides. Bandaranaike was the catalyst. Like many others who played that deadly role in other countries, Bandaranaike was by no means one of the embittered poor himself. He was from an elite background and was skilled in whipping up other people's emotions for his own political purposes.*

Much discussion of policies toward Third World countries proceeds as if the fundamental problem in such countries is poverty and a lack of the skills and knowledge required to raise their standard of living. Supplying money, physical equipment and technocrats with skills might seem to be the answer, as policies to help Third World countries advance. But many, if not most, poor countries already have within their own borders people with the human capital to advance the nation's economy. Yet there are formidable political obstacles to using that human capital, and many political incentives to avoid letting minorities with skills lacking in the majority population have free rein to put their skills to work, with resulting disparities in performances and rewards.

Political Leaders

In the most varied conditions in countries around the world— whether in Third World countries or in economically more advanced countries, and whether in countries where the majority or the

---

* Once his purposes were served— that is, he became prime minister— Bandaranaike was willing to back off the extremism he had aroused. But the emotions he had whipped up could not be turned off, and acquired a life of their own. When Bandaranaike moderated his stance toward the Tamils after getting elected, he was assassinated by a Buddhist extremist and the polarization process continued to escalate into a devastating civil war.

minority has the higher skills— those seeking either the leadership or the votes of lagging groups tend to offer them four things:

1. Assurance that their lags are not their fault.
2. Assurance that their lags are the fault of some more fortunate group that they already envy and resent.
3. Assurance that the lagging group and their culture are just as good as anybody else's, if not better.
4. Assurance that what the lagging group needs and deserves is a demographically defined "fair share" of the economic and other benefits of society, sometimes supplemented with some kind of reparations for past injustices or some special reward for being indigenous "sons of the soil."

In addition, racial or ethnic leaders have every incentive to promote the isolation of the groups they lead— despite the fact that isolation has been a major factor in the poverty and backwardness of many different peoples around the world.

Where a lagging group is concentrated in a particular region of a country, leaders of such groups have incentives to promote secession from the more advanced part of the country, as Slovaks seceded from Czechoslovakia and as East Pakistanis seceded from Pakistan to create the new nation of Bangladesh. Despite the economic losses that poorer groups may sustain when they are no longer part of a more advanced economy, their political leaders gain from acquiring more power as leaders of a nation, and have every incentive to promote national pride in independent nationhood, whether or not that has made the people they lead better off or worse off economically. The people themselves may also benefit psychically by being spared the public embarrassment and private shame of being visibly outperformed repeatedly by others in the same economy and society.

Where the political situation makes secession unlikely to happen, leaders of lagging groups have every incentive to promote cultural isolation, such as laws or policies in parts of the United States requiring the teaching of Hispanic children in the Spanish language, even when their parents want them taught in English, so as to facilitate their rise in the American economy and society.[42]

Perhaps the most culturally isolated of all American ethnic groups are those descendants of the indigenous American Indian population who still live on reservations with great legal autonomy, but with lower per capita incomes than blacks, Hispanics or other American Indians who are not living on reservations. Since the 1980s, American Indians living off reservations— who are a substantial majority of all American Indians— have had per capita incomes slightly higher than those of Hispanic Americans, while American Indians living on reservations have had substantially lower per capita incomes than black or Hispanic Americans and less than half that of the American population as a whole.[43] Yet leaders of American Indian reservations jealously guard their prerogatives and promote the perpetuation of separate cultures among the populations of those reservations.

Racial or ethnic leaders also have incentives to blame advanced groups for the lags of lagging groups. The behavior of advanced groups toward lagging groups has by no means always been exemplary, nor necessarily even decent, so the leaders of lagging groups may have many things to complain about— without those things being the reasons for the economic, educational or other gaps between the advanced groups and the lagging groups.

In particular circumstances, some advanced group may in fact be the cause of holding back some lagging group. But that cannot be assumed *a priori* from the fact that one group is demonstrably more successful economically or in other ways. Even where the advanced group has behaved badly toward the lagging group, as has often happened in many countries around the world, that is still not proof that the lagging group would have been better off economically in the absence of the advanced group.

The ancient Romans certainly behaved abominably toward the ancient Britons whom they conquered. But that is not to say that the Romans were the reason that the Britons lagged. It was only the fact that the Britons lagged *before* the Romans arrived and conquered them that permitted a numerically smaller Roman military force to overwhelm a numerically larger British force, both during the conquest and later, when there was a mass uprising of the British, provoked by the Romans' oppression. In putting down that uprising, the Romans slaughtered Britons by the thousands, and the queen who had led the uprising committed suicide to avoid the retribution she knew she could expect from the Romans. Yet, in modern times, even such a British patriot as Winston Churchill could say, "We owe London to Rome"[44] because the ancient Britons were not yet capable of creating such a city themselves.

No one believes that slaves were always treated well, in the many times and places around the world where there were slaves. There is too much documented evidence that they were not. But the fact that black Americans today have a far higher standard of living than the peoples of sub-Saharan Africa from whom they are descended is not a happenstance. Nor can this outcome retroactively justify slavery, any more than the valuable advantages that Western Europeans' descendants received as a cultural legacy from Roman conquests retroactively justify the Romans' brutal oppression of their ancestors.

Neither can individuals or groups lagging today automatically blame their lags on the injustices inflicted on their ancestors, when the cultural benefits available to them in later times were an unintended by-product of those injustices. *Moral* condemnation is not *causal* explanation, despite how often the two have been combined in a politically attractive package. Despite the tendency of political, and especially ideological, explanations of economic disparities to combine moral and causal factors, the reason so many mountain peoples around the world have been poor has not been that others went up into those mountains and took away their wealth, but that the mountain peoples seldom produced much wealth in the first place. The Spaniards seizing the wealth of the Incas was an exception on a horrific scale, but empirically it was not the rule.

The one thing that can be said unequivocally about the past is that it is irrevocable. When both history and the contemporary world scene show what a challenge it can be to create or maintain decent relations among contemporaries, it is staggering that some people imagine that they can take on the far larger task of righting the wrongs of the past, committed by people long dead, without igniting dangerous new hostilities among the living.

Ethnic or political leaders are not the sole source of polarization in ethnically diverse societies. The political process itself can encourage polarization. Politics is not simply a process that reflects existing attitudes and beliefs among voters. Among some lagging groups especially, causation can go in the opposite direction— that is, politics can shape attitudes and beliefs. The political process can attract and absorb energies that could otherwise go into alternative efforts to advance individuals and groups, such as education, entrepreneurship or the acquisition of job skills.

For lagging groups with a short time horizon, political activities such as rallies, marches and demonstrations offer instant gratification through emotional expression and solidarity with like-minded people, as well as posing issues in terms of a righteous crusade against presumed enemies responsible for the lags of one's group. By contrast, putting time and energies into the acquisition of education and/or work skills, and developing self-discipline, can mean a far longer and more lonely process of unromantic drudgery, with no such immediate gratification as solidarity with others voicing opposition to presumed enemies. Moreover, this alternative to political activity can produce a painful sense of one's own current inadequacies, even if due to circumstances beyond one's control.

Chapter 12

THE WELFARE STATE

*They went to work with unsurpassable efficiency. Full
employment, a maximum of resulting output, and general
well-being ought to have been the consequence. It is true
that instead we find misery, shame and, at the end of it
all, a stream of blood. But that was a chance coincidence.*

Joseph A. Schumpeter

The welfare state is often seen in terms of its effects on the
material well-being of individuals or groups. However, it can also
have an effect on the productivity of a nation as a whole, and therefore
on the standard of living of its people in general. Moreover, the
welfare state's effects extend beyond economics to social behavior with
major impacts on both the recipients of welfare benefits and those
who interact with them. These effects are not due solely to the welfare
state, as such, but often also to the social vision which accompanies
the welfare state, makes it politically possible, and changes the way
many people see the world and their role in it.

THE WELFARE STATE VISION

In a democratic country, a welfare state can be created only after a
welfare state vision is created and prevails politically. Therefore, in
assessing the effects of a welfare state, we must include the effects of
that essential vision, as well as the effects of the particular institutions
and policies created. Among the assumptions behind the welfare state

273

vision, two seem crucial: (1) many people are mired in a degree of poverty that a prosperous society can and should relieve, and (2) many, if not most, of the people in poverty never had the same chance of a better life as others who ended up more prosperous.

The fundamental premise of the welfare state vision, that all individuals in a society should be guaranteed at least some basic necessities of life, is so widely accepted today— among some staunch conservatives, as well as among people on the left— that it may be surprising to some that no such assumption was prevalent a hundred years ago, even among people on the political left. If there was one thing on which socialists and religious conservatives were agreed then, it was the principle that "he who does not work, neither shall he eat." Both would offer charity to those unable to work, but there was to be no general guarantee of basic necessities for those who simply chose not to work. William Jennings Bryan, a populist on the left who was three times the Democrats' candidate for President of the United States, stated plainly in his famous "cross of gold" speech in 1896:

> We cannot insure to the vicious the fruits of a virtuous life; we would not invade the home of the provident in order to supply the wants of the spendthrift; we do not propose to transfer the rewards of industry to the lap of indolence. Property is and will remain the stimulus to endeavor and the compensation for toil. We believe, as asserted in the Declaration of Independence, that all men are created equal, but that does not mean that all men are or can be equal in possessions, in ability or in merit; it simply means that all shall stand equal before the law.[1]

By contrast, today even a conservative or libertarian author, writing a book criticizing the welfare state, nevertheless took it as almost axiomatic that safety nets "to provide a floor of help for the needy and to alleviate human suffering are easily justifiable on moral grounds."[2] Nor did he find it necessary to specify just what those moral grounds were. They had, apparently, become over the years just one of those things that presumably "everybody knows."*

In an earlier era, even those socialists who wanted income redistribution found it necessary to spell out some moral justification, one of which appeared in the influential nineteenth century social novel *Looking Backward* by Edward Bellamy, who saw the poor as people denied their fair share of the prosperity that others enjoyed, largely as a windfall gain from the economic advances inherited from the past. A key character in the novel asks why contemporary producers are able to create so much more output than in the past, and offers this answer:

> Was it not wholly on account of the heritage of the past knowledge and achievements of the race, the machinery of society, thousands of years in contriving, found by you ready-made to your hand? How did you come to be possessors of this knowledge and this machinery, which represent nine parts to one contributed by yourself in the value of your product? You inherited it, did you not? And were not these others, these unfortunate and crippled brothers whom you cast out, joint inheritors, co-heirs with you? What did you do with their share? Did you not rob them when you put them off with crusts, who were entitled to sit with the heirs, and did you not add insult to robbery when you called the crusts charity?[3]

What we inherit from the past, however, is not simply the physical wealth created in the past but, more important, the mental tools— the human capital— with which to replenish that physical wealth as it is used up or wears out. One of the reasons for the poor being poor is that they are not acquiring the same human capital as others— in effect, not claiming their share of the most important part of the common economic inheritance and putting it to work. For example, more than half of the American households in the bottom 20 percent of income recipients have *no one* working, and also have lower educational levels.[4] In an age of widespread access to education, at

---

* The key assumption of an inherent "right" to what others have produced— with no reciprocal obligation, even to observe common decency— breaks the connection between production and consumption in some people's minds, even when that connection remains as unbreakable as ever in the real world.

least in the more prosperous countries, external barriers cannot automatically be assumed to be the reason for low incomes, nor internal cultural patterns automatically ruled out.

It is a question that needs to be examined empirically, despite how widespread is the practice of assuming *a priori* that barriers must be responsible. If the obstacles to be overcome are internal, rather than external, then simply having low-income people sharing in the material output produced by others— who *did* claim their inheritance of human capital and applied it— can reduce the incentives for those who did not do so to change, and to do likewise. Despite what is often said, you cannot "give" anyone an education. The most you can do is make an education available for them to work at acquiring.

Even in a society with rules that are fair, in the sense of judging everyone by the same standards and rewarding or punishing them according to the same criteria, it would still be true that someone born in a rundown South Bronx neighborhood would have nothing like the same probability of achieving economic success— however defined— as someone born in an affluent or wealthy Park Avenue neighborhood. To be fair in the sense of providing equal probabilities of success for people born in unequal social circumstances would be very different. In that sense, life has been unfair in virtually every society of the past or the present. But whether redistributing income will produce greater development of human capital among the poor or will produce even less development of their human capital is an empirical question— and one seldom raised by those promoting the welfare state vision.

The case for that vision has been made in unmistakably clear and contemporary terms by Nicholas Kristof of the *New York Times*:

> One delusion common among America's successful people is that they triumphed just because of hard work and intelligence.
>
> In fact, their big break came when they were conceived in middle-class American families who loved them, read them stories, and nurtured them with Little League sports, library cards and music lessons. They were programmed for success by the time they were zygotes.[5]

The social conditions into which individuals are born and raised are of course not equal, just as the geographic, demographic and cultural conditions in which individuals, groups and nations find themselves are not equal in their economic prospects. This has been true throughout recorded history. No doubt many of us wish that things were different, and some want to "do something" about it. But everything depends on just what specifically is the "something" that is done. The welfare state is just one option among many.

Mr. Kristof's response to the unfairness of life is to criticize those who "are oblivious of their own advantages, and of other people's disadvantages." He accuses them of "a mean-spiritedness in the political world or, at best, a lack of empathy toward those struggling— partly explaining the hostility to state expansion of Medicaid, to long-term unemployment benefits, or to raising the minimum wage to keep up with inflation."[6] In short, Kristof's response to the unfairness of life is a government transfer of resources from those who are more prosperous to those who are less prosperous— with no caveats about the further consequences of such welfare state policies or the accompanying vision, and no apparent apprehension about whether those consequences will make either the less prosperous, or society at large, better off or worse off on net balance.[*]

To blithely assume that the only reason to be against minimum wage laws is a lack of empathy with the poor is to ignore a vast literature on the negative repercussions of minimum wage laws. These repercussions include increased numbers of unemployed young males idle on the streets, which is seldom a benefit to any community. With minimum wage laws, as with other laws and policies, what matters ultimately are not the intentions, hopes or expectations, but empirical evidence as to what actually happens. It is remarkable how seldom that test is applied to minimum wage laws.

---

[*] A century earlier, economist Alfred Marshall warned against "the harm to strength of character and to family life that comes from ill-considered aid to the thriftless"— a warning that proved to be prophetic. Alfred Marshall, *Principles of Economics*, fifth edition, Vol. I (London: Macmillan and Co., Ltd., 1907), p. 44.

Ten years after passage of the federal minimum wage law in the United States— the Fair Labor Standards Act of 1938— the wartime inflation during the intervening decade had so raised prices and wages that the minimum wage specified in that law was below what inexperienced and unskilled workers were already being paid, so that by 1948 it was in most places the same as if there were no minimum wage law. This allows us to see what unemployment was like for inexperienced youths at a time of a virtual absence of a minimum wage law, and then later in its presence, as the minimum wage rate was successively raised over the years to catch up, and then keep up, with inflation.

The unemployment rate among black 16- and 17-year-old males in 1948 was just under 10 percent. The last year in which it was under 10 percent was 1953. But, in later years, as the minimum wage rate was repeatedly raised to keep up with inflation, unemployment among blacks in this age group never again fell below *20 percent*. From 1971 through 1994, the unemployment rate among black 16- and 17-year-old males never fell below *30* percent, and exceeded 40 percent in nine of those years, while 50 percent was exceeded twice. From 1995 on, the 16-17-year-old male category was consolidated into a new 16-19-year-old male category. Unemployment for this new category ranged from a low of 23.8 percent to a high of 52.2 percent from 1995 through 2009.[7]

Despite complications in trying to determine empirically the effects of minimum wage laws on the unemployment rates of black teenage males,* when their unemployment rates under minimum wage rates that keep going up, along with inflation, have for more

---

* One of these complications is that surveying employers before and after a minimum wage increase has the fatal weakness of survey research in general— namely, that you can only survey survivors. Reduced employment of low-skilled workers in the wake of a minimum wage increase can take many forms. If all the businesses employing low-skilled workers were identical, then unemployment resulting from a minimum wage increase might be expected to be found in all the firms surveyed. But a more common circumstance is one in which some firms in an industry are quite profitable, others are less profitable and still others are struggling to stay in business. In these circumstances, an increase in the minimum wage can increase the number of struggling firms that go out of business and reduce the number of new firms that enter the industry to replace them, now that there are higher labor costs. A smaller number of surviving firms may each have no reduction

than half a century been some *multiple* of what their unemployment rate was when inflation rendered the official minimum wage rate ineffective, the results are too blatant to be ignored or evaded.

Empirical evidence has likewise seldom been mentioned by those who make a common claim, advanced by Kristof among many others, that "Slavery and post-slavery oppression left a legacy of broken families" among blacks.[8] But the plain fact is that the proportion of black children living with only one parent was never as great during the first hundred years after slavery as it became in the first thirty-five years after the great expansion of the welfare state, beginning in the 1960s. Yet the "legacy of slavery" argument continues to be blithely repeated, and the legacy of the welfare state ignored. As in all too many other contexts, facts have not made a dent on the prevailing vision. Indeed, the very thought that this often repeated phrase should be subjected to empirical tests seems not to have occurred to many who are content to simply continue to repeat the phrase.

The proportion of black children being raised by a single mother in 1960 was 22 percent. Thirty-five years later, that proportion had risen to 52 percent being raised by a mother alone, 4 percent being raised by a father alone and another 11 percent being raised with neither parent present— altogether, 67 percent of all black children.[9] By 1995, the proportion of black children in poverty-level families who were being raised without a father present was 85 percent.[10] While it is true that the proportion of black children being raised without a father present was higher than the proportion of white children being

---

at all in employment, despite however much reduction of employment there may be in that industry, as a result of marginal firms going out of business without being replaced by as many new firms providing an equal number of jobs.

Another complication is that people working for minimum wages are a small fraction of the people working, so that what happens to the employment of minimum wage workers can be lost in statistics about the total employment in an industry, due to all sorts of other fluctuations in the employment of a larger number of other workers. But if, instead of surveying surviving firms after a minimum wage increase, data are collected on unemployment rates among particular groups of inexperienced and low-skilled workers, such as black teenagers, a more accurate picture of the effects of minimum wages on unemployment can be obtained.

raised without a father, even before the great expansion of the welfare state in the 1960s, for neither race was that proportion anywhere near what it became after the expansion of the welfare state. During those very same post-1960s years, the proportion of *white* children living with only one parent suddenly soared to several times what it had been for decades prior to 1960.[11]

The central rationale for the welfare state is poverty. But, if the word is to have any specific meaning, someone must define it in specific terms. Once that is done, "poverty" means *no more and no less* than those specifications, despite however much the word may conjure up images from a past era when poverty meant hunger, ragged clothing, cramped housing and the like. Today, poverty in America means whatever government statisticians in Washington say it means.

Most people living below the official poverty line in the United States in 2001 had central air conditioning and a microwave oven, for example. In fact, these items were more common among the officially poor in 2001 than they were among the American population as a whole in 1980. Most poverty-level households in 2001 also had cable television and two or more television sets. As of 2003, nearly three-fourths of officially poverty-level households owned at least one motor vehicle and 14 percent owned two or more.[12] In contrast to times past when low-income people lived packed into overcrowded housing, Americans living below the official poverty level today have more housing space per person than the average European— not poor Europeans, but the average European.[13] As a scholar who spent years studying Latin America put it, "the poverty line in the United States is the upper-middle class in Mexico."[14]

This is not to say that Americans living in official poverty have no problems. They have serious and often catastrophic social problems, but these are seldom the result of material deprivation— and are far more often a result of social degeneration, much of it representing social retrogressions during the era of the rising welfare state and of the pervasive, non-judgmental social vision that led to the welfare state, among other social changes.

PROGRESS AND RETROGRESSIONS

Black Americans, a group often identified as beneficiaries of the welfare state in America, made considerable economic progress in the twentieth century but much, if not most, of it was *prior* to the massive expansion of the American welfare state, beginning with the "war on poverty" programs of the 1960s. This is just one of many possible empirical tests of the social vision behind the creation and expansion of the welfare state.

Testing the Prevailing Vision

Progress, for most blacks, can be measured from the time of the Emancipation Proclamation of 1863.* That progress was slow but steady. By 1900, a majority of black Americans were literate— something that would not be true of the population of Romania until decades later, and of the population of India until more than half a century after that. As of 1910, about one-fourth of black farmers were owners or buyers of their land, rather than renters or sharecroppers.[15] Professor Herbert Gutman's monumental treatise, *The Black Family in Slavery and Freedom, 1750-1925* showed that, during the era from 1880 to 1925, "the typical Afro-American family was lower-class in status and headed by two parents." In 1925, just 3 percent of black families in New York were headed by a woman under thirty.[16] The unwed teenage mother became common in a later generation, during the era of the expanded welfare state.

The reasons for black poverty— often very real poverty, in earlier years especially— are not hard to find. It was 1930 before the average black adult had six years of education,[17] mostly in inferior Southern

---

* About ten percent of the black population in America had been free before the Civil War, and these "free persons of color" had a head start that made their descendants so much more experienced and more educated that they remained the elite of the black population on into the middle of the twentieth century. These included historic figures such as W.E.B. Du Bois, Homer Plessy of *Plessy v. Ferguson* and Thurgood Marshall, the attorney who argued the landmark case of *Brown v. Board of Education*.

schools. In Georgia that same year, no more than half the black adult population had reached the third grade.[18] At that time, only 19 percent of black children of high school age in the South actually went to high school.[19] It was 1924 before the first permanent public high school for black children in Atlanta was built,[20] after years of campaigns for such a school by the local black community.

As of 1940, 87 percent of black families in the United States lived below the poverty line. But this declined to 47 percent by 1960, as black education and urban job experience increased in the wake of the mass migrations of blacks out of the South. This 40 percentage point drop in the black poverty rate occurred *prior* to both the civil rights laws and the "war on poverty" social welfare programs of the 1960s. Over the next 20 years, from 1960 to 1980, the black poverty rate dropped an additional 18 points[21]— significant, but the continuation of a pre-existing trend at a slower pace, rather than being a new result from new civil rights laws and welfare state policies, as so often claimed.

There were dramatic increases in the number of black elected officials in the South after passage of the Voting Rights Act of 1965. But nothing similarly dramatic occurred in black economic advancement as a result of the civil rights laws of the 1960s. In some important social ways, actual retrogressions set in.

Arguably the most consequential of these social retrogressions was the decline in two-parent families. We have also seen in Chapter 9 some declines in black educational achievements during this later era, such as a decline in the proportion of black students in New York's selective Stuyvesant High School to *one-tenth* of what that proportion had been in earlier years. In addition, there was an increase in crime and violence, including ghetto riots. The first in a series of such riots across the country erupted in Los Angeles, just days after the Voting Rights Act of 1965 was passed.

This eruption of violence was contrary to the prevailing political and social vision of the times, in which problems among blacks were automatically assumed to be due to deficiencies in the way white people treated them. But such riots were *less* common in the South,[22] where racial discrimination in laws and practices remained more common. By contrast, the worst of these riots— with 43 people killed, 33 of whom were black— occurred in Detroit, where black median family income was 95 percent of white median family income, where the black unemployment rate was 3.4 percent and where black home ownership was higher than in any other major city.[23] Yet no such facts made a dent in the prevailing social vision.

The proliferation of black politicians and of community activists provided a great increase in the number of "leaders" promoting the same kind of vision that ethnic leaders have promoted to many other lagging groups in many other countries around the world. That vision is one in which the lagging group's problems are due primarily, if not solely, to the malign actions of other groups. The answers offered to blacks in America have been in principle— despite local variations— very much like the answers offered to Czechs in nineteenth century Bohemia, Sinhalese in twentieth century Sri Lanka, Maoris in New Zealand and many others elsewhere: group solidarity in pursuit of collective political solutions and, in the meantime, resistance to the cultures of those who are more fortunate, in the name of "pride" in one's own culture.

The actual track record of that approach, as compared to other approaches used by other groups, has received virtually no attention from either black leaders or the black or white intelligentsia in either the media or academia. A list of groups that have risen from poverty to prosperity, in countries around the world— the Chinese, Lebanese, Jews, and Japanese, for example— would usually also be a list of groups that played very little role in politics during their rise, though a few of their members in later times could afford the luxury of political careers. But, even then, those political careers were seldom based on being spokesmen for their respective groups in the political arena.

Germans in Australia, Brazil and the United States were long noted for their unusually *low* interest in politics, while their interest in education and in otherwise advancing themselves economically was the focus of their attention. In the period up through the First World War, Germans in Brazil seldom even bothered to vote.[24] "Political apathy has, in fact, been frequently noted as a characteristic of German immigrants everywhere," according to a scholarly study.[25] Even when some Americans of German ancestry became prominent in politics— the Muhlenbergs in the eighteenth century, Carl Schurz and John Peter Altgeld in the nineteenth century, and Herbert Hoover and Dwight D. Eisenhower in the twentieth century— they did *not* do so as spokesmen for the German American community, but as individuals addressing issues facing the American population as a whole. Even when Germans were politically attacked as a group in nineteenth century Bohemia, their first response was to defend a cosmopolitan outlook, and only belatedly did they defend themselves specifically as Germans.[26]

It was very much the same story with the overseas Chinese, who studiously avoided political careers or political movements during their rise from poverty to affluence, whether in Southeast Asia or in the United States.[27] The immigrant generation of Jews from Eastern Europe "brought with them a skimpy political experience" and many had "the traditional Jewish persuasion that it was best to keep as far away from politics as possible."[28] The same unromantic but very effective concentration on work, education and saving lifted Japanese and Lebanese immigrants from poverty to prosperity in various countries around the world. It also lifted indigenous minorities such as the Ibos in Nigeria, Tamils in Sri Lanka and Armenians in the Ottoman Empire, among others.

Conversely, one of the most politically successful groups in America— the Irish— did not rise from poverty as fast as other groups that were neither as involved politically, nor as successful in politics, as the Irish were. Irish politicians reached influential positions in mid-nineteenth century American cities and, within a few decades, the Irish were dominant in big city political machines in Boston, New York and other cities across the country, and remained so well into the twentieth century. This brought prosperity, prominence and power to a few, but the great majority of the Irish continued to lag behind other Americans economically, and even behind some other immigrant groups.

At the beginning of the twentieth century, 39 percent of the Irish in New York City were unskilled laborers— the highest percentage for any ethnic group in New York at that time. An additional 25 percent were classified as semi-skilled.[29] In the country as a whole during the period from 1899 to 1910, more than three-quarters of all Irish workers were either laborers or servants.[30] From 1850 to 1900, the leading occupation of Irish women in America was as domestic servants.[31] As late as the 1920s, most of the Irish women who worked outside their homes were domestic servants.[32] As of 1930, the proportion of the Irish who paid more than a hundred dollars a month in rent was barely more than half the proportion among Russians— most of whom were Jews during this era— and less than half the proportion among Germans.[33] This was despite the fact that the peak of Irish immigration to America came decades before the peak of Jewish immigration, so that the Irish had had a longer time to rise in American society.

However plausible, or even inspiring, it might seem that a lagging minority needs to unite in solidarity behind political leaders representing their interests to the larger society, in order to get ahead, the historical record shows no such pattern of economic success for politics, as compared to education, job skills and intact families.

Social pathology in black ghettos is often assumed to be due to poverty, discrimination or the larger society's neglect. But the decade in which there was the greatest emphasis on government social programs to help blacks— the 1960s "war on poverty" and civil rights legislation under President Lyndon Johnson— saw the greatest number and severity of ghetto riots in history, while the 1980s Reagan administration, which opposed welfare state programs, saw very few ghetto riots.

Similarly, despite the ease with which many people use the "legacy of slavery" argument to explain negative features of black communities today, there is seldom any attempt to examine the facts as to whether whatever is complained of— whether fatherless families, high crime rates or other social pathology— was in fact worse among blacks in the first hundred years after slavery or in the first generation after the triumph of the welfare state vision in the 1960s. Here again the hard facts about the 1960s go completely counter to the prevailing assumptions of the 1960s. For two consecutive decades— the 1940s and the 1950s— the homicide rate for black males fell significantly, by 18 percent during the 1940s and by 22 percent in the 1950s. Then this downward trend reversed dramatically during the 1960s, wiping out the declines of the two preceding decades, as the homicide rate per 100,000 black males soared by 89 percent.[34]

For the American population as a whole, there was a long decline in homicide victimization rates from 1933 to 1964, followed by a sharp reversal that led to the highest rates in the twentieth century.[35] Nor was homicide the only social problem that had been getting better for years before the 1960s triumph of the social vision which promoted a sense of entitlement and grievance behind the welfare state, as well as a more lenient attitude toward crime and a more non-judgmental attitude toward other social pathology. Venereal diseases and teenage pregnancy, for example, were declining substantially during the 1950s, before this trend sharply reversed as the 1960s social vision spread through schools across the country under the name of "sex education."[36]

Social retrogressions among blacks that followed in the post-1960 era included rising rates of crime,[37] welfare dependency,[38] and unemployment.[39] Cirrhosis of the liver, a sign of alcoholism, was slightly lower among non-whites than among whites from the mid-1930s through the mid-1950s, but rose substantially above that of whites by the mid-1960s.[40] By the early twenty-first century, episodes of organized mob violence by blacks against whites and Asians struck dozens of cities and towns across the country.[41] While black civil rights organizations and the black public in general had long been opposed to racism, nevertheless group identity politics eventually led to a situation in which a public opinion poll in 2013 found that, not only whites but most blacks themselves, saw fellow blacks as racists more often than they saw whites as racists.[42]

Some fundamental cultural changes preceded these social retrogressions in the black community. During the first half of the twentieth century, Northern black newspapers and black civic organizations like the Urban League tried to acculturate less-educated, lower-class black migrants from the South to the norms of the larger society,[43] much as Irish and Jewish civic organizations during the European immigrant era tried to acculturate their respective compatriots to the norms of the larger society.[44] In the second half of the twentieth century, however, with the spread of the non-judgmental multicultural doctrine that all cultures are equally valid, and equally deserved to be respected or celebrated, to repudiate the ghetto culture was now seen as a racial betrayal by blacks who were "acting white."

Now even those blacks who were more educated and more acculturated, especially among the young, felt a need to adopt, or affect, some patterns or norms from the ghetto culture, as a sign of racial solidarity, or at least to avoid internal social friction among blacks. In short, the acculturation process now reversed, in favor of the lowest common denominator, as the influence of the ghetto culture spread up the social scale, leading to social retrogressions visible in many ways. Television documentaries about black communities in the first half of the twentieth century may show noticeably poorer neighborhoods than today, with fewer cars parked on the streets, but usually neighborhoods without graffiti on buildings or bars on windows. Neither the residents of Harlem, nor whites who visited Harlem, faced the level of dangers in the first half of the twentieth century that became common and pervasive in Harlem and other black communities in later years.

During the 1920s, for example, many white celebrities frequented Harlem's entertainment centers and private parties into the wee hours of the morning, before returning to their homes downtown, sometimes just before dawn. Many used their own cars to go back and forth, but music critic Carl Van Vechten— a frequent visitor to Harlem— usually simply went out on the streets, often intoxicated, to hail a cab to take him back to his West 55th Street apartment.[45] In the early 1930s, when Milton Friedman was a graduate student at Columbia University, he and his future wife went dancing at the Savoy Ballroom in Harlem, "with no fear of being mugged or accosted," as he said in later years.[46] A black actress who lived in Harlem and performed in Manhattan's midtown theater district during the 1940s said: "At one in the morning I would be taking the Eighth Avenue subway up, getting off at the top of the Hill. I had no fears whatsoever."[47] It is hard even to imagine such things in Harlem or other ghettos across the country today.

Public housing projects were a particularly striking setting in which social retrogressions among blacks took place. The filthy, crime-ridden, violence-prone housing projects, full of single-parent families on welfare, that became common across the country in the second half of the twentieth century, were by no means the norm during the first half of the twentieth century. There were *de facto* racially segregated projects in both eras. Yet the earlier projects were a striking contrast with the later projects, in an era of non-judgmental admissions policies toward applicants for apartments in the projects. As the *New York Times* reported, looking back on New York's earlier projects:

> These were not the projects of idle, stinky elevators, of gang-controlled stairwells where drug deals go down. In the 1940s, '50s and '60s, when most of the city's public housing was built, a sense of pride and community permeated well-kept corridors, apartments and grounds.[48]

It was not simply the physical setting that was different. So was the way of life in those early housing projects:

> Doors were kept unlocked as kids bounced from one apartment to the next on rainy Saturdays to watch Laurel and Hardy and Hopalong Cassidy on television.[49]

This was an era when not everyone could afford a television set, but when many people in the housing projects of that era who did have a television set felt safe enough to leave their apartment doors unlocked on Saturday mornings, so that their children's friends could come visit to watch television with them.*

There was a similar atmosphere in Philadelphia housing projects of that era, as described by black economist Walter Williams, who grew up in a housing project there:

> Back in the '40s the Homes were not what they were to become— a location known for drugs, killings, and nighttime sounds of gunfire. One of the most noticeable differences back then compared to today was the makeup of the resident families. Most of the children we played with, unlike my sister and I, lived with both parents. More than likely, there were other single-parent households but I can recall none. Fathers worked, and the mothers often did as well. The buildings and yards were well kept.[50]

There was no graffiti in this project. On hot summer nights it was not uncommon for people to sleep out on the balconies or, in the case of first-floor apartments, in their yards. In the adjoining local black neighborhood, it was not uncommon to see old men sitting around a table out on the street on hot summer nights, playing checkers or cards, during an era when most people could not afford air conditioning.[51] The contrast with the housing projects and ghetto neighborhoods of later years could hardly be more stark:

> When the shooting gets bad, children are put to sleep in bathtubs and under beds so they won't be struck by random bullets. Residents must pay tribute to gun-toting teenagers in order to enter their own buildings, get mail, and ride the elevator. Many have become prisoners in their own apartments, afraid to walk hallways strewn with empty crack vials, used condoms, and excrement where the lights have been put out by muggers

---

* Contrast that with today, when most people living in officially defined poverty have central air conditioning, cable television and multiple television sets per household, but who would not dare to leave their apartment doors unlocked. Such retrogressions were not peculiar to housing projects in New York. Similar drastic retrogressions occurred in other black communities. See Stephan Thernstrom and Abigail Thernstrom, *America in Black and White: One Nation, Indivisible* (New York: Simon & Schuster, 1997), pp. 261–263.

and drug dealers. The buildings themselves crumble in decay from neglect and vandalism. Those who can escape do, leaving behind an increasingly poor and demoralized underclass. The projects are increasingly seen as some other America— isolated and feared havens of addiction, violence and "problem" people.[52]

The demographic makeup of the housing projects' residents was also a contrast with that in earlier times. In the Robert Taylor Homes in Chicago, women headed 90 percent of the families with children in 1980, and 81 percent of these households were on welfare. Unemployment was estimated at 47 percent that year. With less than one percent of the population of Chicago, the Robert Taylor Homes had 11 percent of its murders.[53]

The retrogressions in educational achievement among blacks in parts of the United States, as well as the retrogressions represented by family disintegration, rising rates of drug addiction, violence and criminal behavior in general, have been strikingly similar among lower-class whites in England. Moreover, these and other social retrogressions proliferated during the same time period— from the 1960s onward— on both sides of the Atlantic. A whole way of life among lower-class whites in England, remarkably similar to the way of life in black ghettos in the United States, has been detailed in a classic account, *Life at the Bottom* by Theodore Dalrymple, a British physician who worked in a hospital near a low-income housing project and in a prison.

As regards the housing projects, he observed: "The public spaces and elevators of all public housing blocks I know are so deeply impregnated with urine that the odor is ineradicable. And anything smashable has been smashed."[54] The physical degeneration of the premises has been matched by social degeneration among the people living in them. The unmarried mother with multiple children by multiple fathers— none of whom support their children financially or in any other way— has become common in low-income white neighborhoods in England. As for the behavior of such children in England, Dr. Dalrymple recounted the troubles of a 50-year-old lady who lived alone in a slum and was a patient of his:

The children in her street mock her unceasingly when she leaves her house; they push excrement through her mailbox as a joke. She has long since given up appealing to their mothers for help, since they always side with their children and consider any adverse comment on their behavior as an insult to them personally. Far from correcting their children, they threaten her with further violence.[55]

Putting excrement through someone's mailbox was not an isolated aberration but "a common expression of social disapproval" among such people.[56] In the schools, a common expression of social disapproval of those students who seriously try to learn is beating them up— the same treatment meted out in America to some ghetto children who are accused of "acting white." Some of the low-income white children in England were beaten so badly by other low-income white children as to require medical treatment at the hospital where Dr. Dalrymple worked.[57]

Crime in England skyrocketed in the second half of the twentieth century, as it did in the United States, even though England had long been known as one of the world's most law-abiding nations. In 1954 there was a total of 12 armed robberies in London, at a time when anybody could buy a shotgun there. But the number of armed robberies rose to 1,400 by 1981 and 1,600 in 1991,[58] during an era of severe restrictions on the purchase of all firearms. A scholarly study of gun-control laws in England reported: "In the decade after 1957 the use of guns in serious crime increased a hundredfold."[59]

In England, as in the United States, crime rates had been going down for years, before they suddenly reversed and rose sharply during the second half of the twentieth century,[60] as the social vision of the intelligentsia triumphed in both countries— not only as regards the welfare state but also as regards a more lenient, non-judgmental attitude toward criminals and rioters. In England, this was combined with severe restrictions on police that a writer for London's *Daily Telegraph* referred to as "politically correct policing" that has police acting "more like social workers than upholders of law and order."[61] For example, as Professor Joyce Lee Malcolm of George Mason University reported in the *Wall Street Journal*: "Police have been instructed by the British

Home Office to let burglars and first-time offenders who confess to any of some 60 crimes— ranging from assault and arson to sex with an underage girl— off with a caution. That means no jail time, no fine, no community service, no court appearance."[62]

The effect of the prevailing social vision in England has not been limited to officials. That some people are "rich" has been regarded as a grievance for those who are not. A wave of urban riots swept through London, Manchester and other British cities in August 2011— involving thousands of hoodlums, looters and rioters, setting fire to homes and businesses, beating and robbing people on the streets,* and throwing gasoline bombs at police cars.[63] Girls who had participated in the riots, and who were interviewed on BBC said such things as: "It's the rich people, the people that have got businesses and that's why all of this has happened, because of the rich people. So we're just showing the rich people we can do what we want." They were also "showing the police we can do what we want, and now we have."[64]

A *New York Times* account of the British riots of 2011 cited the outlook of a typical 19-year-old male rioter:

> He lives in a government-subsidized apartment in northern London and receives $125 in jobless benefits every two weeks, even though he says he has largely given up looking for work. He says he has never had a proper job and learned to read only three years ago. . . "No one has ever given me a chance; I am just angry at how the whole system works," Mr. James said. He would like to get a job at a retail store, but admits that he spends most days watching television and just trying to get by. "That is the way they want it," he said, without specifying exactly who "they" were. "They give me just enough money so that I can eat and watch TV all day."[65]

A *Wall Street Journal* account provided a similar rioters' eye view of the world:

> The rioters in the news last week had a thwarted sense of entitlement that has been assiduously cultivated by an alliance of intellectuals, governments and bureaucrats. "We're fed up with being broke," one

---

* Some rioters "forced passers-by to strip naked while they stole their clothes." Philip Johnston, "The Long Retreat of Order," *The Daily Telegraph* (London), August 10, 2011, p. 19.

rioter was reported as having said, as if having enough money to satisfy one's desires were a human right rather than something to be earned.

"There are people here with nothing," this rioter continued: nothing, that is, except an education that has cost $80,000, a roof over their head, clothes on their back and shoes on their feet, food in their stomachs, a cellphone, a flat-screen TV, a refrigerator, an electric stove, heating and lighting, hot and cold running water, a guaranteed income, free medical care, and all of the same for any of the children that they might care to propagate. . .The young unemployed Britons not only have the wrong attitude to work, for example regarding fixed hours as a form of oppression, but they are also dramatically badly educated.[66]

Education has been another area in which there have been revealing parallels between England and the United States. Low-income children of immigrants in England have outperformed low-income, native-born children in schools. A study in Britain in 2013 compared test results among children of various ethnic and national backgrounds, all of whom were from families with incomes low enough to qualify for free lunches in school. Children of African immigrants in this economic bracket met the test standards nearly 60 percent of the time, as did children of immigrants from Bangladesh living at the same economic level. Children of black immigrants from the Caribbean at the same economic level met the standards just under 50 percent of the time. *White, native-born children from families at the same economic level met the standards 30 percent of the time.* In the borough of Knowsley, such white children scored lower than black children in any London borough.[67]

These educational results in England may seem very different from those in the United States, in terms of the race of those doing better and those doing worse. But they are remarkably similar in terms of children from a different foreign culture doing much better in school than native-born children from a lower-class culture, whether in England or America. Various reasons offered as explanations of substandard educational performances in black ghetto schools—whether genetics, racial discrimination or "a legacy of slavery"—obviously do not apply to lower-class whites in England. But the outcomes are strikingly similar.

What lower-class whites in England and ghetto blacks in the United States have in common is a legacy of a generations-long indoctrination in a welfare state ideology of entitlement, victimhood, grievances and a vision of barriers stacked against them that make their prospects hopeless. This welfare state ideology is backed up financially by welfare state programs that subsidize an economically counterproductive and socially destructive lifestyle.*

Meanwhile, the children of low-income immigrants, not burdened by the ideology that generations of the low-income, native-born population have been steeped in, do far better in both countries.** In *Life at the Bottom*, Dr. Dalrymple said, "I cannot recall meeting a sixteen-year-old white from the public housing estates that are near my hospital who could multiply nine by seven (I do not exaggerate). Even three by seven often defeats them."[68] He also noted elsewhere that the average young Polish immigrant who has been in Britain six months, "speaks better, more cultivated English" than lower-class young Britons do.[69] Genetic determinism can hardly explain abysmal educational results in children from a race that produced such mental giants as Shakespeare and Newton, but which now turns out many youngsters unable to cope with simple arithmetic. Nor is there a "legacy of slavery" or racial discrimination excuse that would apply.

While the white students who do so badly in England are from that country's lower-income class, poverty is not a sufficient

---

* People who have to work for a living cannot simply abandon themselves to a life of drugs, sex and violence, much less hanging out on the streets at all hours of the night and developing no way of accommodating themselves to a life of implicit and explicit rules in dealing with others.

** This seems particularly clear when the black population in Britain is broken down into those from Africa and those from the Caribbean. Blacks from the Caribbean began arriving in Britain from the 1940s to the 1960s, while blacks from Africa began arriving during the late 1980s. In short, the Caribbean blacks have spent more decades steeped in the welfare state vision. Although the blacks from the Caribbean arrived earlier and are "substantially better off than their African neighbours," according to *The Economist*, as well as being more often socially integrated and intermarried with white Britons, educationally the black Caribbeans "resemble whites in their performance at school— that is, both do pretty badly, after controlling for income" and a far higher proportion of black African students go on to universities. "The Next Generation," *The Economist*, January 30, 2016, pp. 47–48.

explanation either, because such children represent a retrogression from previous generations of children from low-income families,[70] just as in the United States. Dr. Dalrymple's father was born in a slum. But that was in an earlier time, when even a school in the slums maintained educational standards* and did not pander to the poor by nurturing a sense of grievance and of unfair barriers blocking their rise, as schools have in later times.[71] Instead, schools of the earlier era sought to equip youngsters with the human capital needed to rise out of poverty.[72]

Evidences of declining educational achievements in Britain include a report in *The Economist* that young Britons "have worse literacy and numeracy rates than those aged between 30 and 54, a pattern not seen in any other country in the European Union." Here the educational retrogression is seen in less than a generation. In the job market, native-born Britons "are more likely to be unemployed than children of immigrants, another finding not matched in any other European country."[73]

There are other welfare states in Europe, especially in the Scandinavian countries, where social pathology has not been the same as in England and America. Yet here, as in other contexts, *interactions* must be taken into account— in this case, interactions between the welfare state and the differing cultures of different peoples living within the same welfare state. Even within the United States, Asian Americans have the same welfare state benefits available as others do, but the Asians' cultures and educational performances provide them with far better alternatives than the welfare state. In an era when Scandinavians have some of the highest standards of living in the world, life on welfare may not have the same attraction as it does to some lower-class groups in England and the United States. Moreover, a more homogeneous population in Scandinavian countries may not

---

* "When he died, I found his school textbooks still among his possessions, and they were of a rigor and difficulty that would terrify a modern teacher, let alone child." Theodore Dalrymple, *Life at the Bottom*, p. 155. See also Peter Hitchens, *The Abolition of Britain*, Chapter 3.

have developed so many "leaders" of subgroups with a sense of historic grievances as in Britain and the United States.

The specifics of the historic grievances are different in Britain from those in the United States, just as the specifics of the grievances differ between black Americans and American Indians. But what is the same, within the United States and in common between the United States and Britain, is a long-standing pattern of historic grievances dividing ethnic subgroups of their respective populations. In Britain, the historically aggrieved groups include the Welsh, the Irish and the Scots, from whom bitterly eloquent and divisive "leaders" have arisen over the years. When twentieth century Welsh firebrand Aneurin Bevan, for example, entered the British Parliament to which he had been elected, he saw the portraits of many famous British political figures of the past. His reaction was to say that such statesmen of the past should be rejected by a Member of Parliament from a very different social background:

> The first thing he should bear in mind is that these were not his ancestors. His forebears had no part in the past, the accumulated dust of which now muffles his own footfalls. His forefathers were tending sheep or ploughing the land, or serving the statesmen whose names he sees written on the walls around him, or whose portraits look down upon him in the long corridors. It is not the past of his people that extends in colourful pageantry before his eyes. They were shut out from all this; were forbidden to take part in the dramatic scenes depicted in these frescoes. In him his people are there for the first time, and the history he will make will not be merely an episode in the story he is now reading. It must be wholly different; as different as is the social status which he now brings with him.[74]

As in the United States, divisive "leaders" of aggrieved groups in Britain found, in the second half of the twentieth century, far greater receptivity to their claims and demands among political and intellectual elites imbued with a politically correct social vision, of which the welfare state vision and a more non-judgmental leniency toward criminals were part. Among the political concessions that followed were greater political autonomy in Wales, Ireland and

Scotland, including a resurrection of the Welsh language, a separate Scottish Parliament and political concessions in Ulster County, Ireland.

The economic consequences of the welfare state vision in both England and America have included making it unnecessary for many people to develop their own productive capacities— their human capital— when they can live on what was produced by others and given to them. In both countries, the economic loss to society at large is not simply the cost of welfare state benefits that are transferred to non-producing members of society, but includes the perhaps larger value of output that the recipients could produce if they had to support themselves.

In addition, the counterproductive lifestyles developed in subsidized idleness in a non-judgmental society impose serious psychic costs on other members of society, especially those financially unable to escape neighborhoods where the offensive and dangerous behavior of those whom the welfare state and its accompanying social vision have relieved from the norms of civilized behavior on both sides of the Atlantic.[75] This is in addition to the increased financial costs of prisons, drug rehabilitation facilities, foster care for neglected or abused children, and the like.

More than simple mistakes are involved in promoting a culture of dependency among those whom government statisticians have chosen to define as living in poverty. A dependent voting constituency is valuable to politicians, and a paranoid constituency— resentful of social enemies supposedly dedicated to keeping them down— is even more valuable to politicians who play the role of defenders of the downtrodden, in exchange for their votes.

The many welfare state programs to support low-productivity people in their officially defined poverty serve the interests of welfare state institutions, as well as politicians. American welfare state bureaucracies whose jobs, budgets and power are advanced by the existence of a large dependent population have not only created advertising campaigns to promote greater use of their programs,[76] they have also dispatched their employees to supermarkets in low-income neighborhoods, to point out to people buying food that there are government programs that will pay for their food.

Although promoted as a means of helping people trapped by misfortunes beyond their control, welfare state institutions have themselves become traps, even for people who have in fact been victims of unforeseen but transient misfortunes, such as having a costly illness or losing a job. The many uncoordinated welfare state benefits available have, in many American states, added up to a total value far exceeding the official poverty level of income, and exceeding what low-productivity people could earn in the labor market.[77] In Hawaii, the most generous state, an unemployed single mother with two children has been eligible for welfare benefits worth more than $49,000 a year.[78] After recovery from an illness or other transient misfortunes— after jobs become available again, for example— for many who have been absorbed into welfare state dependency, a return to the labor market could involve a significant reduction in their standard of living.

People who promote the welfare state vision often also lament increasing income disparities. But the welfare state itself tends to increase income disparities between those at the top in income and those at the bottom. The welfare state contributes to this disparity by (1) reducing the need for people at the bottom to earn income and (2) by penalizing their earning of income, since higher income leads to a reduction in eligibility for government benefits. If increasing one's earned income by $10,000 would involve a loss of eligibility for $15,000 worth of government-provided benefits, that would be in effect an implicit "tax" rate of more than 100 percent on earned income. Even in less extreme cases, welfare state beneficiaries can face an implicit "tax" rate on earned income that is higher than the tax rate facing millionaires, if the welfare state beneficiaries were to return to gainful employment at the cost of losing their eligibility for various government benefits.

According to the Congressional Budget Office, in a typical state like Pennsylvania, earning an income of $23,000 could cost the loss of benefits worth as much as 95 percent of the earned income— and that did not count a loss of Medicaid and some other benefits,[79] which might well push the loss up to 100 percent or beyond. Such disincentives have long been known and understood, but neither politicians who benefit from welfare state dependency nor the people whose jobs are in the welfare state bureaucracies have any incentive to correct what is a problem only for others— these others including both people receiving welfare state benefits and the taxpayers.

People with political or financial reasons to support the welfare state are by no means the only ones with personal incentives to sing its praises or to ignore, deny or obfuscate its negative consequences. Much of the intelligentsia, whether in the media, academia or elsewhere, are creators or promoters of the vision that makes the welfare state possible— and, not incidentally, places themselves on a higher moral and/or intellectual plane than others, at least in their own estimation. Nicholas Kristof of the *New York Times* is by no means unique in adopting a disdainful attitude toward those who do not share his social vision, saying that people who think otherwise "just don't get it."[80] Nor is he unique in passing sweeping judgments on things like minimum wage laws, without any attempt to examine the actual empirical evidence on the consequences of such laws, much less empirical evidence on the consequences of the welfare state in general.

In short, the welfare state vision is not simply a theory to be tested empirically but a cause to be promoted and defended, ostensibly for the benefit of the less fortunate. But the fervor with which that vision is promoted and defended is by no means as great when it comes to testing empirically its actual effects on the ostensible beneficiaries, or on society at large. What is remarkable is how readily empirical questions about which policies produce which actual results for the poor, or for society at large, are turned into assertions about who among the opposing protagonists is morally and/or intellectually superior. Nor is this a new phenomenon of our times. Those who appoint themselves guardians of the less fortunate have been doing this as far back as the eighteenth century.[81]

The strategic location of the intelligentsia, whether in the mass media or in educational institutions, enables them to filter what information gets through to the general public, protecting the welfare state vision and with it a flattering vision of themselves. Empirical evidence as to what actually happens to the people they claim to be concerned about, after the welfare state vision is implemented, seldom seems to attract either the same interest or the same energy put into promoting that vision, which allows the intelligentsia to go through life feeling good about themselves, even while leaving social havoc in their wake.

The Role of "Leaders"

We have seen how ethnic leaders in many countries have promoted notions beneficial to themselves but often counterproductive for the groups they lead. Perhaps it is significant that groups which have risen from poverty to prosperity, in various countries around the world, have seldom had as many, or as prominent, ethnic leaders as groups that remain at the bottom. Any reasonably well-informed American can name at least three or four black leaders of the past or present, but would find it hard to name even a single comparable Asian or Jewish ethnic leader to whom these groups' dramatic rises from poverty could be attributed.

The triumph of the welfare state vision in the United States, from the 1960s on, included the idea that there should be the "maximum feasible participation" by local poor communities in efforts to shape programs and policies to help lift the poor out of poverty. What that amounted to in practice was that there was now government money available to subsidize the careers and activities of many new community "leaders" across the country. Whatever the beliefs, hopes or rationales behind this development, what mayors in a number of cities complained about was that there was now a new class of government-sponsored "leaders" spreading disaffection and disorder among the poor and minorities.[82] Ghetto riots, which had been sporadic and isolated before, now began to spread in waves across the country. Whatever the particular incident that might set off violence, there was now a whole class of people with a vested interest in escalating racial polarization.

While some aspects of these developments were peculiar to the United States, what was not unique was that a spreading sense of victimhood, grievance and entitlement led to a lashing out at others. The international treatise *Ethnic Groups in Conflict* noted how common such lashing out has been, in countries around the world, and that "backward groups are overwhelmingly initiators and advanced groups are targets of ethnic riot behavior."[83]

Ghetto riots that swept across the United States during the 1960s— the triumphant decade of the welfare state vision— certainly fit that pattern. In later years, there have been various repetitions of such riots from time to time. But a new pattern has also emerged in more recent years— premeditated and organized physical attacks by blacks on whites in such public places as shopping malls, parks and beaches, usually places *not* located in ghettos.

Unlike ghetto riots that erupt as more or less spontaneous reactions to particular incidents— even if later intensified by hoodlums who join in the mayhem and looting, or career racial activists who stir up mob emotions— the new organized attacks on whites are clearly pre-planned and coordinated, as large numbers of young black males suddenly converge in locally overwhelming numbers to physically attack whites at random.

Often the atmosphere among the attackers is more festive than angry,[84] even though serious and sometimes fatal injuries have been inflicted. One victim of such an attack said afterwards, "I heard laughing as they were beating everybody up. They were eating chips like it was a picnic."[85] Nevertheless, some among the intelligentsia continue to use the phrase "troubled youths" to describe exultant young hoodlums enjoying recreational violence— what Professor

Edward C. Banfield once called "rioting mainly for fun and profit,"[86] rather than the righteous rage that many of the intelligentsia choose to attribute to them. A *New York Times* headline, for example, depicted British rioters as "troubled youth" when reporting on mob violence that swept across England in 2011. The headline was: "London Riots Put Spotlight on Troubled, Unemployed Youths in Britain."[87]

In the early twenty-first century, racial attacks have occurred in dozens of cities and smaller communities in every region of the United States, from coast to coast.[88] There has been a pattern not only to these attacks but also to media and political responses. The most common response might be summarized in one word, *denial*.

Where the attacks have been too large, too frequent, or too widely known in a given community to be ignored, the media response has often been to omit the racial aspect[89] that was central to the attackers themselves, who often called their victims "crackers" or said such things as "This is for Trayvon Martin." Where such attacks across the country over the years have been reported in the media, it has often been as if each attack was an isolated local incident, involving unspecified "young people" attacking unspecified "victims" for unspecified reasons.

Where videos reveal the racial makeup of the attackers and their victims, mayors and police officials in community after community across the country have been quick to deny that these were racial attacks.[90] It is usually unnecessary for the media to deny that these attacks are occurring nationwide because few in the media have ever connected the dots, in the first place. *Investor's Business Daily* is one of the very few media outlets to call attention to a nationwide pattern of unprovoked and organized racial attacks: "Across the U.S., mobs of black youths are organizing on Facebook to loot stores and beat whites."[91] This same information was available to others in the media, but it seldom reached the public.

One variant of these black-on-white attacks caught the media's attention briefly— the so-called "knockout game" in which an individual attacker suddenly lets loose a hard punch to the head of an unsuspecting passerby, in an attempt to knock him down and, if possible, out. A series of such knockout punch attacks by blacks against Jews in the New York City area seemed to catch everyone by surprise in 2013,[92] even though a 2012 book about black-on-white violence already had a chapter titled "The Knockout Game, St. Louis-Style."[93] While it may be a game to the attackers, the victims have often ended up in a hospital, or dead. Someone knocked out in a boxing ring lands on canvas; someone knocked out on a city street usually lands on concrete.

Many who deny or downplay such racial attacks may believe that this will avoid a white backlash that could escalate into a truly disastrous race war. But a taste for recreational violence, as a means of inflicting pain and degradation on others, in order to overcome or avenge one's own sense of a stigma of inferiority, is something that is not likely to stop unless it gets stopped. That in turn is unlikely to happen without wider and more honest recognition of the dangers, followed by public pressure on elected officials to do something more substantive— and more honest— than denying that these attacks are racial.

Some people may imagine that one way of showing empathy with less fortunate people, whether blacks in the United States or low-income whites in England, is to take a non-judgmental attitude toward their transgressions, as if exempting any group from the standards of civilized behavior is a net benefit to them or to society at large. Barbarism is hardly a gift to any community, especially a community where crime and violence are directed primarily against its own members. Nor is an eventual violent backlash from others. The history of intergroup backlashes— such as the Czech backlash against German civilians in Czechoslovakia right after the Second World War[94] or the backlash of the Hutus against the Tutsis in Rwanda half a century later[95]— is a history of horrors that no one should want to see repeated on American soil.

Letting organized racial attacks continue across the country, and perhaps escalate, may only delay a larger and more violent racial backlash and polarization, as knowledge of such things spreads, despite the mainstream media, and builds up a growing backlog of resentments, much like the "social dynamite" that James B. Conant warned was building up in many ghettos before a wave of riots erupted there in the 1960s.[96] But, in this as in many other things, political incentives are to postpone the day of reckoning, even if that means that the reckoning will be larger and more catastrophic.

Many Americans today may find it hard to imagine mobs of whites attacking blacks. But it is not necessary to imagine. Mobs of whites attacking blacks is precisely what a "race riot" meant in the United States a hundred years ago, especially in the first two decades of the twentieth century— and in *Northern* cities even more so than in the South.[97] Since the 1960s, the black-initiated riot has become the norm. But things were different before and can become different again. If so, the economic losses may be the least of the problems.

The compassionate concerns for fellow human beings that motivate many people to promote and support the welfare state cannot be presumed to foster similar feelings among the recipients of welfare state benefits. Much evidence from both England and the United States suggests an opposite result— a general coarsening of behavior and a self-centered disregard of a sense of common humanity or common decency. Nor can the desire of many supporters of the welfare state to create more opportunities for welfare state beneficiaries to develop their own human capital be presumed to be shared by the beneficiaries themselves. The degeneration of both educational standards and behavioral standards in schools located in neighborhoods with concentrations of people living on welfare suggests the opposite. Harassment and violence directed toward those students who want to learn speak volumes on both sides of the Atlantic.

Neither individually nor collectively have human beings begun their lives as civilized people. Civilization is a continuous process that has taken place, for millennia, under some of the very incentives and constraints that the welfare state now seeks to remove— including the necessity of earning a living, and the related necessities of taming one's ego and forming social attachments that inhibit impulses and force one's thoughts and actions to take into account what consequences await, beyond the moment and beyond oneself.

Those who promote or support the welfare state vision may see the loosening of such restrictions as "liberation" for the individual who receives sustenance and shelter as "rights" to which all are "entitled," regardless of what they do or fail to do. But, in a world where society as a whole cannot be liberated from physical and social necessities, exempting some segments of society from inherent necessities operates against the dynamic of what Toynbee called "challenge and response" as key factors in the progress of civilization. For some individuals and groups, exemption from the civilizing challenges of life leaves a purposeless void in their lives, a void too often filled by random sex and/or drugs and/or violence.

How all this works out for particular individuals or groups in a given society is ultimately an empirical question. But it is a question that those with the welfare state vision have few reasons to ask and many reasons to avoid, as painful social realities intrude upon an inspiring vision— often heart-breaking realities not only for blacks in America and low-income whites in Britain but perhaps most tragically of all for indigenous peoples living on reservations in the United States.[98] For those who cherish and promote the welfare state vision, it cannot be easy to admit, even to oneself, having promised progress toward "social justice" and having delivered instead retrogressions toward barbarism.

PART V:

CONCLUSIONS

You're entitled to your own opinion, but you're not entitled to your own facts.

Daniel Patrick Moynihan

Questions about facts are obviously very different from questions about values, goals or policies. We can put particular competing explanations of economic disparities to factual tests and, perhaps equally important, define our terms precisely enough so that we can at least know what we disagree about. While differences of opinion on issues may be inevitable, confusion on issues is not.

Now that we have surveyed some of the factors involved in economic and social outcomes, we can at last confront the most fundamental question: What is the reason for differences in income and wealth among individuals, races, nations and civilizations?

The simplest answer is that there is no such thing as "the" reason. There are all sorts of factors— and many combinations and permutations of those factors. Nor have we enumerated them all, and it is by no means certain that anyone could do so. But what is clear from the factors we have considered thus far is that these combinations and permutations are too numerous to reasonably expect equal economic outcomes, either between nations or within nations, when the things that go into creating those outcomes vary so greatly. The all too familiar cliché about "the paradox of poverty in an affluent society" is a paradox only to those who start with (1) a preconception that equality would be a natural outcome, in the absence of some adverse human intervention— a preconception in defiance of both geography and history, and (2) a disregard of the arbitrary nature of the government-defined word "poverty," which changes over time and varies from country to country at a given time.

Much of the egalitarian thrust of contemporary redistributionists is directed toward the reduction or elimination of income or wealth "disparities" or "gaps" between various groups. But, as distinguished economic development economist Peter Bauer of the London School of Economics pointed out, years ago: "The promotion of economic equality and the alleviation of poverty are distinct and often conflicting."[1] If everyone's income doubles, that should certainly reduce poverty, but it would also widen income gaps and disparities.

This applies to gaps and disparities between nations and within nations. The welfare state can reduce, or perhaps even eliminate, poverty in any material sense, but it also reduces the need for many people to earn income— especially when earning income reduces eligibility for government-provided benefits in kind— and therefore widens statistical gaps and disparities in money income, even as these in-kind benefits reduce differences in standards of living.

Perhaps equally or more important, the welfare state reduces the need to develop human capital. But, whether among individuals or nations, receiving the tangible products of other people's human capital is by no means as fundamental as developing one's own human capital. Spain, during its golden age in the sixteenth and seventeenth centuries, received other countries' products, in exchange for the gold and silver it took from the peoples it conquered in the Western Hemisphere, but Spain lagged behind other contemporary Western European countries in such human capital as both craft skills and scientific advances. Moreover, the disdainful attitudes toward productive work that developed in Spain under these conditions were negative human capital, as was the mass export of human capital by the expulsions of Jews and, later, Moriscos, both of whom had skills largely lacking in the general population of Spain. By contrast, the economies of Scotland and Japan rose dramatically by acquiring the human capital of other cultures, rather than by importing their consumer products.

Redistribution of income is not redistribution of human capital. On the contrary, such redistribution of income not only reduces the incentives, of lagging groups especially, to develop human capital, it can also reduce the incentives of more advanced groups to develop and apply their human capital to the fullest, when the rewards for doing so are reduced by confiscatory policies that transfer a substantial share of their rewards to others. Russian aviation pioneer Igor Sikorsky, for example, simply relocated to the United States after the Communists took over in Russia, so that American society received the benefits of the helicopters and other aircraft that Sikorsky developed, which would otherwise have benefitted Russia.

There is no way to know how many other Russians with talents for innovations, but without the financial resources of Sikorsky, were unable to emigrate but had few incentives to innovate within a Communist society. However, we do know that Soviet premier Leonid Brezhnev complained that Soviet enterprise managers shied away from innovation "as the devil shies away from incense."[2] With the considerable risks that go with innovation, but without corresponding rewards in a Communist economy, there was little reason to expect otherwise.

As regards the more general question of economic differences among nations today, all too often the question posed is much like that in a well-known study, *Why Nations Fail*: "Why is Egypt so much poorer than the United States? What are the constraints that keep Egyptians from becoming more prosperous?"[3] This implicitly treats what happens in the United States as a sort of norm, as what happens usually or more or less naturally, leaving the question as to why this usual, normal or natural development has been thwarted somehow in Egypt. But Egypt may be more typical of what has happened around the world, and over the centuries, than is the United States.

In a wider view of the history of the human race since its beginnings, the entire species was very poor, primitive and densely ignorant for more than 90 percent of its existence. The decisive innovation of agriculture, within the last 5 percent or so of the existence of the human species, opened up vast new possibilities for creating cities, civilizations and all the progress in many dimensions that has been built on that foundation. As we have seen, that progress was never equally accessible to all peoples in all geographic locations or equally sought by all cultures, much less equally compatible with all social conditions or political systems.

It is not poverty that needs to be explained but what combinations of circumstances come together in particular places and times to enable economic progress to take place.

Given the many factors that go into the creation of wealth, and the wide variety of combinations and permutations of those factors, there is no more reason to expect such factors to come together in the same way in contemporary Egypt as in the United States than there is to expect that all the factors which come together to produce tornadoes[4] would come together in Egypt as often as they come together in the United States— more so than in any other country, or all other countries combined.

To pursue the analogy with tornadoes, there is nothing absolutely unique that strikes the eye about either the terrain or the climate in the United States that cannot be found, as individual features, in many other places around the world. Wide level plains are among the things that facilitate the development of tornadoes, but wide level plains exist across much of Europe and in India and Argentina, among other places. What is unique about the United States is the *combination* of things that occur together— in the middle of the country rather than on the coasts, in particular seasons of the year, and in the afternoons more so than in the mornings or at night[5]— that cause the vast majority of all the tornadoes in the world to occur within the United States.*

There is no more reason to expect the same particular mix of geographic, cultural, demographic, political and social factors to come together in Egypt as in the United States than there is to expect the same kind of air currents, contrasting air temperatures and other factors to come together in Egypt as in the United States. We would not set out to discover why there are not more tornadoes in Egypt, if we were interested in knowing how tornadoes originate and behave. Similarly, there is not much reason to seek the causes of poverty in Egypt or in any other country. Poverty— genuine poverty— has been the lot of most of the human race for most of the existence of the

---

* In much the same way, the combination of things required for successfully growing coffee beans means that a small group of nations produces the vast majority of all the coffee in the world. At one time, Brazil alone produced more than half the coffee in the world.

species. However, a more reasonable question also appears in *Why Nations Fail*: "Was it historically— or geographically or culturally or ethnically— predetermined that Western Europe, the United States, and Japan would become so much richer than sub-Saharan Africa, Latin America, and China over the last two hundred years or so?"[6]

While nothing predestined particular nations or peoples to be more prosperous than others, many things facilitated or impeded the economic development of some nations and peoples more so than others. Without presuming to find predestination, we can nevertheless seek patterns in the record of what has already happened. Such patterns can also serve as an empirical check on the many theories and policies being discussed or applied.

By starting with *production*— and, more specifically, differences in productivity— as we have here in earlier chapters, we can at least hope to avoid the problems that arise from treating the money flows resulting from the production process (namely income) as if we can rearrange those money flows to our liking, without regard to repercussions on production. Far too often, those preoccupied with "income distribution" leave production with little or no role, as something that just happens *somehow*— no matter how radically differently it happens in different times and places, or how much that difference affects the standard of living of millions.

Wealth is not manna from heaven. In the real world, wealth has to be produced, and how efficiently it is produced determines the standard of living of a whole society. Since both capital and labor respond to economic incentives, third parties cannot blithely change income to suit their own notions, without recognizing that they are changing the incentives to produce, which may well determine how much will in fact be produced.

Once we put production at the center of our attention, our surprise at extremes of income and wealth might suggest the question whether there are comparable extremes in the production of wealth, and whether these two extremes may have something to do with each other. This seems clear in the case of rich and poor nations, where technological differences are blatantly visible, and differences in skill levels not too difficult to uncover, especially when many poor countries have median ages at least a decade or two younger than the median ages in richer countries.

We need not assume that all differences in income and wealth between all individuals, groups or nations are due to productivity differences, but neither is there any reason why that question should be left unasked, while we marvel with dismay at how large these differences in economic outcomes are, and then swiftly move on to discuss how we can "solve" this "problem." But there is much to be said for preceding our attempt at "solutions" by first going back to square one and carefully scrutinizing both the numbers and the words in which the "problem" has been presented. This can be both an enlightening and a disillusioning process. Nevertheless there is much to be said for confronting a situation as it is, rather than how it might appear. For that, we need to get into economics.

Sometimes economics is thought of as a dry, technical and essentially soulless study of *things*, rather than a subject focusing on the vicissitudes of human beings. That is certainly not how the great economist Alfred Marshall saw economics. As a young man in his twenties, Marshall was an accomplished mathematician who earned his living by teaching mathematics. His decision to change his career to that of an economist came after "I visited the poorest quarters of several cities and walked through one street after another, looking at the faces of the poorest people."[7]

Professor Marshall thought that more economists should be involved in dealing with problems of poverty because too many others who dealt with poverty produced "hastily conceived plans which would often increase the evils that they desire to remedy."[8] He saw, back in the nineteenth century, a pattern still common today among those discussing income differences, that many social reformers "in their desire to improve the distribution, are reckless as to the effects of their schemes on the production of wealth." What was needed, he said, were people with not only "warm hearts" but also "cool heads"[9]—

people able to use economics to "cross-examine the facts."[10] There are many assumptions and beliefs, which claim to be facts, that are very much in need of cross-examining when it comes to the study of wealth, poverty and politics. That will be the task in the concluding chapters.

Chapter 13

ECONOMIC DIFFERENCES

> *Measuring the growth of incomes or the inequality of incomes is a little like Olympic figure skating— full of dangerous leaps and twirls and not nearly as easy as it looks. Yet the growth and inequality of incomes are topics that seem to inspire many people to form very strong opinions about very weak statistics.*
>
> *Alan Reynolds*

Few subjects arouse as many passions or inspire as much rhetoric as questions about what is called "income distribution" or the "concentration of wealth." Some see in controversies about economic inequalities a fundamental "underlying struggle" between "worlds of plenty and worlds of want."[1] But the vast outpourings of words about economic differences— whether between nations or within nations— are seldom matched by a careful scrutiny of either the words or the numbers, or the unspoken assumptions that frame these issues. Many of these words, numbers and unspoken assumptions will not stand up under scrutiny, beginning with income statistics.

INCOME STATISTICS

There are two fundamentally different kinds of statistics used to show income trends over time— *and these different kinds of statistics produce diametrically opposite conclusions.*

The people who appear in one kind of income statistics are a set of the same identical individuals, whose incomes are tabulated throughout the years covered by a given study. A very different kind of statistics— and the kind most often cited in the media, in politics and in academia— is based on tabulating the incomes of whatever mix of people happens to be in such categories as the top fifth, the bottom fifth and other brackets in between, in any given year. A series of such tabulations in a series of years then serves as the basis for conclusions about trends in the incomes earned in each of the various brackets.

These latter kinds of statistics are often cited to assert that the incomes of people in the top bracket ("the rich") are increasing relative to the incomes of people in the bottom bracket ("the poor") or relative to incomes of people in other brackets in between. Assertions that "the gap between rich and poor has widened in America" have appeared in the *New York Times*[2] and in innumerable other media outlets, including the *Washington Post*, where columnist E.J. Dionne described "the wealthy" as "people who have made almost all the income gains in recent years" and added that they are "undertaxed."[3] Books like *The Fair Society* by Peter Corning of Stanford University repeat the same theme, that "the income gap between the richest and the poorest members of our society has been growing rapidly."[4]

Although such statements, which abound throughout the media and are echoed in politics and in academia, are *phrased* as if they are comparing the incomes of specific sets of human beings over time— "the rich" and "the poor"— they are in fact comparing the incomes of particular income brackets *containing an ever-changing mix of people* over time, as individuals move massively from one bracket to another in the normal course of their careers, going from entry-level jobs to jobs that pay far more to successively more experienced people. Those who go into business or the professions likewise tend to acquire a larger clientele with the passing years, resulting in rising incomes there as well.

Studies which actually follow a given set of individuals over time produce not only different conclusions, but *opposite* conclusions from studies which follow income brackets, with each bracket containing ever-changing mixes of people, at very different stages of their individual careers. A study at the University of Michigan that followed specific individuals— working Americans— from 1975 to 1991 found that those particular individuals who were initially in the bottom 20 percent in income had their real incomes rise over the years, not only at a higher rate but in a several times larger total amount, than the real incomes of those particular individuals whose incomes were initially in the top 20 percent.[5]

As a result of their rising incomes, 95 percent of those people who were initially in the bottom quintile in 1975 were no longer there in 1991. Twenty-nine percent of the people who were initially in the bottom quintile rose all the way to the top quintile, while just 5 percent remained behind in the bottom quintile where they began. Meanwhile, over that same span of time those people who were initially in the top quintile in 1975 had the *smallest* increase in real income by 1991— smallest in both percentage terms and in absolute amount— of people in any of the quintiles. The amount by which the average income of people initially in the top quintile rose was less than half that in any of the other quintiles.[6]

However radically different this empirical pattern is from the many loudly proclaimed assertions that "the rich" have been getting richer and "the poor" getting poorer over time, there is nothing surprising about the mundane fact that people who start out at the bottom, in entry-level jobs, usually rise over the years to successively higher levels of work and pay. Meanwhile, those who have already reached middle age, where their productivity and earnings are highest, are unlikely to see any comparably large further increases in productivity and pay as time goes on.

A later study, using data from the Internal Revenue Service, found a very similar pattern. This study followed those specific individuals who filed income tax returns over the course of a decade, from 1996 through 2005. Those whose incomes were initially in the bottom 20 percent of this group saw their incomes rise by 91 percent during that decade— that is, their incomes nearly doubled. Those whose incomes were initially in the much-discussed "top one percent" saw their incomes actually *fall* by 26 percent during that same decade.[7] Again, the facts are the opposite of the loudly proclaimed assertions, based on statistics that measure what is happening over time to abstract categories— income brackets containing ever-changing mixes of people, at varying stages of their own individual life cycles— which are then discussed as if they were statistics about what was happening over time to a given set of flesh-and-blood human beings.

It should also be noted that the University of Michigan study dealt with people who were *working*, and the Internal Revenue Service study dealt with people who were earning enough to be filing income tax returns. In other words, neither study included people who were idle and living on welfare state benefits. Questions about the rate of upward social mobility— whether or to what extent people can rise up the income and occupational ladder— can have very different answers for people who are on the ladder, even at low levels, and people who are not.

A more recent study that followed specific individuals over time in Canada, from 1990 through 2009, found patterns very similar to the patterns found in studies of Americans. Those Canadians who were initially in the bottom 20 percent in income had their incomes increase at both a higher rate, and in a higher absolute amount, than those whose incomes were initially in higher brackets.[8] Yet again, what happened over time to a given set of human beings was the opposite of what happened over that same span of time in abstract categories containing ever-changing mixes of people. In Canada, as in the United States, the upper brackets' incomes were rising faster than the lower brackets' incomes— and, as in the United States, this was spoken of as if it represented what was happening to given sets of people.[9]

What are we to make of the undisputed fact that the incomes in the top bracket are increasing over time, not only absolutely but relative to the incomes in lower brackets? It means that incomes being paid for higher levels of economic activity are increasing relative to incomes paid for lower levels of economic activity. This might be alarming if most people in the lower brackets stayed there for life. But most people in all the quintiles do not stay in those same quintiles for even a single decade. What the higher proportion of incomes going to the top brackets mean is that there is a steeper increase in the payoff for working one's way up the ladder. Referring to people in the upper income brackets as if they were permanent residents in those brackets, rather than people who arrived there after working their way up from much lower incomes, fundamentally distorts reality.

Unfortunately, statistical surveys that follow specific individuals over the years are more expensive than statistical surveys that simply compile data over the years in abstract categories, containing ever-changing mixtures of people at highly varying stages of their own individual life cycles. So it is not surprising that the U.S. Bureau of the Census, and numerous other collectors of statistics, turn out far more data on what is happening in abstract categories over time than data on what is happening to specific sets of individuals over time. Nevertheless, what happens in those abstract categories— income brackets, in this case— over time is often discussed just as if that is what is happening to specific sets of people over time, often called "the poor" and "the rich." Transients in the various income brackets are spoken of as if they were continuous residents in those brackets.

Time and Turnover

Understandable and commendable as it may be to be concerned about the fate of fellow human beings, that is very different from being obsessed with the fate of numbers in abstract categories. To say, as Professor Thomas Piketty does in his much acclaimed book, *Capital in the Twenty-First Century*, that "the upper decile is truly a world unto itself"[10] is to fly in the face of the fact that most American households— 53 percent— are in the top decile at some point in their lives,[11] usually in their older years. For most Americans to envy or resent the top ten percent would be to envy or resent *themselves*. This is not even "class warfare," but confusion between social classes and age cohorts.

Statistics on income differences are almost universally and automatically discussed as if these must be differences between social classes— that is, the same people over time— rather than differences between people of different ages. Indeed, there is seldom even a mention of the *possibility* that these numbers can refer to either social classes or age cohorts, much less attempts in the popular media to determine to what extent they refer to people in different age brackets, rather than people in different social classes. Because of this crucial omission, the income and wealth statistics that are paraded with such fervor can be perfectly accurate and yet completely misleading.

If infants have less income or wealth than their parents, who in turn have less income or wealth than their grandparents, that is hardly the same as if individuals are in wealth or poverty over the course of their lives. Yet the latter is a common insinuation, garnished with numbers. As statistics, infants can be the same as grandparents, but only as statistics. Even if the data are limited to adults, younger adults are the same as older adults only as statistics— and again, economic disparities between people of different ages are not the same as economic disparities between different social classes.

Even the vaunted "top one percent," so often discussed in the media, is a level reached by 11 percent of Americans at some point in the course of their lives.[12] What Professor Paul Krugman of Princeton refers to as "the charmed circle of the 1 percent"[13] must have a somewhat fleeting charm, because most of the people in that circle in 1996 were no longer there in 2005.[14] In Professor Piketty's vision, however, the top one percent in income not only live in their own separate world but "stand out in society" and "exert a significant influence on both the social landscape and the political and economic order."[15] According to Piketty, the top one percent sit atop the "hierarchy" and "structure of inequality."[16]

There is, however, a fundamental difference between a fixed *structure* and a fluid *process*. Piketty glosses over the process in which people's incomes change very substantially over the course of their lives— or even in the course of just one decade. More than half of all taxpayers moved to a different income quintile between 1996 and 2005, and the same was true in the preceding decade.[17] Piketty's crucial misstep has the effect of verbally converting a fluid process over time into a rigid structure, with a more or less permanent top one percent living isolated from the rest of society that is supposedly subjected to their influence. It is a vision divorced from demonstrable facts, however consonant it may be with prevailing preconceptions. Among people in the middle quintile, for example, 42 percent moved up to a higher income quintile, while 25 percent dropped to a lower quintile and 33 percent remained in the middle quintile— all this just within one decade.[18]

Turnover is especially pronounced among those with the highest incomes. While fewer than half of the people in the top one percent in 1996 were still there at the end of a decade, only about one-quarter of those in the top one hundredth of one percent in 1996 were still there in 2005.[19] While the average income of those initially in the top one percent fell by 26 percent during that decade, more than half of the people initially in the top one-hundredth of one percent had their average income cut in half or more during that same decade.[20]

The turnover is even faster among those taxpayers with the 400 highest incomes in the country— incomes far higher than among the top one percent as a whole. Fewer than one-fourth of the income tax filers with the top 400 incomes in 1992 were in that same bracket more than once during the years ending in 2000— and only 13 percent were in that extremely high bracket more than twice during those nine years.[21] At very high income levels— whether the top one percent, one-hundredth of one percent or the top 400 incomes— that income is far more likely to come from investments than from salaries, and earnings from investments are far more volatile than salaries.

Income from investments is not only more volatile than income from salaries, it also differs from salaries more fundamentally because capital gains received in a given year are not necessarily earned in that particular year. Often capital gains have accrued over a period of years, and have then been turned into income in a later year, whether by the sale of a home or other property like stock options, or other sources of incomes accrued over a period of years that are turned into cash in a later year. Capital gains may be spoken of as if they were annual incomes like salaries, but the data on highly volatile incomes at the highest levels indicate otherwise. If capital gains accrue over a period of five years, for example, and are then turned into cash income in the fifth year, that obviously averages out to an income per year that is one-fifth of the income received in the fifth year. To tax that fifth year income at the same rate as an annual salary of that same amount would be to tax a lower annual income at a rate that applies to a higher annual income.

In short, even more than most people in other income brackets, most of the people among the top 400 income recipients are transients— in this case, mostly people with a spike in income for just one year out of nine. Whether their one year at this level is due to receiving an inheritance or otherwise cashing in assets accumulated over a previous span of years, or is due to some other reason, the people who are fleeting residents in this income bracket are hardly credible candidates for the powerful and/or sinister roles assigned to them in much ideological and political rhetoric. During just one decade, there can be thousands of people in the "top 400."

This is not to say that there are no enduringly wealthy people who in fact have lives and lifestyles far removed from those in the rest of society. The question is whether they are the *same* people as those who happen to be in particular income brackets at particular times. Otherwise, what is the point of citing those statistics, based on ever-changing mixes of people, and talking about them as if these were data on a given set of human beings? As for the genuinely wealthy—as distinguished from people with a high annual income in a given year— the depiction of them as being in control of the economy is inconsistent with such facts as that the 400 richest people in the world had net losses of $19 billion in 2015.[22] Surely people who actually controlled the economy could do better than that.

Most comparisons of high incomes with low incomes proceed as if similar things are being compared, but that is clearly not so when the very highest incomes are disproportionately capital gains and the lowest are predominantly salaries. Comparing *annual* incomes from salaries with *multi-year* incomes from capital gains received in a given year is comparing apples and oranges. Higher turnover rates in very high income brackets add to the distortions that exaggerate income disparities. When the actual flesh-and-blood individuals whose multi-year accruals of wealth put them in the highest income bracket, in the year when these accruals are turned into cash, keep disappearing from year to year, and being replaced by new individuals with one-year spikes in capital gains incomes, the exaggeration is even more pronounced.

Much has been made of Piketty's voluminous statistics from various countries. But, as J.A. Schumpeter said long ago, "You can travel far and wide and yet wear blinkers wherever you go."[23] Some critics have questioned some of Piketty's statistics.[24] But the most fundamental question is not about the accuracy of the numbers themselves, but about the accompanying misstatements of what the numbers are measuring. However, it may be worth noting in passing that Piketty's repeated statements that the highest income tax rate during President Herbert Hoover's years in the White House was 25 percent are contradicted by an official Internal Revenue Service document, showing that the top income tax rate in 1932 was 63 percent.[25]

Income versus Wealth

Among the many sources of confusion in discussions of people's economic differences is a failure to distinguish income from wealth. Income and wealth are too fundamentally different from each other to make confident inferences about one from statistics about the other. A billionaire has no need to earn any income at all in a given year, and his investments may not in fact be earning anything on net balance during a particular year, depending on the fluctuations of the market. But a billionaire with a low income is not poor in any meaningful sense, regardless of how low his income may be in a given year. Other people with low incomes who are not poor in any meaningful sense would include wives of wealthy husbands and husbands of wealthy wives, young adults being subsidized by their parents while working part-time or in low-paid, entry-level jobs, and elderly retired people living on money received from "reverse mortgages," which is not counted as income, since that money is a loan to be repaid from their estate after death.

Temporary income fluctuations occur not only at the highest income levels but also among people at more modest income levels— and that may have something to do with the statistical anomaly that there have been hundreds of thousands of people with incomes under $20,000 a year living in homes costing $300,000 and up.[26] Obviously this would not be an economically viable situation if they were making under $20,000 every year.

Use of the term "the rich" to describe people in higher income brackets is just one sign of the confusion between income and wealth, since being rich means having an *accumulation* of wealth, rather than simply a high income in a given year. This is not just a matter of semantics. At a practical level, raising income tax rates to make "the rich" pay their undefined "fair share" of taxes is an exercise in futility, since *income taxes do not touch wealth*. They are taxes on the incomes of people who may be trying to accumulate wealth, but people who *already* have accumulations of wealth, whether personally earned or a result of inheritance, are exempt.

Praise for billionaires who say that they are in favor of higher income tax rates is completely misplaced, when those higher tax rates will not touch their billions, even if such tax rate increases are a serious burden to other people, who are trying to get ahead and accumulate something to leave for their families after they are gone.

Raising the tax rate on people with very high incomes, in the belief that this will make them pay their undefined "fair share," can also be an exercise in futility because the government can only set the tax *rate*, which tells us nothing about how much tax *revenue* will result— or even whether that revenue will rise or fall.[27] Sometimes a higher tax rate leads to lower tax revenue, when many people subject to rising tax rates respond by investing in tax-exempt securities or by making their investments in other countries where tax rates are lower. High tax rates on Americans with high incomes may create little more than an inconvenience for high income earners, who can readily transfer their investments overseas electronically— while creating a far more serious problem for working-class Americans who are looking for jobs, and who cannot nearly so easily transfer themselves physically to the overseas countries where jobs have been created by the transfer of American investments, driven out of the country by high tax rates on higher incomes.

Claims that billionaires are paying lower tax rates than their secretaries can likewise be extremely misleading. Seldom, if ever, does anyone become a billionaire from a salary. Almost invariably, very high incomes are results of investments— and investment income differs fundamentally from salaries. The secretary's salary in a given year is earned and paid in the same year, while the billionaire's investment income in a given year may come from investments that have increased in value over a decade or decades. So while the billionaire's tax *rate* in a given year may be lower than that of his secretary, not only is the actual tax *amount* almost certainly a vastly larger sum of money, its annual tax rate— if the tax sum were spread out over all the years during which the return on investment was earned— could undoubtedly also be higher than that of the secretary.

Similar principles apply to people who are not billionaires, but whose incomes also come from capital gains. For the sake of simplicity, consider an author who takes ten years to write a book, receiving no income at all from this investment of time and effort, and having no assurance during those years that he will ever receive anything— since many, and probably most, book-length manuscripts are never accepted for publication. In short, it is a risky investment that may never pay off. But if, at the end of ten years, the book is published and the publisher pays the author $100,000, should the author be taxed as if he earned $100,000 a year from this book or taxed as if he earned $10,000 a year for each of the ten years spent writing it? Very different tax rates would apply when one annual income is defined as ten times the size of another.

In this case, the Internal Revenue Service will tax the author as if he made $100,000 a year on this book, though in reality the $100,000 is a capital gain— an accumulation of wealth— though there may be no way for the author to prove that he spent ten years writing the book. But by no means is this hypothetical author in the same economic situation as a civil servant with a guaranteed annual income of $100,000. Where investments have been made in stocks, bonds, real estate or other assets whose longevity can be documented, capital gains are usually taxed at a lower current annual rate than wages and salaries, simply because only a fraction of the income received during a given year from investment income may actually be produced during that one year. And of course investments involving risk are taxed at a lower rate than guaranteed salaries, since the former involve losses that are rare with the latter.

In income statistics as well, the hypothetical author— like other recipients of capital gains— will be recorded as having a far higher *annual* income rate than the economic facts would warrant, since receiving a decade's income in a given year is not the same as receiving an annual income of the same amount.

Not only may capital gains that are turned into cash in a given year represent money earned over a number of previous years, but often a *different* number of years for different people, extending to decades for elderly people who retire and sell either a business or a home.* When the earnings of multiple years are treated as if they were earned in a single year, that statistically exaggerates the annual income of people who receive capital gains, making statistical comparisons of disparities between people with high and low incomes similarly exaggerated, when very high incomes are far more likely to be predominantly capital gains and low incomes far more likely to be salaries. Moreover, because the turnover of people in very high income brackets is even greater than the turnover of people in other income brackets, the illusion that we are comparing the same sets of flesh-and-blood human beings over time is even more false than with other comparisons of people in other brackets.

The ease with which many people are labeled "rich" or "poor," on the basis of their respective annual incomes, is usually not only conceptually flawed but usually also involves no concrete information on just how high are the incomes of those labeled "rich," or how much the lower incomes of those labeled "poor" are supplemented by large transfers of in-kind benefits from the government, quite aside from the fact that income is not wealth in the first place. Many people who blithely toss around the words "rich" and "poor" often do not even try to say just how much money they are talking about— that is, how much income it takes to be in the top quarter, the top tenth or the top one percent of income earners. Data from the Internal Revenue Service show that the "adjusted gross income" required to be in the top quarter of American income recipients was $70,492 in 2011. To make the top ten percent required an "adjusted gross income" of

---

* A man who retires after running a local neighborhood grocery store for 40 years, and sells that store for $400,000 more than he paid for building it or buying it, has accumulated $10,000 a year in capital gains. But income statistics will record him as earning $400,000 a year, putting him in the much discussed "top one percent." However, the following year the retired grocer will have dropped out of that "top one percent" like many others, and may be unlikely to be in that income bracket again. Someone will of course always be in that bracket, taking his place and sustaining the illusion that a given set of people is being compared with some other given set of people when income and wealth statistics are discussed.

$120,136, and to make the much discussed top one percent required an "adjusted gross income" of $388,905.[28]

People in Professor Piketty's "top decile" of income earners who are supposedly in "a world unto itself"[29] may in fact have all they can do to make ends meet, with a middle-class lifestyle in a high-cost city like San Francisco, especially if they have a child in college. The children of people making over $100,000 a year are often given financial aid at many private colleges with high tuition, and some students whose parents have incomes of $200,000 a year can receive need-based financial aid at Yale.[30] People in the top one percent, with incomes approaching $400,000 a year are obviously in a much more comfortable position, but they can hardly afford the lifestyle of the rich and famous, especially if this is an income that they reached only after rising from lower income levels in previous decades. No one with an income of $400,000 is likely to be able to afford their own private plane or luxury yacht, or other status symbols of the rich and famous.

Statistics on wealth, like statistics on income, can be grossly misleading when it is implicitly assumed that either individuals in particular brackets, or families over the generations, are enduring residents in those statistical categories. When these brackets contain an ever-changing mix of people over time, including an ever-changing set of families over the generations, to say that the 400 wealthiest people in the country have X percent of the wealth of that country, or a rising amount or growing share of the wealth of the country, implicitly assumes that these are the same people over the years or the same families over the generations. But this implicit assumption cannot withstand hard evidence. The descendants of extremely wealthy people may well inherit vast sums of money or extremely valuable property, but that is not the same as saying that most of the extremely rich people in the current generation inherited their wealth.

When *Forbes* magazine ran its first annual issue featuring the 400 wealthiest Americans in 1982, these included 14 Rockefellers, 28 du Ponts and 11 Hunts. But nearly four-fifths of the 400 wealthiest

Americans that year earned their fortunes in their own lifetimes. Twenty years later, the *Forbes* list of the 400 richest Americans included 3 Rockefellers, one Hunt and no du Ponts. By 2006 only two percent of the people on that list had inherited their wealth.[31]

The empirical data from a 2015 study, analyzing the changing mix of particular individuals and families among the top 400 wealthiest Americans on the *Forbes* magazine list, showed results that conflicted with Thomas Piketty's conclusion that the rich are getting richer, and wealth more concentrated. Although the amount of wealth required to be on the list of the top 400 wealthiest Americans increased severalfold over time, the 2015 study pointed out that Piketty's claim is invalid because he "naively assumes that it's the same people getting richer."[32] As with income statistics, the fate of abstract categories of wealth statistics is not the same as the fate of a given set of flesh-and-blood human beings.*

The wealthiest people of today are not simply descendants of the wealthiest families of yesterday. Among the heirs of eight historic fortunes of the nineteenth century— including the enormous fortunes of Cornelius Vanderbilt, John Jacob Astor and Andrew Carnegie— not one made it onto any of the *Forbes* magazine lists, over the years, of the 400 richest Americans.[33] Of the people from families on various other lists of Americans with the largest fortunes in 1918, 1930 and 1957, not one of these families was on the list of the top 30 American fortunes in 2014.[34]

Implicit in much discussion of "income distribution" statistics or "wealth concentration" statistics is the notion that certain income brackets or wealth brackets receive not only a rising share of total income or wealth in a country, but do so *at the expense* of lower

---

* While the *Forbes* magazine list of the wealthiest 400 Americans might not unearth 100 percent of the individuals or families in that category, it seems less likely to miss members of famous wealthy old families like the Rockefellers and the Vanderbilts than to miss some little known individual who amassed a fortune in some obscure part of the economy. Therefore, in so far as there might be a statistical bias in the *Forbes* list, it seems more likely to understate how many of the wealthiest 400 Americans earned their own fortunes.

income brackets or lower wealth brackets. That is, "the poor" are made poorer by "the rich" who become richer at their expense, according to this view. Some, such as *Washington Post* columnist Eugene Robinson, have made this claim explicit, as when he said, "The rich are getting richer at the expense not only of the poor but of the middle class as well." These non-"rich" are referred to as "long-suffering victims" of the "upper crust" who have been "waging an undeclared but devastating war" against them.[35]

Mr. Robinson has, however inadvertently, performed a real service by bringing to the surface a widespread undercurrent of confusion that cannot withstand scrutiny in the light of day. We can put aside for the moment his implicit assumption that trends in statistics about income brackets, with their ever-changing mixes of people, are the same as trends about what is happening to given sets of flesh-and-blood human beings called "the rich" and "the poor." We may, for the sake of argument, leave that particular confusion aside, in order to focus attention on the rest of his argument.

Even during periods when a higher share of total income goes to the top income bracket, that does not prevent the real income received in the bottom bracket from rising absolutely. During the period from 1985 through 2001, for example, the income share of the bottom 20 percent of American households declined from 4 percent of all incomes to 3.5 percent of all incomes. But the average real income of households in the bottom 20 percent *rose* by thousands of dollars.[36] This is not even taking into account the well-documented fact that most people initially in the bottom income quintile move up and out of that quintile over a span of years as long as that in this example. But even if they had all stayed put, the rising amount and share of income of "the rich" would still not have made them poorer, as the data show.

The rising absolute real income in the bottom quintile happened over the same years while the number of billionaires was growing—and, according to people like Eugene Robinson, prospering at the expense of the poor, against whom the rich were "waging war." However, since more than half of the households in the bottom 20 percent in income have *no one* working,[37] it is not clear what "the rich" can be taking from those who are producing nothing.

The production so often ignored in discussions of "income distribution" is what enabled people at both the bottom and the top to have rising real incomes simultaneously in a growing economy. But the practice of discussing what is called "income distribution" as if there were some fixed sum that is actually distributed enables people to speak as if there has been a "transfer of income from the low end of the distribution to the high end" in the United States.[38] But, internationally, as well as within the United States, the idea that the rich have gotten richer by making the poor poorer does not square with the hard data.

If "the rich" grew rich by "exploiting" the masses, as in Marxian theory, the median income in countries with many billionaires should be lower than in countries with few billionaires. Yet hard data show the opposite. Poverty-stricken Africa, with a population several times that of the United States, has only a fraction of the number of American billionaires. In fact, Africa and the Middle East combined had only one-sixth as many billionaires as the United States, as of 2016.[39] Germany, with a population only one-fourth that of the United States, nevertheless has more billionaires than all of Africa and the Middle East combined.[40] The Leninist version of Marxian theory is that the rich nations exploit the poor nations. But most of the investment made by rich countries is in other rich countries, with poor countries receiving very small shares.

PERSPECTIVES ON DISPARITIES

Understanding the basic facts about income and wealth differences is necessary, but not by itself sufficient. Much depends on what is presupposed as causes of those differences. Large divergences from an even or random set of outcomes are regarded by many as signs of something strange, if not sinister. But this is something to be investigated, rather than presupposed. Some see a moral significance in income and wealth differences, and seek to create "social justice." That too needs to be investigated, for its internal logic, as well as in the light of external evidence.

The Randomness Assumption

With very few of the factors that facilitate the creation of economic production being equally available to all— either among nations or within nations— it is hard to understand how the expectation of equality in economic outcomes has acquired such a fierce hold on contemporary thinking that income inequalities— "disparities," "gaps" or "inequities"— are taken as being at least strange, if not sinister. But gross inequalities in outcomes are rampant in all kinds of human endeavors around the world, including those that can hardly be explained by discrimination, exploitation or the many other sins of human beings. Those sins are real, but their *moral* significance does not automatically make them *causal* factors of the same significance in economic outcomes. That is an important empirical question, though one seldom addressed by moral crusaders.

Because the implicit assumption that even or random outcomes are natural is so widespread, and so consequential in its economic, moral, political and even legal implications, it is an assumption that needs to be examined at some length and confronted with many facts about many different kinds of human endeavors. As we have seen in earlier chapters, geographic, demographic and cultural factors behind the creation of wealth are often grossly unequal, including even such simple but economically important factors as skills and honesty. More fundamentally, people in general do not behave randomly but *purposefully.* They do not, for example, immigrate randomly, either in terms of the locations they come from in the countries they leave or in terms of the locations where they settle in the countries they go to. They do not raise their children the same, as shown by the large differences in the number of words people at different socioeconomic levels speak to their children.

Purposeful human activities are seldom random in themselves or in their consequences. Nor are they the same among different groups, whether different by race, sex, religion, birth order or innumerable other variables.

Differences in achievements can be extreme, not only in economic endeavors but in all sorts of other endeavors, from the most mundane to the most exalted. An international study of widely recognized European historic figures in the arts and sciences, from the beginning of the fifteenth century through the middle of the twentieth century, found their geographic origins highly concentrated in particular places. Thus "80 percent of all the European significant figures can be enclosed in an area that does *not* include Russia, Sweden, Norway, Finland, Spain, Portugal, the Balkans, Poland, Hungary, East and West Prussia, Ireland, Wales, most of Scotland, the lower quarter of Italy, and about a third of France."[41]

In the United States, that same study— *Human Accomplishment* by Charles Murray— found that about half of the significant American individuals in the arts and sciences, from the time of the founding of the republic to the middle of the twentieth century, were concentrated in an arc extending from Portland, Maine, to the southern tip of New Jersey. The New England states plus New York, Pennsylvania and New Jersey produced more than *seven times* the number of significant American figures in the arts and sciences as did the thirteen states that had formed the Confederacy during the Civil War. Most of those Southern states had none at all, with Virginia being a notable exception.[42]

Similar extreme disparities have been found in individual accomplishments in sports.

Among professional golfers who had survived to the final two rounds of a Professional Golfers Association (PGA) tournament, there was a rough approximation of a normal bell curve when it came to such individual aspects of golf as the average number of putts per round of play or driving distances off the tee.[43] But there was a radically skewed distribution of results when it came to the ultimate test of the *combinations* of the various golf skills, namely winning PGA tournaments. Even among the above average group of professional golfers who had survived to the final two rounds of a PGA tournament, 53 percent never won a single PGA tournament in their entire careers. Among the 47 percent who did win a PGA tournament, almost all won just one, two or three over the course of a lifetime.[44] But Arnold Palmer, Jack Nicklaus and Tiger Woods each won dozens of PGA tournaments, and more than 200 among the three of them.[45]

There have been similarly very skewed distributions among winners of Grand Slam titles in tennis, batting championships in baseball and winners of points in world chess championships.[46] Of the 100 top-ranked marathon runners in the world in 2012, 68 were Kenyans.[47] When two American boys whose ancestors came from India tied for first place in the U.S. National Spelling Bee in 2014, it was the seventh consecutive year in which the Spelling Bee was won by an Indian American. Indian Americans had also won twelve of the previous sixteen.[48] During the twentieth century, there were eight times when a major league baseball player stole 100 bases or more in a season. All eight times, that player was black.[49]

The same skewed distribution is found among recipients of academic degrees. As of the early twenty-first century, every justice of the U.S. Supreme Court had a degree from one of the eight Ivy League institutions in the northeast, out of the thousands of American colleges and universities across the country. Moreover, at the beginning of the twenty-first century, not one of the nine Supreme Court justices was Protestant, in a country where Protestants are the largest religious denomination.

Among people who earned a Bachelor's degree in the United States in academic year 2011–2012, nearly four-fifths of those with degrees in education were women and nearly four-fifths of those with degrees in engineering were men.[50] Although blacks greatly outnumber

Asians in the American population, and slightly outnumber them among recipients of Bachelor's degrees, Asians received more than twice as many Bachelor's degrees in engineering as blacks.[51] The disparity is even greater at the top engineering schools, where Asians have outnumbered blacks by three-to-one at M.I.T., ten-to-one at Harvey Mudd College and by forty-to-one at Cal Tech.[52] But even the extreme disparity at Cal Tech was not half as large as the disparity between Chinese and Malays earning engineering degrees in Malaysia during the 1960s. During that decade, students from the Chinese minority earned just over a hundred times as many engineering degrees as students from the Malay majority[53]— in a country where the Malays control both the universities and the government that sets university policies.

Examples of such gross disparities in innumerable human endeavors could be extended almost indefinitely, just counting those where the circumstances virtually preclude discrimination, such as American men being struck by lightning several times as often as American women, or politically dominant majorities in many countries being outperformed both educationally and economically by subordinate minorities.[54]

Something as simple as giving names to cities and states has not been random in the United States. Instead, there has been a pattern in which the proportion of particular kinds of names differs east of the Mississippi from the pattern west of the Mississippi. This difference reflects the different times at which different places were being settled and named, as the country expanded from east to west over the centuries, while the orientation of the people themselves gradually changed from the Old World— the Eastern Hemisphere— to the New World.

The early settlers in the New England colonies gave many communities that they founded there names taken from the names of communities in England, from which they came— Boston, Cambridge, Plymouth, Greenwich, Manchester, Portsmouth, Northampton, and Milford, for example. Other places in the northeastern United States were also named for places in England, some with the word "New" simply being added to the familiar names of English communities, such as the cities of New London, Connecticut, and New York City, as well as the states of New York, New Jersey and New Hampshire. Other eastern states were named for English royalty, such as Georgia for King George II, the Carolinas for King Charles I, Maryland for his wife Queen Henrietta Maria, and Virginia for Elizabeth I, the virgin queen.

The Welsh who settled in parts of Pennsylvania created communities there with such Welsh names as Bryn Mawr, Haverford, Radnor, and Merion. The entire region of the United States east of the Mississippi River abounded with names taken from the Old World or Eastern Hemisphere. These names included not only names taken from places in England, such as Birmingham and Oxford, but also the largest city in Louisiana being named for the city of Orleans in France. Other names from the Eastern Hemisphere were derived from the names of historic places in classical antiquity, such as Rome, Athens, Bethlehem, Alexandria, Syracuse, Toledo, Memphis, Cairo, and Ithaca. The early Dutch settlement in Manhattan was named New Amsterdam and a section of Manhattan was named for the Dutch city of Haarlem.

As the country expanded westward beyond the Mississippi River, however, such Eastern Hemisphere names became less common, as more cities began to be named for American heroes such as Houston and Austin in Texas and Lincoln, Nebraska, while other names derived from indigenous American Indian languages became more common in the names of states such as the Dakotas, Wyoming and Oklahoma. Of the 25 states with Indian-derived names, 15 are states west of the Mississippi River[55] (itself an Indian-derived name). Spanish names of cities are common in the southwest and along the west coast— El Paso, San Antonio, San Diego, Los Angeles, San Jose and San Francisco, for example— in territory taken over from Mexico.

As the country was expanding westward from the earliest eastern seaboard settlements, the social and cultural focus of Americans was increasingly in their own country, as the era when the people were largely offshoots of European societies receded into the past. The naming of cities and states was never random but showed a pattern reflecting the changing orientation of the people, as of the times when these places were settled.

Despite these and many other examples of outcomes in many different kinds of human endeavors that are remote from an even or random distribution, in situations where discrimination can be ruled out, the implicit assumption persists that uneven or non-random outcomes are strange and suspicious. Moreover, these are not just casual opinions. They are conclusions that have carried great weight in courts of law, in cases involving "disparate impact" statistics, which show demographic "under-representation" of particular groups that are very different from what would be expected by random chance. Among the intelligentsia in the media, or even in academia, such statistics are often treated as virtually proof of discrimination. Thus this implicit *assumption* of evenness or randomness repeatedly trumps innumerable contrary *facts* showing grossly uneven and non-random outcomes from all sorts of purposeful human endeavors. Moreover, serious laws and policies are based on these assumptions in defiance of facts.

Redistributionists seldom, if ever, offer a principled criterion by which current inequalities might be judged. Few today are prepared to say that there should be absolute equality of income or wealth, but they seldom offer more than ad hoc pronouncements that current inequalities are "too much."

Perhaps the closest they come to some principle is that current inequalities are greater than the inequalities in some other time or place. But this offers no principle on which to choose a particular time or place to serve as a standard for judging other times and places. Moreover, the ignored production processes change over time, making different mixes of skills and talents more in demand than before and others less in demand than before, requiring different patterns of pay as incentives to attract people with the currently more valued qualifications. An obvious example of such changes has been the reduced value of physical strength, as machine power has in many cases replaced human muscle, thereby making the male worker's advantage in physical strength less relevant, reducing the pay gap between the sexes, even before there were equal pay laws.

To say that pay differences between people at the top and people at the bottom have increased over the years means something very different when these are differences between classes than when these are differences between people in different age brackets. When some people are in the bottom quintile for life and others are in the top quintile for life, that is a very different situation from one in which most people move from one quintile to another within a decade. Only 11 percent of Americans 25 years old have been in a household within the top 20 percent of household incomes. But 70 percent of Americans 60 years old have been in such a household at some point in their lives.[56] Since every 60-year-old was once a 25-year-old, increased income differences between age brackets are hardly an injustice to Americans who live out a normal life span.

Increased income differences between those at the top and those at the bottom may in some (or most) situations reflect a greater demand for particular skills relative to unskilled and inexperienced labor, or a greater demand for financial expertise relative to personnel department experience, for example. Increased income disparities may also reflect the fact that an increasing proportion of the population can live without working, or with only sporadic or part-time work, thanks to the many in-kind benefits available from the welfare state. These in-kind benefits *are not counted* in income statistics, even though the value of these benefits— ranging from subsidized housing to medical care— exceeds the recorded money income of people in the bottom 20 percent of income recipients.[57]

In short, income statistics greatly overstate differences in standards of living between people in different income brackets, because income data are reported before taxes, paid largely by upper-income people, and before massive transfers of in-kind benefits, which are an especially large part of the standard of living of those in the lower income brackets.

Not all differences in income are due to age or welfare, of course. But whatever these differences are due to, the changing requirements of the production process imply that there is no reason why a particular pattern of income or wealth differences from a particular time or place should remain unchanged, or serve as a benchmark for people living in other times and places, which may require different incentives to attract people to particular occupations with changing productivities relative to one another. This is especially so when income bracket differences are by no means the same as differences between different social classes.

What usually gets ignored, or at best downplayed, in many laments about income disparities between those at the top and those at the bottom is *production*. When *A* makes a thousand times the income of *B*, the question is seldom asked, much less answered, as to whether *A* produced a thousand times the value produced by *B*. As Stephen Moore pointed out in his book, *Who's the Fairest of Them All?*:

> The fact that Bill Gates and Steve Jobs made billions of dollars in income— more than some whole societies make— has on paper made America a more unequal society. But is the middle class better or worse off for Microsoft and Apple products? Should we curse the invention of the personal computer that is now in nearly every home in America simply because it made these men unthinkably wealthy? Since hundreds of millions of people buy their products willingly, it would seem self-evident that Mr. Gates and Mr. Jobs generated a better world for everyone, not just themselves.[58]

After the voluntary purchases of millions of people put a value on what has been produced, and thus put a value on the income of those who produced it, to then seek a "redistribution" of income or wealth is to say that some third party is to be given the power to override the decisions of millions of other people as to those values— and to do so in the name of equality, despite the gross inequality of power that such a redistribution would require. Moreover, unlike economic inequalities, which are compatible with rising standards of living for all, a concentration of power, which is inherently relative, means that an increase of power for some means a loss of freedom for others— the latter usually being a far larger number of people.

The concentration of power being sought by redistributionists is usually as completely ignored as the productivity differences behind differences in income and wealth. Indeed, a whole vocabulary of camouflage words obscures the concentration of power involved. Thus Professor John Rawls, for example, refers repeatedly to how "society" should "arrange" certain economic outcomes,[59] when only the *government* has the power to *force* millions of people to accept a third party's overriding of the transactions terms agreed to by transactors dealing directly with each other. This overriding of transactions terms may be done either directly or by confiscating a portion of the earnings of whoever's income is deemed to be "too much" by third parties.

The very phrase "income distribution" contributes to the camouflage. Most income in a market economy is not *distributed* at all. It is *earned* individually by millions of people, who are paid directly by millions of other people for goods and services received. In a market economy, there is no central repository of income or wealth from which individual incomes are doled out by someone exercising that power, though that is done in the welfare state portion of a society. One may speak metaphorically of income being "distributed" in some purely statistical sense, as the heights of individuals are distributed in the same statistical sense, with a certain portion of the population being five foot two and others being six foot one, four foot ten and so on. But no one imagines that those heights are initially gathered in some central place and then handed out to individuals.

Why do such semantic issues matter? Because those who seek to concentrate in government officials the power to override the terms of millions of individual transactions prefer to depict this as simply a question of replacing the current "income distribution" X with an alternative "income distribution" Y. But the real difference is between allowing millions of people to make transactions with each other, on such terms as are mutually agreeable, versus having third parties armed with the power of government to impose such terms as the third parties choose to impose.

Many redistributionists glide over the issue of concentrating more power in government by speaking, as philosopher Thomas Nagel did, when he referred to "equalities of an economic nature" such as "the equal apportionment of benefits."[60] Most economic benefits in most modern societies are not *apportioned* at all, whether equally or unequally. They are *earned* directly from those who purchase goods or services from stores, from employees or professional service providers or from manufacturers of industrial products. Those who would prefer a radically different process, one in which a concentration of power in government allows politicians and/or bureaucrats to determine the economic fate of millions of citizens, can argue directly for that change in the whole economic process— instead of camouflaging that change as simply a substitution, *somehow*, of income distribution *Y* for income distribution *X*. Taking away the freedom of millions of human beings is too serious to be camouflaged verbally.

Freedom, like money, is valuable— and, like money, it can be counterfeited. What Woodrow Wilson called a "new freedom"[61] was in fact simply a redefinition of the word, calling some government-supplied things, such as regulations or economic transfers, more "freedom" for the beneficiaries. Far from meaning what freedom had meant for centuries— exemption from the power of others— this new conception of freedom, which has become more widespread among the intelligentsia since President Wilson's time, has become in the United States one of the prime means of expanding the power of the federal government over individuals, private institutions and state and local governments.

By absorbing through taxation a greatly increased share of the nation's income, and then dispensing or withholding vast sums of this money at its own discretion, the federal government has extended its power over more decisions made by many more individuals and institutions than those subject to its power under the limitations of the Constitution. This expansion of government power is a contraction of freedom for those subject to that power. Hence the need for those who favor more expansive government to redefine "freedom" to include government-provided benefits as a "new freedom." As just one example of the expansion of federal government control far beyond its Constitutional limits, the ability of local public schools to discipline unruly and disruptive students has been greatly reduced by federal guidelines, backed by the threat of a loss of federal subsidies if those guidelines are not followed.

Those who favor such expansions of federal power extend well beyond the politicians who benefit directly, and include income redistributionists. In Professor Angus Deaton's *The Great Escape*, for example, he declared: "In this book, when I speak of freedom, it is the freedom to live a good life and to do the things that make life worth living. The absence of freedom is poverty, deprivation, and poor health— long the lot of much of humanity, and still the fate of an outrageously high proportion of the world today."[62] What this redefinition of freedom accomplishes is to verbally camouflage the trade-off of freedom for various government-provided benefits, by incorporating those benefits within a new, counterfeit definition of freedom that includes a *loss* of freedom.

In other words, the loss of freedom as the reach and power of the government are increasingly extended is an issue kept off the agenda by redefining words. Moreover, government-provided benefits are not *net* benefits to society, because the government simply *transfers* wealth, rather than creating it.

International Economic Disparities

Comparisons of economic disparities between nations can be even more complicated than comparisons of disparities within nations. Moreover, questions of "social justice" have been raised about income and wealth disparities between nations, as similar questions have been raised about economic disparities within nations. In both cases, questions of *causation* must be raised separately from *moral* questions about "social justice." Each set of questions is too important to be confused with the other.

Among nations, as among individuals and groups, there is a fundamental difference between measuring what is happening over time to particular statistical categories and what is happening over time to specific sets of human beings. For example, data from the World Bank show that in 1960 the average per capita income of the 20 nations with the highest incomes per capita was about 23 times the average per capita income of the 20 nations with the lowest incomes per capita— and that this ratio rose to about 36 times as high by the year 2000. This fits the familiar notion of a growing gap between "the rich" and "the poor." But, comparing the *same* set of nations initially in the top and bottom categories, and following those particular nations over the same years, leads to the directly *opposite* conclusion, for the ratio between the per capita incomes of the particular nations initially in each category fell from about 23-to-one to less than 10-to-one.[63]

As for the more general question of the reasons for large economic disparities between nations, genetic determinists offer the simplest answer to that question— namely, that some races are genetically superior and others genetically inferior. But, among the problems with that theory is that the same race— the Chinese, for example— has sometimes been a world leader in many endeavors, for centuries at a time, and then later lagged far behind in those same endeavors, also for centuries at a time. Europeans were likewise laggards for centuries, not only as compared to the Chinese, but also laggards behind the Islamic world and yet, within the past few centuries, Europeans have been in the forefront in science, technology and other fields so pervasively that many act as if Europeans have been world leaders— whether in achievements or wickedness— from time immemorial.

Some other peoples have lagged persistently behind the rest of the world for centuries, without ever having been in the forefront, at least during the millennia for which there has been a recorded history. These include peoples in the Amazon jungle, in much of sub-Saharan Africa and among the indigenous peoples of Australia. Such groups would also include Caucasian inhabitants of the Canary Islands who, at the time of their being conquered in the fifteenth century, lagged far behind the existing technological level of most Europeans, Asians or Africans.

There have been, and to some extent still are, peoples defined not by race but by geographic circumstances, who have persistently lagged behind the progress of the rest of the world. It is hard to think of any fundamental development that advanced the human race which came out of secluded mountain communities, isolated islands or other places where geography impeded access to other peoples— even though the total population of such places around the world is greater than the population of the United States. Although Australia was for millennia the classic example of a continent isolated from other continents, with Australian aborigines being regarded as classic lagging peoples, Charles Darwin's first-hand observation of the aborigines led him to see them as intelligent human beings.

Since there are mountains in Europe, Asia, Africa and the Western Hemisphere, it is striking that there has been a similar pattern of poverty and backwardness, among other social and political similarities, between mountain peoples who were too isolated from each other on different continents to have had any genetic connection during the millennia before the transportation revolutions of the past few centuries.

That particular individuals from poor societies can emigrate and prosper elsewhere, as Nigerians have in the United States, suggests that circumstances rather than genes often account for poverty and backwardness. So too has the worldwide success of such groups as the overseas Chinese and the overseas Indians, even during eras when their native lands have been among the poorest in the world.

Aside from these causal questions, there have also been moral questions raised about international disparities in wealth. One of the moral questions raised by some commentators is why some countries, such as the United States, consume a disproportionate share of the world's wealth. Here, as in other contexts, production fades into the background, and a verbally collectivized "world's wealth" appears, having originated *somehow*, and whose "distribution" is the issue. But the United States, like other countries, essentially produces the amount of output it consumes. Imports are paid for out of American income and wealth, in transactions that are voluntary on both sides, so that what is paid compensates the sellers of these imports, and so is no deduction from the wealth of that country or the wealth of the rest of the world.

Historically, there have of course also been uncompensated transfers of wealth, such as Spain's extraction of vast amounts of gold and silver from its subjugated Western Hemisphere colonies. But, like internal uncompensated transfers through slavery, serfdom and other exploitative systems, these past injustices have usually left the exploiting nations with little or no residue today of wealth acquired in the past and consumed in the past. Uncompensated wealth transfers today are usually from wealthier countries to poorer countries, whether as foreign aid or as remittances from people from poorer countries working in wealthier countries.

Sometimes wealth transferred to foreign investors is depicted as deductions from the national wealth of the country where that wealth was produced. But such investments are usually voluntary transactions that would not have taken place unless both parties expected to benefit from receiving a share in the *increased* production resulting from the investment. Either or both sides can miscalculate in particular cases, but the continuance of international investments suggests that this is not the usual outcome. The payment of a share of the increased wealth created by the investment is no net reduction of the recipient country's wealth, compared to what that wealth would have been without the investment. Nevertheless foreign investments in poor countries have been described by Professor Deaton as money sent "to poor countries to seek profits, not to seek better lives for the locals," often leaving the poor countries with "a legacy of foreign ownership and internal inequality."[64]

In this formulation investors' motives, inequality and foreign ownership are treated as major concerns, rather than the actual effects of foreign investments on the incomes of people living in poor countries. Among the many indications of rising incomes among Third World people working for multinational companies was a 2013 report in *The Economist* magazine, showing that, among employees of foreign companies, "Wages in China and India have been going up by 10–20% a year for the past decade." A decade earlier, "wages in emerging markets were a tenth of their level in the rich world." But between 2001 and 2011, the difference between what computer programmers in India were paid and what computer programmers in the United States were paid constantly narrowed.[65]

Such effects of market competition for workers who have increasing amounts of human capital, gained working in the modern production processes used by multinational companies, remain in the dim background like production in general. Instead, Professor Deaton's focus is on profit-seeking motives and ownership statistics, neither of which necessarily affects the Third World economy adversely, while rising wages are a clear, if unheralded, benefit.

Countries which have confiscated foreign investments— these confiscations often being called "nationalization"— have seldom prospered as a result. In some countries, such as Zimbabwe, the whole economy has collapsed after mass confiscations of foreign investments.[66] What cannot be confiscated is the human capital required to generate, operate, maintain and renew the physical capital as it is used up or wears out. Foreign investments have aided the development of many economies around the world, including some less-developed economies in Asia, whose growth rates increased dramatically in the late twentieth century after they opened their economies to more investment from abroad.

The history of foreign investments in Argentina has been more complicated. Early in the twentieth century, foreign investments were

40 percent of all investments in Argentina. But years of anti-foreign investment political rhetoric and policies, such as that epitomized by the charismatic dictator Juan Perón, reduced the share of foreign investment in Argentina to 5 percent by the 1950s.[67] Over that same span of time, Argentina went from being one of the most prosperous nations in the world to being one of the most economically troubled nations, and it has never recovered the economic standing among the world's nations that it had in the early twentieth century.

Chapter 14

IMPLICATIONS AND PROSPECTS

The study of history is a powerful antidote to contemporary arrogance. It is humbling to discover how many of our glib assumptions, which seem to us novel and plausible, have been tested before, not once but many times and in innumerable guises; and discovered to be, at great human cost, wholly false.

Paul Johnson

Whether trying to understand the present or to foresee or shape the future, facts are necessary but by no means sufficient. There must also be some principles to guide our goals and by which to judge the validity of those goals and the extent to which such goals have been achieved, or can be achieved— and at what cost. It may be easier to gain general agreement on the desirability of increasing the economic prospects of fellow human beings than to gain agreement on what to sacrifice in pursuit of such goals. However desirable a higher Gross Domestic Product per capita might be, few are likely to be willing to achieve that by methods which simply sacrifice some people for the benefit of other people. There are questions of justice to be raised and— hopefully— answered, or at least clarified.

IMPLICATIONS

One of the more heartening implications of our survey of the history of groups, nations and civilizations around the world is how often and how far some poverty-stricken and socially backward peoples have risen, even to the forefront of human achievement. However, this was seldom, if ever, a quick and easy process, or a path equally open to all. The various geographic, demographic, cultural and other factors have made equal chances all but impossible at a given time, though times change and chances change with them, complicating both causal and moral principles.

Some observers have been struck by economic differences between racial or ethnic groups, and from this have concluded that genes are responsible, while others have concluded that racism is responsible. But, where there have been equal or greater economic differences between groups defined by non-racial criteria, then neither of these blanket explanations seems conclusive. The striking similarities among mountain peoples on different continents around the world— and therefore of different races— and the economic and other differences between these mountain peoples in general and their respective lowland compatriots often greatly exceed economic and other differences between races.

Perhaps the most widely accepted, and most politically powerful, explanation of economic disparities in the twentieth century was that the rich exploited the poor. Marxism alone swept many revolutionary movements into political power, and other variations on the theme of exploitation, such as "dependency" theory in Latin America, acquired great political influence on the policies of governments, even where exponents of that theory did not directly seize control of governments themselves. But, again, did people from the lowlands go up into mountains and seize the wealth created by the people there, or did the mountain people simply fail to produce as much in the first place? Have the centuries-long economic disparities between Eastern Europe and Western Europe been a result of Western Europeans seizing wealth produced in Eastern Europe or of Eastern Europeans not producing as much wealth as Western Europeans, for any number of geographic, historic and other reasons?

Among human beings in general, impersonal explanations of economic differences have seldom had the same mass appeal as explanations that involve some people doing other people wrong, whether by depriving them of the fruits of their own labor or by preempting access to paths that would otherwise lead to prosperity and wealth, such as higher education, political influence and others. Given the enormous range of circumstances in places and times around the world, many examples that seem to confirm particular explanations can often be found somewhere, without those explanations being valid in general. Despite the political success in the twentieth century of Marxist theories that the working class has been made poor as a result of their being exploited by capitalists, it would be difficult to find an example where working-class people had as high a standard of living in a Communist country as that of working-class people in a number of capitalist countries.

While many beliefs cannot survive a thorough examination of facts, there are also moral considerations which require considerations that extend beyond facts, though these considerations cannot defy both facts and logic without becoming simply arbitrary dogmas. One of the dominant moral concerns of our times has been what is called "social justice."

"Social Justice"

Perhaps the best-known contemporary exposition of moral principles relevant to differences in income and wealth has been that in John Rawls' influential treatise *A Theory of Justice*. Professor Rawls' conception of "social justice" in the economy is that "those who are at the same level of talent and ability, and have the same willingness to use them, should have the same prospects of success regardless of their initial place in the social system, that is, irrespective of the income class into which they are born."[1]

Perhaps few Americans or other Western peoples would object to this ideal, even if they might disagree as to how or whether it can be put into practice. However, that ideal is almost immediately modified by Rawls, with the proviso that "the advantages of persons with greater natural endowments are to be limited to those that further the good of the poorer sectors of society."[2] That is because "Justice is prior to efficiency," according to Rawls,[3] and differences in natural ability are as undeserved, and therefore as unjust, as being born an heir to a fortune.

To say, as Rawls does, that unjust rewards may be tolerated only to the extent necessary to benefit people in "the poorer sectors of society," raises both factual and moral issues. As we have seen, the poorer sectors of American society, as defined by income, are a transient group disproportionately of the younger and less experienced workers, and no one remains younger for life. Among that small proportion— 5 percent— of those in the bottom income quintile who remain there over the years, while the other 95 percent of those initially in that quintile move on up, it cannot be arbitrarily assumed that this unusual fate can have nothing to do with the way they have chosen to live their lives.

To say, as Rawls does, that morally nothing should be done to benefit the rest of society if it does not also help those at the bottom can amount to enshrining a veto on progress, on behalf of those with a counterproductive lifestyle, unless that lifestyle is subsidized still further. Many conclusions that might make sense in a world of predestination do not make sense in a world that includes individual choices. That such choices may be influenced by past social conditions does not mean that they cannot also be influenced by current rewards or penalties for current or future conduct— especially when these rewards include non-judgmental subsidies of counterproductive behavior.

Our survey of peoples and places around the world in earlier chapters, in search of reasons for disparities in income and wealth— whether between nations or within nations— has been, implicitly, a search for reasons behind differences in *productivity*. Others who are more interested in redistributing incomes and wealth often leave the *production* of these incomes and this wealth somewhere in the dim background. By pushing the production process off into the background, redistributionists avoid confronting the question whether income inequalities might be matched by corresponding inequalities in economic productivity.

What redistributionists seek to suggest, or to proclaim, is the injustice of existing rewards, given that so much of what a given individual receives originated in some windfall gain or windfall loss, of which "the accident of birth" is central. In short, redistributionists seek to judge merit, more so than productivity— or even in some cases to the exclusion of productivity, given the Rawlsian principle that justice is more important than economic efficiency. Professor Thomas Piketty offers a slight variation on this Rawlsian theme by saying that "if inequality is due, at least in part, to factors beyond the control of individuals, such as inequality of initial endowments owing to inheritance or luck (which cannot be attributed to individual effort), then it is just for the state to seek in the most efficient way possible to improve the lot of the least well-off (that is, of those who have had to contend with the most adverse factors)."[4]

Professor Piketty rightly says that this represents "a certain consensus" as regards "the fundamental principles of social justice"[5]— which makes it all the more important to examine the logic and implicit assumptions behind that consensus. Like so many things said by redistributionists, Piketty's argument puts a burden of proof on only one side. That is, the heir must establish that he deserves his inheritance— and forfeits his claim if even a significant *part* of his inheritance is not due to his own efforts— but "the state" need establish *nothing whatever* to justify confiscating what the original owner intended to leave to his heir. Nor need the state establish any basis for assuming that putting the property in question in the hands of politicians or bureaucrats will serve the interests of "social justice"— however defined— rather than the political interests of government officials.

As with many other redistributionist arguments, production remains in the dim background, except for an incidental proviso by Professor Piketty that the property confiscated by the government be used "in the most efficient way possible." But there is not even a pretense of an argument that politicians or bureaucrats will be more efficient than the designated heir— or the free market in which the heir may choose to sell his inheritance. Moreover, arbitrarily limiting questions of efficiency to events subsequent to the death of the original owner ignores the fact that one of the incentives for the creation of inherited wealth in the first place may well have been a desire to leave something behind for one's family and loved ones. Once that hope is jeopardized or thwarted, the incentives to produce and to save seem unlikely to remain the same.

Such philosophic arguments for "social justice" are not fundamentally different from common political rhetoric which says to business owners "You didn't create that!" because a business was not 100 percent due to the unaided efforts of its founder. In both cases, there is the same asymmetric burden of proof, where the owner must prove everything and the prospective government confiscator must prove nothing.

Similarly, Piketty simply assumes that those at the bottom of the income pyramid are there due to having to contend with "the most adverse" conditions— when in fact many, and perhaps most, are there because they are young and inexperienced, a condition usually remedied by the passage of time. The desire to earn higher rewards by developing one's own human capital seems unlikely to be as effective when young people are rewarded with unearned transfers of money or in-kind benefits from what others have produced. Moreover, redistributionists in general tend to act as if social policy decisions are to focus on the redress of past unfairness, rather than on the incentive effects of those decisions on future productivity.

Nevertheless, in some contexts we can use the criteria of "social justice" advocates, for the sake of argument. Imagine a man who was born to parents who were not merely poor but alcoholic, irresponsible and neglectful or abusive toward their children. For such an individual, born in such a family, to somehow have wrenched himself away from the culture of such an environment and become a very decent and hard-working man, acquiring a skill such as carpentry to support himself and his family, whom he treats far better than he was treated as a child, would certainly be a meritorious achievement.

Imagine now a different man born in very different circumstances, to loving and caring parents, raised in an affluent or wealthy home, with all the advantages that social position can confer, in terms of private education and a wider cultural exposure. For such a man to go on to become a brain surgeon would certainly be commendable, but by no means necessarily more of a meritorious achievement than that of the carpenter.

In a world where rewards were based solely on merit, there would be no obvious reason to pay the brain surgeon any more than the carpenter was paid. But, in a world where *productivity* matters, this is no longer simply a question of the relative merits of individuals. Merit-based "social justice" to particular income recipients must be weighed against the well-being of all the people in the society who stand to benefit from what they produce. Introducing *production* into the discussion makes a crucial difference. It is now a question of the relative urgency of brain surgery and carpentry, and of providing incentives for young people of high ability— however acquired— to choose the long and challenging preparation to become brain surgeons out of the many options they have, however unjust it may be that some people have so many more options than others have.

Instead of limiting ourselves to weighing the relative economic fates of particular individuals or groups as income recipients, a discussion of the goods and services *produced* by those individuals or groups weighs as well the fate of those other members of society at large who benefit from the goods and services produced by those who are the sole or primary focus of income redistributionists.

To call the fate of consumers of goods and services a matter of "efficiency," while calling the fate of those who receive incomes for producing those goods and services a matter of "social justice"— and then making "social justice" *categorically* more important than "efficiency," as Rawls does[6]— is to make a distinction without a difference. If income is redistributed in a way that reduces efficiency, which is what makes the distinction relevant, then the economic losses of some as consumers have simply and arbitrarily been declared to be less important than the economic gains of others from "social justice." But what is an injustice, if not an undeserved cost of some sort inflicted on people? It is hard to see how an undeserved cost inflicted on people in their role as consumers is morally different from an undeserved cost inflicted on people in their role as income recipients.

On the international stage as well, preoccupation with "social justice," defined as reductions of income and wealth gaps between nations, ignores the distinction— and the trade-off— between reducing these gaps and reducing poverty. Game theorist Herman Kahn presented the distinction incisively back in the 1970s:

> The increasing disparity between average incomes in the richest and poorest nations is usually seen as an unalloyed evil to be overcome as rapidly as possible through enlightened policies by the advanced nations and international organizations. If this occurred because the poor were getting poorer, we would agree, but when it occurs at all, it is almost always because the rich are getting richer. This is not necessarily a bad thing for the poor, at least if they compare themselves with their own past or their own present rather than with a mythical theoretical gap.[7]

Between nations, as within nations, we must consider the *production* that often gets left in the dim background by redistributionists. The benefits of economic advances made by the more fortunate nations are by no means confined to the more fortunate nations themselves. The increased output they produce, or simply improve qualitatively, or make more available quantitatively by lower prices reflecting lower costs of production as efficiency increases, affects consumers around the world.

Medical advances produced in the more prosperous nations save lives in the poorer nations. The percentage decline in mortality rates and the percentage increases in longevity have been greater in the poorer nations.[8] Medical advances benefit people in their role as patients— in other words, as consumers rather than producers or income recipients. But this does not make such benefits axiomatically less important than benefits to them in their role as income recipients, despite the Rawlsian arbitrary priority to the contrary, based on pronouncing "efficiency" to be less important than "justice."

There is a crucial difference, in the real world, between saying that justice is very desirable and saying that it is categorically preemptive. On a sinking ship, with more passengers than life preservers, the only truly just solution available is that everyone drowns. But most of us might prefer the unjust solution that as many lives as possible be saved, even if those saved are no more deserving than those who perish. We might prefer that outcome, even if we knew that those saved in the panic and chaos of the situation were likely to be the strongest, most ruthless and most calloused. Abstract principles can often conflict with a sense of common humanity in the real world. The history of what has happened in places and times where an abstract principle— whether of justice, religion or ideology— has triumphed over a sense of common humanity is a history often written in blood and punctuated by horrors.

Much of what is called "social justice" extends beyond what any society actually controls. It might more aptly be called *cosmic* justice, the kind of justice we might want if we were creating our own universe. But, in a universe that was here long before our remotest ancestors arrived on the scene, and in societies that evolved for millennia before we were born, we are, as it were, entering the game very late in the game, and what has already happened is irrevocable. The score can be changed, as it has changed before, but we cannot proceed as if we were present at the beginning. The quest for cosmic justice can be another example of the best being the enemy of the good, when pursuing the unattainable can forfeit much progress and happiness, and inflict needless suffering— as has already happened in too many times and places.

"Solutions"

One of the difficulties with trying to create "solutions" is the uncertainty of defining what is a "problem." When *A* and *B* make a transaction between themselves that *C* does not like, is that a problem to be solved?

A and *B* may be employer and employee, landlord and tenant or lender and borrower. No doubt each of the primary parties to any of these transactions would prefer terms more favorable to himself or herself, but the transactions would not have taken place unless at least one, and probably both, were willing to accept something less than they might hope for.

But many among the intelligentsia press for government to "do something" about transactions terms that the parties themselves have agreed to, this call for government intervention often being based on ideas similar to those expressed by John Rawls in *A Theory of Justice*. However, the question must be raised as to the basis for arming intellectual coteries with the massive powers of government to forcibly undo economic transactions terms made by millions of people intimately familiar with their own individual circumstances and alternatives, in a way that distant intellectuals or government functionaries cannot possibly be familiar.

What if those millions of people do not share Rawls' notion that justice is more important than efficiency? Indeed, if any two things each have some value, one cannot be *categorically* more valuable than the other, as Rawls claims.[9] A diamond may be worth far more than a penny, but enough pennies will be worth more than any diamond.

Comfortable academics on ivy-covered campuses may be able to afford a preoccupation with statistical patterns and a preference for income numbers that fit their preconceptions. But that is very different from saying that people mired in poverty— genuine poverty, perhaps in the Third World— are wrong to welcome some billionaire investor who wants to set up a factory near them that will provide jobs enabling them to give their families things they have never been able to afford before,* just because that billionaire's investment will also make him richer than before, to the discomfort of those reading statistics on distant academic campuses or in distant editorial offices.

Those among the intelligentsia and other "social justice" advocates may prefer a statistically more equal society to a more prosperous society, even one that is better able to subsidize the poor. But, while that is the right of those who hold such views, it is also the right of others, including low-income people, to prefer a more prosperous society. If the aversion of the intelligentsia to the level of inequality in the United States were shared by the poor in other countries, it would be hard to account for the long-standing, massive and sometimes desperate efforts of poor immigrants from around the world to reach America.

The very idea that millions of fellow human beings must be forced to arrange themselves in a tableau** pleasing to a relative handful of intellectuals or politicians is not only grotesque in itself, but still more amazing as part of a claim of higher morality, equality or humanitarianism under the name of "social justice." Nor does the actual track record of intellectuals in many other aspects of life inspire general confidence in either their assumptions or their conclusions.***

---

* Multinational corporations typically pay higher wages than local employers in the Third World.
** Often what is sought is symbolic conformity to a preconception, regardless of what the human reality may be. Thus, for example, a school may be racially "integrated," in a symbolic sense, if it presents a tableau of black and white students attending the same school, even if they are not only socially separate within the school but mutually hostile.
*** It was, after all, not the unwashed masses but exquisitely educated intellectuals who urged Western democracies to disarm in the 1930s, while Hitler was building a massive war machine in Germany and while imperial Japan was doing the same in Asia. Back in the seventeenth century, most of the judges who condemned 20 people to death for witchcraft in Salem had been educated at Harvard. In the twentieth century, it was the triumph of the intellectuals' social vision in America during the 1960s that was followed by sharp reversals of long downward trends in murder rates and in rates of venereal diseases and teenage pregnancy in the population at large, as well as the disintegration of two-parent black families, which had been the norm for a hundred years after slavery, but not after 30 years following the expanded welfare state of the 1960s. This list could be extended almost indefinitely.

One of the reasons for paying people for their productivity, rather than their merits, is that productivity is far easier to determine than merit. This is especially so in a market economy, where the value of what is produced is judged by whoever chooses to buy it and use it. Few can have anything approaching a comparable knowledge or understanding of someone else's merit, especially when they have not "walked in his shoes."

This, of course, does not mean that nothing whatever should be done to widen the options of those born into less fortunate circumstances, and who consequently have had fewer options for developing their productivity. Indeed, there has never been a time in the entire history of the United States when nothing whatever was being done for such people. American society is one where major voluntary philanthropy has been going on for centuries. The United States has been, and is, unique in the extent to which private philanthropy has created schools, libraries, scholarships, colleges, foundations, hospitals and other civic institutions that are elsewhere provided by government or by religious organizations.

Nor have all contributions been in money. Vast amounts of time have been donated to many civic causes, including those aimed at extending the options available to the less fortunate. The thousands of whites from the North who went into the South after the Civil War, to teach the children of newly freed slaves in private institutions established by philanthropists, were a classic example. These teachers, usually young women, braved nearly impossible conditions, including the hostility of Southern white society, from which they were often ostracized and sometimes threatened, and many utterly unprepared black students, handicapped both by the experience of slavery and by the general Southern culture in which education was by no means a high priority. W.E.B. Du Bois called the work of these white volunteers from the North the "finest thing in American history."[10]

Much of such philanthropic activity as this is ignored by those who largely ignore productivity in general, whether economically or socially motivated productivity. But such voluntary civic-minded activities cannot be taken as given, natural or something that just happens *somehow*. It differs as greatly as the economic production that is so often also treated as something that just happens *somehow*, in disregard of how very differently it happens in different places and times, with correspondingly different effects on people's standards of living. But such civic-minded activities do *not* occur equally in all societies around the world, or even to the same extent throughout Western civilization.

Nineteenth century French visitor Alexis de Tocqueville was struck by the extent of voluntary civic activities among Americans, as he reported in his classic, *Democracy in America*.[11] But distinguished American scholar Edward C. Banfield found no such widespread attitudes or practices in the Italian mountain village where he stayed in the middle of the twentieth century, where "some find the idea of public-spiritedness unintelligible." No one would "lift a finger to assist a nun carrying a heavy burden to the orphanage at the top of the mountain," and though the local monastery was crumbling, "none of the many half-employed stone masons has ever given a day's work to its repair."[12]

A twenty-first century study of Russian society likewise found very little civic-mindedness, or even organized voluntary social activities in general, as compared to the United States. This study of "non-governmental associations" in 60 countries found that "Russia's best ranking was in sports and recreation, where the country rose as far as 9th from the very bottom." In that category, "nearly 4% of the adults surveyed said they were involved in a sports club or some other athletic voluntary association." But fewer than 2 percent were involved in voluntary social welfare activities to help others.

Among Americans, the study found that "participation is roughly ten times higher in sports and social welfare organizations; roughly twenty times higher in environmental, religious, and professional organizations; roughly thirty times higher in cultural/educational and women's organizations, and roughly fifty times higher in human rights organizations."[13]

The limiting factor in the success of efforts to raise the educational and economic levels of those born into less fortunate circumstances can be the degree of *receptivity* of many of the people born and raised in a culture that does not provide them with the same desire, habits or discipline required to make the most of expanded opportunities that some other groups have. Here the leadership of lagging groups is often a major impediment to those groups' advancement, since such leaders have every incentive to promote a vision in which the group's problems are caused primarily, if not exclusively, by the sins of other people. What incentive is that to engage in the arduous process of trying to change oneself by abandoning the habits and values acquired early in life?

Although isolation is a major handicap, creating or perpetuating poverty and backwardness, ethnic leaders have every incentive to keep their followers isolated from other peoples and cultures. Nor does this have to be strictly a matter of cynical calculation, since the extraordinary ability of the human mind to rationalize has been demonstrated in many ways and on many occasions. The great eighteenth century philosopher David Hume could urge his fellow Scots to learn English precisely because his career was *not* that of an ethnic leader. When you want to help people, you tell them the truth. When you want to help yourself, you tell them what they want to hear. People with careers as ethnic leaders usually tell their followers what they want to hear.

Those who have promoted the prevailing social vision, in which lags, gaps or disparities to the detriment of black people are the fault of white people, are trapped in the corollary that these lags, gaps or disparities should disappear, once those other people are constrained by civil rights laws and policies. But nothing of the sort has happened in the wake of the civil rights revolution of the 1960s. However dramatic the increase of black political representation at local and national levels, there were no correspondingly dramatic reductions in economic disparities. Economic progress continued, but the rise out of poverty was not at as fast a pace as in the years *preceding* the civil rights revolution of the 1960s.[14]

This leaves those who cling to the prevailing vision little alternative but to claim that even an absence of concrete evidence that continuing black lags, gaps or disparities can be traced to what others are doing to them only shows that these continuing gaps must be due to the diabolical cleverness with which "covert" or "institutional" racism has been concealed. When an absence of tangible evidence is assumed to prove the same proposition that tangible evidence would also prove, that is essentially an arbitrary heads-I-win-and-tails-you-lose argument. But, given the initial premises of those who are driven to this desperate expedient, genetic determinism might seem to loom in the background. Hence the fierce but strained and unconvincing attempts to come up with alternative explanations.

A more realistic set of initial assumptions, rather than the prevailing civil rights vision, could have spared those who argue this way from having painted themselves into a corner, where they have had to resort to such strained and unconvincing claims. The economic gap between Eastern Europeans and Western Europeans is greater than the economic gap between blacks and whites in America[15]— and has persisted for centuries, even though Western Europeans have been in no position to thwart the economic rise of Eastern Europeans. Yet those who expected blacks to rise to parity with whites in a few decades had obviously left many things out of their calculations.

Given the specific historical circumstances of American blacks, their record has by no means been something calling for some esoteric apologetics or blame-shifting. As a white Southern scholar observed in the early twentieth century, "no race has come further against greater handicaps." A race "peremptorily shorn of its cultural heritage, became in three generations" a group "substantially comparable to the peasant classes of our western culture." The failure to advance further at that time "may be due mainly to contacts restricted by inescapable physical stigmata"— that is, social isolation based on color. Though "limited in cultural opportunities, encircled by race prejudice as by a barrier of fire, the Negro's rise to partial land ownership, to industrial position, and to a modicum of success in the arts and sciences is frankly a notable achievement for any race."[16]

This was said at a time when most black adults had only an elementary school education, and in inferior Southern schools at that. Whatever may be said about the pace of black progress in the first hundred years after slavery, that progress was not marred by the kinds of stark and tragic, nationwide retrogressions* in behavior that set in among lower-class blacks in the 1960s and then spread to others. The unwillingness to acknowledge these internal retrogressions, much less try to deal with them, makes the further progress of blacks needlessly more difficult.

What is remarkable about many crusades to have the government intervene in the terms of economic transactions involving incomes is the contrast between the fervor of the campaigns for these interventions and the far lesser interest, or no visible interest at all, in empirical evidence about how these interventions turn out. When Nicholas Kristof of the *New York Times* sweepingly condemned those who opposed minimum wage laws, while showing no interest in, or even awareness of, empirical evidence on the actual consequences of such laws— on which there is voluminous evidence— he was following a quite familiar pattern among crusaders for third-party interventions. Although rent control laws were passed in San Francisco in 1979, it was 2001 before local authorities produced an empirical study of its actual consequences.[17] Although affirmative action in college admissions began in the 1960s, efforts of independent researchers to gain access to raw data with which to test the educational consequences have been impeded for decades.[18]

---

* There were *regional* retrogressions in black communities in Northern cities, in the wake of the massive migrations of blacks out of the South in the late nineteenth and early twentieth centuries. But, while there were retrogressions in race relations that led to contracting opportunities for the small black population already living in these Northern cities, the move meant progress for the much larger number of black migrants moving into these cities. See my *Black Rednecks and White Liberals*, pp. 46–49.

FACING THE FACTS— AND THE FUTURE

In dealing with the social and economic problems involving wealth, poverty and politics, specific policy prescriptions are not necessarily the most urgent need. Blueprints for Utopia are available in abundance. What are not nearly so abundant are prerequisites for rational thinking about current problems and future alternatives. The most important of these prerequisites is the *truth*. Whatever destination we are seeking, either literally or figuratively, we can only get there from where we are. This means that we must first know the truth about where we are, in order to advance toward our destination.

If our physical destination is Hawaii, then we must first know whether we are currently east, west, north or south of Hawaii. Otherwise we are likely to head in the wrong direction to get there. If the destination we wish to reach is figurative and social, rather than geographic, the same principle applies. If we wish to promote the economic or other advancement of black Americans, for example, we first need to know the truth about where black Americans are now— not where we might wish they were, or where some blacks might prefer to believe they are, or to have others believe they are, but where they are in fact, in *truth*. Wrong premises seldom lead to correct conclusions.

What are the obstacles to knowing the truth?

Unfortunately, these obstacles are all too plain and all too numerous. They include things you cannot say, even with a mountain of empirical evidence behind you, and other things you can shout from the rooftops, without a speck of evidence behind you, and in defiance of whatever evidence exists to the contrary. This is nowhere more true than on college and university campuses, where either a student or a professor publicly speaking unpalatable truths about any minority group currently in favor risks adverse reactions, ranging from becoming an instant social pariah to punishment under campus "speech codes" to physical harassment and threats of violence. Meanwhile, there are other things that can be said, no matter how demonstrably false, with little risk of even criticism, much less discrediting.

Unfortunately, arbitrary premises that are demonstrably false and misleading abound in all too many settings, whether in academia, the media or in government. One of the most pervasive of these false premises is one that we have already noted in Chapter 8— the assumption that disparities in economic outcomes imply external restrictions imposed by others. This implicit assumption of equal outcomes in the absence of external restrictions flies in the face of evidence from around the world that geographic, demographic, cultural and other factors influencing outcomes are not even approximately equal. Nor are performances in purely individual endeavors that can be objectively measured, such as individual performances in sports, chess or spelling bees— all of which show highly skewed distributions of success.

Words versus Realities

Professor Joseph Stiglitz of Columbia University says that one way of "looking at equality of opportunity is to ask to what extent the life chances of a child are dependent on the education and income of his parents." More specifically, he asks, "Is it just as likely that a child of poor or poorly educated parents gets a good education and rises to the middle class as someone born to middle-class parents with college degrees?" As evidence of unequal opportunities, he says, "Latinos and African-Americans still get paid less than whites, and women still get paid less than men." According to Professor Stiglitz, "Americans are coming to realize that their cherished narrative of social and economic mobility is a myth."[19]

If equal *opportunity* and equal *probability* of success are used interchangeably, what does that accomplish? It finesses aside the question whether some people make better use of their opportunities than other people do. When Asian students outnumber white students by more than two-to-one in each of New York City's three elite public high schools— Stuyvesant, Bronx Science and Brooklyn Tech[20]— are we to say that whites are being denied equal opportunity?

Are we to say that this must mean that Asians have higher incomes and more education than whites, even when we know that Chinese immigrants from Fujian province have neither? Are we to equate equal opportunity with equal chances, even when we know that the children of black doctors and lawyers in affluent Shaker Heights neglect their studies?[21] Or that black schoolchildren from the same ghetto neighborhood in New York, taught in the very same school building— but some in successful charter school programs and the others in the regular public school environment— score respectively far above average on educational tests and far below average on those same tests?[22]

More fundamentally, are we advocating changes in government policy or changes in child-rearing practices— and, if the latter, through voluntary means or by government imposition of its preferences on families? Are we saying that the circumstances of *life* are unfair or that particular institutions where we collect statistics are unfair?

Words matter. So does the slippery use of words, which can insinuate what they cannot substantiate. To people who are seeking the truth, it is a crucial question whether, or to what extent, those groups who are less successful are being thwarted by external barriers— that is, by less *opportunity*— or instead are less successful because of their own internal deficiencies in knowledge, discipline, values or other things that affect their *life chances*. But to redistributionists who are seeking ideological victory, that is precisely the question to be kept off the agenda.

If Stiglitz prefers to make life chances his issue, that is his prerogative. But to claim that *other people's* belief in social mobility has been refuted as a "myth" is to impute his conception of social mobility to those other people. And to cite as evidence income differences between blacks and whites, or between women and men, is to add to the confusion, when many— if not most— Americans would take that to mean that he is saying that the external factor of discrimination must be the reason. Yet innumerable empirical studies have shown that blacks and whites, as groups, do *not* have the same job qualifications and that women and men likewise differ in many of the things that go into economic advancement, beginning with the simple fact that women average fewer hours of employment per year and fewer years of continuous employment— *among many other consequential differences.*[23]

As far back as 1971, those single women who had worked continuously from high school into their thirties were earning slightly *more* than men of the same description,[24] even though women as a group were not earning as much as men as a group. As far back as academic year 1972–73, while black academics as a group earned lower incomes than white academics as a group, nevertheless those black academics with Ph.D.s from equally high-ranked departments in their respective fields as whites, and with equal numbers of articles published, earned *more* than white academics of the same description.[25]

The approach of Professor Stiglitz is by no means unique. Redefining words is a major part of the ideological arsenal of income redistributionists in general, whether discussing the less successful or the more successful members of society. When discussing the latter, the very concept of achievement is often replaced by the concept of privilege. For example, another writer has argued that income statistics show "unambiguously" that "persons of Irish-Catholic ethnicity were the second most privileged group in U.S. society, adjudged on the basis of annual income, educational level and occupational prestige," with Jews being "the most privileged."[26]

What makes this statement grotesque is that Irish and Jewish immigrants were among the most desperately poor of the immigrants who arrived in the United States in the nineteenth century, and lived in a poverty and squalor unseen today and virtually inconceivable today.

That the Irish and the Jews rose from such painful beginnings to prosperity in the next century is an *achievement*, not a privilege. That they did so in the face of once common employers' notices that said

"No Irish Need Apply," and in the face of quota limits on how many Jewish students would be admitted to Harvard[27] and other elite universities, and even smaller limits— usually zero— on how many Jewish professors would be appointed during the pre-World War II era, makes their achievements more striking, even though others now try to make those achievements vanish by the verbal magic of calling them "privileges." Even middle-class blacks have been described as "privileged,"[28] though their ancestors were by no means brought to America as doctors, lawyers or teachers.

The same word games are played in discussions of group differences in outcomes in foreign countries— and not simply by politicians or journalists, but in serious academic publications. Thus Malays in Malaysia, for example, have been referred to as "deprived"[29] and non-Malays as having "privilege,"[30] despite pervasive government-mandated preferences for Malays in both public and private institutions. Similarly, Canadians of Japanese ancestry in Toronto have been described as "privileged," because they have achieved higher incomes than others in that city[31]— despite a prior history of severe anti-Japanese discrimination in Canada, climaxed by internment during the Second World War for longer than Japanese Americans were interned.[32]

In short, the achievements of these and other groups, after long and hard struggles upward, are made to vanish from discussion by a simple substitution of the word "privilege" for the word "achievement"— even though privilege refers to a condition that exists *ex ante* and achievement refers to a condition that exists *ex post*.* Other words

---

* The same tactic of calling achievements "privilege" extends beyond human beings to cultural products such as books, music and motion pictures. Classic movies like "The Wizard of Oz" or "Citizen Kane," whose appeal has endured over successive generations, or the writings of Shakespeare and the music of Beethoven that have remained viable for centuries, are referred to as "privileged." Thus the judgment of successive ages can be replaced by the vogues of the moment, as the power to anoint is transferred from a broader constituency over time to contemporary elites in strategic positions in educational institutions or in the arts. As in a political context, deception is a means to power and verbal dexterity a key instrument of deception.

that confuse the *ex ante* with the *ex post*, such as "advantage" or "access," are part of the same verbal arsenal of evasion.

In an article titled "The Asian Advantage," the *New York Times'* Nicholas Kristof, for example, explains the academic and economic success of Asian Americans by asserting that they "started with one advantage: They are highly educated, more so even than the average American."[33] But most Asian American groups have *not* "started" as immigrants on American soil "highly educated."

Although there were substantial numbers of Chinese immigrants in the United States by the middle of the nineteenth century, as late as 1940 fewer than 2 percent of Chinese American males had completed college.[34] The earliest generations of Chinese in nineteenth century America worked as manual laborers, whether on farms or in cities or as workers helping build the transcontinental railroad.[35] Chinese men— there were very few women— lived poverty-stricken lives, often sleeping ten or twelve to a room.[36] By the 1920s, the primary occupation of Chinese Americans was in laundries, usually small, one-man, hand laundries.[37] In the twenty-first century, as we have seen, immigrants from Fujian province in China began working as hotel maids, restaurant laborers and in other similar low-level, low-paid jobs, often with long hours of exhausting work, while having their children tutored to be able to get into New York's elite public high schools, from which they could go on to elite colleges.

Japanese immigrants to the United States had a similar history, beginning in the nineteenth century as agricultural laborers in Hawaii and California. Those arriving around the turn of the century had with them an average of eleven dollars in 1896 to a high of twenty-six dollars in 1904.[38] Many of the Vietnamese "boat people" who fled as refugees to the United States in the 1970s arrived destitute and often with little knowledge of English. Such were the "advantages" with which Asian Americans began.

While Asian Americans as a whole are today college-educated more often than the American population as a whole, even today that is not true of all the constituent groups within this heterogeneous category. Even in the year 2000, not quite as high a proportion of Vietnamese in the United States had a Bachelor's degree as the proportion of the American population as a whole had.[39] Yet the economic and educational rise of the Vietnamese refugees in the United States has been another of the striking achievements of Asian Americans— again, achievements not to be confused with "advantages" or other synonyms for privileges.

Even when the early generations of various Asian American groups did not themselves have much education, they came from a culture that valued education highly, and their children were raised with great emphasis on doing well in school. Teachers in New York's Chinatown rated the Chinese children "better behaved, more obedient, and more self-reliant" than their white classmates.[40] The same would be said of other Asian students in educational institutions across the country. But these are matters of behavioral choice and work efforts, not conferred privileges. This is not a question of semantics, but a question of whether we are trying to (1) discover evidence as to what behaviors help or hurt, or (2) verbally obscure such evidence.

Mr. Kristof closes by saying: "But let's not use the success of Asians to pat ourselves on the back and pretend that discrimination is history."[41] Discrimination is apparently the automatic default setting. But Asian Americans have had a considerable past history of being discriminated against in the United States, both by laws and practices, as well as a history of rising from poverty to a position where their success could then be attributed by people like Kristof to the "advantage" provided by their achievements. It is not a question of patting ourselves on the back, but of trying to determine what actually works, as distinguished from what has been asserted by elite groupthink.

The verbal tactics of elite groupthink tend to remove behavioral choices, efforts and productivity from discussions of intergroup economic disparities. So too does the tactic of arbitrarily dismissing any negative information about particular groups as "stereotypes."

Verbal virtuosity is an obstacle to truth, by corrupting the words that might otherwise convey unwelcome truths that redistributionists avoid. The fundamental issue is not how to grade or rank different groups, but how to discover what things work and what things turn out to be counterproductive. Making excuses for counterproductive behavior does not help any group advance, though it may enable those elites responsible for promoting counterproductive social policies to escape responsibility in the eyes of others or of themselves.

The Role of Productivity

By focusing on the *rewards* received for achievements, redistributionists ignore the benefits of those achievements for *others*, which is the very reason that those others— whether employers, patients, customers, or other recipients of the goods or services that people with these achievements produce— are willing to pay their own money to receive those benefits. As in many other contexts, *productivity* vanishes into thin air by verbal sleight of hand, when discussing the "income distribution" that results from that productivity. It is as if all that matters is the income difference between *A* and *B*, ignoring the benefits of their respective achievements for *C, D, E* and many others. Ultimately, it is as if the internal distribution of the fruits of production is more important than the amount of production itself— on which the standard of living of a whole society depends.

Preoccupation with the differential benefits to those with various achievements too often obscures the benefits of those achievements for society as a whole. Back in prehistoric times, whoever invented the wheel, or whoever first figured out how to start a fire, may well have acquired an "advantage" over others, but surely what is most important is that those things were major additions to the human capital of mankind in its infancy. It might well have been even better if everyone, all over the world, had acquired such advances at the same time. But surely what is far more important than this theoretical possibility is that these fundamental advances were in fact made in the real world, as the human species began its millennia-long advance toward civilization. Was that less important than the question whether it was "fair" for some people to have fire or the wheel before others?

When some children today are raised in ways that make it easier for them to become doctors, engineers or scientists, that is not simply a *differential advantage* over other children who are raised in ways that make it more likely that they will become welfare recipients or criminals. These are differences that affect the well-being of the whole society. Yet there are academics who deplore college admissions decisions based on the academic qualifications of individual applicants because, in their view, this is simply rewarding those who have already been "privileged."

A former director of Stanford's college admissions office, for example, said that requiring certain tests from all applicants "could unfairly penalize disadvantaged students in the college admissions process." She said, "These students, through no fault of their own, often find themselves in high schools that provide inadequate preparation for the Achievement Tests."[42] The consequences *for society* of different admissions criteria are considerations that seem to vanish into thin air. In a similar vein, the admissions committee was reluctant to give special consideration to some students with special abilities:

> The possibility of broadening the identification process to include other talents actually made some of my staff nervous. There was some consideration given to the question of access— an applicant who was fluent in four or five languages would bring a vibrancy to the academic community at the university, but such a student would either have grown up abroad or have been in a school system that consistently offered multiple foreign language courses from elementary school on. These options were not available to most applicants, and it seemed misguided to begin to attach value in the admissions process to opportunities that relatively few applicants could consistently attain.[43]

Here again, the issue is arbitrarily confined to equalizing the chances between applicant *A* and applicant *B*, in utter disregard of the effect on outside individuals *C, D, E* and many others. Such arbitrary restrictions on the considerations taken into account would be dismissed as ridiculous in fields where the *end result* is what matters, whether in sports, in war or in many other kinds of endeavors. No National Football League team would have hesitated for a moment to choose Eli Manning or Peyton Manning over some less qualified quarterback because the Mannings' father had been a professional NFL quarterback, who was able to give them grooming for that position that not one other quarterback in a hundred could get. No one would have chosen some less qualified general over General Douglas MacArthur to command troops in battle because General MacArthur had the unfair advantage of being groomed from an early age by a father who was a general before him.

But, in academia, among admissions committee members who pay no price for being wrong, here again the consequences *for society* of different admissions criteria are considerations that virtually vanish into thin air, just as with the group activist in Nigeria who deplored "the tyranny of skills."[44]

In a sense, there is indeed a tyranny of skills, though it exists independently of a given institution or a given society, because of inherent realities beyond our control. The presence or absence of medical skills, for example, can be the difference between life and death for millions of people. That is an inherent reality— or tyranny— we cannot escape. All that a given institution or society can do is recognize the value of skills— or else subordinate skills to social preconceptions or political expediency. Skills confer benefits, even on those who do not have skills. When a graduate of a selective public high school and a selective city college in New York created a polio vaccine, that was a boon to people of every income level, every ability level, and of every race, color, creed and nationality around the world.*

---

* Intellectuals preoccupied with such things as differences in life expectancy between people in the affluent countries and people in the Third World seem not to notice that the vast increase in life expectancy in the Third World has been largely due to medical and public health advances that originated in the more affluent countries.

Maybe there was some other applicant to these selective educational institutions who was not as qualified academically as Jonas Salk, but who had overcome more handicaps, and thus would be considered more deserving by some admissions committees. But the real question is: Would that other student be equally likely to create a polio vaccine? The ultimate purpose of an educational institution, especially one supported by taxpayers, is not to confer benefits on individual selected applicants but to serve the larger society by turning out graduates with knowledge and skills that benefit others.

Frequent expressions of astonishment at how large the differences in rewards are between individuals, groups or nations seldom lead to questions as to whether what is produced by those who receive these rewards differs correspondingly. It is not so much that redistributionists give different answers to that question than others might give. More fundamentally, that question is seldom asked, much less answered. Here again, production usually remains somewhere in the dim background, as something that just happens *somehow*.

Studies of people who became genuinely rich, with huge fortunes, like that of John D. Rockefeller, may abound with assertions about their "greed." But those who use such characterizations seldom pose the most basic question: What did Rockefeller supply to others that caused so many of those others to turn their own individually modest sums of money over to him, adding up to his vast fortune?

Despite the frequency with which "greed" is invoked in this context, it explains absolutely nothing— unless you believe that an insatiable desire for money will itself cause others to pay you that money. But regardless of how often this causally meaningless explanation— greed— has passed muster among the intelligentsia, a more old-fashioned expression conveys a more fundamental truth: "If wishes were horses, beggars would ride." Greed may or may not be an accurate characterization of any given individual, but his or her wishes cannot explain why others provide the money to satisfy those wishes.

Nor is the amount of wealth received even a barometer of greed: A small-time criminal who robs a little mom-and-pop store and kills the owner, to keep from being identified, is surely greedy, even if the money received from the robbery is trivial compared to what an engineer or a surgeon earns honestly in a month.

In the case of John D. Rockefeller, his fortune began in the nineteenth century, with his reducing the price of kerosene to a fraction of what it was before his innovations in production and distribution greatly reduced the cost of producing and delivering this product to consumers.[45] For example, the units in which we measure oil today are barrels, even though oil is no longer actually shipped in barrels but in tankers, due to Rockefeller's cost-saving shift to railroad tanker cars long ago.

As of the time when this happened, light bulbs had not yet been invented, so the ancient saying, "The night cometh when no man can work," still applied to all who could not afford to use candles, gaslight or oil-burning sources of light for hours at a time each night. Many working-class people had few options besides going to bed when nightfall came. Only after Rockefeller's innovations in production and distribution cut the cost of kerosene, to a fraction of what it had been before, were ordinary people able to afford to stay up for hours after dark, using kerosene lamps. What such people were purchasing were hundreds of hours of additional light per year. It is hardly surprising that millions of people were willing to pay to enlarge their lives in this way.

We take so many of the benefits of today's world for granted that it is hard to conceive of how different life was in the world of earlier times— much less grasp the full impact of landmark economic advances that enabled people to transcend the severe limitations of those times. It has been estimated, for example, that most Americans in the early nineteenth century lived out their entire lives and died within a fifty-mile radius of where they were born.[46] The railroad and the automobile expanded their world to vastly larger dimensions, especially in the early twentieth century, after Henry Ford's mass-production methods drastically reduced the cost of producing an automobile. This changed cars from being luxuries of the rich to being accessible to the masses.

The fortune made by Henry Ford was an incidental by-product of this historic expansion of productivity that expanded the lives of millions. Why third parties should imagine themselves entitled to intervene in such processes, to which they contributed nothing, and to preempt the decisions of others— decisions for which the interventionists pay no price when they are wrong— is one of the many mysteries of our time.

Many fortunes of historic dimensions came from producing a new product or making an old product either better or cheaper, or both. In less spectacular ways as well, other people who have acquired other skills are paid for what those skills add to the lives of other people, whether these are the skills of doctors curing diseases or the skills of pilots transporting people thousands of miles. Acquiring valuable skills to do these and other things is an *achievement* that benefits others, rather than a "privilege" that benefits only themselves at the expense of others. The difference is fundamental, regardless of how much verbal cleverness goes into obscuring that difference.

Redistributionists may demand proof that all fortunes, or all high incomes, are earned that way, but this is putting the burden of proof on others, instead of putting the burden of proof on those who seek to restrict the freedom of their fellow human beings to live their own lives and make their own economic decisions as they see fit. There is no reason why the divine right of kings, from earlier centuries, should be inherited by today's intelligentsia or politicians.

Are there imperfections in a market economy? Yes! There are imperfections in all things human, including alternatives to the market economy. As a distinguished scholar put it: "The study of human institutions is always a search for the most tolerable imperfections."[47]

None of this means that the status quo must be maintained. It cannot be and has not been, except in isolated, poor and backward societies. Even leading conservative figures in Western societies, ranging from Edmund Burke in the eighteenth century to Milton Friedman in the twentieth century, have advocated major social changes.* The fact that they opposed some other changes does not mean that they opposed change as such. But the word "change" is not a blank check for self-indulgence— least of all self-indulgence in the notion that disparities imply villainy, which in turn implies a crusade on the side of the angels against the forces of evil, despite how self-flattering such a vision of the world might be.

An even more dangerous illusion is that the undoubted unfairness of life chances is a reason to give politicians ever more control of a nation's resources and ever more power over our individual lives. The track record of that approach is— at the very least— sobering, when even most socialist and communist governments had been forced by counterproductive consequences to abandon economic central planning by the end of the twentieth century, and when the material benefits of an expansive welfare state to some in England and the United States have been accompanied by painful social retrogressions to the detriment of each society as a whole.

Most important of all, whatever changes are made in economic or social policies must begin with the truth about our current situation, whether that truth is palatable or unpalatable, if "change" is to mean progress. Drawing up policy blueprints is a task for which there has never been a shortage of eager candidates. We can only hope that those policies will be based on hard facts about the real world, rather than on rhetoric or preconceptions.

---

* In addition to devoting years to the impeachment of the British viceroy of India, on grounds that he oppressed the native peoples, Burke advocated the abolition of slavery at a time when that was a distinctly minority view in Western civilization and virtually a non-existent view in non-Western societies. Burke even drew up plans for preparing slaves for freedom and providing them with property with which to begin their lives as free people. Milton Friedman proposed sweeping changes in public schools and in the Federal Reserve System, as well as a negative income tax to transfer money to low-income people. Burke said, "A state without the means of some change is without the means of its conservation" and Milton Friedman wrote a book titled *The Tyranny of the Status Quo*. See also Edmund Burke, *Reflections on the Revolution in France and Other Writings*, edited by Jesse Norman (New York: Everyman's Library, 2015), pp. 328–349, 420–424, 441–442, 1003–1004.

CAUSATION VERSUS BLAME

The strong emotions surrounding issues of income and wealth make careful— and honest— uses of words especially important. Among the careful distinctions we need to make is the distinction between causation and blame. We also need to distinguish between the general unfairness of life and the question of specific unfairness in particular institutions or in particular societies. "The world has never been a level playing field," as Professor David S. Landes put it. Geography alone is enough to prevent equal prospects for all, but "No one can be praised or blamed for the temperature of the air, or the volume and timing of rainfall, or the lay of the land."[1]

THE DIRECTION OF CAUSATION

Differences in geography, demography, culture and other factors can make economic and other prospects or outcomes unequal for different individuals and groups, even if particular institutions or societies were to treat everyone the same. Nevertheless, many people blame statistical inequalities on the institutions where the statistics that convey these inequalities happened to be collected. Others blame some factor with which negative outcomes are correlated— blaming crime on poverty, for example. Statisticians have long warned against confusing correlation with causation, but too often those warnings have been ignored. Even when there is in fact a causal relationship between two things, that by itself does not tell us the *direction* of causation— that is, whether X caused Y or Y caused X, or whether both were caused by some other factor Z. It is possible that poverty causes crime, but it is also possible that the same set of attitudes and behavior— or the same lack of human capital— that lead to poverty can also lead to crime.

Empirical studies have often found a substantial correlation between the socioeconomic level into which an individual was born and the later educational, economic or other achievements of that individual. From this many have concluded that social mobility is a "myth." But when not only particular individuals, but whole groups, rise dramatically from the same low socioeconomic levels in which other groups remain largely mired, that raises questions about the direction of causation. Have the same *internal* factors which led one generation of a particular group to be poor also led their offspring to remain poor? Or have *external* factors kept poor people in general from rising very much? Clearly it is not always the latter, for both in England and in the United States students from some low-income immigrant families do much better in school than low-income native-born students, whether the latter are black in the United States or white in England. Low-income immigrants as a group rise economically more readily than low-income native-born groups.

In theory, when low-income students score lower on academic tests than high-income students, that might be because the effects of poverty cause low-income students to have lower educational outcomes. But another possibility is that the same cultural or other factors which inhibited low-income students' performances on academic tests also inhibited their economic success as adults. Again, the correlation between X and Y might be because X causes Y or because X and Y are both caused by Z.

One way to tell which of these possibilities fits the facts is to compare academic test results between students in groups which each have both low-income families and high-income families.

In 1981 and in 1995, for example, the average SAT score of black high school students on the mathematics portion of the test was lower than the average score of either white or Asian high school students. Since black students come from families with lower average incomes than either white or Asian students, this establishes correlation but does not help us determine causation, much less the direction of causation. However, when in 1981 black students from families with incomes of $50,000 or more scored slightly *below* white students from families with incomes under $6,000, and even further below Asian students with incomes under $6,000,[2] clearly the cause of the test score differences was not differences in income. A very similar pattern appeared in 1995.

Nor did this pattern change much when the three groups were compared in terms of how much education their respective parents had. Black students whose parents had postgraduate degrees scored lower on the mathematics portion of the SAT than white students whose parents had only high school diplomas, and far lower than Asian students whose parents had high school diplomas.[3] In short, despite the correlation between the socioeconomic position of families and their children's educational performances— a correlation that holds for all three groups— a finer breakdown of the data by family income among all three groups shows that correlation is not causation. This raises the question as to what other factor could be affecting both educational and economic outcomes. The evidence suggests that there are behavioral differences between groups with different cultures.

One sign of cultural differences, as noted earlier, is that various cultural groups around the world have had very different propensities to buy books.[4] Black Americans with high incomes have fewer books in their homes than white Americans with lower incomes.[5] Other evidences of cultural differences include the fact that black children in the upscale community of Shaker Heights, Ohio, spend less time on their studies than white students in the same community.[6]

The hostility of many people in Washington's black community toward Dunbar High School during its era of academic ascendancy and, in a later era, the nationwide phenomena of hostility by black students toward their more academically inclined black classmates, who are accused of "acting white," are among other indicators of a culture that is not oriented toward intellectual achievement or toward the behavior that leads to intellectual achievement. That this is a cultural, rather than a genetic, phenomenon is suggested by the fact that, in England, low-income black immigrant students outperform low-income native-born white students.[7]

A very different social outcome— imprisonment— also shows a correlation between what happens to parents and what happens to their children. A critic of high imprisonment rates pointed out that children whose parents have been in prison are seven times more likely to be imprisoned themselves than other children are.[8] This may well indicate an unfairness of life, without necessarily demonstrating unfairness in the criminal justice system. How often can the police know the parental history of most of the people they arrest? Judges and juries are even less likely to know. But when the kinds of attitudes, behavior and associates that the parents had are socially "inherited" by the children, it is hardly surprising that similar results follow. It is a painful unfairness of life, since children do not have the option of choosing their parents. But here, as in other contexts, we cannot simply assume that the unfairness occurred where the statistics were collected.

Many people who cite statistics on higher rates of disciplining of young black males in schools proceed on the assumption that this indicates racial prejudices by school authorities, rather than different behavior on the part of young black males. Such assumptions seem especially untenable when the school authorities themselves are black, as is often the case. Nor is this some abstract philosophical issue. If young black males are exempted from the same standards of behavior as other students, in order to achieve statistical parity in rates of disciplining, this hardly seems likely to lead to better behavior. If anything, getting away with disruptive and violent behavior when young seems more likely to lead to similar behavior as adults, which in turn can lead to prison. Such a policy can make both black males and society as a whole worse off in the end, despite however much it may enhance the prospects of politicians or racial "leaders" who assume the role of protectors against the discrimination of others.

When there are internal factors behind lower educational performances, socioeconomic performances or criminal behavior, whether the factors involved are genetic or cultural does not necessarily matter much in this context, since both genes and cultures are passed on from parents to children. Internal factors can prevent people from rising, even when there are no serious external barriers to overcome. Nor is there any reason for arbitrarily refusing to consider internal factors as things that can lead to crime and punishment. Nor should internal factors behind counterproductive behavior be considered unchangeable, especially when such behavior was not nearly as prevalent in earlier generations— either among low-income blacks in the United States or low-income whites in England.

As regards upward socioeconomic mobility, we cannot arbitrarily assume, either explicitly or implicitly, that all groups have the same desire for, or focus on, upward mobility,* even if they might all welcome it, if it happened, just as they might welcome winning a

---

* As a personal note, my life began in 1930 in the culture of the South, at a time when the Southern culture was a handicap to both blacks and whites. Among other things, it was a culture that put little emphasis on education or on striving for upward mobility. Neither when I went to school in the South, nor to school in Harlem at the age of nine, was I seriously focused on what education would mean to me as an adult. Adulthood, in my mind at that time, was some far off, exotic place, much like Tahiti or Antarctica, and something that I would deal with when the time came, but which had no urgent connection in my mind with what I was doing as a kid in school.

Fortunately, the adults in the family in which I was raised, though not well educated themselves, understood that I would have access to more and better education in New York than they had in the South, and better opportunities as an adult than they ever had. They tried to convey that to me as a reason to do my best in school. Their message was reinforced by some other adults I encountered along the way, and later by kids from a more educated, and more education-minded, background in a predominantly white junior high school, who gave me a new perspective that I seldom encountered in the culture of the neighborhood where I lived. Knowing today that most youngsters in Harlem back then (or now) never had the same influences and guidance that I happened to have had, I find it hard to believe that those youngsters' outcomes are due solely to either their innate potential or to external barriers thwarting the same upward thrust as that of other youngsters from different cultures.

lottery or any other windfall gain. Indeed, some redistributionists argue as if economic success is in fact like winning a lottery, rather than being one of the fruits of years of developing human capital.

Conversely, in very different circumstances, when and where there are sufficiently unyielding barriers to opportunity, internal qualifications for upward mobility may not matter. There have been times and places where no one was going to let someone who was Jewish or black become head of state in either Europe or the United States, or let either rise to various other highly valued roles, regardless of their potential or achievements.

In short, there is no *a priori* answer to the question of why the offspring of some families do dramatically better than the offspring of other families. The only real choice is between answering that question on the basis of widespread beliefs— what "everybody knows"— or by examining empirical evidence. For black Americans, for example, the most widely accepted belief today— what "everybody knows"— is that racial prejudice is the principal factor in the under-representation of blacks in high quality educational institutions, in the highest paying and most prestigious careers, or their over-representation in prisons.

One of the ways of testing this belief would be by seeing whether other people who are black do significantly better than native-born black Americans in educational institutions, in job markets or elsewhere. According to a 2004 report, most of the black students at Harvard were not native-born American blacks but were either West Indian or African immigrants or their children, or the children of biracial couples— groups disproportionately represented at various other elite universities around the country.[9] Nigerians, for example, have been greatly over-represented among black students in a number of elite educational institutions in America,[10] as they outperform native-born white students in British schools.[11] Economically, nearly one-fourth of Nigerian households in the United States have annual incomes of more than $100,000, compared to 10.6 percent of black American households.[12] If white racism is the cause of lower educational and economic outcomes for black Americans, why are black Nigerians exempt?

CAUSATION, CONVEYANCE AND BLAME

Both moral and causal arguments are important, but amalgamating the two, even implicitly, is a formula for confusion, perhaps exemplified in the catch phrase, "blaming the victim." Whether particular individuals, groups or nations with poorer outcomes are in fact victims of other people is precisely the question that is preempted by this phrase. There is no question that for an individual to be born blind or crippled can be a tragic misfortune, but that in itself does not mean that someone has victimized that individual. There are, after all, causes besides humans— various diseases or other geographic features being obvious examples. For a group, a race or a nation to be located in a geographic setting that affords far less promising prospects of either prosperity or progress can be a major, fundamental misfortune, but that in itself does not mean that some other *people* have victimized them.

Determining where some disadvantage to particular individuals or groups originated is often no easy matter. Because data collected at a given institution may *convey* a certain negative outcome does not mean that the institution where those data were collected *caused* that outcome. Some hospitals have significantly higher death rates than others precisely because they have the most highly-skilled doctors and the most advanced medical technology— and therefore treat patients with the most difficult, life-threatening medical problems that some other hospitals are simply not equipped to handle. A hospital that treats mostly people with such routine medical conditions as childbirth or broken legs may well have a lower death rate than a hospital which performs operations like brain surgery or heart transplants. Higher death rates at more advanced hospitals *convey* a reality that these hospitals did not *cause*. That reality in this case is that its patients have more severe afflictions, for which neither the patients nor the hospital are to blame.

Similarly with outcomes in economic and social institutions, where negative outcomes at particular institutions are often more or less automatically taken to mean that it was these institutions which *caused* negative results that the data collected there *conveyed*. When, for example, statistics on the employment, pay and promotion of people from different ethnic backgrounds are collected at a particular business, differences in these respects from one group to another do not mean that the *cause* of such differences must have originated at those businesses where data *conveying* these differences originated.

Often other data, or just common observations, show children being raised differently in different groups, and behaving and performing differently in schools or in society as they grow up, years before they reached a particular employer. Yet U.S. courts of law have accepted "disparate impact" statistics collected at particular businesses as evidence of discrimination by those particular businesses. In the same vein, group differences in results on particular tests are often taken to mean that those tests are "biased," when the scores on these tests *convey* differences among the participants which these tests are accused of *causing* by asking questions geared to a white culture, for example— even when Asian Americans in fact score higher than whites on these tests.

Individuals, groups, races and nations may be handicapped by their cultural settings, as they have been handicapped by their geographic settings. In either case, their misfortunes do not necessarily mean victimhood, which requires people who are victimizing others. While cultures are man-made, they were usually made jointly by people long dead before the present generation was born, and these cultures were certainly not made with malice against future descendants. In short, misfortunes cannot automatically be transmuted into victimhood by a catch phrase, not if one is serious about the truth, rather than fencing with words. To suggest that there can be cultural patterns inconsistent with progress in the world as it has evolved is not to "blame the victim," except for those who are preoccupied with trying to verbally turn the tables on people who speak unwelcome truths.

THE LOCALIZATION OF BLAME

People who seek to find blame, as distinct from causation, often also seek a *localized* source of evil to blame. Professor Paul Krugman, for example, refers to slavery as "America's original sin."[13] But it would be hard to find an evil less localized than slavery. Though universally condemned today, slavery was an institution accepted as a fact of life for thousands of years, by even moral and religious leaders around the world. Christian monasteries in Europe and Buddhist monasteries in Asia had slaves.[14] Reformers could urge better treatment of slaves, or call for the exemption of particular peoples from being enslaved, but it was extremely rare to call for condemnation and abolition of slavery, as such. Ironically, among the times and places where this rare phenomenon occurred was the newly formed United States of America in the eighteenth century. This was by no means a majority view among Americans at that time, but it was a view not without consequences.

In the wake of the war for American independence, in the name of freedom, a number of Northern states abolished slavery and, even in the South, tens of thousands of slaves were voluntarily set free by individual slaveowners— though by no means most slaveowners— in the decades that followed American independence.[15] Though human beings often fail to live up to their ideals, this does not mean that those ideals have had no effect. The ideal of freedom behind the American Revolution had its effect in freeing thousands of people from slavery in the newly formed United States, something that was happening nowhere else in the world at that time. To call slavery "America's original sin" is to turn reality upside down. Would anyone refer to cancer as "America's horrible disease," when it is a dreadful affliction for human beings around the world? [16]

Slavery was not peculiar to the United States, to white society or to Western civilization. What was peculiar to Western civilization was not that it had slavery, like non-Western societies around the world, but that Western civilization was where the drive to destroy slavery began— a drive that lasted more than a century, was fought on many fronts around the world and succeeded over the opposition of non-Western societies.[17] Only the military dominance of the West in the nineteenth and early twentieth centuries allowed the West to impose the abolition of slavery on the countries it conquered, along with many other things— good, bad or mixed— imposed during the era of worldwide Western imperialism.

Evils and failings common to human beings around the world may not provide as promising a target for ideological crusades as evils attributable to an identifiable, localized source of evil that can be removed and replaced by some favored alternative. But universal evils or failings of humans can mean that even the most sweeping, devastating and bloody victory over those currently in power locally may produce only a change in the cast of characters, without changing the tragic story itself. The tyranny and carnage that followed the French Revolution were at least as bad as the horrors of the old regime it replaced. In the twentieth century, the replacement of oppressive, monarchical dynasties by Communist and Fascist dictatorships was a major change for the worse, whether measured by the amount of slaughters or by the amount of oppression of the living.

The false narrative of "America's original sin"— as distinguished from humanity's worldwide sin— has led to other false narratives, including "the legacy of slavery" as a blanket explanation of various forms of social pathology in today's black ghettos. This has served not only to insulate counterproductive behaviors from criticism but, in a larger context, has directed attention away from the welfare state vision and the welfare state policies that have left such social havoc in their wake on both sides of the Atlantic. The fundamental problem is not that some people were not familiar with certain historical facts. The fundamental problem is that they chose to make sweeping assertions without bothering to check the facts— and that their sweeping assertions have been widely accepted on the basis of repetition, in the absence of supporting facts and in defiance of readily available contrary facts.

MULTIPLE CAUSATION

The fact that the human species achieved nothing that we today would consider to be civilization, until well within the last 10 percent of its existence, has weighty implications for our times. Even races and nations that are today considered the most backward are more advanced than any race was during most of the existence of the human species. Were all the races of the world genetically inferior for all those scores of millennia? Or was some other factor or factors holding them back?

The most obvious factor behind backwardness was isolation in prehistoric times, as in later times. Hunter-gatherers could travel only so far, and could interact with only so many other hunter-gatherers in ancient times. How could a hunter-gatherer in Scandinavia even suspect the existence of other hunter-gatherers in Asia or even Southern Europe, much less interchange goods or thoughts with them across continents, and certainly not interchange genes? Even today, we look in vain for breakthroughs on the frontiers of knowledge from people living on isolated islands or in remote mountain villages, or from people living anywhere who are culturally isolated by illiteracy. Such people may have all they can do to survive, much less try to match the achievements of other people in more favorable settings.

At a minimum, this suggests that the truly isolated human being, denied even vicarious contact with the rest of his species through reading about them, is incapable of achieving even a significant fraction of what his potential might be if immersed in the knowledge created by his contemporaries and heir to the knowledge of the many generations that went before him. Indeed, even a hundred, or a thousand, isolated human beings, knowing only each other, and nothing about other contemporaries or predecessors, have seldom, if ever, produced anything the world has bothered to notice.

Yet there is no evidence that human genes changed drastically within the last 5 or 10 percent of human existence. Nor is there any hard evidence that the specific races that made the first world-changing advances in agriculture— in the Middle East, on the Indian subcontinent or in ancient China— were genetically superior then or now. These are certainly not the most prosperous, nor the most advanced, regions today.

What seems far more likely, in this context as in many others, is that multiple factors had to come together and interact, in order to produce a particular complex outcome, such as civilization. Most of those factors might well have been present for millennia, but impotent without the other factor or factors needed to complete the prerequisites for civilization. Yet, once agriculture was established, on a scale sufficient to permit or promote urbanization, there began many advances, within the last few millennia of recorded history, across a wide sweep of human endeavors, by descendants of people who in prehistoric times did not even know how to plant seeds to grow food.

Yet this development of civilization led ultimately to people who can now travel to the moon and send complex scientific instruments throughout the solar system and beyond into outer space. This enormous disparity of achievements between different eras of human existence dwarfs disparities between rich and poor contemporaries in the world of today. Yet this vast disparity between the achievements of different eras hardly seems explicable by either victimhood or genetics.

This scenario of progress has yet to be played out fully in the Amazon jungles or in other isolated places around the world, even though people in such places have benefitted as consumers of products created by fellow human beings in more fortunate settings.

If a number of factors have to come together, in order to produce a given outcome— whether tornadoes or economic advances— then it is possible that a number of those factors may come together in a number of places, while all of the factors come together in very few places, or even in only one. If there are ten factors required for success in a particular endeavor, individuals or groups with nine of those factors will not necessarily do 90 percent as well. They may be utter failures. The net result can be a very skewed distribution of outcomes, whether the particular outcome is most of the world's tornadoes occurring in just one country or a trio of professional golfers winning more than 200 PGA tournaments between them, while most professional golfers never win even a single PGA tournament in their entire careers.

Most notable economic, technological or intellectual achievements involve multiple factors— beginning with a desire to succeed in the particular endeavor, without which all the ability and opportunity mean nothing, just as the desire and the opportunity mean nothing without the ability. What this implies, among other things, is that an individual, a people, or a nation may have some, many or most of the prerequisites for a given achievement without having any real success in producing that achievement. And yet that individual, that people or that nation may suddenly burst upon the scene with spectacular success when whatever the missing factor or factors are finally get added to the mix.

Poor and backward nations that suddenly moved to the forefront of human achievements include Scotland in the nineteenth century and Japan in the twentieth century. But there have been other social phenomena pointing in the same direction, as examples of the consequences of multiple causation.

We have become so used to seeing numerous world-class performances by Jewish intellectual figures that it is necessary to reflect that this has been a phenomenon that burst upon the world in the nineteenth and twentieth centuries. There were individual Jewish intellectuals of international stature here and there in earlier centuries, but the proliferation of Jewish Nobel Prize winners across numerous fields in the twentieth century was a new and unpredictable phenomenon. Since Jews existed as a separate people for thousands of years before, and had a long tradition of reverence for learning, most of the factors required for their breakout in the nineteenth century may already have been present. But, for centuries, Jews were denied the rights of Christians in Europe or the rights of Muslims in the Middle East— and these denials included access to universities.

The first Christian nation in which Jews had the same rights as other people was the United States, late in the eighteenth century, when the American Constitution simply forbad religious distinctions in the law. After the French Revolution in 1789, France also granted equal rights to Jews. As restrictions against Jews began to erode in Europe, Jews began to flow, and then to flood, into universities. The missing ingredient had apparently been added.

Conversely, when a given individual, group, institution or nation has already had a highly successful combination of factors for many years, either internal changes in just one of those factors, or changes in external circumstances, can suddenly drop that institution, that people or that nation out of the top ranks in the particular endeavor. Thus the Eastman Kodak Company's global dominance in photographic equipment and supplies for more than a century came to a sudden end in the early twenty-first century, including a decline into bankruptcy, when the worldwide shift to digital cameras made film, film cameras and the chemicals and equipment for developing and processing film obsolete.*

China's historic decline, over the centuries, from an advanced nation in the forefront of human progress, to a Third World country, prey to more powerful nations in many ways, began with a decision by its fifteenth century rulers to isolate China from the outside world.

---

* The irony in all this is that Eastman Kodak could hardly have been caught by surprise by the emergence of digital cameras, since the digital camera was *invented* within Eastman Kodak. As in many other contexts, having facts is not the same as seeing the implications of those facts.

Loss of just one prerequisite— rulers rational enough to avoid irreparably self-destructive policies— was sufficient to negate the effects of all the other positive factors that had for centuries given China historic achievements.

Just as a combination of prerequisites for success in a particular endeavor may deny success to individuals, groups, institutions or nations that may have most of those prerequisites, but not all, so may variations in the number or kind of prerequisites from one endeavor to another let individuals or groups seriously lagging in some or most other endeavors nevertheless be not merely competent but outstanding or even dominant in particular endeavors that do not require the particular qualities or circumstances that they do not have, even if there is fierce competition within the particular endeavor in which they compete and excel.

Thus, during the era when Irish American immigrants and their offspring were over-represented among unskilled laborers and domestic servants, they were also among the leading performers in such sports as boxing and baseball, and among popular entertainers. Sports and entertainment are highly competitive fields, with many trying but few succeeding. Yet the crucial qualities, skills and talents required tend to be individual, and do not require an elaborate infrastructure of formal education or long years of training by specialists, which few poor people can afford.

Other low-income Americans, lacking in educational traditions or high-level industrial or commercial experience, have followed in the footsteps of Irish Americans, not only in sports and entertainment in general, but even in many of the very same kinds of sports and entertainment in which Irish Americans once excelled so strikingly— that is, boxing and baseball rather than polo or golf, popular music rather than symphonic music, vaudeville performers rather than ballet dancers or Shakespearean actors.

However demanding the skills or talents, and however rare the individuals able to reach the peaks, when the prerequisites for success in particular endeavors did not include an elaborate formal infrastructure, such as that required to become a scientist, a surgeon or an engineer, economically and educationally lagging groups have often been over-represented not only numerically but especially among the star performers.

A whole succession of Irish American heavyweight boxing champions in the nineteenth and early twentieth centuries, from the era of John L. Sullivan to that of Gene Tunney, was followed by a succession of black American heavyweight boxing champions, beginning in the 1930s with the legendary Joe Louis,* who still holds the record for one-round knockouts in heavyweight championship fights. Decades later, the era of black boxing champions was succeeded by an era of Hispanic American boxing champions. Similarly in baseball where, despite a ban on black players in the major leagues until 1947— which is to say, more than half a century after major league baseball began— there were seven consecutive years when no white man won the National League's Most Valuable Player award,[18] and now 5 of the top 10 players who hit the most home runs in their careers are black.[19]

Here too, the era of black dominance among baseball stars was followed by an era when a wholly disproportionate number of baseball stars have been Hispanic. In 1990, 17 percent of major league baseball players were black and 13 percent were Hispanic. By 2014, however, only 8.2 percent of major league baseball players were black and 28.4 percent were Hispanic.[20] For 12 consecutive years— from 2001 through 2012— there was an American League home run leader with a Hispanic surname, though one year another player with a Portuguese surname (Teixeira) tied for leadership.[21]

---

* There was an isolated black heavyweight champion— Jack Johnson— beginning in 1908, but the succession of black heavyweight champions began with Joe Louis. There were some black boxing champions in lower weight divisions in the early twentieth century, but there were few opportunities for black boxers to fight for championships in any weight divisions in the wake of negative public reactions to Jack Johnson's becoming a highly controversial figure because of his behavior outside of the ring. But Joe Louis' sportsmanship in the ring, and his dignity outside the ring, acquired respect among both blacks and whites, leading to more acceptance of black champions in other weight divisions as well.

It was not only among some ethnic groups, but also among white Southerners, that a lagging group, in economic and educational terms, produced many stars in sports and entertainment. Although white Southerners have long been no more than one-third of the white population of the country, in baseball four of the five highest lifetime batting averages were achieved by white players born in the South— Ty Cobb (.367) in Georgia, Rogers Hornsby (.358) in Texas, Shoeless Joe Jackson (.356) in South Carolina and Tris Speaker (.345) in Texas.

The lone non-Southerner among the top five, Ed Delahanty, had a lifetime batting average of .346.[22] His career began earlier, in the late nineteenth century and continued into the early twentieth century, encompassing an era with such other Irish baseball stars as Wee Willie Keeler (.343 lifetime batting average), Eddie Collins (.333), John J. McGraw (.333), James Edward (Tip) O'Neill (.326), Roger Connor (.317), Jim O'Rourke (.310) and Michael (King) Kelly (.308) who, at his peak, led the National League in batting with .354 in 1884 and .388 in 1886.[23] Among the Irish pitching stars of that era was "Iron Man" McGinnity, who led the National League in games pitched in six different seasons, was a 35-game winner with an earned run average of 1.61 in 1904, and became renowned for sometimes pitching both games of a double-header, as he did three times in one month, winning all six games.[24]

While some might imagine that sports involve only physical skills, that is harder to believe when it comes to entertainers, and especially musicians and musical composers. Here again, there has been a fault line between the kinds of entertainment requiring a formal infrastructure of education and specialized training, such as ballet and classical music versus popular music and dance, where individual talents and creativity are key. Among musical instruments, the violin requires formal training, while the piano can be self-taught, even though becoming a top popular pianist has been a rare triumph. Here black American musicians have not merely held their own but excelled and created musical genres that became popular across America and even internationally. Black composers emerged early in the twentieth century, with Scott Joplin and W.C. Handy, followed later by a new, more sophisticated musical genre created by Duke Ellington and others.

Here again, with entertainment as with sports, what blacks achieved was preceded by similar achievements by the Irish before them, Hispanics after them and by white Southerners. A whole line of famous Irish American singers in the early twentieth century was climaxed by Bing Crosby as the leading entertainer in the first half of the twentieth century and, in 1947, he was named "Most Popular Living Person" in a radio poll.[25] It was said that, through his recordings, radio broadcasts and movies, his voice was heard by more people around the world than the voice of any other human being at that time. Later there were famous Hispanic entertainers, and white Southern entertainers went from being regionally prominent to being nationally famous, with Elvis Presley becoming an international icon. *Billboard* magazine's 2010 rankings of the "Top 100 Artists 1955–2009" had Elvis Presley first, with a large lead over The Beatles in second place.[26]

Even within sports, there are areas where the skills required for success are clearly and unmistakably *not* physical. These would include baseball broadcasters whose renown put them in the Baseball Hall of Fame, such as Red Barber, Mel Allen, Russ Hodges and Ernie Harwell— all four of whom were from the 1940s and 1950s heyday of radio sportscasters,* and all of them white Southerners.[27] What is especially remarkable is that these broadcasters became famous in an era when there was not one major league baseball team in the entire South. To become major league broadcasters, they had to move to other regions of the country and compete with people living there, in order to get a job, and then go on to become renowned in their field.

Despite the poverty and backwardness of many mountain peoples on every inhabited continent, there have been areas in which they too excelled. A sweeping spectrum of elegant handicrafts has for centuries

---

* Televised sports obviously reduced the crucial role of the radio sportscaster in conveying what was happening.

poured out of mountain communities around the world. Among the mountain handicraft products in demand internationally have been shawls from Kashmir and watches and clocks from the Swiss Alps and mountainous regions of France and the Black Forest region of southern Germany.[28] Because of high transportation costs from mountains to the outside world, only articles with a high value concentrated in a small physical size could find a market in the lowlands, and be sold successfully in competition with products produced in the lowlands. Yet, at one time, in centuries past, villagers in the Pindus Mountains of Greece developed high skills in metalworking and wool processing, producing "fine handiwork in gold and silver" and "exquisitely embroidered woolens," which found markets from Istanbul to Vienna. Silk handicrafts also flourished for a time in the mountains of Greece, Italy and Morocco, though these eventually succumbed to competition from Asia, where silk originated.[29]

In the Andes, weaving techniques were adapted to the hair of the llamas.[30] From the mountains of Tibet came many high quality handicraft products based on the same social circumstances as in other mountains around the world— namely, great amounts of free time in the winters, spent indoors, where special skills could be developed and practiced. From the deposits of silver and gold in their region, Tibetans made jewelry, and from local woods various artistic objects were designed and carved. In other parts of the world, other mountain and highland peoples also used local resources to produce various local specialties such as dolls, rugs, lace and violin strings. As a distinguished geographer once noted: "Most of these mountain industries merely supplement the scant agricultural resources; they represent the efforts of industrious but hard pressed people to eke out their meager subsistence."[31] In the process, many became skilled weavers, potters, dye makers, wood carvers, stone carvers, and jewelers.[32]

No matter how lagging, poor or backward particular peoples may be at particular times, or even for centuries, it is hard to find large groups of human beings so lacking in skills or talents as to be fit only to be the proverbial "hewers of wood and drawers of water," though some welfare state policies and practices have reduced some people to a level where they cannot, or will not, come up to even that modest level of productivity.

While it may be readily understandable that lagging groups can find some niche in which they can hold their own, what is striking is that such groups often do not merely hold their own, but are especially successful in reaching the peaks, more so than the population at large, including other groups who greatly outperform them in many other kinds of endeavors. This pattern, however, seems consistent with lagging groups and advanced groups being innately not very different, if different at all, but different in outcomes primarily according to whether they have or do not have the full ensemble of factors required for success in various fields, even if the lagging group has most of these factors but lacks part of the ensemble that comes from either internal culture or external circumstances.

If so, then it is not surprising that a backlog, as it were, of innate potential unable to come to fruition in other fields would be concentrated in the fields where the prerequisites are met, and therefore make groups lagging elsewhere be among the top performers in the fields accessible to them. What is also consistent with this hypothesis is that when social groups in America rise out of the status of lagging groups— Irish Americans being a classic example— and become part of the mainstream of American achievements in a variety of fields, they tend also to forfeit their predominance among the stars in sports and entertainment.

Against this background, many current assumptions and beliefs are hard to sustain. One of these current notions is that lagging groups require a lowering of existing standards, so that more of their members can advance via various forms of "affirmative action." Yet the fields in which many lagging groups have had their greatest success— especially sports and entertainment— include fields notorious for severe competition, in which even star performers whose performances begin to decline are ruthlessly cast aside. In short, lagging minorities have flourished in endeavors whose conditions are the direct opposite of those of affirmative action. They have had real achievements against unsparing competition, rather than make-believe achievements based on affirmative action quotas.

Against the background of British historian Arnold Toynbee's "challenge and response" thesis, that the necessity to overcome obstacles has spurred human achievements, what income redistributionists propose, in the form of a welfare state guarantee of "basic necessities," is to remove fundamental and long-standing challenges from the lives of some people by guaranteeing them a livelihood without their having to lift a finger— much less develop human capital, even in the form of common decency. Among the consequences of a need to work to *earn* a living is that behavior is constrained on the job by the need to keep a job, and behavior off the job is constrained by a need to be fit to go to work without being incapacitated by a lack of sleep or by the repercussions of alcoholism or drugs.

Because the redistributionists' argument is presented as a moral imperative for an affluent society to see that everyone has "basic necessities"— however defined— their proposal often escapes empirical tests of what such policies actually produce, compared to what is produced by policies based on the thesis that "challenge and response" spurs human achievements. The many examples of social degeneration in the wake of the all-encompassing welfare state, in both England and America, might have painfully sobering implications, if so many advocates of the welfare state were not still ignoring painful social consequences, while basking in the glow of a sense of moral superiority. This fits a more general pattern described by T.S. Eliot:

> Half the harm that is done in this world is due to people who want to feel important. They don't mean to do harm— but the harm does not interest them. Or they do not see it, or they justify it because they are absorbed in the endless struggle to think well of themselves.[33]

It is never easy to disentangle people's motives. However, to the extent that one's primary concern is for the well-being of the less fortunate, it is not sufficient to put great efforts into formulating "solutions" and promoting their acceptance and implementation. The crucial step that remains is determining the actual empirical consequences that follow. Whether minimum wage laws, gun control laws, higher tax rates on "the rich" or innumerable other policies actually produce the results desired is the ultimate bottom line. But when that final test is often given little or no attention, then it is hard to avoid the conclusion that the process stopped at the point where the goal of thinking well of oneself has been achieved.

The "legacy of slavery" argument is often presented as if to excuse bad behavior in black communities by depicting such behavior as results of the past sins of whites. But the "legacy of slavery" argument also serves as an exemption from scrutiny for counterproductive social trends in the wake of welfare state policies and the vision behind those policies. Tactically, these arguments have been very successful in a political sense. But, empirically, to say that a "legacy of slavery" has kept black communities from rising above their current level of behavior is to defy historical evidence that many black communities had a higher level of civilized behavior *generations ago*, before the triumph of the welfare state vision. Moreover, a very similar retrogression in the behavior of low-income whites in England, in the wake of very similar policies and visions there, suggests that similar policies and visions have produced very similar results on both sides of the Atlantic.

In the bitter battles between those who ascribe unequal economic and social outcomes to external barriers and those who ascribe them to internal deficiencies, both often ignore the possibility that what people *want* to do, or *do not* want to do is a factor not to be overlooked. These culturally shaped preferences can make the ability-versus-barriers dichotomy irrelevant in particular cases. With all the innate ability in the world, and with all the doors of opportunity wide open, people who have no desire to do X have very little likelihood of doing *X*, either well or badly, and are unlikely to be statistically well represented in that endeavor.*

Given multiple factors required for success in many endeavors, including some in which people with most, or perhaps almost all, of these factors may nevertheless be complete failures, there is no reason to expect either even or random patterns of success. Nor is there any basis for expecting a persistence of a given uneven pattern of success over time— especially when the particular prerequisites can change over time. Nor can a general presumption of malign actions by others being behind the fate of the less fortunate be sustained with logic, much less evidence, despite how common that implicit but unsubstantiated assumption has become in American courts of law, under the "disparate impact" theory of discrimination, or how common that same presumption has been in other nations as well.

The presumption of equal outcomes in the absence of malign actions can lead to incorrect— and disastrous— conclusions in other circumstances. When Dr. Marcus Whitman treated both indigenous American Indians and white Americans for measles in the Pacific northwest in 1847, the estimated death rate among the whites was about 15 percent at most, while among the Indians the death rate was about 50 percent. Other Indians did not regard this pattern, which involved the deaths of their loved ones, as just a matter of random chance. Blaming their deaths on some malign action by Dr. Whitman, they killed him and his wife, among other whites massacred or enslaved.[34] However, the whites and the Indians who were ill differed in one crucial factor, the greater exposure of people of European origin to many diseases with which the Indians had historically had no contact, and therefore had developed no biological resistance.

---

* People who are quick to depict any "under-representation" of minorities as evidence or proof of discrimination overlook one of the most blatant examples of "under-representation" of blacks. One may watch years of National Football League games without seeing a single black player kick a single extra point after a touchdown. But the great number of black football stars in other, more remunerative football roles would show what a farce the "under-representation" theory of discrimination is.

Something similar sometimes happened in medieval Europe, when epidemics struck. When the rate of infection and death was noticeably lower among Jews than among Gentiles, demagogues were able to convince some people that Jews must somehow be behind the epidemic and were sparing themselves. Where enough people believed this story, it could lead to mass violence against Jews. What no one knew at the time was that unseen microorganisms were the cause of these epidemics. Because Jewish religious practices required them to pray before every meal and, since they could not go before God with dirty hands, they also had to wash their hands before every meal. Neither Jews nor Gentiles knew about germs at this point but their cultural differences had serious consequences in their susceptibility to communicable diseases.

These were neither the first nor the last times when statistical disparities led people to jump to conclusions about villainy being the cause. False assumptions as to causation are more than intellectual errors, and their consequences go far beyond economic losses.

Chapter 16

GOALS

While goals are in principle quite different from facts— we may all agree on the facts and yet desire to pursue very different goals— many goals are based on a particular set of beliefs about what the existing facts are. If the less fortunate peoples of the world are less fortunate primarily because they are victims of the more fortunate, then the goal to pursue in trying to make things right can be very different from what the goal would be if the less fortunate are seen as people lacking the geographic, cultural or other advantages enjoyed by other peoples, which may be largely through no fault of theirs or of others. Not only may goals differ between people with these very different conceptions of the facts, so may the criteria by which progress is measured.

We have seen how the constraints of geography can doom some peoples not only to poverty but, even worse, can severely limit their development of human capital by restricting their access to the on-going advances of the human race in technology, science, medicine and innumerable other activities. Dramatic rises and falls of whole peoples over the centuries— the British, the Chinese and the peoples of the Islamic world, for example— suggest that their relative positions in the world are not set in concrete by genetics or other unchangeable factors.

Even the historic lags of peoples who have never been in the forefront of human achievement are further evidence of the same thesis, since such peoples have almost invariably lived for centuries or millennia in very isolated geographic settings, such as secluded mountain villages, tropical jungles or on islands far from the nearest mainland. Even countries with outstanding advances at the time, such as China and Japan, fell disastrously behind after they decided to isolate themselves, centuries ago. Both eventually reconnected themselves with the outside world in many ways and rose economically— Japan in the second half of the nineteenth century and China in the late twentieth century.

Impersonal or morally neutral factors have seldom, if ever, had the same attraction for either the elites or the masses as explanations that feature the inhumanity of human beings to fellow human beings. Monstrously appalling things done by some peoples to others darken the history of every region of the planet, but descendants of peoples guilty of the worst or most extensive villainies of the past are by no means always the most prosperous peoples today. Conversely, few peoples have been persecuted for so many centuries, in so many parts of the world as the Jews, who today prosper and achieve. None of this suggests that persecution has no economic effects, but only that how much is an empirical question, not a forgone conclusion.

Nevertheless, no explanation of glaring economic differences by geography, demography, culture or other impersonal factors has ever enjoyed the sudden worldwide acceptance and devotion as Marxism had in the twentieth century— a theory, belief system and agenda based on the assumption that the poor are poor because the rich exploit them. Yet none of the Communist countries established around the world ever achieved a standard of living for ordinary people equal to that in a number of capitalist economies.

Even after communist countries became generally discredited by the end of the twentieth century, the idea that the wealth of the wealthy derived from the poverty of the poor continued to influence both beliefs and goals.

ECONOMIC GOALS

Some might regard the spread of prosperity among human beings in general as the prime criterion of economic success. Others, especially those who believe that the poor are poor because the rich are getting richer at their expense, may be more likely to see the prime criterion as being a reduction or elimination of economic "gaps" and "disparities," which are equated with "inequities." Many people may be in favor of both these things, and think of them as complementary goals, when in fact beyond some point there are inescapable trade-offs that can make the two goals incompatible in practice, however desirable they might seem together in theory. If everyone's income doubles, for example, that will almost certainly reduce poverty, but it will also increase economic "gaps," "disparities" and "inequities."

Gaps may decline because the more advanced group's outcomes decline, without the lagging group's outcomes improving, so that no one is any better off as a result of reducing these gaps in this way. These outcomes may be in educational test results or mortality rates or other variables. Making a reduction of statistical gaps a major goal can make such apparent progress a poor indicator of benefits to flesh-and-blood human beings.

Obviously, some people may value the spread of prosperity more than the reduction of inequality, while others prefer the opposite. When China, after the death of Mao, abandoned the original Communist emphasis on economic egalitarianism and adopted more market-oriented reforms under Deng Xiaoping— who said, "Let some people get rich first"[1]— the economic growth rate hit new highs and literally hundreds of millions of people rose out of poverty.[2] That a country historically plagued by famines, including a famine under Mao in which tens of millions died, became a country in which about one-fourth of the adult population is now overweight, is one measure of the change. But such market-driven rises in per capita real income have not been evenly spread in China, any more than in other places and times, whether within nations or between nations.

When prosperity is widespread, even if not equalized, that may be of more significance to those released from the worst deprivations of grinding poverty than would reductions in the statistical gaps between the poor and the rich. A low-income mother whose sick baby's chances of dying in infancy have been cut in half, as a result of rising prosperity, is unlikely to think of this as inconsequential, much less a grievance, even if she learns that a rich mother's baby's smaller chances of dying in infancy have also been cut in half or perhaps by more than half.

Preoccupation with "disparities," "gaps" and "inequities" has largely been the hallmark of the intelligentsia, the media and politicians. Yet the people whose lives have been most changed by rising levels of prosperity around the world have often been those who were most lacking in basic things before, people living on the fringes of survival. Thus even a redistributionist has noted that the population growth in low-income countries has increased at a higher rate than in more affluent countries.[3] This has largely been due to growing economic prosperity and advances in medical knowledge originating in more affluent countries.

If the desperately poor people in the Italian mountain village described by Professor Banfield in the mid-twentieth century were later enabled to add some meat to their diet— even if only hamburgers or frankfurters— that might be a more meaningful benefit to them than if people in a more affluent society could afford more lobster or filet mignon.* Being able to afford motor scooters might add more to the range of the mountain villagers' mobility than

---

* On a personal note, at a dire time in my life as a young man, I pawned my one suit, in order to get money to be able to eat. After emerging from a pawn shop on the Lower East Side of New York, which was a predominantly Jewish neighborhood at that time, I went into a nearby eating place and ordered a knish and an orange soda. Many years later, I would eat at the Waldorf Astoria, in Parisian restaurants and in the White House. But no meal ever topped that knish and orange soda. Moreover, my happiness as I sat in that little eatery on the Lower East Side was not spoiled for a moment by thoughts that somebody else, somewhere else, in far more elegant surroundings, was probably enjoying a multi-course meal of the most exquisite food.

if a rich family bought a second Rolls Royce. In their book *Free to Choose*, Rose and Milton Friedman pointed out such patterns more generally:

> Industrial progress, mechanical improvement, all of the great wonders of the modern era have meant relatively little to the wealthy. The rich in Ancient Greece would have benefited hardly at all from modern plumbing: running servants replaced running water. Television and radio— the patricians of Rome could enjoy the leading musicians and actors in their home, could have the leading artists as domestic retainers. Ready-to-wear clothing, supermarkets— all these and many other modern developments would have added little to their life. They would have welcomed the improvements in transportation and in medicine, but for the rest, the great achievements of Western capitalism have redounded primarily to the benefit of the ordinary person.[4]

Back in 1836, Nathan Rothschild— one of the richest men in the world, and perhaps *the* richest— died from an infection that defied the efforts of leading doctors summoned to his side.[5] Today, a child of the poorest welfare mother in America is unlikely to die from that same infection, because economic and medical advances present routine cures for such things. This happened not because governments intervened to prevent people from becoming as rich as Nathan Rothschild, but because people in some countries remained free to work out their own lives and make their own mutual accommodations on such terms as they could with their fellow human beings— and it was largely from such countries that the technological and medical advances came.

Emphasis on "income distribution"— and especially *redistribution*— to the neglect of *production* downplays the benefits to society at large, and to the poor especially, from what is produced in the course of earning higher incomes.* As new, better and often cheaper products spread throughout societies around the world, much of this output benefitted people of all sorts, which is the very reason

---

* It is not that money income "trickles down" to the poor— a proposition advocated by no one, but used as a straw man by many. See my monograph, *"Trickle-Down" Theory and "Tax Cuts for the Rich"*.

why millions of people were willing to pay for it, and thus helped create vast fortunes such as that of Bill Gates and others.

Since the reduction of poverty and the closing of economic gaps are competing goals, on what basis can we choose between them? One basis might be what is actually achievable and at what cost. There is a serious question as to whether economic equality— even approximate equality— can be achieved at all, since economic achievements can depend on things largely beyond any government's control, such as geography, or totally beyond anyone's control, such as the past. A government might, of course, simply divorce rewards from productivity, but that experiment has been tried at various times and places over the centuries, usually with results ranging from economic failure to social catastrophe.[6] This does not mean that we can do nothing, but it does suggest that we cannot do everything that strikes us as desirable.

Even leaving aside all practical issues arising from conflicts between the goal of increasing prosperity and the goal of reducing gaps, the achievement of equal incomes can be literally impossible, when equality in one sense is inherently incompatible with equality in another sense.

To take the most extreme case, even if every American man, woman and child had equal individual incomes, that would still leave substantial inequalities in *household* incomes, because households that are in the top 20 percent of income recipients today contain millions more people than households in the bottom 20 percent. These larger households would remain in higher income brackets if incomes were made equal among all individuals. If we restrict income equality to adults, there would be even more inequality between households, since households consisting of a single mother with multiple children would not have nearly as much income— either total income or income per person— as households consisting of two parents and two children, even if welfare paid the single mother as much as other adults received for working.

Putting aside the case of literal equality between every individual or every individual adult, if by some miracle it were possible to have all individuals in all groups attain both the same quantitative levels of education, as measured by the number of years in educational institutions, and also the same qualitative levels as measured by mastery of subjects of the same difficulty and economic rewards, that would still leave intractable differences in age, which would mean inescapable differences in experience since, when the age of adulthood is eighteen, a forty-year-old worker has more than ten times as much work experience as a twenty-year-old worker*— and has probably advanced to successively more responsible and better rewarded positions, while compiling a longer track record on which prospective employers can judge a prospective employee's qualifications.

In these circumstances, even if every twenty-year-old Puerto Rican in the United States had identical incomes with every twenty-year-old Japanese American, and similar equality at every other age, that would still leave a major income inequality between these two groups, because the average Japanese American is more than twenty years older than the average Puerto Rican. In short, even extraordinary and unprecedented degrees of equalization among comparable individuals could still leave major statistical inequalities among groups.

In one sense, the redistributionists can be said to be trying to do more than is possible, given the variety of factors that go into economic productivity and the many differences in the extent to which those factors are present in different groups and nations. But,

---

* If the twenty-year-old worker does not enter the workforce until after additional years spent completing college and postgraduate education, the disparities in years of experience would be even greater— and the annual income required to financially compensate such workers for the additional time, expense and delay of earnings, due to these extra years would increase the inequalities of annual incomes. In other words, part of what may be statistically recorded as annual earnings in later years are in fact capital gains compensating the accumulated efforts made in previous years. As in other contexts, speaking of capital gains received during a given year as if they were the same as incomes earned that same year distorts the economic reality and statistically exaggerates economic inequalities. Delayed compensation, whether for additional education or additional job experience, makes lifetime inequalities less than inequalities measured annually.

in another sense, what the redistributionists are trying to redistribute is insufficient, because it is not fundamental, in either economic or psychic terms. The welfare state redistributes tangible output produced by some to others who have produced less, or have produced nothing at all. But the ultimate wealth of a society does not consist of its tangible output, as such, but the *ability*— the human capital— to produce that tangible output.

That is why nations whose tangible output has been largely destroyed by war, along with most of the physical machinery which produced that output, have nevertheless been able to recover economically within a few years after peace is restored— and why some poorer nations, undisturbed by war, have been unable to achieve comparable prosperity even after decades of being presented with financial capital and physical capital through foreign aid. Transferring the fruits of human capital is not as fundamental as spreading the human capital itself. Such spectacular rises from poverty and backwardness to the forefront of economic achievements as occurred in Scotland in the eighteenth and nineteenth centuries, and in Japan in the nineteenth and twentieth centuries, were achieved by their acquiring human capital from more economically and technologically advanced societies, rather than receiving gifts of end products produced by other peoples' human capital.

Where nations instead receive vast tangible wealth, without having to produce and supply an equivalent, this does *not* promote the development of their own human capital. This unearned wealth can even permit the development of a disdainful attitude toward work in general or toward the development of commercial, industrial or scientific skills, all of which require sustained efforts, rather than the leisurely, luxurious and free-spending lifestyle that unearned wealth permits or promotes. Great conquering nations which have extracted wealth from those they subjugated, or ruling elites who did the same to serfs or slaves within their own country, could indulge in the luxury of pride in being non-productive themselves. During the heyday of the Spanish empire, the vast amounts of gold and silver that poured into Spain enabled Spaniards to purchase the products of other nations, rather than having to produce those products themselves. As one proud Spaniard said of his country, "all the world serves her and she serves nobody."[7]

This disdain toward those who were economically productive extended to such displays of bigotry as the mass expulsions of Jews in the fifteenth century and of Moriscos in the seventeenth century— mass exports of human capital in both cases. Such attitudes were not unique to Spain. It was said of serfdom in Russia that it simply put "much wealth in the hands of a spendthrift nobility."[8] In America, the plantation owners in the antebellum South were likewise noted for a spendthrift lifestyle and the region for lagging in the skills, work ethic and entrepreneurship more common in the rest of America. Those who seek to depict slavery as the basis for American prosperity fail to explain why the region where slavery was concentrated and flourished was the poorest and least progressive region of the country, as was also true in Brazil, the second largest slave-owning nation in the Western Hemisphere.

Some nations acquire unearned wealth from an abundance of rich natural resources, such as vast oil reserves in the Middle East, and hire foreigners to supply the technological expertise to develop those resources, as well as hiring other foreigners to do more mundane tasks— in either case doing little to develop the human capital of their own people. The era when the Islamic civilization of the Middle East exceeded European civilization in various achievements was *before* the industrial revolution that made Middle Eastern oil enormously valuable in the world market. The era when the elite human capital of the Middle East could stand comparison with that anywhere else in the world was an era before petroleum made the development of human capital unnecessary for a life of luxury among the Middle Eastern elites. As for the effect on the people at large, in the late twentieth century the average life expectancy in oil-rich countries like Saudi Arabia and Iran was decades shorter than in countries with few natural resources like Japan and Israel.[9]

Within nations as well, spreading human capital is more fundamental than spreading the tangible fruits of human capital— not only economically but also psychically, because the development of human capital enables the creation of both self-respect and the respect of others. No amount of make-believe "self-esteem," dispensed in schools or from other sources, can substitute for earned self-respect. The largesse of others is no substitute, whether that largesse takes the form of foreign aid to lagging nations or welfare state benefits to lagging groups internally. Moreover, self-respect does not depend on preoccupation with invidious comparisons that are at the heart of the redistributionist vision.

Even someone with a modest and unexciting job can nevertheless take pride in being the one who puts food on the table and a roof over the heads of loved ones. But the old-fashioned phrase, the "respectable poor," has faded away in the era of the welfare state vision, where those who work at "menial" jobs for "chump change" can be disdained by those around them, who can receive comparable living standards without working at all. To imagine that human well-being can be reduced to the kinds of numbers with which the intelligentsia are preoccupied is to treat people in general, and the poor in particular, as if they were livestock to be fed and herded according to whatever notions are in vogue among their betters.

The assumption that wealth consists of physical assets which can be seized from those who have supposedly acquired those assets unjustly from others has been put to the test in many times and places around the world, when people regarded as "exploiters" have been expelled and forced to leave behind the great bulk of their physical wealth. After the entrepreneurial Gujaratis from India were expelled from Uganda in the 1970s, and arrived destitute in England, they rose to affluence and wealth again in England, while the Ugandan economy collapsed.[10] After Germans were expelled from Czechoslovakia following the Second World War, the Sudeten region in which they had been concentrated had still not recovered decades later.[11] In these and other cases, tangible physical wealth could be seized, but not the human capital which had created that wealth before and could create it again. Meanwhile, the seized wealth gets used up by the nation that seized it and those who created it are no longer there to replenish it.

Another crucial question must be faced: What are the consequences of fervently and incessantly proclaiming an unreachable goal, or bitterly denouncing a failure to achieve an equality of outcomes— in a world where outcomes in innumerable endeavors have seldom been equal and have frequently been grossly unequal, even in circumstances where discrimination or other sins can hardly explain these outcomes? Treating equal or random outcomes as a norm, in defiance of evidence from innumerable kinds of endeavors, in societies around the world and down through history, creates innumerable occasions for complaints and denunciations of mundane facts of life. This may be convenient for political or ideological purposes, but it generates much angst of questionable social value over matters large and small, such as an example of the latter which appeared in the *New York Times*:

> The numbers are stunning: From 2007 through 2014, women made up only 30.2 percent of all speaking or named characters in the 100 top-grossing fictional films released in the United States. . . . That is one of the findings in a study, "Inequality in 700 Popular Films," being released on Wednesday, that looks at gender, race, ethnicity and what one of the report's researchers, Stacy L. Smith, describes as an "epidemic" when it comes to lack of diversity.[12]

Since choosing which movies to watch is a wholly voluntary activity for males and females alike, the fact that the speaking or named characters in the most often chosen movies are male, young and white is yet another example of innumerable non-random outcomes, though it is treated as reason for bitter complaints about "hurdles facing female directors" and "deeply racist practices" among movie-makers. But movie producers, like other producers, tend to produce whatever their customers will pay for. When movie-goers' choices do not correspond to others' preconceptions about even or random outcomes, that is taken as a sign that there is something wrong in the real world, since presumably there cannot be anything wrong with others' preconceptions. Such thinking— or lack of thinking— often prevails in far weightier matters than movies, creating far more serious social consequences.*

The goal of equality may be literally impossible when even perfect equality of outcomes for comparable individuals means inequality of outcomes for groups, races or nations— when those groups, races or nations differ in median age alone, quite aside from differences in the quantity or quality of their education, or differences in their respective cultural priorities as to what they want to do, or differences in the geographic or social settings into which they are born. Theoretically, everyone could get together and agree on which particular definition of equality they would use. But what incentive would there be to do that, in an atmosphere where disparities or gaps are seen as intolerable grievances, redeemable for various free benefits to be supplied by others?

ECONOMIC AND SOCIAL CONSEQUENCES

Whatever the merits of any particular definition of equality of outcomes, what must be faced are the consequences of perpetually promoting a fervent crusade, perpetually frustrated by its own internal contradictions— but whose frustration is instead blamed on enemies of a sacred cause.

Those who are in the business of protesting grievances are not going to stop protesting, or taking disruptive or violent action, because equality has been achieved by one definition, when equality by one definition precludes equality by some other definitions. In this context, such phrases as "No justice, no peace" amount to a declaration of unending internal strife, since justice by one definition

---

* A society constantly being assailed from schools, colleges and the media, because its outcomes do not present a tableau fitting the preconceptions of the intelligentsia, can become a society of disgruntled people, unwilling to defend it from internal or external threats that would turn it into a far worse society.

is injustice by another. But no society has inexhaustible patience with unending turmoil. If history is any guide, it is only a matter of time before patience is exhausted and severe repressive measures are imposed, to the ultimate detriment of the whole society.

Again, if history is any guide, no amount of progress toward an unreachable goal can satisfy fiercely promoted aspirations seen as sacred, so that all remaining unfulfilled hopes are seen as intolerable impositions of injustice. Some have argued from history that major social upheavals have often occurred when social problems were in fact lessening, but not at a pace comparable to rising expectations. If so, it may be more than coincidence that the wave of ghetto riots that swept across the United States in the 1960s began just days after passage of the Voting Rights Act of 1965, the capstone of historic civil rights legislation that had preceded it.

Preoccupation with income differences, and with political crusades against them, have not seized the minds and emotions of the general public to anything like the degree to which such preoccupations have dominated the thinking of the intelligentsia.* The obsession of the intelligentsia with economic "gaps" and "disparities" has not usually been shared by the public at large. This has been true even in countries with the most poisonous form of this obsession, resentment and hatred of ethnic minorities who are more productive, and therefore more prosperous, than the population at large. A scholarly study of Romania between the two World Wars, for example, found that the "anti-Jewish mood proved most rampant among the middle and upper classes and among the intellectuals."[13] It was much the same story of hostile reactions to other minority businessmen and professionals in other countries around the world.

An international treatise on ethnic conflicts found that "the supposed economic resentments of businessmen by their customers often do not exist."[14] Malays often preferred dealing with Chinese shopkeepers, for example.[15] In India, Maharashtrians preferred

---

* This has long been the pattern. See, for example, R.H. Tawney, *Equality* (London: George Allen & Unwin, Ltd., 1931), pp. 29, 35, 39.

shopping at businesses run by non-Maharashtrians in Bombay (now Mumbai) in the late twentieth century.[16] In Indonesia and Burma, indigenous farmers often preferred dealing with Arab money-lenders (in Indonesia) and Indian money-lenders (in Burma) to dealing with government money-lenders of their own ethnicity, even though the latter offered lower interest rates.[17] Boycotts of Indian businesses in Uganda in 1959–1960 and of Japanese businesses in Peru in 1930 likewise lacked public support.[18] Even in Nazi Germany, Hitler's 1933 call for a boycott of Jewish businesses failed and had to be called off when it proved to be a politically embarrassing failure.[19]

Such boycotts and other reactions against minority businesses have often been supported, however, by indigenous business rivals in these and other countries, as an obvious matter of self-interest— and by the respective intelligentsia, on ideological grounds. African university students have been hostile toward Indian businessmen in Uganda; Lebanese businessmen in Nigeria, Ghana and Senegal; and Armenian businessmen in Ethiopia.[20] The Third World intelligentsia have seldom had any business experience, and tend to greatly prefer government jobs to working in the private sector.[21] Similar hostility to business has long been common among intellectuals in more prosperous industrial societies as well. It is not surprising that the goal of reducing economic inequalities has often permeated their advocacies and actions. With sufficient time, persistence and fervor, the obsessions of the intelligentsia can of course spread to the public at large, but that is seldom where such zeal originates.

More generally, the crucial question in economic and social issues is whether the success of whatever goal is being pursued is measured by its tangible effects on human well-being, or is instead measured by abstract numbers or other indicators of approaching some preconceived tableau. Despite all the horrors under totalitarian Communist governments in the twentieth century, it should not be forgotten that the Communist movements which led to such governments included people dedicated to equality, to "ending exploitation" and to other humane goals. Many in such movements were willing to risk or sacrifice their livelihoods, or if necessary their lives, in pursuit of those goals. The willingness of many to also sacrifice their own integrity and the truth, in order to forward the cause, was a key factor in the political success of ruthless Communist leaders in imposing horrors with impunity.

This was not unique to Communist movements. Similar phenomena have existed in smaller messianic movements, such as that which led to the Jonestown massacre in 1978. But the Communist movement was the largest and most thoroughly documented example of a movement's implacable pursuit of an unachievable ideal, and the demonizing of all who got in the way, while lionizing ruthless leaders with unbridled powers, including the power to make a mockery of the ideals of the movement itself and exterminate any of its members he chose. As Edward Gibbon said, in his *The Decline and Fall of the Roman Empire*, "fanaticism obliterates the feelings of humanity."[22] This eighteenth century observation, based on looking back on earlier centuries, still applies in the twenty-first century.

Communists are of course an extreme example. But, under any movement or set of collective beliefs, a feeling of being on the side of the angels can be a dangerous self-indulgence in a heedless willfulness that is sometimes called idealism. This kind of idealism can replace realities with preconceptions, and make the overriding goal the victory of some abstract vision, in defiance of reality or in disregard of the fate of fellow human beings. The symbols of the preconception can become goals in themselves. For example, symbolic confiscatory tax rates on "the rich" in America— *which are not actually collected*[23]— benefit neither the U.S. Treasury nor the poor, however much they may benefit people in other countries, who take the jobs created there by American investments that have fled to countries with lower tax rates. The educationally futile mass busing of black and white children to create a tableau of racially "integrated" schools, even when the races remained socially separate and even hostile to one another within the school, is yet another of many examples of symbolism's triumph over reality.

Regardless of the extent to which economic equality can or cannot be achieved or approximated, making equality a moral touchstone has meant fomenting resentments of others who are better off, in whatever way and for whatever reasons. In addition to worldwide examples of resentments toward high-achieving minorities, even when they created businesses and industries where these had not existed before, benefitting the larger society around them, there has also been hostility toward fellow members of lagging groups who are acquiring educational and other prerequisites for overcoming their lags. This has been common on both sides of the Atlantic, among low-income whites in England and among ghetto blacks in the United States, among others.

Equality of outcomes as a fact in the real world is not what poses a danger. It is the perpetually frustrated attempts to achieve this unachievable goal which produce such poisonous by-products as unprovoked lashing out at people who have more. Whether this takes the form of ghetto mobs destroying small businesses owned by Asian Americans, or blacks in school beating up their Asian American classmates, none of the usual excuses apply. Even the hostility toward fellow black students who attended Dunbar High School during the years of its academic ascendancy was grotesque, at a time when blacks needed all the highly educated people possible, to break down all the racial barriers that they could and did.

There is of course no need to promote *in*equality of achievement or reward, nor to accept it as anything other than a fact of life, resulting from geographic, cultural and other influences, some within human control and some not. However commendable the desire to extend more opportunities to those born into less promising circumstances, what is less commendable— indeed, irresponsible— is to pretend to have more power than we do to create equality of achievement for all.*

---

* Particular nations, or particular groups within nations, have risen from dire poverty to achieve not merely equality but above average income and wealth. However, the impetus for this has almost always come from within these particular nations or groups themselves.

What is truly reprehensible are attempts to pull down those who have achieved more, instead of facilitating the rise of those less fortunate who seek to rise through their own achievements. The idea that those who have less can be presumed to be victims of those who have more is an idea whose consequences have a worldwide history written in the blood of millions.

Ideas have consequences, even when they have no validity. The many wide-ranging and mutually contradictory meanings of the word "equality" make it politically attractive to large numbers of people with substantively very different values and beliefs, who can coalesce around a word, even when they mean different things by that word. While this is a political or ideological advantage to those who seek to mobilize a large constituency, and the unattainability of a treasured goal ensures longevity to the crusades of that constituency, the actual social consequences of heady crusades for unattainable goals have been painfully sobering, at best. Fortunately, many less pretentious activities, including the cumulative effects of economic, medical and technological advances, have had a far more successful record of improving and expanding the scope of human life.

In the United States, during the twentieth century alone, many luxuries of the rich spread to virtually all, not by redistribution of income, but by the normal processes of a market economy. To begin with the most basic things, only 10 percent of American homes had flush toilets in 1900 but 98 percent had them by 1997.[24] In 1900 the primary source of lighting for 88 percent of U.S. families was either kerosene or coal oil lamps, while another 9 percent had gas lighting and only 3 percent had electric lights. But, by 1990, more than 99 percent of American families had electric lights.[25] In 1900, only 8 percent of American homes had central heating, as distinguished from being heated by stoves, fireplaces or other devices such as kerosene heaters. By 1997, however, 93 percent of American homes had central heating systems.[26] Infant mortality rates were 165 per thousand in 1900 and 7 per thousand in 1997, as fatal childhood diseases like measles and diphtheria had declined to the vanishing point by the middle of the twentieth century.[27]

Beyond these most basic things, only one percent of American families owned an automobile in 1910, but 86 percent did by 1983.[28] Only 5 percent of American residences in 1900 had a telephone but 83 percent did by 1970.[29] Among the things that nobody had in 1900 but which virtually every American household had before the end of the twentieth century were radios and refrigerators. Other things that nobody had in 1900 but which most American households had by 1987 included air conditioning (62 percent), washing machines (73 percent) and television sets (93 percent).[30] Other things that did not exist at the beginning of the twentieth century, but which were ubiquitous by the end of that century would include airplanes and computers. The scope of people's lives was expanded not only by technological advances but also by rising incomes. The number of people who visited Yellowstone National Park in 1904 was 13,727 but, in 1998, there were more than 3 million visitors. The number of Americans who visited a foreign country in 1919 was 152,000 but, in 1997, there were 22 million.[31]

Most of the people who were responsible for creating such major advances and expansions in the scope of human life in the United States in the twentieth century are largely unknown to the American public today, except for a few individuals known simply for having become rich, *somehow*. The mundane progress driven by ordinary economic and social processes in a free society becomes dramatic only when its track record is viewed in retrospect over a span of years.

It is by no means obvious why we should prefer trying to equalize incomes to putting our efforts into increasing output. People in general, and the poor in particular, seem to "vote with their feet" by moving to where there is greater prosperity, rather than where there is greater economic equality. Rising standards of living, especially for those at the bottom economically, have resulted not so much from changing the relative sizes of different slices of the economic pie as from increasing the size of the pie itself— which has largely been accomplished without requiring heady rhetoric, fierce emotions or bloodshed.

Does it not matter if the hungry are fed, if slums are replaced by decent and air-conditioned housing, if infant mortality rates are reduced to less than a tenth of what they were before? Are invidious "gaps" and "disparities" all that matter? In a world where we are all beneficiaries of enormous windfall gains that our forebears never had, are we to tear apart the society that created all this, because some people's windfall gains are greater or less than some other people's windfall gains?

ACKNOWLEDGEMENTS

One of the most general acknowledgements that needs to be made, more often than it is, is that we all stand on the shoulders of giants. I am especially awed, and indebted to, those who have obviously invested great amounts of time, effort and wisdom writing monumental treatises on subjects ranging from the Chinese in Southeast Asia to the geographic histories of nations around the world to landmark human achievements in the arts and sciences over the centuries.

There would of course be no point standing on the shoulders of giants if we saw only what they saw and simply repeated what they had already said, often quite well. But we can at least look in different directions from the vantage points they give us, and seek answers to other questions with the benefit of the knowledge and insight they provided. At the opposite end of the spectrum are the many wrong-headed publications, including painfully specious Supreme Court decisions, which have spurred my re-examination of issues that I might not have noticed otherwise. Both valid and invalid arguments can spur deeper examinations of important issues.

Closer to home, it would be hard to exaggerate how much I owe to my research assistants of many years, Na Liu and Elizabeth Costa. They have not simply gotten research material that I asked for but have participated more actively by seeking out and evaluating other material on their own initiative. In addition, Ms. Costa has done the painstaking copy-editing and fact-checking, while Ms. Liu has created the Quark computer files from which the finished manuscript can be printed directly into books— sparing me interactions with publishers' copy-editors, and sparing them interactions with me.

All of this takes place with the support, and under the auspices, of the Hoover Institution, utilizing the vast library resources of Stanford University. My wife Mary and my friend of many years, Joseph Charney, gave helpful critiques of parts of both the first edition of *Wealth, Poverty and Politics* and this revised and enlarged edition.

All conclusions, and whatever errors there may be, are solely my responsibility.

Thomas Sowell
The Hoover Institution
Stanford University

NOTES

Preface

Epigraph: John Adams: A Biography in His Own Words, edited by James Bishop Peabody (New York: Newsweek, 1973), Volume I, pp. 121–122.

1. Charles Sanders Peirce, *Essays in the Philosophy of Science* (New York: Liberal Arts Press, 1957), p. 35.

Chapter 1: Issues

Epigraph: Alexander Hamilton, "Defects of the Present Confederation," Alexander Hamilton, James Madison, and John Jay, *The Federalist*, Number 21, edited by Benjamin Fletcher Wright (Cambridge, Massachusetts: Harvard University Press, 1961), p. 189.

1. Theodore Caplow, Louis Hicks and Ben J. Wattenberg, *The First Measured Century: An Illustrated Guide to Trends in America, 1900–2000* (Washington: The AEI Press, 2001), p. 99; Stanley Lebergott, *Pursuing Happiness: American Consumers in the Twentieth Century* (Princeton: Princeton University Press, 1993), p. 120.

2. See, for example, N.J.G. Pounds, *An Historical Geography of Europe* (Cambridge: Cambridge University Press, 1990), p. 21.

3. Ibid., p. 27. The advanced state of ancient civilizations in Egypt, India and China during the same era has been covered in many books and articles by many authors, including Margaret Oliphant, *The Atlas of the Ancient World: Charting the Great Civilizations of the Past* (New York: Simon & Schuster, 1992), pp. 38–41, 146–149, 162–165.

4. Mark Casson, *The Growth of International Business* (London: George Allen & Unwin, 1983), p. 106.

5. Luigi Barzini, *The Europeans* (New York: Simon and Schuster, 1983), p. 47.

6. Charles O. Hucker, *China's Imperial Past: An Introduction to Chinese History and Culture* (Stanford: Stanford University Press, 1975), p. 65; Jacques Gernet, *A History of Chinese Civilization*, second edition, translated by J.R. Foster and Charles Hartman (New York: Cambridge University Press, 1996), pp. 69, 138, 140.

7. David S. Landes, *The Wealth and Poverty of Nations: Why Some Are So Rich and Some So Poor* (New York: W.W. Norton & Company, 1998), pp. 93–95;

William H. McNeill, *The Rise of the West: A History of the Human Community* (Chicago: University of Chicago Press, 1991), p. 526.

8. Charles Murray, *Human Accomplishment: The Pursuit of Excellence in the Arts and Sciences, 800 B.C. to 1950* (New York: Harper Collins, 2003), pp. 355–361.

9. Ellen Churchill Semple, *Influences of Geographic Environment* (New York: Henry Holt and Company, 1911), p. 20. According to Fernand Braudel: "The mountains are as a rule a world apart from civilizations, which are an urban and lowland achievement. Their history is to have none, to remain almost always on the fringe of the great waves of civilization, even the longest and most persistent, which may spread over great distances in the horizontal plane but are powerless to move vertically when faced with an obstacle of a few hundred metres." Fernand Braudel, *The Mediterranean and the Mediterranean World in the Age of Philip II*, translated by Siân Reynolds (Berkeley: University of California Press, 1995), Vol. I, p. 34.

10. Fernand Braudel, *The Mediterranean and the Mediterranean World in the Age of Philip II*, translated by Siân Reynolds, p. 35.

11. *The World Almanac and Book of Facts: 2014* (New York: World Almanac Books, 2014), pp. 748, 771, 779–780, 821, 831, 839, 846.

12. Ibid., pp. 764, 786, 793.

13. The Economist, *Pocket World in Figures: 2013 Edition* (London: Profile Books, Ltd., 2012), p. 25.

14. According to the authors of *Why Nations Fail*, "World inequality today exists because during the nineteenth and twentieth centuries some nations were able to take advantage of the Industrial Revolution and the technologies and methods of organization that it brought while others were unable to do so." Daron Acemoglu and James A. Robinson, *Why Nations Fail: The Origins of Power, Prosperity, and Poverty* (New York: Crown Business, 2012), p. 271. But economic inequalities among nations did not begin with the industrial revolution, and the international inequalities of ancient times were by no means necessarily less than the inequalities of the nineteenth and twentieth centuries, or the inequalities of today.

15. Herbert Heaton, *Economic History of Europe* (New York: Harper & Brothers, 1936), p. 246; Saskia Sassen, *Territory, Authority, Rights: From Medieval to Global Assemblages* (Princeton: Princeton University Press, 2006), p. 83.

16. Carlo M. Cipolla, *Before the Industrial Revolution: European Society and Economy, 1000–1700,* second edition (New York: W.W. Norton, 1980), p. 252.

17. David S. Landes, *The Wealth and Poverty of Nations,* p. 250.

18. U.S. Bureau of the Census, *Historical Statistics of the United States: Colonial Times to 1970* (Washington: Government Printing Office, 1975), Part 1, p. 382.

19. The Economist, *Pocket World in Figures: 2003 Edition* (London: Profile Books, 2002), p. 26; U.S. Bureau of the Census, "Money Income in the United States: 2000," *Current Population Reports,* P60–213 (Washington: U.S. Bureau of the Census, 2001), p. 2.

20. The phrase "income distribution" leads some people to reason as if there is some pre-existing block of income or wealth— created "somehow"— that is then divided up among individuals or groups. In reality, it is the process of creating wealth that leads to individual incomes being received in exchange for individual productivity in that process. These individual incomes may later be added up by others into a verbally collectivized "national income," which is then spoken of as being "distributed" to individuals or groups. Sometimes the same way of thinking is applied internationally, leading to laments about such things as how Americans, for example, consume a disproportionate share of "the world's output." But there is no one named "World" who produces all output, or indeed any output at all. Americans essentially consume what Americans produce, using a portion of what they produce to exchange for an equivalent amount of imported goods from others. In a purely figurative statistical sense, income can be said to be "distributed" in the same sense in which there is a statistical "distribution" of heights in a population, without anyone imagining that these heights exist collectively and are then sent out to individuals. Those who believe that income or wealth *should* be collectivized in reality, and then be shared out, are of course free to advocate such an economic system explicitly, but that is very different from insinuating such a process with words that have more than one meaning.

21. Henry Hazlitt, *The Wisdom of Henry Hazlitt* (Irvington-on-Hudson, New York: The Foundation for Economic Education, 1993), p. 224.

22. Ellsworth Huntington, "Climate and Civilization," *Harper's Monthly Magazine,* February 1915, pp. 367–373.

23. Ellen Churchill Semple, *Influences of Geographic Environment,* p. 125.

24. Darrel Hess, *McKnight's Physical Geography: A Landscape Appreciation*, eleventh edition (Upper Saddle River, New Jersey: Pearson Education, 2014), pp. 100–101; E.A. Pearce and C.G. Smith, *The Times Books World Weather Guide* (New York: Times Books, 1984), pp. 129, 130, 131, 132, 142, 376.

25. E.A. Pearce and C.G. Smith, *The Times Books World Weather Guide*, pp. 132, 376. In none of the winter months— from December through March— is the average daily low temperature in Washington warmer than in London, and the lowest temperature ever recorded in Washington is lower for each of those winter months than in London.

26. Daron Acemoglu and James A. Robinson, *Why Nations Fail*, p. 62.

27. Fernand Braudel, *The Structures of Everyday Life: The Limits of the Possible*, translated by Siân Reynolds (Berkeley: University of California Press, 1992), p. 101.

28. See, for example, Richard Lynn and Tatu Vanhanen, *IQ and Global Inequality* (Augusta, Georgia: Washington Summit Publishers, 2006), pp. 105–111.

29. Richard Lynn, *The Global Bell Curve: Race, IQ, and Inequality Worldwide* (Augusta, Georgia: Washington Summit Publishers, 2008), p. 5.

30. Richard Lynn and Tatu Vanhanen, *IQ and Global Inequality*, pp. 105–111.

31. Ellsworth Huntington, "Climate and Civilization," *Harper's Monthly Magazine*, February 1915, pp. 367–373.

32. Attributed to John Maynard Keynes, without specific citation. A very similar statement appeared earlier in Carveth Read, *Logic: Deductive and Inductive*, third edition (London: Alexander Moring Limited, The De La More Press, 1909), p. 320.

Part I: Geographic Factors

Epigraph: David S. Landes, *The Wealth and Poverty of Nations: Why Some Are So Rich and Some So Poor* (New York: W.W. Norton & Company, 1998), p. 6.

1. Darrell Hess, *McKnight's Physical Geography: A Landscape Appreciation*, eleventh edition (Upper Saddle River, New Jersey: Pearson Education, Inc., 2014), p. 200.

2. Monica and Robert Beckinsale, *Southern Europe: The Mediterranean and Alpine Lands* (London: University of London Press, 1975), p. 33.

3. Alan H. Strahler, *Introducing Physical Geography*, sixth edition (Hoboken, New Jersey: Wiley, 2013), pp. 402–403.

4. Fred Punzo, *Desert Arthropods: Life History Variations* (New York: Springer, 2000), p. 73.

5. Carl H. Ernst and Jeffrey E. Lovich, *Turtles of the United States and Canada*, second edition (Baltimore: Johns Hopkins University Press, 2009), pp. 17–18, 50.

6. Andrew H. Brown, "Saving Earth's Oldest Living Things," *National Geographic*, May 1951, p. 691.

7. Antony R. Orme, "Coastal Environments," *The Physical Geography of Africa*, edited by William M. Adams, Andrew S. Goudie, and Antony R. Orme (Oxford: Oxford University Press, 1996), p. 247.

8. Monica and Robert Beckinsale, *Southern Europe*, pp. 42–43, 228.

9. James S. Gardner, et al., "People in the Mountains," *Mountain Geography: Physical and Human Dimensions*, edited by Martin F. Price, et al (Berkeley: University of California Press, 2013), p. 268.

10. See, for example, Jeffrey D. Sachs and Andrew M. Warner, "The Curse of Natural Resources," *European Economic Review*, Vol. 45, Issues 4–6 (2001), pp. 827–838; Roland Hodler, "The Curse of Natural Resources in Fractionalized Countries," *European Economic Review*, Vol. 50, Issue 6 (2006), pp. 1367–1386; Raymond F. Mikesell, "Explaining the Resource Curse, with Special Reference to Mineral-Exporting Countries," *Resources Policy*, Vol. 23, No. 4 (December 1997), pp. 191–199; Macatran Humphreys, Jeffrey D. Sachs, and Joseph Stiglitz, *Escaping the Resource Curse* (New York: Columbia University Press, 2007); Michael L. Ross, *The Oil Curse: How Petroleum Wealth Shapes the Development of Nations* (Princeton: Princeton University Press, 2012); *Resource Curse or Blessing? Africa's Management of Its Extractive Industries*, Hearing before the Subcommittee on African Affairs of the Committee on Foreign Relations, United States Senate, One Hundred Tenth Congress, second session, September 24, 2008 (Washington: Government Printing Office, 2009).

11. See, for example, Frederick R. Troeh and Louis M. Thompson, *Soils and Soil Fertility*, sixth edition (Ames, Iowa: Blackwell, 2005), p. 330; Xiaobing Liu, et al., "Overview of Mollisols in the World: Distribution, Land Use and

Management," *Canadian Journal of Soil Science*, Vol. 92 (2012), pp. 383–402; Darrell Hess, *McKnight's Physical Geography*, eleventh edition, pp. 362–363.

12. William S. Maltby, *The Rise and Fall of the Spanish Empire* (New York: Palgrave Macmillan, 2009), p. 18; Peter Pierson, *The History of Spain* (Westport, Connecticut: Greenwood Press, 1999), pp. 7–8.

13. John H. Chambers, *A Traveller's History of Australia* (New York: Interlink Books, 1999), p. 35.

14. Ellen Churchill Semple, *Influences of Geographic Environment* (New York: Henry Holt and Company, 1911), pp. 442–443; Don Funnell and Romola Parish, *Mountain Environments and Communities* (London: Routledge, 2001), p. 115.

15. The total area of all 50 states is 3,678,190 square miles. Subtracting the area of Alaska (590,693 square miles) and Hawaii (6,468 square miles) leaves 3,081,029 square miles as the area of the remaining 48 contiguous states. The area of the Sahara Desert is 3,320,000 square miles or approximately 8 percent larger than the 48 contiguous states. *Time Almanac: 2013* (Chicago: Encyclopedia Britannica, 2012), pp. 173, 466, 582–583, 587.

16. Antony R. Orme, "Coastal Environments," *The Physical Geography of Africa*, edited by William M. Adams, Andrew S. Goudie, and Antony R. Orme, p. 238.

17. Fernand Braudel, *A History of Civilizations*, translated by Richard Mayne (New York: The Penguin Group, 1994), p. 124. Likewise, a geographer said, "Enlightenment filtering in here was sadly dimmed as it spread." Ellen Churchill Semple, *Influences of Geographic Environment*, p. 392.

18. William H. McNeill, *History of Western Civilization: A Handbook*, sixth edition (Chicago: University of Chicago Press, 1986), p. 247.

19. Gregory Veeck, et al., *China's Geography: Globalization and the Dynamics of Political, Economic, and Social Change*, second edition (Lanham, Maryland: Rowman & Littlefield, 2011), p. 220.

20. Darrell Hess, *McKnight's Physical Geography*, pp. 336–338.

21. Ellen Churchill Semple, *The Geography of the Mediterranean Region: Its Relation to Ancient History* (New York: Henry Holt and Company, 1931), pp. 289–292.

22. J.R. McNeill, *The Mountains of the Mediterranean World: An Environmental History* (New York: Cambridge University Press, 1992), p. 349.

23. Ellen Churchill Semple, *The Geography of the Mediterranean Region*, p. 91.

24. Charles Murray, *Human Accomplishment: The Pursuit of Excellence in the Arts and Sciences, 800 B.C. to 1950* (New York: Harper Collins, 2003), pp. 355–361.

25. N.J.G. Pounds, *An Historical Geography of Europe* (Cambridge: Cambridge University Press, 1990), p. 1.

26. Ellen Churchill Semple, *Influences of Geographic Environment*, pp. 29, 131.

27. Ibid., p. 25.

28. Oscar Handlin, "Introduction," *The Positive Contribution by Immigrants*, edited by Oscar Handlin (Paris: United Nations Educational, Scientific and Cultural Organization, 1955), p. 13.

29. Ulrich Bonnell Phillips, *The Slave Economy of the Old South: Selected Essays in Economic and Social History* (Baton Rouge: Louisiana State University Press, 1968), p. 269.

Chapter 2: Waterways

Epigraph: Fernand Braudel, *The Mediterranean and the Mediterranean World in the Age of Philip II*, translated by Siân Reynolds (Berkeley: University of California Press, 1995), Vol. II, p. 773.

1. Ellen Churchill Semple, *Influences of Geographic Environment* (New York: Henry Holt and Company, 1911), p. 84.

2. Jeffry A. Frieden, *Global Capitalism: Its Fall and Rise in the Twentieth Century* (New York: W.W. Norton, 2006), p. 5. Similar disparities between the cost of land transport and water transport were found in eighteenth century America. Ellen Churchill Semple, *American History and Its Geographic Conditions* (Boston: Houghton, Mifflin and Company, 1903), p. 87.

3. Daniel Yergin, *The Prize: The Epic Quest for Oil, Money, and Power* (New York: Simon & Schuster, 1991), p. 60.

4. Jack Chen, *The Chinese of America* (San Francisco: Harper & Row, Publishers, 1980), pp. 65–66.

5. Fernand Braudel, *The Structures of Everyday Life: The Limits of the Possible*, translated by Siân Reynolds (Berkeley: University of California Press, 1992), p. 421.

6. William A. Hance, *The Geography of Modern Africa* (New York: Columbia University Press, 1964), p. 5.

7.   Jocelyn Murray, editor, *Cultural Atlas of Africa* (New York: Facts on File Publications, 1981), p. 10.

8.   Ellen Churchill Semple, *Influences of Geographic Environment*, p. 255. The ratio of Africa's coastline to its area is in fact less than that for any other continent. Asia, the largest continent, is 50 percent larger than Africa, but its coastline is more than twice as long as the coastline of Africa. Antony R. Orme, "Coastal Environments," *The Physical Geography of Africa*, edited by William M. Adams, Andrew S. Goudie, and Antony R. Orme (Oxford: Oxford University Press, 1996), p. 238.

9.   Robert Stock, *Africa South of the Sahara: A Geographical Interpretation*, third edition (New York: The Guilford Press, 2013), p. 29; Robert O. Collins and James M. Burns, *A History of Sub-Saharan Africa*, second edition (New York: Cambridge University Press, 2014), p. 17.

10.   Robert Stock, *Africa South of the Sahara*, third edition, p. 129; Ellen Churchill Semple, *American History and Its Geographic Conditions*, p. 246.

11.   Jacques Gernet, *A History of Chinese Civilization*, second edition, translated by J.R. Foster and Charles Hartman (New York: Cambridge University Press, 1996), p. 321.

12.   Ellen Churchill Semple, *Influences of Geographic Environment*, p. 260.

13.   Ellen Churchill Semple, *American History and Its Geographic Conditions*, pp. 180–181.

14.   Ibid., p. 137.

15.   Carl Ortwin Sauer, *Geography of the Pennyroyal* (Frankfort: The Kentucky Geological Survey, 1927), p. 210.

16.   Darrell Haug Davis, *The Geography of the Mountains of Eastern Kentucky* (Frankfort: The Kentucky Geological Survey, 1924), p. 106.

17.   Ibid.

18.   Rupert B. Vance, *Human Geography of the South: A Study in Regional Resources and Human Adequacy* (Chapel Hill: University of North Carolina Press, 1932), p. 451.

19.   William Howarth, "The St. Lawrence: A River of Boundaries," National Geographic Society, *Great Rivers of the World*, edited by Margaret Sedeen (Washington: National Geographic Society, 1984), pp. 415–416, 420; Ronald

Stagg, *The Golden Dream: A History of the St. Lawrence Seaway* (Toronto: Dundurn Press, 2010), p. 233.

20. U.S. Navy Hydrographic Office, *Africa Pilot*, Vol. II: *South and East Coasts of Africa from Cape of Good Hope to Ras Hafun* (Washington: Government Printing Office, 1916), p. 248.

21. William A. Hance, *The Geography of Modern Africa*, second edition (New York: Columbia University Press, 1975), pp. 497–498.

22. Virginia Thompson and Richard Adloff, *French West Africa* (Stanford: Stanford University Press, 1957), p. 305.

23. Edwin O. Reischauer and John K. Fairbank, *A History of East Asian Civilization*, Volume I: *East Asia: The Great Tradition* (London: George Allen & Unwin, Ltd., 1960), pp. 20–21.

24. Ellen Churchill Semple, *Influences of Geographic Environment*, p. 341.

25. William H. McNeill, *History of Western Civilization: A Handbook*, sixth edition (Chicago: University of Chicago Press, 1986), p. 247.

26. Jocelyn Murray, editor, *Cultural Atlas of Africa*, p. 13.

27. F.J. Pedler, *Economic Geography of West Africa* (London: Longmans, Green and Co., 1955), p. 118.

28. Ellen Churchill Semple, *The Geography of the Mediterranean Region: Its Relation to Ancient History* (New York: Henry Holt and Company, 1931), pp. 83, 85, 90, 103–104.

29. See E.A. Pearce and C.G. Smith, *The Times Books World Weather Guide* (New York: Times Books, 1984), pp. 154, 304; Ellen Churchill Semple, *The Geography of the Mediterranean Region*, p. 83; Amalie Jo Orme, "The Mediterranean Environment of Greater California," *The Physical Geography of North America*, edited by Antony R. Orme (Oxford: Oxford University Press, 2002), pp. 402–424; Harriet D. Allen, "Mediterranean Environments," *The Physical Geography of Africa*, edited by William M. Adams, Andrew S. Goudie, and Antony R. Orme, p. 307.

30. E.A. Pearce and C.G. Smith, *The Times Books World Weather Guide*, pp. 380, 393, 415. These summer rainfall differences are also reflected in annual rainfall differences between many cities in the eastern and western Mediterranean. See Ellen Churchill Semple, *The Geography of the Mediterranean Region*, p. 90.

31. E.A. Pearce and C.G. Smith, *The Times Books World Weather Guide*, pp. 389, 393.

32. Ellen Churchill Semple, *The Geography of the Mediterranean Region*, p. 117.

33. Ibid., p. 124.

34. Jean W. Sedlar, *East Central Europe in the Middle Ages, 1000–1500* (Seattle: University of Washington Press, 1994), p. 335.

35. Ellen Churchill Semple, *The Geography of the Mediterranean Region*, pp. 91–92; See also Ellen Churchill Semple, *Influences of Geographic Environment*, pp. 450–451.

36. David S. Landes, *The Wealth and Poverty of Nations: Why Some Are So Rich and Some So Poor* (New York: W.W. Norton & Company, 1998), p. 295.

37. Nicholas Wollaston, "The Zaire," *Great Rivers of the World*, edited by Alexander Frater (Boston: Little, Brown and Company, 1984), p. 80.

38. Rupert B. Vance, *Human Geography of the South*, p. 261.

39. Robert E. Gabler, et al., *Physical Geography*, ninth edition (Belmont, California: Brooks/Cole Cengage Learning, 2009), p. 470.

40. Ellen Churchill Semple, *Influences of Geographic Environment*, p. 343.

41. Darrell Haug Davis, *The Geography of the Mountains of Eastern Kentucky*, p. 111.

42. Ellen Churchill Semple, *The Geography of the Mediterranean Region*, p. 186.

43. Rupert B. Vance, *Human Geography of the South*, p. 264.

44. Ellen Churchill Semple, *Influences of Geographic Environment*, pp. 349–350.

45. Darrel Hess, *McKnight's Physical Geography: A Landscape Appreciation*, eleventh edition (Upper Saddle River, New Jersey: Pearson Education, 2014), p. 271.

46. Jonathan B. Tourtellot, "The Amazon: Sailing a Jungle Sea," *Great Rivers of the World*, edited by Margaret Sedeen, p. 299.

47. Ellen Churchill Semple, *The Geography of the Mediterranean Region*, p. 579.

48. Rondo Cameron, *A Concise Economic History of the World: From Paleolithic Times to the Present* (New York: Oxford University Press, 1989), p. 98.

49. Ellen Churchill Semple, *Influences of Geographic Environment*, pp. 56, 330.

50. Ibid., p. 331.

51. Ibid.

52. Fernand Braudel, *The Mediterranean and the Mediterranean World in the Age of Philip II*, translated by Siân Reynolds, Vol. I, pp. 95, 144.

53. William H. McNeill, *History of Western Civilization*, sixth edition, p. 246.

54. Fernand Braudel, *The Mediterranean and the Mediterranean World in the Age of Philip II*, translated by Siân Reynolds, Vol. I, p. 138; Don Hinrichsen, *Coastal Waters of the World: Trends, Threats, and Strategies* (Washington: Island Press, 1998), p. 75.

55. Fernand Braudel, *The Mediterranean and the Mediterranean World in the Age of Philip II*, translated by Siân Reynolds, Vol. I, p. 138.

56. Ibid.

Chapter 3: Lands

Epigraph: Tim Marshall, *Prisoners of Geography: Ten Maps That Explain Everything About the World* (New York: Scribner, 2015), p. 1.

1. Jared Diamond, *Guns, Germs, and Steel: The Fates of Human Societies* (New York: W.W. Norton, 1997), p. 367.

2. J.D. Mackie, *A History of Scotland*, second edition, revised and edited by Bruce Lenman and Geoffrey Parker (New York: Penguin Books, 1978), p. 13.

3. Darrell Haug Davis, *The Geography of the Mountains of Eastern Kentucky* (Frankfort: The Kentucky Geological Survey, 1924), p. ix.

4. Ibid., p. 4.

5. Ibid., p. 61.

6. James S. Gardner, et al., "People in the Mountains," *Mountain Geography: Physical and Human Dimensions*, edited by Martin F. Price, et al (Berkeley: University of California Press, 2013), pp. 268, 269.

7. See, for example, J.R. McNeill, *The Mountains of the Mediterranean World: An Environmental History* (New York: Cambridge University Press, 1992), pp. 27, 44–46, 104, 142–143; Ellen Churchill Semple, *Influences of Geographic Environment* (New York: Henry Holt and Company, 1911), pp. 530, 531, 599, 600; Fernand Braudel, *The Mediterranean and the Mediterranean World in the Age of Philip II*, translated by Siân Reynolds (Berkeley: University of California Press, 1995), Vol. I, pp. 38, 57, 97; Rupert B. Vance, *Human Geography of the South: A Study in Regional Resources and Human Adequacy* (Chapel Hill: University of North Carolina Press, 1932), pp. 242, 246–247.

8. Ellen Churchill Semple, *Influences of Geographic Environment*, p. 532.

9. Rupert B. Vance, *Human Geography of the South*, p. 242. See also Darrell Haug Davis, *The Geography of the Mountains of Eastern Kentucky*, pp. 23, 25. The

isolation between mountain villages does not imply isolation within those villages, where homes or farms may be close together.

10. "Each settlement. . . constitutes a world within itself, for it is insulated from its neighbors by one or two thousand feet of steep wooded ridge." Rupert B. Vance, *Human Geography of the South*, p. 242. See also Ibid., pp. 243, 246.

11. Jean W. Sedlar, *East Central Europe in the Middle Ages, 1000–1500* (Seattle: University of Washington Press, 1994), p. 335.

12. Fernand Braudel, *The Mediterranean and the Mediterranean World in the Age of Philip II*, translated by Siân Reynolds, Vol. I, p. 283.

13. J.R. McNeill, *The Mountains of the Mediterranean World*, p. 44.

14. Ellen Churchill Semple, *Influences of Geographic Environment*, pp. 531–532.

15. James S. Gardner, et al., "People in the Mountains," *Mountain Geography*, edited by Martin F. Price, et al., p. 269.

16. Douglas W. Freshfield, "The Great Passes of the Western and Central Alps," *The Geographical Journal*, Vol. 49, No. 1 (Jan. 1917), pp. 2–22; James S. Gardner, et al., "People in the Mountains," *Mountain Geography*, edited by Martin F. Price, et al., p. 288; Ellen Churchill Semple, *American History and Its Geographic Conditions* (Boston: Houghton, Mifflin and Company, 1903), p. 52; N.J.G. Pounds, *An Historical Geography of Europe* (Cambridge: Cambridge University Press, 1990), pp. 15, 110, 140; Ellen Churchill Semple, *Influences of Geographic Environment*, p. 535.

17. Ellen Churchill Semple, *Influences of Geographic Environment*, p. 539.

18. Ibid., pp. 532–536.

19. H. Tyler Blethen and Curtis W. Wood, Jr., *From Ulster to Carolina: The Migration of the Scotch-Irish to Southwestern North Carolina*, revised edition (Raleigh: North Carolina Department of Cultural Resources, Division of Archives and History, 1998), p. 40.

20. J.R. McNeill, *The Mountains of the Mediterranean World*, p. 143.

21. Ibid., pp. 27, 54.

22. Darrell Haug Davis, *The Geography of the Mountains of Eastern Kentucky*, pp. 103, 105.

23. Ibid., p. 107.

24. Ibid., p. 114.

25. J.R. McNeill, *The Mountains of the Mediterranean World*, p. 27.

26. Alton C. Byers, et al., "An Introduction to Mountains," *Mountain Geography*, edited by Martin F. Price, et al., p. 6.

27. James S. Gardner, et al., "People in the Mountains," Ibid., p. 267.

28. Martin F. Price and Thomas Kohler, "Sustainable Mountain Development," Ibid., p. 336.

29. Edward C. Banfield, *The Moral Basis of a Backward Society* (New York: The Free Press, 1958), pp. 10, 17, 35, 46.

30. Ibid., pp. 46–47.

31. J.R. McNeill, *The Mountains of the Mediterranean World*, p. 47.

32. Ibid., p. 29.

33. See for example, Don Funnell and Romola Parish, *Mountain Environments and Communities* (London: Routledge, 2001), p. 99; James S. Gardner, et al., "People in the Mountains," *Mountain Geography*, edited by Martin F. Price, et al., pp. 276, 306; Ellen Churchill Semple, *Influences of Geographic Environment*, pp. 595–596.

34. Alton C. Byers, et al., "An Introduction to Mountains," *Mountain Geography*, edited by Martin F. Price, et al., p. 2.

35. J.R. McNeill, *The Mountains of the Mediterranean World*, p. 206; William H. McNeill, *The Age of Gunpowder Empires: 1450–1800* (Washington: The American Historical Association, 1989), p. 38.

36. Ellen Churchill Semple, *Influences of Geographic Environment*, pp. 490–492, 586–588; Ellen Churchill Semple, *The Geography of the Mediterranean Region: Its Relation to Ancient History* (New York: Henry Holt and Company, 1931), pp. 26, 140–141; J.R. McNeill, *The Mountains of the Mediterranean World*, pp. 118–119, 228–229, 268; Larry J. Hoefling, *Chasing the Frontier: Scots-Irish in Early America* (Lincoln, Nebraska: iUniverse, Inc., 2005), pp. 1–2; Robert Bartlett, *The Making of Europe: Conquest, Colonization and Cultural Change, 950–1350* (New York: Penguin Press, 1993), p. 78. In 1915, Arnold Toynbee said that the British "have debarred the hill tribes from making a livelihood by raiding the Plains" in India. Arnold J. Toynbee, *Nationality & The War* (London: J.M. Dent & Sons, 1915), p. 389.

37. Edward C. Banfield, *The Moral Basis of a Backward Society*, p. 35.

38. Peter Levi, *Atlas of the Greek World* (New York: Facts on File, Inc., 1980), p. 13.

39. Ellen Churchill Semple, *Influences of Geographic Environment*, p. 46.

40. J.R. McNeill, *The Mountains of the Mediterranean World*, pp. 126, 127, 129.

41. Ibid., p. 133.

42. Fernand Braudel, *The Mediterranean and the Mediterranean World in the Age of Philip II*, translated by Siân Reynolds, Vol. I, p. 42.

43. Rupert B. Vance, *Human Geography of the South*, p. 247.

44. Don Funnell and Romola Parish, *Mountain Environments and Communities*, p. 206.

45. Amy Chua and Jed Rubenfeld, *The Triple Package: How Three Unlikely Traits Explain the Rise and Fall of Cultural Groups in America* (New York: The Penguin Press, 2014), p. 169.

46. Kevin D. Williamson, "Left Behind," *National Review*, December 16, 2013, p. 26.

47. Darrell Haug Davis, *The Geography of the Mountains of Eastern Kentucky*, p. 159.

48. Martin F. Price and Thomas Kohler, "Sustainable Mountain Development," *Mountain Geography*, edited by Martin F. Price, et al., p. 339.

49. J.R. McNeill, *The Mountains of the Mediterranean World*, pp. 116, 117, 139. See also Ellen Churchill Semple, *Influences of Geographic Environment*, p. 570.

50. See, for example, J.R. McNeill, *The Mountains of the Mediterranean World*, p. 144.

51. Josip Roglič, "The Geographical Setting of Medieval Dubrovnik," *Geographical Essays on Eastern Europe*, edited by Norman J.G. Pounds (Bloomington: Indiana University Press, 1961), p. 150.

52. Fernand Braudel, *The Mediterranean and the Mediterranean World in the Age of Philip II*, translated by Siân Reynolds, Vol. I, p. 46; Don Funnell and Romola Parish, *Mountain Environments and Communities*, pp. 225, 227; J.R. McNeill, *The Mountains of the Mediterranean World*, pp. 41–42 (note 48), 110; Lionel Obadia, "The Impact of Modernisation Processes in the Himalayas: Tibetan and Nepalese Traditions in Transition?" *Religious Transformation in Modern Asia: A Transnational Movement*, edited by David W. Kim (Leiden: Brill, 2015), p. 144.

53. James N. Gregory, *The Southern Diaspora: How The Great Migrations of Black and White Southerners Transformed America* (Chapel Hill: University of North Carolina Press, 2005), p. 76.

54. Mandel Sherman and Cora B. Key, "The Intelligence of Isolated Mountain Children," *Child Development*, Vol. 3, No. 4 (1932), pp. 279–290. A similar

pattern among black youngsters was found in Otto Klineberg, "Mental Testing of Racial and National Groups," *Scientific Aspects of the Race Problem*, edited by H.S. Jennings, et al (Washington: Catholic University Press, 1941), p. 280.

55. "The highlands of the Southern Appalachians... are peopled by the purest English stock in the United States, descendants of the backwoodsmen of the late eighteenth century. Difficulty of access and lack of arable land have combined to discourage immigration. In consequence, foreign elements, including the elsewhere ubiquitous negro, are wanting, except along the few railroads which in recent years have penetrated this country." Ellen Churchill Semple, *Influences of Geographic Environment*, p. 45.

56. Lester R. Wheeler, "A Comparative Study of the Intelligence of East Tennessee Mountain Children," *Journal of Educational Psychology*, Vol. XXXIII, No. 5 (May 1942), pp. 322, 324.

57. Rupert B. Vance, *Human Geography of the South*, p. 256.

58. Ibid., p. 243.

59. Fernand Braudel, *The Mediterranean and the Mediterranean World in the Age of Philip II*, translated by Siân Reynolds, Vol. I, p. 44.

60. Martin F. Price and Thomas Kohler, "Sustainable Mountain Development," *Mountain Geography*, edited by Martin F. Price, et al., p. 340; Don Funnell and Romola Parish, *Mountain Environments and Communities*, pp. 111, 217; James N. Gregory, *The Southern Diaspora*, p. 36; Darrell Haug Davis, *The Geography of the Mountains of Eastern Kentucky*, p. 53.

61. James S. Gardner, et al., "People in the Mountains," *Mountain Geography*, edited by Martin F. Price, et al., p. 272; Stephen F. Cunha and Larry W. Price, "Agricultural Settlement and Land Use in Mountains," Ibid., pp. 304–305; Don Funnell and Romola Parish, *Mountain Environments and Communities*, p. 213; Ellen Churchill Semple, *Influences of Geographic Environment*, pp. 579–580.

62. See, for example, Don Funnell and Romola Parish, *Mountain Environments and Communities*, p. 215; James S. Gardner, et al., "People in the Mountains," *Mountain Geography*, edited by Martin F. Price, et al., p. 268; Stephen F. Cunha and Larry W. Price, "Agricultural Settlement and Land Use in Mountains," Ibid., p. 304; J.R. McNeill, *The Mountains of the Mediterranean World*, pp. 54, 107, 134, 175, 213.

63. Don Funnell and Romola Parish, *Mountain Environments and Communities*, pp. 223–224; J.R. McNeill, *The Mountains of the Mediterranean World*, pp. 119, 213; James S. Gardner, et al., "People in the Mountains," *Mountain Geography*, edited by Martin F. Price, et al., p. 272; Ellen Churchill Semple, *Influences of Geographic Environment*, p. 581.

64. J.R. McNeill, *The Mountains of the Mediterranean World*, p. 213; N.J.G. Pounds, *An Historical Geography of Europe*, p. 264.

65. Ellen Churchill Semple, *Influences of Geographic Environment*, p. 582.

66. Charles A. Price, *Southern Europeans in Australia* (Melbourne: Oxford University Press, 1963), p. 24. See also pp. 16, 17n.

67. Ibid., p. 58.

68. E. Richards, "Highland and Gaelic Immigrants," *The Australian People: An Encyclopedia of the Nation, Its People and Their Origins*, edited by James Jupp (North Ryde, NSW, Australia: Angus & Robertson Publishers, 1988), pp. 765–769; Kenneth E. Nilsen, "Celtic Languages in North America, Scottish Gaelic," *The Celts: History, Life, and Culture*, edited by John T. Koch (Santa Barbara: ABC-CLIO, 2012), Volume 1, p. 167; Sara M. Evans and Harry C. Boyte, *Free Spaces: The Sources of Democratic Change in America* (New York: Harper & Row, 1986), p. 153.

69. Alton C. Byers, et al., "An Introduction to Mountains," *Mountain Geography*, edited by Martin F. Price, et al., p. 1.

70. J.R. McNeill, *The Mountains of the Mediterranean World*, pp. 20, 35, 41.

71. Monica and Robert Beckinsale, *Southern Europe: The Mediterranean and Alpine Lands* (London: University of London Press, 1975), pp. 42, 43, 228.

72. Alton C. Byers, et al., "An Introduction to Mountains," *Mountain Geography*, edited by Martin F. Price, et al., p. 1.

73. Ellen Churchill Semple, *Influences of Geographic Environment*, pp. 578–579; J.R. McNeill, *The Mountains of the Mediterranean World*, pp. 223–227.

74. American Petroleum Institute, *Basic Petroleum Data Book*, Volume XX, Number 2 (Washington: American Petroleum Institute, 2000), Section II, Table 1.

75. Vance Packard, *The Waste Makers* (New York: D. McKay, Co., 1960), p. 200; American Petroleum Institute, *Basic Petroleum Data Book*, Volume XX, Number 2, Section II, Table 1.

76. Burton W. Folsom, Jr. and Anita Folsom, *Uncle Sam Can't Count: A History of Failed Government Investments, from Beaver Pelts to Green Energy* (New York: HarperCollins, 2014), p. 171.

77. "A Survey of Oil," part of a special section on oil, *The Economist*, April 30, 2005, p. 19; Russell Gold, "As Prices Surge, Oil Giants Turn Sludge into Gold," *Wall Street Journal*, March 27, 2006, p. A1; Jad Mouawad, "Oil Innovations Pump New Life into Old Wells," *New York Times*, March 5, 2007, p. A1; "Building on Sand," *The Economist*, May 26, 2007, p. 72.

78. Richard A. Oppel, Jr., "The Other Oil Economy," *New York Times*, February 19, 2000, p. C1.

79. John K. Fairbank and Edwin O. Reischauer, *China: Tradition & Transformation* (Boston: Houghton Mifflin, 1978), p. 17.

80. Frederick R. Troeh and Louis M. Thompson, *Soils and Soil Fertility*, sixth edition (Ames, Iowa: Blackwell, 2005), p. 330; Xiaobing Liu, et al., "Overview of Mollisols in the World: Distribution, Land Use and Management," *Canadian Journal of Soil Science*, Vol. 92 (2012), pp. 383–402; H.J. de Blij, et al., *Physical Geography: The Global Environment*, third edition (New York: Oxford University Press, 2004), pp. 316, 321–323.

81. Uzo Mokwunye, "Do African Soils Only Sustain Subsistence Agriculture?" *Villages in the Future: Crops, Jobs and Livelihood*, edited by Detlef Virchow and Joachim von Braun (New York: Springer, 2001), p. 175.

82. World Bank Independent Evaluation Group, *World Bank Assistance to Agriculture in Sub-Saharan Africa* (Washington: The World Bank, 2007), p. 14.

83. Rattan Lal, "Managing the Soils of Sub-Saharan Africa," *Science*, May 29, 1987, p. 1069.

Chapter 4: Climate, Animals and Diseases

1. "Top of the World," *National Geographic Magazine*, October 1949, p. 528; Paul Carell, *Hitler's War on Russia: The Story of the German Defeat in the East*, translated by Ewald Osers (London: George G. Harrap & Co., Ltd., 1964), p. 415.

2. *The World Almanac and Book of Facts: 2013* (New York: World Almanac Books, 2013), p. 335.

3. E.A. Pearce and C.G. Smith, *The Times Books World Weather Guide* (New York: Times Books, 1984), p. 19.

4. Ibid., pp. 19, 130, 219, 413.

5. Ibid., pp. 279, 380, 413.

6. Robert E. Gabler, et al., *Physical Geography*, ninth edition (Belmont, California: Brooks/Cole Cengage Learning, 2009), p. 98.

7. E.A. Pearce and C.G. Smith, *The Times Books World Weather Guide*, pp. 26, 41, 47, 54, 57. Although there is little cloud cover over the Sahara Desert, there is more cloud cover over the equatorial regions of Africa. Andrew S. Goudie, "Climate: Past and Present," *The Physical Geography of Africa*, edited by William M. Adams, Andrew S. Goudie, and Antony R. Orme (Oxford: Oxford University Press, 1996), p. 40.

8. *The World Almanac and Book of Facts: 2015* (New York: World Almanac Books, 2015), p. 322.

9. E.A. Pearce and C.G. Smith, *The Times Books World Weather Guide*, pp. 130, 199, 357.

10. George W. Hoffman, "Changes in the Agricultural Geography of Yugoslavia," *Geographical Essays on Eastern Europe*, edited by Norman J.G. Pounds (Bloomington: Indiana University Press, 1961), p. 114.

11. Andrew J. Bach and Larry W. Price, "Mountain Climate," *Mountain Geography: Physical and Human Dimensions*, edited by Martin F. Price, et al (Berkeley: University of California Press, 2013), p. 41.

12. David S. Landes, *The Wealth and Poverty of Nations: Why Some Are So Rich and Some So Poor* (New York: W.W. Norton & Company, 1998), p. 5.

13. Ibid.

14. Ellen Churchill Semple, *Influences of Geographic Environment* (New York: Henry Holt and Company, 1911), p. 27.

15. Ellsworth Huntington, "Climate and Civilization," *Harper's Monthly Magazine*, February 1915, pp. 367–373.

16. Ellen Churchill Semple, *The Geography of the Mediterranean Region: Its Relation to Ancient History* (New York: Henry Holt and Company, 1931), p. 382.

17. E.A. Pearce and C.G. Smith, *The Times Books World Weather Guide*, p. 199.

18. Don Funnell and Romola Parish, *Mountain Environments and Communities* (London: Routledge, 2001), pp. 142–143, 145–146.

19. Samuel P. Huntington, *The Clash of Civilizations and the Remaking of World Order* (New York: Simon & Schuster, 1996), p. 49; Fernand Braudel, *The Mediterranean and the Mediterranean World in the Age of Philip II*, translated by Siân Reynolds (Berkeley: University of California Press, 1995), Vol. II, pp. 773–774.

20. Robert J. Sharer, *The Ancient Maya*, fifth edition (Stanford: Stanford University Press, 1994), p. 455.

21. Jared Diamond, *Guns, Germs, and Steel: The Fates of Human Societies* (New York: W.W. Norton, 1997), p. 367.

22. Ibid., p. 262.

23. Ibid., p. 367.

24. Ibid., p. 366.

25. Fernand Braudel, *The Structures of Everyday Life: The Limits of the Possible*, translated by Siân Reynolds (Berkeley: University of California Press, 1992), p. 343.

26. Ibid., pp. 345–346.

27. Ibid., pp. 341–342.

28. *The World Almanac and Book of Facts: 2014* (New York: World Almanac Books, 2014), p. 733; Barbara F. Grimes, editor, *Ethnologue: Languages of the World* (Dallas: SIL International, 2000), Volume I, p. 846.

29. Gordon F. McEwan, *The Incas: New Perspectives* (Santa Barbara, California: ABC-CLIO, 2006), p. 89.

30. Donald P. Whitaker, et al., *Area Handbook for Australia* (Washington: Government Printing Office, 1974), p. 34.

31. "The Rivers of Australia," National Geographic Society, *Great Rivers of the World*, edited by Margaret Sedeen (Washington: National Geographic Society, 1984), p. 278.

32. Ellen Churchill Semple, *Influences of Geographic Environment*, p. 434.

33. Ibid.

34. William S. Maltby, *The Rise and Fall of the Spanish Empire* (New York: Palgrave Macmillan, 2009), p. 18; Eric R. Wolf, *Europe and the People Without History* (Berkeley: University of California Press, 1982), p. 196.

35. Ellen Churchill Semple, *Influences of Geographic Environment*, p. 63.

36. Ibid., p. 144.

37. Ellsworth Huntington, *The Character of Races: As Influenced by Physical Environment, Natural Selection and Historical Development* (New York: Charles Scribner's Sons, 1924), p. 74.

38. "The Indigenous People," *The Australian People: An Encyclopedia of the Nation, Its People and Their Origins*, edited by James Jupp (Cambridge: Cambridge University Press, 2001), p. 4.

39. Darrel Hess, *McKnight's Physical Geography: A Landscape Appreciation*, eleventh edition (Upper Saddle River, New Jersey: Pearson Education, 2014), p. 324.

40. Nicholas Wade, *A Troublesome Inheritance: Genes, Race and Human History* (New York: The Penguin Press, 2014), p. 93.

41. Alfred W. Crosby, "An Ecohistory of the Canary Islands: A Precursor of European Colonialization in the New World and Australasia," *Environmental Review*, Vol. 8, No. 3 (Autumn 1984), p. 217.

42. Charles Darwin, *The Voyage of the Beagle* (Washington: National Geographic Society, 2004), pp. 385–386.

43. Donald P. Whitaker, et al., *Area Handbook for Australia*, pp. 46, 361–362.

44. J.M. Roberts, *A History of Europe* (New York: The Penguin Press, 1997), p. 139.

45. Fernand Braudel, *The Structures of Everyday Life*, translated by Siân Reynolds, pp. 81–82.

46. Burr Cartwright Brundage, *Empire of the Inca* (Norman: University of Oklahoma Press, 1963), pp. 261–262.

47. Francis Jennings, *The Invasion of America: Indians, Colonialism, and the Cant of Conquest* (Chapel Hill: University of North Carolina Press, 1976), p. 22.

48. Charles Darwin, *The Voyage of the Beagle*, p. 386.

49. Ibid., pp. 386–387.

50. Rupert B. Vance, *Human Geography of the South: A Study in Regional Resources and Human Adequacy* (Chapel Hill: University of North Carolina Press, 1932), p. 396.

51. Josef Joffe, "European Culture: What It Was, Where It Is Going," *Culture Matters in Russia— and Everywhere: Backdrop for the Russia-Ukraine Conflict*, edited by Lawrence Harrison and Evgeny Yasin (Lanham, Maryland: Lexington Books, 2015), p. 39.

52. Caroline Golab, *Immigrant Destinations* (Philadelphia: Temple University Press, 1977), p. 102.

53. Donald L. Horowitz, *Ethnic Groups in Conflict* (Berkeley: University of California Press, 1985), p. 663.

54. Ellen Churchill Semple, *Influences of Geographic Environment*, pp. 426–429.

Part II: Cultural Factors

Epigraph: David S. Landes, "Culture Makes Almost All the Difference," *Culture Matters: How Values Shape Human Progress*, edited by Lawrence E. Harrison and Samuel P. Huntington (New York: Basic Books, 2000), p. 2.

1. "Africa's Testing Ground," *The Economist*, August 23, 2014, p. 59.

2. Carlo M. Cipolla, "Editor's Introduction," *The Economic Decline of Empires*, edited by Carlo M. Cipolla (London: Methuen & Co., 1970), p. 9.

3. Ibid., p. 8.

4. Jaime Vicens Vives, "The Decline of Spain in the Seventeenth Century," Ibid., pp. 127, 147.

5. Ibid., p. 127.

6. Ibid., p. 126.

7. Ibid., pp. 130, 133.

8. "A strong challenge often provokes a highly creative response, but there comes a point where its severity is no longer stimulating but overwhelming." Arnold Toynbee, *A Study of History*, a new edition revised and abridged by the author and Jane Caplan (New York: Oxford University Press, 1972), p. 83. See also, Ibid., pp. 113, 115, 119; Arnold Toynbee, *A Study of History: Abridgement of Volumes VII–X*, edited by D.C. Somervell (New York: Oxford University Press, 1957), Volume 2, p. 362.

Chapter 5: Culture and Economics

Epigraph: Samuel P. Huntington, *The Clash of Civilizations and The Remaking of World Order* (New York: Simon & Schuster, 1996), p. 41.

1. See, for example, Richard Lynn, *The Global Bell Curve: Race, IQ, and Inequality Worldwide* (Augusta, Georgia: Washington Summit Publishers, 2008).

2. Arnold J. Toynbee, *Nationality & The War* (London: J.M. Dent & Sons, Ltd. 1915), p. 7.

3. Victor Wolfgang von Hagen, *The Germanic People in America* (Norman: University of Oklahoma Press, 1976), p. 326; Alfred Dolge, *Pianos and Their Makers* (Covina, California: Covina Publishing Company, 1911), pp. 172, 264; Edwin M. Good, *Giraffes, Black Dragons, and Other Pianos: A Technological History from Cristofori to the Modern Concert Grand* (Stanford: Stanford University Press, 1982), p. 137n; W.D. Borrie, "Australia," *The Positive Contribution by Immigrants*, edited by Oscar Handlin (Paris: United Nations Educational, Scientific and Cultural Organization, 1955), p. 94.

4. Adam Giesinger, *From Catherine to Khrushchev: The Story of Russia's Germans* (Winnipeg, Manitoba, Canada: Adam Giesinger, 1974), pp. 143–144.

5. Larry V. Thompson, Book Review, *Journal of Latin American Studies*, Vol. 8, No. 1 (May 1976), p. 159. See also Victor Wolfgang von Hagen, *The Germanic People in America*, pp. 242–243; Ronald C. Newton, *German Buenos Aires, 1900–1933: Social Change and Cultural Crisis* (Austin: University of Texas Press, 1977), pp. 7–8, 22.

6. T.N. Dupuy, *A Genius for War: The German Army and General Staff, 1807–1945* (Englewood Cliffs, New Jersey: Prentice-Hall, Inc., 1977), p. 4.

7. Carlo M. Cipolla, *Literacy and Development in the West* (Baltimore: Penguin Books, 1969), pp. 24, 28, 30–31, 70.

8. Richard Sallet, *Russian-German Settlements in the United States*, translated by Lavern J. Rippley and Armand Bauer (Fargo: North Dakota Institute for Regional Studies, 1974), p. 14; Carlo M. Cipolla, *Literacy and Development in the West*, pp. 11, 72, 93, 120, 128.

9. T. Lynn Smith, *Brazil: People and Institutions*, revised edition (Baton Rouge: Louisiana State University Press, 1963), p. 134.

10. Thomas W. Merrick and Douglas H. Graham, *Population and Economic Development in Brazil: 1800 to the Present* (Baltimore: The Johns Hopkins University Press, 1979), p. 111.

11. Carlo M. Cipolla, *Literacy and Development in the West*, p. 17.

12. Irina Livezeanu, *Cultural Politics in Greater Romania: Regionalism, Nation Building, & Ethnic Struggle, 1918–1930* (Ithaca: Cornell University Press, 1995), pp. 230, 231.

13. Hain Tankler and Algo Rämmer, *Tartu University and Latvia: With an Emphasis on Relations in the 1920s and 1930s* (Tartu: Tartu Ülikool, 2004), pp. 23–24; F.W. Pick, "Tartu: The History of an Estonian University," *American Slavic and East European Review*, Vol. 5, No. 3/4 (November 1946), p. 159; Toivo U. Raun, "The Role of Tartu University in Estonian Society and Culture, 1860–1914," *Die Universitäten Dorpat/Tartu, Riga und Wilna/Vilnius 1579–1979*, edited by Gert von Pistohlkors, et al (Köln: Böhlau Verlag, 1987), p. 135.

14. Anders Henriksson, *The Tsar's Loyal Germans: The Riga German Community: Social Change and the Nationality Question, 1855–1905* (New York: Columbia University Press, 1983), pp. 6–7, 32, 49; Ingeborg Fleischhauer and Benjamin Pinkus, *The Soviet Germans: Past and Present* (London: C. Hurst & Company, 1986), p. 16.

15. Victor Purcell, *The Chinese in Southeast Asia*, second edition (London: Oxford University Press, 1965); Jack Chen, *The Chinese of America* (San Francisco: Harper & Row, Publishers, 1980), Duvon Clough Corbitt, *A Study of the Chinese in Cuba, 1847–1947* (Wilmore, Kentucky: Asbury College, 1971); Watt Stewart, *Chinese Bondage in Peru: A History of the Chinese Coolie in Peru, 1849–1874* (Durham: Duke University Press, 1951); Cecil Clementi, *The Chinese in British Guiana* (Georgetown, British Guiana: "The Argosy" Company, Ltd., 1915); David Lowenthal, *West Indian Societies* (New York: Oxford University Press, 1972), pp. 202–208.

16. Albert Hourani, "Introduction," *The Lebanese in the World: A Century of Emigration*, edited by Albert Hourani and Nadim Shehadi (London: The Centre for Lebanese Studies, 1992), pp. 3–11; Clark S. Knowlton, "The Social and Spatial Mobility of the Syrian and Lebanese Community in Sao Paulo, Brazil," Ibid., pp. 285–311; Trevor Batrouney, "The Lebanese in Australia, 1880–1989," Ibid., pp. 413–442; Said Boumedouha, "Change and Continuity in the Relationship between the Lebanese in Senegal and Their Hosts," Ibid., pp. 549–563; Alixa Naff, "Lebanese Immigration into the United States: 1880 to the Present," Ibid., pp. 141–165.

17. Paul Johnson, *A History of the Jews* (New York: Harper & Row, 1987); Jonathan I. Israel, *European Jewry in the Age of Mercantilism: 1550–1750* (Oxford: Clarendon Press, 1985); Ezra Mendelsohn, *The Jews of East Central*

Europe between the World Wars (Bloomington: Indiana University Press, 1983); Bernard Lewis, *The Jews of Islam* (Princeton: Princeton University Press, 1984); Moses Rischin, *The Promised City: New York's Jews, 1870–1914* (Cambridge, Massachusetts: Harvard University Press, 1962); Louis Wirth, *The Ghetto* (Chicago: University of Chicago Press, 1956); Irving Howe, *World of Our Fathers: The Journey of the East European Jews to America and the Life They Found and Made* (New York: Harcourt Brace Jovanovich, 1976); Hilary L. Rubinstein, *Chosen: The Jews in Australia* (Sydney: Allen & Unwin, 1987); Daniel J. Elazar and Peter Medding, *Jewish Communities in Frontier Societies: Argentina, Australia, and South Africa* (New York: Holmes & Meier, 1983).

18. Hugh Tinker, *The Banyan Tree: Overseas Emigrants from India, Pakistan, and Bangladesh* (Oxford: Oxford University Press, 1977); "Going Global," *The Economist*, December 19, 2015, pp. 105–107.

19. Victor Purcell, *The Chinese in Southeast Asia*, second edition, pp. 277–279.

20. Jack Chen, *The Chinese of America*, Chapters 12–18; Stanford M. Lyman, *Chinese Americans* (New York: Random House, 1974), Chapter 4; Betty Lee Sung, *The Chinese in America* (New York: Macmillan Publishing, 1972), Chapter 3.

21. Watt Stewart, *Chinese Bondage in Peru*, p. 98.

22. Duvon Clough Corbitt, *A Study of the Chinese in Cuba, 1847–1947*, pp. 79–80; United States House of Representatives, "Coolie Trade," Report No. 443, 36th Congress, 1st Session, April 16, 1860, p. 10.

23. Duvon Clough Corbitt, *A Study of the Chinese in Cuba, 1847–1947*, p. 80.

24. Ibid.

25. Stanford M. Lyman, *Chinese Americans*, p. 152.

26. Jack Chen, *The Chinese of America*, p. 18.

27. Ellen Churchill Semple, *Influences of Geographic Environment* (New York: Henry Holt and Company, 1911), p. 621.

28. Kay S. Hymowitz, "Brooklyn's Chinese Pioneers," *City Journal*, Spring 2014, pp. 21, 23.

29. William Easterly, *The Tyranny of Experts: Economists, Dictators, and the Forgotten Rights of the Poor* (New York: Basic Books, 2013), p. 79.

30. Kay S. Hymowitz, "Brooklyn's Chinese Pioneers," *City Journal*, Spring 2014, pp. 26, 27.

31. Irving Howe, *World of Our Fathers*, pp. 156–159; Jacob Riis, *How the Other Half Lives: Studies Among the Tenements of New York* (New York: Charles Scribner's Sons, 1914), p. 125.

32. Simon Kuznets, "Immigration of Russian Jews to the United States: Background and Structure," *Perspectives in American History*, Vol. IX (1975), pp. 115–116.

33. Reports of the Immigration Commission, *The Children of Immigrants in Schools* (Washington: Government Printing Office, 1911), Vol. I, p. 110.

34. Carl C. Brigham, *A Study of American Intelligence* (Princeton: Princeton University Press, 1923), p. 190.

35. Charles Murray, *Human Accomplishment: The Pursuit of Excellence in the Arts and Sciences, 800 B.C. to 1950* (New York: Harper Collins, 2003), pp. 291–292.

36. Carl C. Brigham, "Intelligence Tests of Immigrant Groups," *Psychological Review*, Vol. 37, Issue 2 (March 1930), p. 165.

37. Clark S. Knowlton, "The Social and Spatial Mobility of the Syrian and Lebanese Community in Sao Paulo, Brazil," *The Lebanese in the World*, edited by Albert Hourani and Nadim Shehadi, p. 298.

38. Luz Maria Martinez Montiel, "The Lebanese Community in Mexico: Its Meaning, Importance and the History of Its Communities," Ibid., pp. 380, 385.

39. Trevor Batrouney, "The Lebanese in Australia, 1880–1989," Ibid., p. 419.

40. H. Laurens van der Laan, "A Bibliography on the Lebanese in West Africa, and an Appraisal of the Literature Consulted," *Kroniek van Afrika*, 1975/3, No. 6, p. 285.

41. H.L. van der Laan, *The Lebanese Traders in Sierra Leone* (The Hague: Mouton & Co, 1975), p. 249.

42. Ibid., p. 236.

43. Ibid., pp. 237–240.

44. Ibid., pp. 41, 105; Albert Hourani, "Introduction," *The Lebanese in the World*, edited by Albert Hourani and Nadim Shehadi, p. 7; Charles Issawi, "The Historical Background of Lebanese Emigration, 1800–1914," Ibid., p. 31; Alixa Naff, "Lebanese Immigration into the United States: 1880 to the Present," Ibid., p. 145; Trevor Batrouney, "The Lebanese in Australia, 1880–1989," Ibid., p. 421.

45. Albert Hourani, "Introduction," *The Lebanese in the World*, edited by Albert Hourani and Nadim Shehadi, p. 7.

46. Alixa Naff, "Lebanese Immigration into the United States: 1880 to the Present," Ibid., pp. 144, 145, 147.

47. Ibid., p. 148.

48. H.L. van der Laan, *The Lebanese Traders in Sierra Leone*, p. 112.

49. Milton & Rose D. Friedman, *Two Lucky People: Memoirs* (Chicago: University of Chicago Press, 1998), pp. 20–21.

50. Alixa Naff, "Lebanese Immigration into the United States: 1880 to the Present," *The Lebanese in the World*, edited by Albert Hourani and Nadim Shehadi, p. 157.

51. Ignacio Klich, "*Criollos* and Arabic Speakers in Argentina: An Uneasy *Pas de Deux*, 1888–1914," Ibid., p. 265.

52. Trevor Batrouney, "The Lebanese in Australia, 1880–1989," Ibid., p. 421.

53. H.L. van der Laan, *The Lebanese Traders in Sierra Leone*, pp. 106–109.

54. David Nicholls, "Lebanese of the Antilles: Haiti, Dominican Republic, Jamaica, and Trinidad," *The Lebanese in the World*, edited by Albert Hourani and Nadim Shehadi, pp. 345, 351, 352, 355.

55. Alixa Naff, "Lebanese Immigration into the United States: 1880 to the Present," Ibid., pp. 141–165.

56. H.L. van der Laan, *The Lebanese Traders in Sierra Leone*, pp. 210, 240, 276; Albert Hourani, "Introduction," *The Lebanese in the World*, edited by Albert Hourani and Nadim Shehadi, p. 4; Clark S. Knowlton, "The Social and Spatial Mobility of the Syrian and Lebanese Community in Sao Paulo, Brazil," Ibid., pp. 300, 304, 305; Boutros Labaki, "Lebanese Emigration During the War (1975–1989)," Ibid., p. 625; Marwan Maaouia, "Lebanese Emigration to the Gulf and Saudi Arabia," Ibid., p. 655.

57. Amy Chua and Jed Rubenfeld, *The Triple Package: How Three Unlikely Traits Explain the Rise and Fall of Cultural Groups in America* (New York: The Penguin Press, 2014), p. 6.

58. Ibid., pp. 38–39.

59. Ibid., pp. 39, 40.

60. Andrew Tanzer, "The Bamboo Network," *Forbes*, July 8, 1994, pp. 138–144; "China: Seeds of Subversion," *The Economist*, May 28, 1994, p. 32.

61. See, for example, P.T. Bauer, *Equality, the Third World and Economic Delusion* (Cambridge, Massachusetts: Harvard University Press, 1981), Chapters 5, 6, 7; William Easterly, *The White Man's Burden: Why the West's Efforts to Aid the Rest Have Done So Much Ill and So Little Good* (New York: Penguin Press, 2006).

62. Rondo Cameron, *A Concise Economic History of the World: From Paleolithic Times to the Present* (New York: Oxford University Press, 1989), p. 108.

63. Fernand Braudel, *The Mediterranean and the Mediterranean World in the Age of Philip II*, translated by Siân Reynolds (Berkeley: University of California Press, 1995), Vol. II, p. 795.

64. Charles Darwin, *The Voyage of the Beagle* (Washington: National Geographic Society, 2004), p. 384.

65. Lawrence E. Harrison, *Underdevelopment Is a State of Mind: The Latin American Case* (Cambridge, Massachusetts: The Center for International Affairs, Harvard University, 1985), p. 103.

66. *The World Almanac and Book of Facts: 2014* (New York: World Almanac Books, 2014), pp. 750, 754.

67. Robert F. Foerster, *The Italian Emigration of Our Times* (New York: Arno Press, 1969), p. 236; Carl Solberg, *Immigration and Nationalism: Argentina and Chile, 1890–1914* (Austin: University of Texas Press, 1970), p. 38.

68. Robert F. Foerster, *The Italian Emigration of Our Times*, p. 230.

69. Ibid., p. 243.

70. Fred C. Koch, *The Volga Germans: In Russia and the Americas, from 1763 to the Present* (University Park: Pennsylvania State University Press, 1977), p. 227; Timothy J. Kloberdanz, "Plainsmen of Three Continents: Volga German Adaptation to Steppe, Prairie, and Pampa," *Ethnicity on the Great Plains*, edited by Frederick C. Luebke (Lincoln: University of Nebraska Press, 1980), pp. 66–67.

71. Carl Solberg, *Immigration and Nationalism*, p. 51.

72. Robert F. Foerster, *The Italian Emigration of Our Times*, p. 261.

73. Mark Jefferson, *Peopling the Argentine Pampa* (New York: American Geographical Society, 1926), p. 1.

74. Carl Solberg, *Immigration and Nationalism*, pp. 49–50.

75. Robert F. Foerster, *The Italian Emigration of Our Times*, pp. 254–259.

76. Gino Germani, "Mass Immigration and Modernization in Argentina," *Studies in Comparative International Development*, Volume 2, Issue 11 (November 1966), p. 170; Laura Randall, *An Economic History of Argentina in the Twentieth Century* (New York: Columbia University Press, 1978), p. 116.

77. Mark Jefferson, *Peopling the Argentine Pampa*, p. 76.

78. Gino Germani, "Mass Immigration and Modernization in Argentina," *Studies in Comparative International Development*, Volume 2, Issue 11 (November 1966), p. 178.

79. Carl E. Solberg, "Peopling the Prairies and the Pampas: The Impact of Immigration on Argentine and Canadian Agrarian Development, 1870–1930," *Journal of Interamerican Studies and World Affairs*, Vol. 24, No. 2 (May 1982), pp. 136, 152; Gloria Totoricagüena, *Basque Diaspora: Migration and Transnational Identity* (Reno: Center for Basque Studies, University of Nevada, 2005), pp. 171, 180. See also Lawrence E. Harrison, *The Pan-American Dream: Do Latin America's Cultural Values Discourage True Partnership with the United States and Canada?* (New York: Basic Books, 1997), p. 151.

80. Adam Giesinger, *From Catherine to Krushchev*, p. 229; Fred C. Koch, *The Volga Germans*, pp. 222, 224.

81. Fred C. Koch, *The Volga Germans*, pp. 226, 227.

82. "A Century of Decline," *The Economist*, February 15, 2014, p. 20.

83. "The End of Populism," *The Economist*, November 28, 2015, p. 31.

84. Emilio Willems, "Brazil," *The Positive Contribution by Immigrants*, edited by Oscar Handlin, p. 123.

85. Eric N. Baklanoff, "External Factors in the Economic Development of Brazil's Heartland: The Center-South, 1850–1930," *The Shaping of Modern Brazil*, edited by Eric N. Baklanoff (Baton Rouge: Louisiana State University Press, 1969), p. 31; Thomas Sowell, *The Economics and Politics of Race: An International Perspective* (New York: William Morrow and Company, Inc., 1983), p. 52.

86. Warren Dean, *The Industrialization of São Paulo: 1880–1945* (Austin: University of Texas Press, 1969), p. 49.

87. Ibid., p. 35.

88. See, for example, Emilio Willems, "Brazil," *The Positive Contribution by Immigrants*, edited by Oscar Handlin, pp. 128, 133; Rollie E. Poppino, *Brazil: The Land and the People* (New York: Oxford University Press, 1968), pp. 31–35; Seymour Martin Lipset, *Revolution and Counterrevolution: Change and Persistence in Social Structures* (New York: Basic Books, 1968), pp. 90–91.

89. Jean Roche, *La Colonisation Allemande et le Rio Grande do Sul* (Paris: Institut Des Hautes Études de L'Amérique Latine, 1959), pp. 388–389.

90. Warren Dean, *The Industrialization of São Paulo*, p. 54.

91. Adam Giesinger, *From Catherine to Krushchev*, p. 229; Frederick C. Luebke, *Germans in the New World: Essays in the History of Immigration* (Urbana: University of Illinois Press, 1990), pp. 94, 96; Gabriel Paquette, *Imperial Portugal in the Age of Atlantic Revolutions: The Luso-Brazilian World, c. 1770–1850* (Cambridge: Cambridge University Press, 2013), p. 80; Carl E. Solberg, "Peopling the Prairies and the Pampas: The Impact of Immigration on Argentine and Canadian Agrarian Development, 1870–1930," *Journal of Interamerican Studies and World Affairs*, Vol. 24, No. 2 (May 1982), pp. 131–161.

92. Carl Solberg, *Immigration and Nationalism*, Chapter 1; George F.W. Young, "Bernardo Philippi, Initiator of German Colonization in Chile," *Hispanic American Historical Review*, Vol. 51, No. 3 (August 1971), p. 490; Fred C. Koch, *The Volga Germans*, pp. 231–233.

93. Carl Solberg, *Immigration and Nationalism*, p. 40; George F.W. Young, *The Germans in Chile: Immigration and Colonization, 1849–1914* (New York: Center for Immigration Studies, 1974), pp. 111–114.

94. George F.W. Young, *The Germans in Chile*, p. 115.

95. Carl Solberg, *Immigration and Nationalism*, p. 63.

96. Fernand Braudel, *A History of Civilizations*, translated by Richard Mayne (New York: Penguin Books, 1993), p. 440.

97. Gino Germani, "Mass Immigration and Modernization in Argentina," *Studies in Comparative International Development*, Volume 2, Issue 11 (November 1966), pp. 171–172.

98. Fred C. Koch, *The Volga Germans*, pp. 231–232; M.G. and E.T. Mulhall, *Handbook of Brazil* (Buenos Ayres, 1877), pp. 148–149.

99. See, for example, Gino Germani, "Mass Immigration and Modernization in Argentina," *Studies in Comparative International Development*, Volume 2,

Issue 11 (November 1966), pp. 173–174; Eric N. Baklanoff, "External Factors in the Economic Development of Brazil's Heartland: The Center-South, 1850–1930," *The Shaping of Modern Brazil*, edited by Eric N. Baklanoff, p. 30; Eugene W. Ridings, "Predominance among Overseas Traders in Nineteenth-Century Latin America," *Latin American Research Review*, Vol. 20, No. 2 (1985), p. 18.

100. J.F. Normano and Antonello Gerbi, *The Japanese in South America: An Introductory Survey with Special Reference to Peru* (New York: The John Day Company, 1943), pp. 38–39.

101. C. Harvey Gardiner, *The Japanese and Peru: 1873–1973* (Albuquerque: University of New Mexico Press, 1975), p. 25; J.F. Normano and Antonello Gerbi, *The Japanese in South America*, p. 70.

102. C. Harvey Gardiner, *The Japanese and Peru*, pp. 62, 64; Toraji Irie and William Himel, "History of Japanese Migration to Peru, Part II," *Hispanic American Historical Review*, Vol. 31, No. 4 (November 1951), p. 662.

103. C. Harvey Gardiner, *The Japanese and Peru*, pp. 61–62.

104. William R. Long, "New Pride for *Nikkei* in Peru," *Los Angeles Times*, April 28, 1995, p. A1.

105. C. Harvey Gardiner, *The Japanese and Peru*, p. 75; Pablo Macera and Shane J. Hunt, "Peru," *Latin America: A Guide to Economic History, 1830–1930*, edited by Roberto Cortés Conde and Stanley J. Stein (Berkeley: University of California Press, 1977), p. 566.

106. C. Harvey Gardiner, *The Japanese and Peru*, p. 68; J.F. Normano and Antonello Gerbi, *The Japanese in South America*, pp. 109–110.

107. C. Harvey Gardiner, *The Japanese and Peru*, p. 68.

108. J.F. Normano and Antonello Gerbi, *The Japanese in South America*, pp. 77, 113–114.

109. Jaime Vicens Vives, "The Decline of Spain in the Seventeenth Century," *The Economic Decline of Empires*, edited by Carlo M. Cipolla (London: Methuen & Co., 1970), p. 127.

110. Norman R. Stewart, *Japanese Colonization in Eastern Paraguay* (Washington: National Academy of Sciences, 1967), p. 153.

111. Harry Leonard Sawatzky, *They Sought a Country: Mennonite Colonization in Mexico* (Berkeley: University of California Press, 1971), p. 365.

112. Lawrence E. Harrison, *The Pan-American Dream*, p. 83.

113. Oscar Árias Sánchez, "Quo Vadis, Latin America? Four Cultural Obstacles to Economic Development," *Culture Matters in Russia— and Everywhere: Backdrop for the Russia-Ukraine Conflict*, edited by Lawrence Harrison and Evgeny Yasin (Lanham, Maryland: Lexington Books, 2015), pp. 49, 50.

Chapter 6: Cultural Diffusion

Epigraph: Ellen Churchill Semple, *The Geography of the Mediterranean Region: Its Relation to Ancient History* (New York: Henry Holt and Company, 1931), p. 13.

1. Robert Bartlett, *The Making of Europe: Conquest, Colonization and Cultural Change, 950–1350* (New York: The Penguin Press, 1993), pp. 60, 70–84, 281, 283; Paul Robert Magocsi, *Historical Atlas of Central Europe*, revised and expanded edition (Seattle: University of Washington Press, 2002), pp. 54–55; Jean W. Sedlar, *East Central Europe in the Middle Ages, 1000–1500* (Seattle: University of Washington Press, 1994), p. 116; N.J.G. Pounds, *An Historical Geography of Europe: 1800–1914* (Cambridge: Cambridge University Press, 1985), pp. 75, 449–458; Walter Nugent, *Crossings: The Great Transatlantic Migrations, 1870–1914* (Bloomington: Indiana University Press, 1992), p. 84; Roy E.H. Mellor and E. Alistair Smith, *Europe: A Geographical Survey of the Continent* (New York: Columbia University Press, 1979), p. 92; *The Oxford Encyclopedia of Economic History*, edited by Joel Mokyr (Oxford: Oxford University Press, 2003), Vol. 2, pp. 247–248.

2. Stasys Goštautas, "The Early History of the University of Vilnius: A Crossroads between East and West," *Die Universitäten Dorpat/Tartu, Riga und Wilna/Vilnius 1579–1979*, edited by Gert von Pistohlkors, et al (Köln: Böhlau Verlag, 1987), pp. 1, 3; Ramunas Kondratas, "Medical Reforms at the University of Vilnius in the Beginning of the Nineteenth Century," Ibid., p. 92.

3. John A. Armstrong, "Mobilized Diaspora in Tsarist Russia: The Case of the Baltic Germans," *Soviet Nationality Policies and Practices*, edited by Jeremy R. Azrael (New York: Praeger, 1978), pp. 69–70.

4. Glenn T. Trewartha, *Japan: A Geography* (Madison: University of Wisconsin Press, 1965), pp. 78–79.

5. Edwin O. Reischauer, *The Japanese* (Cambridge, Massachusetts: Harvard University Press, 1980), p. 5.

6. Ibid., p. 8.

7. Ibid., p. 9.

8. Tetsuro Nakaoka, "The Transfer of Cotton Manufacturing Technology from Britain to Japan," *International Technology Transfer: Europe, Japan and the USA, 1700–1914*, edited by David J. Jeremy (Aldershot, Hants, England: Edward Elgar, 1991), p. 184.

9. John K. Fairbank, Edwin O. Reischauer and Albert M. Craig, *East Asia: Tradition & Transformation*, revised edition (Boston: Houghton-Mifflin Company, 1989), p. 410.

10. Irokawa Daikichi, *The Culture of the Meiji Period*, translated and edited by Marius B. Jansen (Princeton: Princeton University Press, 1985), p. 7.

11. Yasuo Wakatsuki, "Japanese Emigration to the United States, 1866–1924: A Monograph," *Perspectives in American History*, Vol. XII (1979), p. 431. See also p. 434.

12. Ibid., pp. 414, 415.

13. John K. Fairbank, Edwin O. Reischauer and Albert M. Craig, *East Asia*, revised edition, p. 532.

14. Ibid., p. 530.

15. David S. Landes, *The Wealth and Poverty of Nations: Why Some Are So Rich And Some So Poor* (New York: W.W. Norton, 1998), p. 472.

16. Sydney and Olive Checkland, *Industry and Ethos: Scotland 1832–1914* (Edinburgh: Edinburgh University Press, 1989), p. 147; William R. Brock, *Scotus Americanus: A Survey of the Sources for Links between Scotland and America in the Eighteenth Century* (Edinburgh: Edinburgh University Press, 1982), p. 114.

17. T.C. Smout, *A History of the Scottish People, 1560–1830* (New York: Charles Scribner's Sons, 1969), pp. 480–489; Alexander Bain, *James Mill: A Biography* (London: Longmans, Green, and Co., 1882), Chapter 1; Michael St. John Packe, *The Life of John Stuart Mill* (London: Secker and Warburg, 1954), p. 9n.

18. Henry Thomas Buckle, *On Scotland and the Scotch Intellect* (Chicago: University of Chicago Press, 1970), p. 154.

19. Fernand Braudel, *A History of Civilizations*, translated by Richard Mayne (New York: The Penguin Press, 1994), pp. 80–81.

20. "The Tragedy of the Arabs," *The Economist*, July 5, 2014, p. 9.

21. Fernand Braudel, *The Mediterranean and the Mediterranean World in the Age of Philip II*, translated by Siân Reynolds (Berkeley: University of California Press, 1995), Vol. I, p. 83.

22. Rondo Cameron, *A Concise Economic History of the World: From Paleolithic Times to the Present* (New York: Oxford University Press, 1989), p. 80.

23. Edward Nawotka, "Translating Books into Arabic," *Los Angeles Times*, January 4, 2008, p. E24.

24. United Nations Development Programme, *Arab Human Development Report 2003* (New York: United Nations Development Programme, 2003), p. 67.

25. "Self-doomed to Failure," *The Economist*, July 6, 2002, pp. 24–26.

26. David C. Lindberg, "The Transmission of Greek and Arabic Learning to the West," *Science in the Middle Ages*, edited by David C. Lindberg (Chicago: University of Chicago Press, 1978), pp. 52–90.

27. Freeman Dyson, "The Case for Blunders," *New York Review of Books*, March 6, 2014, p. 6.

28. Niall Ferguson, *Civilization: The West and the Rest* (New York: The Penguin Press, 2011), p. 47.

29. Jürgen Osterhammel, *The Transformation of the World: A Global History of the Nineteenth Century*, translated by Patrick Camiller (Princeton: Princeton University Press, 2014), p. 786.

30. Toivo U. Raun, *Estonia and the Estonians*, second edition (Stanford: Hoover Institution Press, 1991), pp. 55, 56.

31. Pieter Judson, "When Is a Diaspora Not a Diaspora? Rethinking Nation-Centered Narratives about Germans in Habsburg East Central Europe," *The Heimat Abroad: The Boundaries of Germanness*, edited by Krista O'Donnell, Renate Bridenthal and Nancy Reagin (Ann Arbor: University of Michigan Press, 2005), p. 231.

32. Derek Sayer, *The Coasts of Bohemia: A Czech History* (Princeton: Princeton University Press, 1998), p. 77.

33. Ibid., p. 90.

34. Gary B. Cohen, *The Politics of Ethnic Survival: Germans in Prague, 1861–1914*, second edition (West Lafayette: Purdue University Press, 2006), p. 1.

35. Toivo U. Raun, "The Role of Tartu University in Estonian Society and Culture: 1860–1914," *Die Universitäten Dorpat/Tartu, Riga und Wilna/Vilnius 1579–1979*, edited by Gert von Pistohlkors, et al., p. 124.

36. Paul Robert Magocsi, *Historical Atlas of Central Europe*, revised and expanded edition, pp. 37–41; Sidney Pollard, *Marginal Europe: The Contribution of Marginal Lands Since the Middle Ages* (Oxford: Oxford University Press, 1997), p. 153; Robert Bartlett, *The Making of Europe*, pp. 128–132; Péter Gunst, "Agrarian Systems of Central and Eastern Europe," *The Origins of Backwardness in Eastern Europe: Economics and Politics from the Middle Ages Until the Early Twentieth Century*, edited by Daniel Chirot (Berkeley: University of California Press, 1989), p. 64.

37. Anders Henriksson, *The Tsar's Loyal Germans: The Riga German Community: Social Change and the Nationality Question, 1855–1905* (New York: Columbia University Press, 1983), p. 15.

38. Thomas Sowell, *Migrations and Cultures: A World View* (New York: Basic Books, 1996), pp. 181–213.

39. Myron Weiner, *Sons of the Soil: Migration and Ethnic Conflict in India* (Princeton: Princeton University Press, 1978), p. 250.

40. A.A. Ayoade, "Ethnic Management in the 1979 Nigerian Constitution," *Canadian Review of Studies in Nationalism*, Spring 1987, p. 127.

41. *Encyclopedia of Human Rights*, edited by David P. Forsythe (Oxford: Oxford University Press, 2009), Volume 1, p. 58.

42. Cacilie Rohwedder, "Germans, Czechs Are Hobbled by History as Europe Moves Toward United Future," *Wall Street Journal*, November 25, 1996, p. A15; Ulla Dahlerup, "Sojourn in Sudetenland," *Sudeten Bulletin/Central European Review*, December 1965, pp. 395–403; Robert Bideleaux and Ian Jeffries, *A History of Eastern Europe: Crisis and Change* (London: Routledge, 1998), p. 548.

43. J.H. Elliott, *Spain and Its World, 1500–1700: Selected Essays* (New Haven: Yale University Press, 1989), pp. 225–226; Rondo Cameron, *A Concise Economic History of the World*, p. 108.

44. Solomon Grayzel, *A History of the Jews: From the Babylonian Exile to the End of World War II* (Philadelphia: The Jewish Publication Society of America, 1947), pp. 355–356, 386–394; Jonathan I. Israel, *European Jewry in the Age of Mercantilism: 1550–1750* (Oxford: Clarendon Press, 1985), pp. 5, 6.

45. W. Cunningham, *Alien Immigrants to England* (London: Frank Cass & Co., Ltd., 1969), Chapter 6.

46. Simon Kuznets, "Immigration of Russian Jews to the United States: Background and Structure," *Perspectives in American History*, Vol. IX (1975), p. 39.

47. Donald L. Horowitz, *Ethnic Groups in Conflict* (Berkeley: University of California Press, 1985), pp. 176–177.

48. Hugh LeCaine Agnew, *Origins of the Czech National Renascence* (Pittsburgh: University of Pittsburgh Press, 1993), p. 51.

49. Derek Sayer, *The Coasts of Bohemia*, p. 50.

50. Gary B. Cohen, *The Politics of Ethnic Survival*, pp. 87, 91.

51. Donald L. Horowitz, *Ethnic Groups in Conflict*, p. 176.

52. Camille Laurin, "Principles for a Language Policy," *Cultural Diversity and Canadian Education: Issues and Innovations*, edited by John R. Mallea and Jonathan C. Young (Ottawa: Carleton University Press, 1990), pp. 186, 189.

53. Donald L. Horowitz, *Ethnic Groups in Conflict*, pp. 176–177.

54. Will Pavia, "French Zealots Just Don't Fancy an Italian," *The Times* (London), February 22, 2013, p. 28; Jeremy King, *Budweisers Into Czechs and Germans: A Local History of Bohemian Politics, 1848–1948* (Princeton: Princeton University Press, 2002), pp. 4, 128.

55. See, for example, Stuart Buck, *Acting White: The Ironic Legacy of Desegregation* (New Haven: Yale University Press, 2010).

56. For other examples, see Ellen Churchill Semple, *Influences of Geographic Environment* (New York: Henry Holt and Company, 1911), p. 625.

57. Donald L. Horowitz, *Ethnic Groups in Conflict*, p. 153.

58. Arnold J. Toynbee, *Nationality & The War* (London: J.M. Dent & Sons, Ltd. 1915), p. 488.

59. See, for example, "Are Jews Generic?" in my *Black Rednecks and White Liberals* (San Francisco: Encounter Books, 2005), pp. 65–110.

60. W.E.B. Du Bois, *The Souls of Black Folk: Essays and Sketches* (Chicago: A.C. McClurg & Co., 1903), p. vii.

61. David E. Cunningham, *Barriers to Peace in Civil War* (Cambridge: Cambridge University Press, 2011), p. 137.

62. Ian Jeffries, *The Former Yugoslavia at the Turn of the Twenty-First Century: A Guide to the Economies in Transition* (London: Routledge, 2002), p. 38.

63. Gyanendra Pandey, *Remembering Partition: Violence, Nationalism and History in India* (Cambridge: Cambridge University Press, 2001), p. 68.

64. Ben Kiernan, *The Pol Pot Regime: Race, Power, and Genocide in Cambodia under the Khmer Rouge, 1975–79*, third edition (New Haven: Yale University Press, 2008), p. 460.

65. William L. Shirer, *The Rise and Fall of the Third Reich: A History of Nazi Germany* (New York: Simon and Schuster, 1960), p. 978.

Chapter 7: Culture and Progress

Epigraph: Charles Murray, *Human Accomplishment: The Pursuit of Excellence in the Arts and Sciences, 800 B.C. to 1950* (New York: Harper Collins, 2003), p. 392.

1. Archie Brown, Michael Kaser, and Gerald S. Smith, *The Cambridge Encyclopedia of Russia and the Former Soviet Union*, second edition (Cambridge: Cambridge University Press, 1994), p. 5.

2. Ibid., pp. 17–18.

3. Jonathan P. Stern, "Soviet Natural Gas in the World Economy," *Soviet Natural Resources in the World Economy*, edited by Robert G. Jensen, et al (Chicago: University of Chicago Press, 1983), p. 372.

4. Russell B. Adams, "Nickel and Platinum in the Soviet Union," Ibid., p. 536.

5. Theodore Shabad, "The Soviet Potential in Natural Resources: An Overview," Ibid., p. 269.

6. Nikolai Shmelev and Vladimir Popov, *The Turning Point: Revitalizing the Soviet Economy* (New York: Doubleday, 1989), pp. 128–129.

7. John Stuart Mill, *The Collected Works of John Stuart Mill*, Volume III: *Principles of Political Economy with Some of Their Applications to Social Philosophy* (Toronto: University of Toronto Press, 1965), p. 882.

8. John P. McKay, *Pioneers for Profit: Foreign Entrepreneurship and Russian Industrialization 1885–1913* (Chicago: University of Chicago Press, 1970), pp. 176, 187.

9. Karl Stumpp, *The German-Russians: Two Centuries of Pioneering* (Bonn: Edition Atlantic-Forum, 1971), p. 68.

10. Alec Nove, *The Soviet Economic System* (London: George Allen & Unwin, Ltd., 1977), pp. 100–101; Linda M. Randall, *Reluctant Capitalists: Russia's Journey Through Market Transition* (New York: Routledge, 2001), pp. 56–57.

11. Raghuram G. Rajan and Luigi Zingales, *Saving Capitalism from the Capitalists* (New York: Crown Business, 2003), p. 57.

12. Bryon MacWilliams, "Reports of Bribe-Taking at Russian Universities Have Increased, Authorities Say," *The Chronicle of Higher Education*, April 18, 2002 (online).

13. "Problems at the Pump," *The Economist*, May 30, 2015, p. 44.

14. Seymour Martin Lipset, "Values, Education, and Entrepreneurship," *Elites in Latin America,* edited by Seymour Martin Lipset and Aldo Solari (New York: Oxford University Press, 1967), p. 15.

15. "Five-Fingered Discounts," *The Economist*, October 23, 2010, p. 81.

16. See, for example, Warren Dean, *The Industrialization of São Paulo: 1880–1945* (Austin: University of Texas Press, 1969), p. 63.

17. Renée Rose Shield, *Diamond Stories: Enduring Change on 47th Street* (Ithaca: Cornell University Press, 2002), p. 94.

18. Susan Wolcott, "An Examination of the Supply of Financial Credit to Entrepreneurs in Colonial India," *The Invention of Enterprise: Entrepreneurship from Ancient Mesopotamia to Modern Times*, edited by David S. Landes, et al (Princeton: Princeton University Press, 2010), p. 458.

19. S. Gordon Redding, *The Spirit of Chinese Capitalism* (Berlin: Walter de Gruyter, 1990), p. 213.

20. H.L. van der Laan, *The Lebanese Traders in Sierra Leone* (The Hague: Mouton & Co, 1975), pp. 42–43, 190, 191–192.

21. "The World's Least Honest Cities," *The Telegraph.UK*, September 25, 2013.

22. "Scandinavians Prove Their Honesty in European Lost-Wallet Experiment," *Deseret News*, June 20, 1996; Eric Felten, "Finders Keepers?" *Reader's Digest*, April 2001, pp. 102–107; "So Whom Can You Trust?" *The Economist*, June 22, 1996, p. 51.

23. Michael Booth, *The Almost Nearly Perfect People: Behind the Myth of the Scandinavian Utopia* (New York: Picador, 2014), p. 40.

24. Eric Felten, "Finders Keepers?" *Reader's Digest*, April 2001, p. 105.

25. See Raymond Fisman and Edward Miguel, "Cultures of Corruption: Evidence from Diplomatic Parking Tickets," Working Paper 12312, National Bureau of Economic Research, June 2006, Table 1.

26. Transparency International, *Transparency International Corruption Perceptions Index 2013* (Berlin: Transparency International Secretariat, 2013).

27. Ellen Churchill Semple, *Influences of Geographic Environment* (New York: Henry Holt and Company, 1911), p. 510.

28. "Aspiring Africa," *The Economist,* March 2, 2013, p. 12.

29. Nicholas Eberstadt, *Russia's Peacetime Demographic Crisis: Dimensions, Causes, Implications* (Seattle: National Bureau of Asian Research, 2010), p. 282.

30. Ibid., pp. 232, 233.

31. Donald L. Horowitz, *Ethnic Groups in Conflict* (Berkeley: University of California Press, 1985), p. 663.

32. Feroz Ahmad, "Unionist Relations with the Greek, Armenian, and Jewish Communities of the Ottoman Empire, 1908–1914," *Christians and Jews in the Ottoman Empire: The Functioning of a Plural Society,* Volume I: *The Central Lands,* edited by Benjamin Braude and Bernard Lewis (New York: Holmes & Meier, 1982), pp. 411, 412.

33. Mohamed Suffian bin Hashim, "Problems and Issues of Higher Education Development in Malaysia," *Development of Higher Education in Southeast Asia: Problems and Issues,* edited by Yip Yat Hoong (Singapore: Regional Institute of Higher Education and Development, 1973), Table 8, pp. 70–71.

34. Sarah Gordon, *Hitler, Germans and the "Jewish Question"* (Princeton: Princeton University Press, 1984), p. 13; Peter Pulzer, *The Rise of Political Anti-Semitism in Germany & Austria,* revised edition (Cambridge, Massachusetts: Harvard University Press, 1988), pp. 10–13, *passim.*

35. Leon Volovici, *Nationalist Ideology and Antisemitism: The Case of Romanian Intellectuals in the 1930s,* translated by Charles Kormos (Oxford: Pergamon Press, 1991), p. 60; Irina Livezeanu, *Cultural Politics in Greater Romania: Regionalism, Nation Building, & Ethnic Struggle, 1918–1930* (Ithaca: Cornell University Press, 1995), pp. 63, 115; Howard M. Sachar, *Diaspora: An Inquiry into the Contemporary Jewish World* (New York: Harper & Row, 1985), pp. 297, 299; Australian Government Commission of Inquiry into Poverty, *Welfare of Migrants* (Canberra: Australian Government Publishing Service, 1975), p. 107.

36. Jason L. Riley, *Please Stop Helping Us: How Liberals Make It Harder for Blacks to Succeed* (New York: Encounter Books, 2014), p. 49.

37. Gary B. Cohen, *The Politics of Ethnic Survival: Germans in Prague, 1861–1914*, second edition (West Lafayette: Purdue University Press, 2006), p. 28.

38. See, for example, Gunnar Myrdal, *Asian Drama: An Inquiry Into the Poverty of Nations* (New York: Pantheon, 1968), Vol. III, p. 1642; Myron Weiner and Mary Fainsod Katzenstein, *India's Preferential Policies: Migrants, the Middle Classes, and Ethnic Equality* (Chicago: University of Chicago Press, 1981), p. 99.

39. Leon Volovici, *Nationalist Ideology and Antisemitism*, translated by Charles Kormos, p. 60.

40. Mary Fainsod Katzenstein, *Ethnicity and Equality: The Shiv Sena Party and Preferential Policies in Bombay* (Ithaca: Cornell University Press, 1979), pp. 48–49; Myron Weiner and Mary Fainsod Katzenstein, *India's Preferential Policies*, pp. 10–11, 44–46.

41. Ezra Mendelsohn, *The Jews of East Central Europe between the World Wars* (Bloomington: Indiana University Press, 1983), pp. 98–99, 106.

42. Larry Diamond, "Class, Ethnicity, and the Democratic State: Nigeria, 1950–1966," *Comparative Studies in Society and History*, Vol. 25, No. 3 (July 1983), pp. 462, 473; Donald L. Horowitz, *Ethnic Groups in Conflict*, p. 225.

43. Anatoly M. Khazanov, "The Ethnic Problems of Contemporary Kazakhstan," *Central Asian Survey*, Vol. 14, No. 2 (1995), pp. 244, 257.

44. Leon Volovici, *Nationalist Ideology and Antisemitism*, translated by Charles Kormos, *passim*; Joseph Rothschild, *East Central Europe between the Two World Wars* (Seattle: University of Washington Press, 1992), p. 293; Irina Livezeanu, *Cultural Politics in Greater Romania*, *passim*.

45. Gunnar Myrdal, *Asian Drama*, Vol. I, p. 348; Donald L. Horowitz, *Ethnic Groups in Conflict*, p. 133; Donald L. Horowitz, *The Deadly Ethnic Riot* (Berkeley: University of California Press, 2001), pp. 144–145.

46. Conrad Black, "Canada's Continuing Identity Crisis," *Foreign Affairs*, March/April 1995, p. 100.

47. See, for example, Gary B. Cohen, *The Politics of Ethnic Survival*, pp. 26–28, 32, 133, 236–237; Ezra Mendelsohn, *The Jews of East Central Europe between*

the World Wars, p. 167; Hugh LeCaine Agnew, *Origins of the Czech National Renascence* (Pittsburgh: University of Pittsburgh Press, 1993), *passim*.

48. Some examples can be found, among other places, in John H. Bunzel, *Race Relations on Campus: Stanford Students Speak* (Stanford: Stanford Alumni Association, 1992).

49. Philip Nobile, "Uncovering Roots," *Village Voice*, February 23, 1993, p. 34. Another devastating critique of *Roots* is that of Gary B. Mills and Elizabeth Shown Mills, "'Roots' and the New 'Faction': A Legitimate Tool for Clio?" *The Virginia Magazine of History and Biography*, Vol. 89, No. 1 (January 1981), pp. 3–26.

50. Donald L. Horowitz, *Ethnic Groups in Conflict*, p. 72; See also Keith Windschuttle, "The Fabrication of Aboriginal History," *The New Criterion*, Vol. 20, No. 1 (September 2001), pp. 41–49.

51. Nathan Glazer and Daniel Patrick Móynihan, *Beyond the Melting Pot: The Negroes, Puerto Ricans, Jews, Italians, and Irish of New York City*, second edition (Cambridge, Massachusetts: MIT Press, 1970), p. 241.

52. Joseph Rothschild, *East Central Europe between the Two World Wars*, p. 385.

53. Chandra Richard de Silva, "Sinhala-Tamil Relations and Education in Sri Lanka: The University Admissions Issue— The First Phase, 1971–7," *From Independence to Statehood: Managing Ethnic Conflict in Five African and Asian States*, edited by Robert B. Goldmann and A. Jeyaratnam Wilson (London: Frances Pinter, Ltd. 1984), p. 126.

54. Donald L. Horowitz, *Ethnic Groups in Conflict*, p. 225.

55. Robert A. Kann and Zdeněk V. David, *The Peoples of the Eastern Habsburg Lands, 1526–1918* (Seattle: University of Washington Press, 1984), p. 201.

56. Gary B. Cohen, *The Politics of Ethnic Survival*, p. 148. Derek Sayer, *The Coasts of Bohemia: A Czech History* (Princeton: Princeton University Press, 1998), p. 101.

57. Jeremy King, *Budweisers Into Czechs and Germans: A Local History of Bohemian Politics, 1848–1948* (Princeton: Princeton University Press, 2002), p. 4.

58. Philip Authier, "Camille Laurin, Father of Bill 101, Dies," *The Gazette* (Montreal, Quebec), March 12, 1999, p. A1; Guy Dumas, "Quebec's Language Policy: Perceptions and Realities," *Language and Governance*, edited by Colin Williams (Cardiff: University of Wales Press, 2007), pp. 250–262.

59. Robert Bothwell, et al., *Canada Since 1945: Power, Politics, and Provincialism*, revised edition (Toronto: University of Toronto Press, 1989), pp. 375–376; Graham Fraser, *Sorry, I Don't Speak French: Confronting the Canadian Crisis That Won't Go Away* (Toronto: McClelland & Stewart, 2006), pp. 121–122; John English, *Just Watch Me: The Life of Pierre Elliott Trudeau, 1968–2000* (Toronto: Alfred A. Knopf Canada, 2009), pp. 304–305.

60. Grady McWhiney, *Cracker Culture: Celtic Ways in the Old South* (Tuscaloosa: University of Alabama Press, 1988), pp. 45–47, 49; David Hackett Fischer, *Albion's Seed: Four British Folkways in America* (New York: Oxford University Press, 1989), pp. 365–366, 740–743; Lewis Cecil Gray, *History of Agriculture in the Southern United States to 1860* (Washington: Carnegie Institution of Washington, 1933), Vol. I, p. 484; Frederick Law Olmsted, *The Cotton Kingdom: A Traveller's Observations on Cotton and Slavery in the American Slave States* (New York: Alfred A. Knopf, 1953), pp. 12, 65, 147, 527; Alexis de Tocqueville, *Democracy in America* (New York: Alfred A. Knopf, 1989), Vol. I, pp. 363, 369; Forrest McDonald, "Cultural Continuity and the Shaping of the American South," *Geographic Perspectives in History*, edited by Eugene D. Genovese and Leonard Hochberg (London: Basil Blackwell, Ltd., 1989), pp. 231–232; Lewis M. Killian, *White Southerners*, revised edition (Amherst: University of Massachusetts Press, 1985), pp. 108–109.

61. Robert E. Lee, *Lee's Dispatches: Unpublished Letters of General Robert E. Lee, C.S.A. to Jefferson Davis and the War Department of the Confederate States of America, 1862–65*, edited by Douglas Southall Freeman, New Edition (New York: G.P. Putnam's Sons, 1957), p. 8.

62. Ulrich Bonnell Phillips, *The Slave Economy of the Old South: Selected Essays in Economic and Social History*, edited by Eugene D. Genovese (Baton Rouge: Louisiana State University Press, 1968), p. 107.

63. Grady McWhiney, *Cracker Culture*, p. 19; Virginia Brainard Kunz, *The Germans in America* (Minneapolis: Lerner Publications Co., 1966), pp. 11–12.

64. Lewis Cecil Gray, *History of Agriculture in the Southern United States to 1860*, Vol. II, p. 831.

65. Rupert B. Vance, *Human Geography of the South: A Study in Regional Resources and Human Adequacy* (Chapel Hill: University of North Carolina Press, 1932), p. 168. See also Grady McWhiney, *Cracker Culture*, p. 83.

66. P.T. Bauer, *Reality and Rhetoric: Studies in the Economics of Development* (London: Weidenfeld and Nicolson, 1984), p. 7.

67. G.M. Trevelyan, *English Social History: A Survey of Six Centuries, Chaucer to Queen Victoria* (Middlesex, England: Penguin Books, 1986), pp. 140–141.

68. Fernand Braudel, *The Mediterranean and the Mediterranean World in the Age of Philip II*, translated by Siân Reynolds (Berkeley: University of California Press, 1995), Vol. II, p. 715.

69. Christopher Hibbert, *The English: A Social History 1066–1945* (New York: W.W. Norton & Co., 1987), p. 509.

70. W.E.B. Du Bois, *The Philadelphia Negro: A Social Study* (Philadelphia: University of Pennsylvania Press, 1899), pp. 33–35.

71. Robert F. Foerster, *The Italian Emigration of Our Times* (New York: Arno Press, 1969), p. 314.

72. William H. McNeill, *History of Western Civilization: A Handbook*, sixth edition (Chicago: University of Chicago Press, 1986), p. 252.

73. David S. Landes, *The Wealth and Poverty of Nations: Why Some Are So Rich And Some So Poor* (New York: W.W. Norton, 1998), p. 214.

74. W.A. Armstrong, "The Countryside," *The Cambridge Social History of Britain: 1750–1950*, Vol. 1: *Regions and Communities*, edited by F.M.L. Thompson (Cambridge: Cambridge University Press, 1993), p. 87.

75. G.M. Trevelyan, *English Social History*, pp. 243, 271–272, 315, 325, 335, 386–387, 393n, 409, 414, 419–420.

76. Carl K. Eicher, "Facing Up to Africa's Food Crisis," *Foreign Affairs*, Fall 1982, p. 166.

77. Ibid., p. 170.

78. Gunnar Myrdal, *Asian Drama: An Inquiry Into the Poverty of Nations*, abridged edition (New York: Pantheon, 1972), p. 296. The great British economist Alfred Marshall observed in 1909: "The notion that it is more dignified to hold a pen and keep accounts than to work in a high grade engineering shop seems to me the root of India's difficulties." Alfred Marshall, "Letters," *Memorials of Alfred Marshall*, edited by A.C. Pigou (New York: Kelley & Millman, Inc., 1956), p. 457.

79. Daniel J. Boorstin, *The Americans*, Vol. II: *The National Experience* (New York: Random House, 1965), p. 176.

80. Grady McWhiney, *Cracker Culture*, p. 253. As of 1860, the total population of the South was 39 percent of the total population of the United States. Since slaves were about one-third of the population of the South, and were usually in no position to invent, that leaves white Southerners as 26 percent of the total population of the country and approximately one-third of the white population. For population statistics, see Lewis Cecil Gray, *History of Agriculture in the Southern United States to 1860*, pp. 656, 811.

81. Rupert B. Vance, *Human Geography of the South*, p. 279.

82. Grady McWhiney, *Cracker Culture*, p. 256.

83. Ibid., pp. 253–258.

84. Rupert B. Vance, *Human Geography of the South*, p. 280.

85. Ibid., p. 281.

86. Ibid., p. 305.

87. Ellen Churchill Semple, *American History and Its Geographic Conditions* (Boston: Houghton, Mifflin and Company, 1903), p. 346.

88. Paul Johnson, *A History of the American People* (New York: Harper Collins, 1998), p. 462.

89. Rupert B. Vance, *Human Geography of the South*, pp. 301–303.

90. Ibid., pp. 304–305.

91. Ibid., pp. 112–116, 127–128.

92. Ibid., p. 292.

93. David S. Landes, *The Wealth and Poverty of Nations*, pp. 516–517.

Part III: Social Factors

Epigraph: Fernand Braudel, *A History of Civilizations*, translated by Richard Mayne (New York: The Penguin Press, 1994), p. 17.

1. Charles Murray, *Human Accomplishment: The Pursuit of Excellence in the Arts and Sciences, 800 BC to 1950* (New York: HarperCollins, 2003), p. 291.

2. Frederick Law Olmsted, *The Cotton Kingdom: A Traveller's Observations on Cotton and Slavery in the American Slave States* (New York: Alfred A. Knopf, 1953), pp. 366, 396. See also pp. 330, 520, 591 and Arthur M. Schlesinger, "Editor's Introduction," Ibid., pp. liv–lv.

3.   Daniel J. Boorstin, *The Americans*, Vol. I: *The Colonial Experience* (New York: Random House, 1958), pp. 302, 303, 304.

4.   Arthur Herman, *How the Scots Invented the Modern World: The True Story of How Western Europe's Poorest Nation Created Our World & Everything In It* (New York: Crown Publishers, 2001), p. 20.

5.   [Robert M. Yerkes,] National Academy of Sciences, *Psychological Examining in the United States Army* (Washington: Government Printing Office, 1921), Vol. XV, Part III, p. 697.

6.   Many expressions of such views can be found in my *Intellectuals and Race* (New York: Basic Books, 2013), pp. 28–37.

Chapter 8: Population

1.   Ellen Churchill Semple, *Influences of Geographic Environment* (New York: Henry Holt and Company, 1911), pp. 462–463, 584–585.

2.   Ibid., pp. 582–585.

3.   Ibid., pp. 579–580.

4.   Thomas Robert Malthus, *An Essay on the Principle of Population* (London: J. Johnson, 1798), p. 14; Thomas Robert Malthus, *Population: The First Essay* (Ann Arbor: University of Michigan Press, 1959), p. 5; Thomas Robert Malthus, "An Essay on the Principle of Population, As It Affects the Future Improvement of Society with Remarks on the Speculations of Mr. Godwin, M. Condorcet and Other Writers," *On Population*, edited by Gertrude Himmelfarb (New York: The Modern Library, 1960), p. 9.

5.   Eduardo Porter, "Old Forecast of Famine May Yet Come True," *New York Times*, April 2, 2014, p. B1.

6.   See my *On Classical Economics* (New Haven: Yale University Press, 2006), pp. 57–63, 120–122.

7.   *Geography of Sub-Saharan Africa*, third edition, edited by Samuel Aryeetey Attoh (New York: Prentice Hall, 2010), p. 182; *The World Almanac and Book of Facts: 2013* (New York: World Almanac Books, 2013), p. 793.

8.   P.T. Bauer, *Equality, the Third World and Economic Delusion* (Cambridge, Massachusetts: Harvard University Press, 1981), p. 43.

9.   Paul Robert Magosci, *A History of Ukraine* (Seattle: University of Washington Press, 1996), p. 6; Norman Davies, *Europe at War, 1939–1945: No Simple*

Victory (London: Macmillan, 2006), p. 32; Tony Judt, *Postwar: A History of Europe Since 1945* (New York: Penguin Books, 2006), p. 648.

10. Shirley S. Wang, "Obesity in China Becoming More Common," *Wall Street Journal*, July 8, 2008, p. A18.

11. The Economist, *Pocket World in Figures: 2014 edition* (London: Profile Books, 2013), p. 18.

12.

GROUPS	MEDIAN AGE
BLACK	32.9
CAMBODIAN	31.0
CHINESE	38.0
CUBAN	39.8
JAPANESE	49.5
MEXICAN	26.0
PUERTO RICAN	28.4
WHITE	40.2
TOTAL	37.4

SOURCE: U.S. Census Bureau, 2012 American Community Survey 1-Year Estimates

13. W. Michael Cox and Richard Alm, "By Our Own Bootstraps: Economic Opportunity & the Dynamics of Income Distribution," *Annual Report 1995*, Federal Reserve Bank of Dallas, p. 16.

14. "Choose Your Parents Wisely," *The Economist*, July 26, 2014, p. 22.

15. Leila Morsy and Richard Rothstein, *Five Social Disadvantages That Depress Student Performance: Why Schools Alone Can't Close Achievement Gaps* (Washington: Economic Policy Institute, 2015), p. 6.

16. Ibid., p. 7.

17. "Choose Your Parents Wisely," *The Economist*, July 26, 2014, p. 22.

18. Ibid., pp. 21, 22.

19. Helen Ware, *A Profile of the Italian Community in Australia* (Melbourne: Australian Institute of Multicultural Affairs and Co.As.It Italian Assistance Association, 1981), p. 12.

20. Charles A. Price, *Southern Europeans in Australia* (Melbourne: Oxford University Press, 1963), p. 162. This pattern was typical of Southern

Europeans as a whole. In the era before the Second World War, over 90 percent of Australia's immigrants from Southern Europe "came not as a broad scatter from southern Europe as a whole but in concentrated streams from relatively small and restricted areas of origin" and "the great majority of immigrants settled fairly close together." Ibid., p. 276; Charles A. Price, *The Methods and Statistics of 'Southern Europeans in Australia'* (Canberra: The Australian National University, 1963), p. 21.

21. Philip Taylor, *The Distant Magnet: European Emigration to the USA* (New York: Harper & Row, 1971), pp. 210, 211; Jonathan Gill, *Harlem: The Four Hundred Year History from Dutch Village to Capital of Black America* (New York: Grove Press, 2011), p. 139; Robert F. Foerster, *The Italian Emigration of Our Times* (New York: Arno Press, 1969), p. 393; Dino Cinel, *From Italy to San Francisco: The Immigrant Experience* (Stanford: Stanford University Press, 1982), pp. 28, 117–120.

22. Samuel L. Baily, "The Adjustment of Italian Immigrants in Buenos Aires and New York, 1870–1914," *American Historical Review*, April 1983, p. 291; John E. Zucchi, *Italians in Toronto: Development of a National Identity, 1875–1935* (Kingston, Ontario: McGill-Queen's University Press, 1988), pp. 41, 53–55, 58.

23. Frederick C. Luebke, *Germans in the New World: Essays in the History of Immigration* (Urbana: University of Illinois Press, 1990), p. 99.

24. Theodore Huebener, *The Germans in America* (Philadelphia: Chilton Company, 1962), p. 84.

25. Hildegard Binder Johnson, "The Location of German Immigrants in the Middle West," *Annals of the Association of American Geographers*, edited by Henry Madison Kendall, Volume XLI (1951), pp. 24–25.

26. LaVern J. Rippley, "Germans from Russia," *Harvard Encyclopedia of American Ethnic Groups*, edited by Stephan Thernstrom, et al (Cambridge, Massachusetts: Harvard University Press, 1980), p. 427.

27. Frederick C. Luebke, *Germans in the New World*, pp. 99–100.

28. Iris Barbara Graefe, "Cultural Changes Among Germans from Russia in Argentina, 1967–1977," *Germans from Russia in Colorado*, edited by Sidney Heitman (Fort Collins, Colorado: The Western Social Science Association, 1978), p. 58.

29. Louise L'Estrange Fawcett, "Lebanese, Palestinians and Syrians in Colombia," *The Lebanese in the World: A Century of Emigration*, edited by Albert Hourani and Nadim Shehadi (London: The Centre for Lebanese Studies, 1992), p. 368.

30. Jack Chen, *The Chinese of America* (San Francisco: Harper & Row, Publishers, 1980), p. 18.

31. Kay S. Hymowitz, "Brooklyn's Chinese Pioneers," *City Journal*, Spring 2014, pp. 20–29.

32. Edward C. Banfield, *The Unheavenly City Revisited* (Boston: Little, Brown and Company, 1974), p. 91.

33. E. Franklin Frazier, "The Impact of Urban Civilization Upon Negro Family Life," *American Sociological Review*, Vol. 2, No. 5 (October 1937), p. 615.

34. Jonathan Gill, *Harlem*, p. 284; E. Franklin Frazier, *The Negro in the United States*, revised edition (New York: The Macmillan Company, 1957), pp. 239, 257–258; Willard B. Gatewood, *Aristocrats of Color: The Black Elite, 1880–1920* (Bloomington: Indiana University Press, 1990), pp. 194–195; Stephen Birmingham, *Certain People: America's Black Elite* (Boston: Little, Brown and Company, 1977), pp. 196–197; "Sugar Hill: All Harlem Looks Up to 'Folks on the Hill'," *Ebony*, November 1946, pp. 5–11.

35. Philip Taylor, *The Distant Magnet*, p. 57.

36. Josip Roglič , "The Geographical Setting of Medieval Dubrovnik," *Geographical Essays on Eastern Europe*, edited by Norman J.G. Pounds (Bloomington: Indiana University Press, 1961), p. 148; Jean W. Sedlar, *East Central Europe in the Middle Ages, 1000–1500* (Seattle: University of Washington Press, 1994), p. 8.

37. Carlo M. Cipolla, *Clocks and Culture: 1300–1700* (New York: Walker and Company, 1967), pp. 66–69; David S. Landes, *Revolution in Time: Clocks and the Making of the Modern World* (Cambridge, Massachusetts: Harvard University Press, 1983), pp. 237–238.

38. As to the role of the scientists in getting President Franklin D. Roosevelt to create the Manhattan Project that produced the first atomic bomb, see Richard Rhodes, *The Making of the Atomic Bomb* (New York: Simon & Schuster, 1986), pp. 305–314. As for these particular scientists being Jewish, see Ibid., pp. 13, 106, 188–189; Silvan S. Schweber, *Einstein and Oppenheimer: The Meaning of Genius* (Cambridge, Massachusetts: Harvard University Press,

2008), p. 138; Michio Kaku, *Einstein's Cosmos: How Albert Einstein's Vision Transformed Our Understanding of Space and Time* (New York: W.W. Norton, 2004), pp. 187–188; Howard M. Sachar, *A History of the Jews in America* (New York: Alfred A. Knopf, 1992), p. 527; American Jewish Historical Society, *American Jewish Desk Reference* (New York: Random House, 1999), p. 591.

39. Fernand Braudel, *A History of Civilizations*, translated by Richard Mayne (New York: Penguin Books, 1993), p. 440.

40. Angus Deaton, *The Great Escape: Health, Wealth, and the Origins of Inequality* (Princeton: Princeton University Press, 2013), p. 207.

41. W. Michael Cox and Richard Alm, "By Our Own Bootstraps: Economic Opportunity & the Dynamics of Income Distribution," *Annual Report 1995*, Federal Reserve Bank of Dallas, p. 8; "Movin' On Up," *Wall Street Journal*, November 13, 2007, p. A24. Similar patterns exist in Canada. See Niels Veldhuis, et al., "The 'Poor' Are Getting Richer," *Fraser Forum*, January/February 2013, pp. 24, 25.

42. Thomas A. Hirschl and Mark R. Rank, "The Life Course Dynamics of Affluence," *PLoS ONE*, January 28, 2015, p. 5.

43. The Pew Charitable Trusts, *Pursuing the American Dream: Economic Mobility Across Generations* (Washington: Economic Mobility Project, an initiative of The Pew Charitable Trusts, 2012), p. 1. This is called "absolute mobility" in both the 2008 and the 2012 Pew studies. Ibid.; Isabel V. Sawhill, "Overview," Julia B. Isaacs, Isabel V. Sawhill and Ron Haskins, *Getting Ahead or Losing Ground: Economic Mobility in America* (Washington: Economic Mobility Project, an initiative of The Pew Charitable Trusts, 2008), p. 2.

44. The Pew Charitable Trusts, *Pursuing the American Dream*, p. 2.

45. Ibid., p. 1. This is called "relative mobility" in both studies. Ibid.; Isabel V. Sawhill, "Overview," Julia B. Isaacs, Isabel V. Sawhill and Ron Haskins, *Getting Ahead or Losing Ground*, p. 2.

46. The Pew Charitable Trusts, *Pursuing the American Dream*, p. 2.

47. Ibid., p. 28. A similar caveat appears in the 2008 study on page 105.

48. Isabel V. Sawhill, "Overview," Julia B. Isaacs, Isabel V. Sawhill and Ron Haskins, *Getting Ahead or Losing Ground*, p. 6.

Chapter 9: Mental Capabilities

Epigraph: Charles Murray, *Real Education: Four Simple Truths for Bringing America's Schools Back to Reality* (New York: Crown Publishing, 2008), p. 11.

1. "Great Expectations," *The Economist*, April 4, 2015, p. 12; "Unequal Beginnings," Ibid., pp. 57–58.

2. Charles Murray, *Human Accomplishment: The Pursuit of Excellence in the Arts and Sciences, 800 B.C. to 1950* (New York: Harper Collins, 2003), pp. 355–361.

3. See, for example, Ibid., Chapter 13; David S. Landes, *The Wealth and Poverty of Nations: Why Some Are So Rich and Some So Poor* (New York: W.W. Norton & Company, 1998), *passim*; Ellen Churchill Semple, *Influences of Geographic Environment* (New York: Henry Holt and Company, 1911), *passim*.

4. Eligio R. Padilla and Gail E. Wyatt, "The Effects of Intelligence and Achievement Testing on Minority Group Children," *The Psychosocial Development of Minority Group Children*, edited by Gloria Johnson Powell, et al (New York: Brunner/Mazel, Publishers, 1983), p. 418.

5. Mandel Sherman and Cora B. Key, "The Intelligence of Isolated Mountain Children," *Child Development*, Vol. 3, No. 4 (December 1932), p. 283; Lester R. Wheeler, "A Comparative Study of the Intelligence of East Tennessee Mountain Children," *Journal of Educational Psychology*, Vol. XXXIII, No. 5 (May 1942), pp. 322, 324.

6. Otto Klineberg, *Race Differences* (New York: Harper & Brothers, 1935), p. 182.

7. A.G. Hopkins, *An Economic History of West Africa* (New York: Columbia University Press, 1973), p. 44; William S. Maltby, *The Rise and Fall of the Spanish Empire* (New York: Palgrave Macmillan, 2009), p. 18; Peter Pierson, *The History of Spain* (Westport, Connecticut: Greenwood Press, 1999), pp. 7–8; Ellen Churchill Semple, *Influences of Geographic Environment*, p. 434.

8. George W. Pierson, *The Moving American* (New York: Alfred A. Knopf, 1973), pp. 14–15.

9. Ellen Churchill Semple, *Influences of Geographic Environment*, p. 96.

10. *Griggs et al. v. Duke Power Co.*, 401 U.S. 424 (1971), at 432.

11. Heather Mac Donald, "How Gotham's Elite High Schools Escaped the Leveller's Ax," *City Journal*, Spring 1999, p. 74.

12. Jason L. Riley, *Please Stop Helping Us: How Liberals Make It Harder for Blacks to Succeed* (New York: Encounter Books, 2014), p. 49.

13. Susan Jacoby, "Elite School Battle," *Washington Post*, May 28, 1972, p. B4.

14. Kerri MacDonald, "A Nobel Laureate Returns Home to Bronx Science," *New York Times*, October 16, 2010, p. A16.

15. Dennis Saffran, "The Plot Against Merit," *City Journal*, Summer 2014, pp. 81–82.

16. Reginald G. Damerell, *Education's Smoking Gun: How Teachers Colleges Have Destroyed Education in America* (New York: Freundlich Books, 1985), p. 164.

17. Maria Newman, "Cortines Has Plan to Coach Minorities into Top Schools," *New York Times*, March 18, 1995, p. 1.

18. Fernanda Santos, "Black at Stuy," *New York Times*, February 26, 2012, Metropolitan Desk, p. 6.

19. See the title essay in my *Black Rednecks and White Liberals* (San Francisco: Encounter Books, 2005), as well as *Cracker Culture: Celtic Ways in the Old South* (Tuscaloosa: University of Alabama Press, 1988) by Grady McWhiney and *Albion's Seed: Four British Folkways in America* (New York: Oxford University Press, 1989) by David Hackett Fischer.

20. H.J. Butcher, *Human Intelligence: Its Nature and Assessment* (New York: Harper & Row, 1968), p. 252.

21. President Wm. W. Patton, "Change of Environment," *The American Missionary*, Vol. XXXVI, No. 8 (August 1882), p. 229; James D. Anderson, *The Education of Blacks in the South, 1860–1935* (Chapel Hill: University of North Carolina Press, 1988), p. 46.

22. See my *Black Rednecks and White Liberals*, pp. 38–40.

23. Henry S. Robinson, "The M Street High School, 1891–1916," *Records of the Columbia Historical Society*, Washington, D.C., Vol. 51 (1984), p. 122.

24. T. Rees Shapiro, "Vanished Glory of an All-Black High School," *Washington Post*, January 19, 2014, p. B6.

25. See Table 4, School Code 0508/0598 [Dunbar High School] in my "Assumptions versus History in Ethnic Education," *Teachers College Record*, Volume 83, No. 1 (Fall 1981), p. 47.

26. Mary Gibson Hundley, *The Dunbar Story: 1870–1955* (New York: Vantage Press, 1965), p. 25.

27. Ibid., p. 75.

28. Ibid., p. 78. Mary Church Terrell, "History of the High School for Negroes in Washington," *Journal of Negro History*, Vol. 2, No. 3 (July 1917), p. 262.

29. Department of Defense, *Black Americans in Defense of Our Nation* (Washington: U.S. Department of Defense, 1985), p. 153.

30. Mary Church Terrell, "History of the High School for Negroes in Washington," *Journal of Negro History*, Vol. 2, No. 3 (July 1917), p. 264.

31. Louise Daniel Hutchison, *Anna J. Cooper: A Voice from the South* (Washington: The Smithsonian Institution Press, 1981), p. 62.

32. The first black federal judge was William H. Hastie, the first black general was Benjamin O. Davis, Sr., and the first black Cabinet member was Robert C. Weaver.

33. Mary Gibson Hundley, *The Dunbar Story*, p. 57.

34. Alison Stewart, *First Class: The Legacy of Dunbar, America's First Black Public High School* (Chicago: Lawrence Hill Books, 2013), pp. 91–93.

35. Jervis Anderson, "A Very Special Monument," *The New Yorker*, March 20, 1978, p. 93.

36. Ibid., p. 113.

37. Tucker Carlson, "From Ivy League to NBA," *Policy Review*, Spring 1993, p. 36.

38. T. Rees Shapiro, "Vanished Glory of An All-Black High School," *Washington Post*, January 19, 2014, p. B6.

39. See the title article in my *Black Rednecks and White Liberals*.

40. Jason L. Riley, *Please Stop Helping Us*, p. 43.

41. John U. Ogbu, *Black American Students in an Affluent Suburb: A Study of Academic Disengagement* (Mahwah, New Jersey: Lawrence Erlbaum Associates, 2003), Chapters 1, 2.

42. Ibid., p. 179.

43. Jason L. Riley, *Please Stop Helping Us*, p. 45.

44. Ibid., p. 46.

45. Ibid., p. 47.

46. See the data in my "Assumptions versus History in Ethnic Education," *Teachers College Record*, Volume 83, No. 1 (Fall 1981), pp. 40, 41.

47. Stephan Thernstrom and Abigail Thernstrom, *America in Black and White: One Nation, Indivisible* (New York: Simon & Schuster, 1997), p. 357.

48. *KIPP: 2014 Report Card* (San Francisco: KIPP Foundation, 2014), pp. 10, 19. See also Mathematica Policy Research, *Understanding the Effect of KIPP as it Scales: Volume I, Impacts on Achievement and Other Outcomes* (Washington: Mathematica Policy Research, 2015).

49. Daniel Bergner, "Class Warfare," *New York Times Magazine*, September 7, 2014, p. 62.

50. Ibid., pp. 63, 66.

51. Alison Stewart, *First Class*, p. 90.

52. Ibid., pp. xii, 32, 33, 34, 35, 69.

53. U.S. Census Bureau, "Table 4. Poverty Status of Families, by Type of Family, Presence of Related Children, Race, and Hispanic Origin: 1959 to 2013," downloaded on October 23, 2014:

   http://www.census.gov/hhes/www/poverty/data/historical/families.html

54. John H. Bunzel, "Affirmative-Action Admissions: How It 'Works' at UC Berkeley," *The Public Interest*, Fall 1988, pp. 124, 125.

55. Richard Sander and Stuart Taylor, Jr., *Mismatch: How Affirmative Action Hurts Students It's Intended to Help, and Why Universities Won't Admit It* (New York: Basic Books, 2012), p. 154.

56. None of the book's many tables separates black students who were admitted under the normal standards and those admitted under affirmative action standards. See William G. Bowen and Derek Bok, *The Shape of the River: Long-Term Consequences of Considering Race in College and University Admissions* (Princeton: Princeton University Press, 1998), pp. ix–xix.

57. Ibid., p. 61. See also p. 259.

58. Stephan Thernstrom and Abigail Thernstrom, *America in Black and White*, p. 408.

59. William G. Bowen and Derek Bok, *The Shape of the River*, p. 60n.

60. Citations from these other empirical studies, as well as a more extended critique of *The Shape of the River*, can be found in my *Affirmative Action Around the World: An Empirical Study* (New Haven: Yale University Press, 2004), pp. 152–159.

61. Stephan Thernstrom and Abigail Thernstrom, "Reflections on *The Shape of the River*," *UCLA Law Review*, Vol. 46, No. 5 (June 1999), p. 1589.

62. Mark H. Haller, *Eugenics: Hereditarian Attitudes in American Thought* (New Brunswick: Rutgers University Press, 1963), p. 11.

63. Gunnar Myrdal, *An American Dilemma: The Negro Problem and Modern Democracy* (New York: Harper & Brothers, 1944), p. 99.

64. See, for example, Edward Alsworth Ross, *The Old World in the New: The Significance of Past and Present Immigration to the American People* (New York: The Century Company, 1914); Francis A. Walker, "Methods of Restricting Immigration," *Discussions in Economics and Statistics*, Volume II: *Statistics, National Growth, Social Economics*, edited by Davis R. Dewey (New York: Henry Holt and Company, 1899); Kenneth L. Roberts, *Why Europe Leaves Home* (Bobbs-Merrill Company, 1922); George Creel, "Melting Pot or Dumping Ground?" *Collier's*, September 3, 1921, pp. 9 ff.

65. Rudolph Pintner, *Intelligence Testing: Methods and Results*, new edition (New York: Henry Holt and Co., 1939), p. 453.

66. Carl C. Brigham, "Intelligence Tests of Immigrant Groups," *Psychological Review*, Vol. 37, Issue 2 (March 1930), p. 165.

67. H.J. Butcher, *Human Intelligence*, p. 252.

68. For details, compare Carl C. Brigham, *A Study of American Intelligence* (Princeton: Princeton University Press, 1923), pp. 16–19, 36–38; [Robert M. Yerkes,] National Academy of Sciences, *Psychological Examining in the United States Army* (Washington: Government Printing Office, 1921), Vol. XV, Part III, pp. 874, 875; Thomas Sowell, "Race and IQ Reconsidered," *Essays and Data on American Ethnic Groups*, edited by Thomas Sowell and Lynn D. Collins (Washington: The Urban Institute, 1978), pp. 226–227.

69. James R. Flynn, "The Mean IQ of Americans: Massive Gains 1932 to 1978," *Psychological Bulletin*, Vol. 95, No. 1 (1984), pp. 29–51; James R. Flynn, "Massive IQ Gains in 14 Nations: What IQ Tests Really Measure," *Psychological Bulletin*, Vol. 101, No. 2 (1987), pp. 171–191.

70. James R. Flynn, *Where Have All the Liberals Gone? Race, Class, and Ideals in America* (Cambridge: Cambridge University Press, 2008), pp. 72–74, 87.

71. Joseph J. Ryan, "Intelligence," *21st Century Psychology: A Reference Handbook*, edited by Stephen F. Davis and William Buskist (Los Angeles: SAGE Publications, 2008), Vol. 1, p. 418.

72. Robert William Fogel, *The Escape from Hunger and Premature Death, 1700–2100: Europe, America, and the Third World* (Cambridge: Cambridge University Press, 2004), pp. 55–57.

73. Daniel Schwekendiek, "Height and Weight Differences Between North and South Korea," *Journal of Biosocial Science*, Vol. 41, No. 1 (January 2009), pp. 51–55. *The Economist* reported that North Koreans were "on average three inches shorter" than South Koreans. "We Need to Talk About Kim," *The Economist*, December 31, 2011, p. 8.

74. Robert William Fogel, *The Escape from Hunger and Premature Death, 1700–2100*, p. 41.

75. Kenneth L. Roberts, "Lest We Forget," *Saturday Evening Post*, April 28, 1923, pp. 3 ff; Kenneth L. Roberts, *Why Europe Leaves Home*; Kenneth L. Roberts, "Slow Poison," *Saturday Evening Post*, February 2, 1924, pp. 8 ff; George Creel, "Melting Pot or Dumping Ground?" *Collier's*, September 3, 1921, pp. 9 ff; George Creel, "Close the Gates!" *Collier's*, May 6, 1922, pp. 9 ff.

76. Clifford Kirkpatrick, *Intelligence and Immigration* (Baltimore: The Williams & Wilkins Company, 1926), pp. 24, 31, 34.

77. Philip E. Vernon, *Intelligence and Cultural Environment* (London: Methuen & Co., Ltd., 1970), p. 155; Lester R. Wheeler, "A Comparative Study of the Intelligence of East Tennessee Mountain Children," *Journal of Educational Psychology*, Vol. XXXIII, No. 5 (May 1942), p. 322; Mandel Sherman and Cora B. Key, "The Intelligence of Isolated Mountain Children," *Child Development*, Vol. 3, No. 4 (1932), p. 283; Hugh Gordon, *Mental and Scholastic Tests Among Retarded Children* (London: His Majesty's Stationery Office, 1923), p. 38.

78. See, for example, Richard Lynn and Tatu Vanhanen, *IQ and Global Inequality* (Augusta, Georgia: Washington Summit Publishers, 2006).

79. Wolf H. Berger, *Ocean: Reflections on a Century of Exploration* (Berkeley: University of California Press, 2009), p. 151.

80. Arthur R. Jensen, "How Much Can We Boost IQ and Scholastic Achievement?" *Harvard Educational Review*, Winter 1969, p. 95.

81. Quoted in Rupert B. Vance, *Human Geography of the South: A Study in Regional Resources and Human Adequacy* (Chapel Hill: University of North Carolina Press, 1932), pp. 464–465.

82. See, for example, Grady McWhiney, *Cracker Culture,* pp. 196, 253; Lewis Cecil Gray, *History of Agriculture in the Southern United States to 1860* (Washington: Carnegie Institution of Washington, 1933), Vol. II, pp. 656, 811; Hinton Rowan Helper, *The Impending Crisis of the South: How to Meet It* (Cambridge, Massachusetts, Harvard University Press, 1968), pp. 69, 284, 285, 288–291, 338.

83. Richard Lynn, *The Global Bell Curve: Race, IQ, and Inequality Worldwide* (Augusta, Georgia: Washington Summit Publishers, 2008), p. 51.

Part IV: Political Factors

Epigraph: Freeman Dyson, "The Case for Blunders," *New York Review of Books,* March 6, 2014, p. 6.

1. Bryan Ward-Perkins, *The Fall of Rome and the End of Civilization* (Oxford: Oxford University Press, 2005), p. 98.

2. Ibid., pp. 104–106.

3. N.J.G. Pounds, *An Historical Geography of Europe* (Cambridge: Cambridge University Press, 1990), p. 91. See also Ibid., pp. 69–70.

4. Ibid., p. 165; N.J.G. Pounds, *An Historical Geography of Europe: 1500–1840* (Cambridge: Cambridge University Press, 1979), pp. 134–135.

5. N.J.G. Pounds, *Hearth & Home: A History of Material Culture* (Bloomington: Indiana University Press, 1989), p. 95.

6. N.J.G. Pounds, *An Historical Geography of Europe,* pp. 161, 165, 374; N.J.G. Pounds, *An Historical Geography of Europe: 1800–1914* (Cambridge: Cambridge University Press, 1985), p. 146.

7. Karl Polanyi, *The Great Transformation: The Political and Economic Origins of Our Time* (Boston: Beacon, 1957), p. 45.

8. See, for example, my *Knowledge and Decisions* (New York: Basic Books, 1980), for a fuller treatment of this consideration.

Chapter 10: Political Institutions

Epigraph: Alfred Marshall, *Industry and Trade* (London: Macmillan and Co., 1923), pp. 647–648.

1. Ellen Churchill Semple, *Influences of Geographic Environment* (New York: Henry Holt and Company, 1911), p. 327.

2. Ibid., p. 523.

3. See, for example, Ibid., pp. 595, 596. Alton C. Byers, et al., "Introduction to Mountains," *Mountain Geography: Physical and Human Dimensions*, edited by Martin F. Price, et al (Berkeley: University of California Press, 2013), p. 2; James S. Gardner, et al., "People in the Mountains," Ibid., p. 276.

4. See, for example, Ellen Churchill Semple, *Influences of Geographic Environment*, pp. 237, 591, 593, 599; J.R. McNeill, *The Mountains of the Mediterranean World: An Environmental History* (New York: Cambridge University Press, 1992), p. 48.

5. Ellen Churchill Semple, *Influences of Geographic Environment*, pp. 592, 593.

6. Ibid., p. 597.

7. James S. Gardner, et al., "People in the Mountains," *Mountain Geography*, edited by Martin F. Price, et al., p. 288; Ellen Churchill Semple, *Influences of Geographic Environment*, p. 535; Fernand Braudel, *The Mediterranean and the Mediterranean World in the Age of Philip II*, translated by Siân Reynolds (New York: Harper & Row, 1972), Vol. I, pp. 41, 207.

8. Ellen Churchill Semple, *Influences of Geographic Environment*, pp. 535, 548.

9. Gordon F. McEwan, *The Incas: New Perspectives* (Santa Barbara: ABC-CLIO, 2006), p. 3; The Economist, *Pocket World in Figures: 2014 edition* (London: Profile Books, Ltd., 2013), pp. 148, 150, 222.

10. Gordon F. McEwan, *The Incas*, p. 23; Jeffrey Quilter, *The Ancient Central Andes* (New York: Routledge, 2014), p. 32; Thomas E. Weil, et al., *Area Handbook for Peru* (Washington: Government Printing Office, 1972), p. 36.

11. The fate of people in mountains with this kind of physical layout, in various parts of the world, is contrasted with the fate of people in mountains whose topography provides larger level valleys and mountain passes providing greater communication with the outside world in Ellen Churchill Semple, *Influences of Geographic Environment*, pp. 533–536.

12. *The World Almanac and Book of Facts: 2014* (New York: World Almanac Books, 2014), p. 696.

13. Ellen Churchill Semple, *Influences of Geographic Environment*, p. 374.

14. Gordon F. McEwan, *The Incas*, p. 3.

15. Alan L. Kolata, *Ancient Inca* (Cambridge: Cambridge University Press, 2013), pp. 128, 129–130; Gordon F. McEwan, *The Incas*, pp. 84–85, 121–122; John H.

Bodley, *Cultural Anthropology: Tribes, States, and the Global System* (Mountain View, California: Mayfield Publishing Company, 1997), pp. 215–216.

16. Ellen Churchill Semple, *Influences of Geographic Environment,* p. 419.

17. Fernand Braudel, *A History of Civilizations,* translated by Richard Mayne (New York: The Penguin Press, 1994), pp. 128–129.

18. Fernand Braudel, *The Structures of Everyday Life: The Limits of the Possible,* translated by Siân Reynolds (Berkeley: University of California Press, 1992), pp. 92–93.

19. Ellen Churchill Semple, *Influences of Geographic Environment,* pp. 110–111.

20. Orlando Patterson, *Slavery and Social Death: A Comparative Study* (Cambridge, Massachusetts: Harvard University Press, 1982), pp. 406–407 (note 172); W. Montgomery Watt, *The Influence of Islam on Medieval Europe* (Edinburgh: Edinburgh University Press, 1972), p. 19; Bernard Lewis, *Race and Slavery in the Middle East: An Historical Enquiry* (New York: Oxford University Press, 1990), p. 11; Daniel Evans, "Slave Coast of Europe," *Slavery & Abolition,* Vol. 6, Number 1 (May 1985), p. 53 (note 3); William D. Phillips, Jr., *Slavery from Roman Times to the Early Transatlantic Trade* (Minneapolis: University of Minnesota Press, 1985), p. 57.

21. Daniel Evans, "Slave Coast of Europe," *Slavery & Abolition,* Vol. 6, No. 1 (May 1985), p. 42.

22. Ellen Churchill Semple, *Influences of Geographic Environment,* p. 90.

23. Martin A. Klein, "Introduction: Modern European Expansion and Traditional Servitude in Africa and Asia," *Breaking the Chains: Slavery, Bondage, and Emancipation in Modern Africa and Asia,* edited by Martin A. Klein (Madison: University of Wisconsin Press, 1993), p. 8.

24. Ibid., pp. 19, 20. As of 1840, there were still more slaves in India than those emancipated by the British in the Caribbean. David Brion Davis, *The Problem of Slavery in the Age of Revolution: 1770–1823* (Ithaca: Cornell University Press, 1975), p. 63.

25. Martin A. Klein, "Introduction: Modern European Expansion and Traditional Servitude in Africa and Asia," *Breaking the Chains,* edited by Martin A. Klein, p. 11.

26. Adam Smith, *An Inquiry into the Nature and Causes of the Wealth of Nations* (New York: Modern Library, 1937), p. 365.

27. Ellen Churchill Semple, *Influences of Geographic Environment*, p. 275; A. Sheriff, "Localisation and Social Composition of the East African Slave Trade, 1858–1873," *The Economics of the Indian Ocean Slave Trade in the Nineteenth Century*, edited by William Gervase Clarence-Smith (London: Frank Cass and Company, 1989), pp. 133–134, 142, 144; R.W. Beachey, *The Slave Trade of Eastern Africa* (New York: Barnes & Noble Books, 1976), p. 182; Robert Stock, *Africa South of the Sahara: A Geographical Interpretation*, third edition (New York: The Guilford Press, 2013), pp. 179, 180.

28. See, for example, Harold D. Nelson, et al., *Nigeria: A Country Study* (Washington: U.S. Government Printing Office, 1982), p. 16; François Renault, "The Structures of the Slave Trade in Central Africa in the 19th Century," *The Economics of the Indian Ocean Slave Trade in the Nineteenth Century*, edited by William Gervase Clarence-Smith, pp. 146–165; Paul E. Lovejoy and Jan S. Hogendorn, "Slave Marketing in West Africa," *The Uncommon Market: Essays in the Economic History of the Atlantic Slave Trade*, edited by Henry A. Gemery and Jan S. Hogendorn (New York: Academic Press, 1979), pp. 221–223, *passim*; Martin A. Klein, "Introduction: Modern European Expansion and Traditional Servitude in Africa and Asia," *Breaking the Chains*, edited by Martin A. Klein, p. 10; James F. Searing, *West African Slavery and Atlantic Commerce: The Senegal River Valley, 1700–1860* (Cambridge: Cambridge University Press, 1993), p. 69.

29. François Renault, "The Structures of the Slave Trade in Central Africa in the 19th Century," *The Economics of the Indian Ocean Slave Trade in the Nineteenth Century*, edited by William Gervase Clarence-Smith, p. 148; Edward A. Alpers, *Ivory and Slaves: Changing Pattern of International Trade in East Central Africa to the Later Nineteenth Century* (Berkeley: University of California Press, 1975), pp. 191–193; R.W. Beachey, *The Slave Trade of Eastern Africa*, pp. 182, 183, 189.

30. Robert C. Davis, *Christian Slaves, Muslim Masters: White Slavery in the Mediterranean, the Barbary Coast, and Italy, 1500–1800* (New York: Palgrave Macmillan, 2003), p. 23; Philip D. Curtin, *The Atlantic Slave Trade: A Census* (Madison: University of Wisconsin Press, 1969), pp. 72, 75, 87.

31. Jean W. Sedlar, *East Central Europe in the Middle Ages, 1000–1500* (Seattle: University of Washington Press, 1994), p. 97.

32. Ehud R. Toledano, *The Ottoman Slave Trade and Its Suppression: 1840–1890* (Princeton: Princeton University Press, 1982), pp. 18, 59, 168, 171, 188, 189.

33. See, for example, Eric Williams, *Capitalism & Slavery* (New York: Russell & Russell, 1961), pp. vii–viii and *passim*.

34. Roger Anstey, "The Volume and Profitability of the British Slave Trade, 1761–1807," *Race and Slavery in the Western Hemisphere: Quantitative Studies*, edited by Stanley L. Engerman and Eugene D. Genovese (Princeton: Princeton University Press, 1975), pp. 22–23.

35. David Eltis, "Europeans and the Rise and Fall of African Slavery in the Americas: An Interpretation," *American Historical Review*, Vol. 98, Issue 5 (December 1993), p. 1400.

36. John Stuart Mill, "Considerations on Representative Government," *Collected Works of John Stuart Mill*, Volume XIX: *Essays on Politics and Society*, edited by J.M. Robson (Toronto: University of Toronto Press, 1977), p. 395.

37. Simon Robinson and Nancy Palus, "An Awful Human Trade," *Time*, April 30, 2001, pp. 40–41; Andrew Cockburn, "21st Century Slaves," *National Geographic*, September 2003, pp. 2–25; "Slave Trade in Africa Highlighted by Arrests," *New York Times*, August 10, 1997, Foreign Desk, p. 9.

38. Christopher Hibbert, *The English: A Social History, 1066–1945* (New York: W. W. Norton, 1987), p. 121.

39. John Stuart Mill, "Considerations on Representative Government," *Collected Works of John Stuart Mill*, Volume XIX: *Essays on Politics and Society*, edited by J.M. Robson, p. 571.

40. Donald L. Horowitz, *Ethnic Groups in Conflict* (Berkeley: University of California Press, 1985), p. 5.

41. Ibid., p. 76.

42. "Secret Weapon," *The Economist*, June 20, 2015, "Special Report: Nigeria," p. 8.

43. Amy Chua and Jed Rubenfeld, *The Triple Package: How Three Unlikely Traits Explain the Rise and Fall of Cultural Groups in America* (New York: The Penguin Press, 2014), p. 42.

44. Ibid., p. 43. Details can be found in U.S. Bureau of the Census, American Factfinder, Table DP03, "Selected Economic Characteristics," 2006–2010 American Community Survey Selected Population Tables."

45. Richard Lynn and Tatu Vanhanen, *IQ and the Wealth of Nations* (Westport, Connecticut: Praeger, 2002), p. 179.

46. Amy Chua and Jed Rubenfeld, *The Triple Package*, p. 7.

47. "The Worldwide Web," part of a special report on India, *The Economist*, May 23, 2015, p. 15.

48. N.J.G. Pounds, *An Historical Geography of Europe: 1800–1914* (Cambridge: Cambridge University Press, 1985), pp. 457–458.

49. Walter Nugent, *Crossings: The Great Transatlantic Migrations, 1870–1914* (Bloomington: Indiana University Press, 1992), p. 84.

50. Rupert B. Vance, *Human Geography of the South: A Study in Regional Resources and Human Adequacy* (Chapel Hill: University of North Carolina Press, 1932), p. 251.

51. The Economist, *Pocket World in Figures: 2015 edition* (London: Profile Books, Ltd., 2014), pp. 26, 228.

52. Ibid., pp. 26, 112.

53. V.I. Lenin, *Imperialism, The Highest Stage of Capitalism* (New York: International Publishers, 2013), p. 64.

54. Mira Wilkins, *The History of Foreign Investment in the United States to 1914* (Cambridge, Massachusetts: Harvard University Press, 1989), p. 609.

55. U. S. Bureau of the Census, *Historical Statistics of the United States: Colonial Times to 1970* (Washington: Government Printing Office, 1975), Part 2, p. 870.

Chapter 11: Politics and Diversity

Epigraph: Milton Friedman, *Free to Choose: A Personal Statement* (New York: Harcourt Brace Jovanovich, 1980), p. 132.

1. See, for example, *Coming Apart: The State of White America, 1960–2010* (New York: Crown Forum, 2012), by Charles Murray.

2. The principle, but not the phrase, came from William Graham Sumner's 1906 book *Folkways*. Decades later, Gunnar Myrdal paraphrased Sumner's "legislation cannot make mores" as "stateways cannot change folkways." William Graham Sumner, *Folkways: A Study of the Sociological Importance of Usages, Manners, Customs, Mores, and Morals* (Boston: Ginn and Company, 1906), p. 77; Shirley Moody-Turner, *Black Folklore and the Politics of Racial Representation* (Jackson: University Press of Mississippi, 2013), pp. 18, 169

(note 1); Gunnar Myrdal, *An American Dilemma: The Negro Problem and Modern Democracy* (New York: Harper & Brothers, 1944), p. 1049.

3. Sarah Gordon, *Hitler, Germans and the "Jewish Question"* (Princeton: Princeton University Press, 1984), p. 8.

4. Raphael Patai, *The Vanished Worlds of Jewry* (New York: Macmillan, 1980), p. 57. See also Donald L. Niewyk, *The Jews in Weimar Germany* (Baton Rouge: Louisiana State University Press, 1980), p. 98.

5. Carl Wittke, *We Who Built America: The Saga of the Immigrant* (Cleveland: Case Western Reserve University Press, 1967), p. 329; Eric E. Hirshler, "Jews from Germany in the United States," *Jews from Germany in the United States*, edited by Eric E. Hirshler (New York: Farrar, Straus and Cudahy, 1955), pp. 42–45; Frederick C. Luebke, *Germans in the New World: Essays in the History of Immigration* (Urbana: University of Illinois Press, 1990), p. 170; Tobias Brinkmann, "Jews, Germans, or Americans? German-Jewish Immigrants in the Nineteenth-Century United States," *The Heimat Abroad: The Boundaries of Germanness*, edited by Krista O'Donnell, Renate Bridenthal, and Nancy Reagin (Ann Arbor: University of Michigan Press, 2005), pp. 112, 115, 116, 119, 120, 132.

6. Judith Laikin Elkin, *Jews of the Latin American Republics* (Chapel Hill: University of North Carolina Press, 1980), p. 37; Ezra Mendelsohn, *The Jews of East Central Europe between the World Wars* (Bloomington: Indiana University Press, 1983), p. 133.

7. Albert Bernhardt Faust, *The German Element in the United States* (New York: Arno Press, 1969), Vol. I, p. 45. Frederick C. Luebke, *Germans in Brazil: A Comparative History of Cultural Conflict During World War I* (Baton Rouge: Louisiana State University Press, 1987), p. 81. There has been challenge to the idea that Germans in the United States had amicable relations with blacks, or were abolitionist in their view of slavery. See, for example, the papers in *States of Progress: Germans and Blacks in America Over 300 Years*, edited by Randall M. Miller (Philadelphia: German Society of Pennsylvania, 1989). However, the issue is not whether the Germans met some absolute standard in either their relations with blacks or in their views of slavery. The point is that their record compares favorably with that of other contemporary whites. Even this volume devoted to re-assessing the history of Germans' relations with blacks in the United States,

and their attitudes toward slavery, does not claim that the Germans were more racist than other whites, and some of the historical facts cited in that volume include the admission of some blacks as members of German churches in colonial Pennsylvania and the Moravians' missionary work among slaves (p. 6) and the fact that it would be difficult "to find any significant German leaders who were advocates of slavery" during the antebellum era (p. 57).

8. Clement Eaton, *The Freedom-of-Thought Struggle in the Old South* (New York: Harper & Row, 1964), pp. 33, 239, 247.

9. John Hope Franklin, *The Free Negro in North Carolina, 1790–1860* (New York: W.W. Norton & Company, 1971), pp. 5–6, 8, 113–114.

10. Albert Bernhardt Faust, *The German Element in the United States*, Vol. I, pp. 98–99, 103, 112, 213, 240; Ibid., Vol. II, p. 423; Joseph Wandel, *The German Dimension of American History* (Chicago: Nelson-Hall, Inc., 1979), pp. 15, 16, 20, 27, 51, 65; R.L. Biesele, "The Relations between the German Settlers and the Indians in Texas, 1844–1860," *Southwestern Historical Quarterly*, Vol. 31, No. 2 (October 1927), pp. 116–129; Philip Raine, *Paraguay* (New Brunswick, New Jersey: Scarecrow Press, 1956), p. 304.

11. Ian Harmstorf and Michael Cigler, *The Germans in Australia* (Melbourne: AE Press, 1985), pp. 49, 80–81.

12. Frederick Law Olmsted, *The Cotton Kingdom: A Traveller's Observations on Cotton and Slavery in the American Slave States* (New York: Alfred A. Knopf, 1953), pp. 114–116, 119–120; Herbert S. Klein, *Slavery in the Americas: A Comparative Study of Virginia and Cuba* (Chicago: University of Chicago Press, 1967), p. 188; Frederick Law Olmsted, *A Journey in the Seaboard Slave States* (New York: New American Library, 1969), p. 127.

13. Herbert S. Klein, *Slavery in the Americas*, p. 188; Frederick Law Olmsted, *A Journey in the Seaboard Slave States*, p. 127.

14. Claudia Goldin, *Urban Slavery in the American South, 1820–1860: A Quantitative History* (Chicago: University of Chicago Press, 1976) pp. 38–39; Robert S. Starobin, *Industrial Slavery in the Old South* (New York: Oxford University Press, 1970), pp. 135–137; Herbert S. Klein, *Slavery in the Americas*, p. 188; Frederick Law Olmsted, *A Journey in the Seaboard Slave States*, p. 127; William L. Westermann, *The Slave Systems of Greek and Roman Antiquity* (Philadelphia: American Philosophical Society, 1955), pp. 12, 121.

15. Murray Gordon, *Slavery in the Arab World* (New York: New Amsterdam Books, 1989), p. 94.

16. Quoted in Joseph S. Berliner, "The Prospects for Technological Progress," *Soviet Economy in a New Perspective: A Compendium of Papers*, submitted to the Joint Economic Committee of Congress (Washington: Government Printing Office, 1976), p. 437.

17. John Stuart Mill, *Principles of Political Economy*, edited by W.J. Ashley (New York: Longmans, Green and Company, 1909), p. 947.

18. Allan H. Meltzer, *A History of the Federal Reserve* (Chicago: University of Chicago Press, 2003), p. 3.

19. See my *Affirmative Action Around the World: An Empirical Study* (New Haven: Yale University Press, 2004), pp. 2, 3, 5–6, 7, 23, 34–35, 49, 63, 74.

20. Ibid., pp. 3, 5–6, 23, 34–35, 49, 63, 74.

21. Mahathir bin Mohamad, *The Malay Dilemma* (Singapore: Asia Pacific Press, 1970), p. 25.

22. Ibid., p. 44.

23. Donald L. Horowitz, *Ethnic Groups in Conflict* (Berkeley: University of California Press, 1985), p. 226.

24. Pyong Gap Min, *Ethnic Business Enterprise: Korean Small Business in Atlanta* (New York: Center for Migration Studies, 1988), p. 104.

25. Illsoo Kim, *New Urban Immigrants: The Korean Community in New York* (Princeton: Princeton University Press, 1981), p. 114.

26. Elissa Gootman, "City to Help Curb Harassment of Asian Students at High School," *New York Times*, June 2, 2004, p. B9; Joe Williams, "New Attack at Horror HS: Top Senior Jumped at Brooklyn's Troubled Lafayette," *New York Daily News*, December 7, 2002, p. 7; Maki Becker, "Asian Students Hit in Rash of HS Attacks," *New York Daily News*, December 8, 2002, p. 7; Samuel G. Freedman, "Students and Teachers Expect a Battle in Their Visits to the Principal's Office," *New York Times*, November 22, 2006, p. B7; Kristen A. Graham and Jeff Gammage, "Two Immigrant Students Attacked at Bok," *Philadelphia Inquirer*, September 21, 2010, p. B1; Jeff Gammage and Kristen A. Graham, "Feds Find Merit in Asian Students' Claims Against Philly School," *Philadelphia Inquirer*, August 28, 2010, p. A1; Kristen A. Graham and Jeff Gammage, "Report Released on Racial Violence at S. Phila.

High," *Philadelphia Inquirer*, February 24, 2010, p. A1; Kristen A. Graham, "Other Phila. Schools Handle Racial, Ethnic Tensions," *Philadelphia Inquirer*, February 4, 2010, p. A1; Kristen A. Graham and Jeff Gammage, "Attacking Immigrant Students Not New, Say Those Involved," *Philadelphia Inquirer*, December 18, 2009, p. B1; Kristen A. Graham, "Asian Students Describe Violence at South Philadelphia High," *Philadelphia Inquirer*, December 10, 2009, p. A1; Colin Flaherty, *'White Girl Bleed A Lot': The Return of Racial Violence to America and How the Media Ignore It* (Washington: WND Books, 2013), Chapter 5.

27. Myron Weiner, *Sons of the Soil: Migration and Ethnic Conflict in India* (Princeton: Princeton University Press, 1978), pp. 45–46, 102–136; Mary Fainsod Katzenstein, *Ethnicity and Equality: The Shiv Sena Party and Preferential Policies in Bombay* (Ithaca: Cornell University Press, 1979), pp. 28–29; Myron Weiner and Mary Fainsod Katzenstein, *India's Preferential Policies: Migrants, The Middle Classes, and Ethnic Equality* (Chicago: University of Chicago Press, 1981), pp. 114–115; David Marshall Lang, *The Armenians: A People in Exile* (London: George Allen and Unwin, 1981), pp. 3, 10, 37; David Lamb, *The Africans* (New York: Vintage Books, 1987), pp. 307–308; Donald L. Horowitz, *Ethnic Groups in Conflict*, pp. 46, 153, 155–156, 212–213; Donald L. Horowitz, *The Deadly Ethnic Riot* (Berkeley: University of California Press, 2001), pp. 4–5, 195, 198.

28. Larry Diamond, *Class, Ethnicity and Democracy in Nigeria: The Failure of the First Republic* (Syracuse: Syracuse University Press, 1988), p. 50.

29. Irina Livezeanu, *Cultural Politics in Greater Romania: Regionalism, Nation Building, & Ethnic Struggle, 1918–1930* (Ithaca: Cornell University Press, 1995), pp. 30–31, 218–231.

30. Martin Meredith, *The First Dance of Freedom: Black Africa in the Postwar Era* (New York: Harper & Row, 1984), pp. 229–230.

31. P.T. Bauer, *Reality and Rhetoric: Studies in the Economics of Development* (London: Weidenfeld and Nicolson, 1984), p. 46.

32. Amy Chua, *World on Fire: How Exporting Free Market Democracy Breeds Ethnic Hatred and Global Instability* (New York: Doubleday, 2003), p. 50.

33. Derek Sayer, *The Coasts of Bohemia: A Czech History* (Princeton: Princeton University Press, 1998), pp. 168–169, 221–248.

34. Amy Chua, *World on Fire*, p. 4.

35. Ibid., p. 2.

36. Lord Kinross, *The Ottoman Centuries: The Rise and Fall of the Turkish Empire* (New York: William Morrow, 1977), p. 558.

37. David Marshall Lang, *The Armenians*, pp. 31, 34. A fuller account of these atrocities can be found in Ambassador Morgenthau's book *Ambassador Morgenthau's Story* (Detroit: Wayne State University Press, 2003), pp. 202–223.

38. "To Hell and Back," *The Economist*, April 5, 2014, p. 53.

39. "Devils and Enemies," *Far Eastern Economic Review*, July 7, 1994, p. 53.

40. Paul Mojzes, *Balkan Genocides: Holocaust and Ethnic Cleansing in the Twentieth Century* (Lanham, Maryland: Rowman & Littlefield, 2011), p. 2.

41. As a Sri Lankan scholar described the situation: "In striking contrast to other parts of South Asia (including Burma), Sri Lanka in 1948 was an oasis of stability, peace and order. The transfer of power was smooth and peaceful, a reflection of the moderate tone of the dominant strand in the country's nationalist movement. More important, one saw very little of the divisions and bitterness which were tearing at the recent independence of the South Asian countries. In general, the situation in the country seemed to provide an impressive basis for a solid start in nation-building and national regeneration." K.M. de Silva, "Historical Survey," *Sri Lanka: A Survey*, edited by K.M. de Silva (Honolulu: The University Press of Hawaii, 1977), p. 84. "Sri Lanka had better prospects than most new states when independence came in 1948." Donald L. Horowitz, "A Splitting Headache," *The New Republic*, February 23, 1987, p. 33. "In general, relations among these main communities in Ceylon are cordial, unmarred by the sort of friction that exists between Hindus and Moslems in India. Except for one sad episode in 1915, racial riots have been unknown." I.D.S. Weerawardana, "Minority Problems in Ceylon," *Pacific Affairs*, Vol. 25, No. 3 (September 1, 1952), p. 279. See also Robert N. Kearney, *Communalism and Language in the Politics of Ceylon* (Durham: Duke University Press, 1967), p. 27.

42. Linda Chavez, *Out of the Barrio: Toward a New Politics of Hispanic Assimilation* (New York: Basic Books, 1991), p. 29; Rosalie Pedalino Porter, *Forked Tongue: The Politics of Bilingual Education*, second edition (New Brunswick: Transaction Publishers, 1996), pp. 33, 35.

43. Randall K.Q. Akee and Jonathan B. Taylor, *Social and Economic Change on American Indian Reservations: A Databook of the U.S. Censuses and the American Community Survey, 1990–2010* (Sarasota, Florida: Taylor Policy Group, Inc., 2014), pp. 6, 7, 16.

44. Winston S. Churchill, *A History of the English-Speaking Peoples* (London: Cassell and Company, Ltd., 1956), Vol. I, p. 31.

Chapter 12: The Welfare State

Epigraph: Joseph A. Schumpeter, Review of Keynes' General Theory, *Journal of the American Statistical Association*, Vol. 31, No. 196 (December 1936), p. 795.

1. *Life and Speeches of Hon. Wm. Jennings Bryan* (Baltimore: R.H. Woodward Company, 1900), pp. 253–254.

2. Stephen Moore, *Who's The Fairest of Them All? The Truth about Opportunity, Taxes, and Wealth in America* (New York: Encounter Books, 2012), p. 2.

3. Edward Bellamy, *Looking Backward: 2000–1887* (Boston: Houghton-Mifflin Company, 1926), p. 136.

4. U.S. Census Bureau, "Table HINC–05. Percent Distribution of Households, by Selected Characteristics within Income Quintile and Top 5 Percent in 2010," from the Current Population Survey, downloaded on October 28, 2014: https://www.census.gov/hhes/www/cpstables/032011/hhinc/new05_000.htm; W. Michael Cox and Richard Alm, *Myths of Rich & Poor: Why We're Better Off Than We Think* (New York: Basic Books, 1999), p. 85.

5. Nicholas Kristof, "Is a Hard Life Inherited?" *New York Times*, August 10, 2014, Sunday Review section, p. 1.

6. Ibid.

7. Walter E. Williams, *Race and Economics: How Much Can Be Blamed on Discrimination?* (Stanford: Hoover Institution Press, 2011), Table 3.2.

8. Nicholas Kristof, "When Whites Just Don't Get It, Part 2," *New York Times*, September 7, 2014, Sunday Review section, p. 11.

9. Stephan Thernstrom and Abigail Thernstrom, *America in Black and White: One Nation, Indivisible* (New York: Simon & Schuster, 1997), p. 238.

10. Ibid., p. 237.

11. Charles Murray, *Coming Apart: The State of White America 1960–2010* (New York: Crown Forum, 2012), p. 160. "An investigation conducted just before the

First World War in the then predominately Irish Middle West Side of New York found that about half the families there were fatherless." Edward C. Banfield, *The Unheavenly City: The Nature and Future of Our Urban Crisis* (Boston: Little, Brown and Company, 1970), p. 72.

12. Nicholas Eberstadt, *The Poverty of "The Poverty Rate": Measure and Mismeasure of Want in Modern America* (Washington: AEI Press, 2008), Chapter 6.

13. Robert Rector and Rachel Sheffield, "Air Conditioning, Cable TV, and an Xbox: What Is Poverty in the United States Today?" *Backgrounder*, No. 2575, Heritage Foundation, July 18, 2011, p. 10.

14. Lawrence E. Harrison, *The Pan-American Dream: Do Latin America's Cultural Values Discourage True Partnership with the United States and Canada?* (New York: Basic Books, 1997), p. 207.

15. E. Franklin Frazier, *The Negro in the United States*, revised edition (New York: The Macmillan Company, 1957), p. 166.

16. Herbert G. Gutman, *The Black Family in Slavery and Freedom, 1750–1925* (New York: Pantheon Books, 1976), pp. 455–456.

17. James P. Smith and Finis Welch, *Race Differences in Earnings: A Survey and New Evidence* (Santa Monica: Rand, 1978), p. 10.

18. John Dittmer, *Black Georgia in the Progressive Era, 1900–1920* (Urbana: University of Illinois Press, 1977), p. 148.

19. Gunnar Myrdal, *An American Dilemma: The Negro Problem and Modern Democracy* (New York: Pantheon Books, 1975), Volume II, p. 950.

20. John Dittmer, *Black Georgia in the Progressive Era, 1900–1920*, pp. 147–148. See also Henry Reid Hunter, *The Development of the Public Secondary Schools of Atlanta, Georgia 1845–1937* (Atlanta: Office of School System Historian, Atlanta Public Schools, 1974), pp. 51–54.

21. Stephan Thernstrom and Abigail Thernstrom, *America in Black and White*, pp. 233–234.

22. Ibid., pp. 159, 164–165.

23. Ibid., pp. 160, 162; Barry Latzer, *The Rise and Fall of Violent Crime in America* (New York: Encounter Books, 2016), p. 127.

24. Frederick C. Luebke, *Germans in Brazil: A Comparative History of Cultural Conflict During World War I* (Baton Rouge: Louisiana State University Press, 1987), pp. 64, 66.

25. Ibid., p. 65.

26. Gary B. Cohen, *The Politics of Ethnic Survival: Germans in Prague, 1861–1914*, second edition (West Lafayette: Purdue University Press, 2006), Chapters 1 and 2. See also Pieter Judson, "When Is a Diaspora Not a Diaspora? Rethinking Nation-Centered Narratives about Germans in Habsburg East Central Europe," *The Heimat Abroad: The Boundaries of Germanness*, edited by Krista O'Donnell, Renate Bridenthal, and Nancy Reagin (Ann Arbor: University of Michigan Press, 2005), p. 221.

27. Victor Purcell, *The Chinese in Southeast Asia*, second edition (London: Oxford University Press, 1965), pp. 94, 96; Ivan H. Light, *Ethnic Enterprise in America: Business and Welfare Among Chinese, Japanese, and Blacks* (Berkeley: University of California Press, 1973), p. 174.

28. Irving Howe, *World of Our Fathers: The Journey of the East European Jews to America and the Life They Found and Made* (New York: Harcourt Brace Jovanovich, 1976), p. 360.

29. Lawrence J. McCaffrey, "Forging Forward and Looking Back," *The New York Irish*, edited by Ronald H. Baylor and Timothy J. Meagher (Baltimore: Johns Hopkins University Press, 1996), p. 229.

30. Caroline Golab, *Immigrant Destinations* (Philadelphia: Temple University Press, 1977), p. 56.

31. Kevin Kenny, "Labor and Labor Organizations," *Making the Irish American: History and Heritage of the Irish in the United States*, edited by J.J. Lee and Marion R. Casey (New York: New York University Press, 2006), p. 357.

32. Patrick J. Blessing, "Irish," *Harvard Encyclopedia of American Ethnic Groups*, edited by Stephan Thernstrom (Cambridge, Massachusetts: Harvard University Press, 1980), p. 531.

33. Appendix Table A.11, *The New York Irish*, edited by Ronald H. Baylor and Timothy J. Meagher, p. 562.

34. Barry Latzer, *The Rise and Fall of Violent Crime in America*, p. 93.

35. Ibid., p. 19.

36. See, for example, John Kobler, "Sex Invades the Schoolhouse," *The Saturday Evening Post*, June 29, 1968, p. 26; Jacqueline R. Kasun, *The War Against Population: The Economics and Ideology of World Population Control* (San Francisco: Ignatius Press, 1988), pp. 142, 144; Cheryl D. Hayes, editor, *Risking the Future: Adolescent Sexuality, Pregnancy, and Childbearing* (Washington: National Academy Press, 1987), p. 66; Hearings Before the Select Committee on Population, Ninety-Fifth Congress, Second Session, *Fertility and Contraception in America: Adolescent and Pre-Adolescent Pregnancy* (Washington: U.S. Government Printing Office, 1978), Volume II, pp. 253, 625.

37. Jason L. Riley, *Please Stop Helping Us: How Liberals Make It Harder for Blacks to Succeed* (New York: Encounter Books, 2014), pp. 67–73.

38. Kay S. Hymowitz, "The Black Family: 40 Years of Lies," *City Journal*, Summer 2005, p. 21.

39. U.S. Bureau of the Census, *Historical Statistics of the United States: Colonial Times to 1970* (Washington: Government Printing Office, 1975), Part I, p. 135; *Economic Report of the President, 2014* (Washington: U.S. Government Printing Office, 2014), p. 380; Walter E. Williams, *Race and Economics*, pp. 42–43.

40. Barry Latzer, *The Rise and Fall of Violent Crime in America*, p. 88. During these years, prior to the change in immigration laws in 1965, "non-whites" in the United States were overwhelmingly black, so that blacks and whites together constituted almost the total population of the United States.

41. See, for example, Sarah-Blake Morgan, "Construction Worker Recalls Uptown Charlotte Attack," *WBTV.com* (Charlotte), March 2, 2016; Lisa Rantala, "Marine Corps Veteran Says He Became Target of Hate Crime," *ABC 6/FOX 28* (Columbus, Ohio), February 29, 2016; John P. Wise, "Parental Guidance Required at Mall St. Matthews, Oxmoor," *KMOV.com* (St. Louis), December 30, 2015; Lauren Adams, "Changes Coming to Mall St. Matthews After 'Chaotic Night,'" *WLKY.com* (Kentucky), December 31, 2015; Angela Price, "3 Charged with Hate Crime over Alleged Attack," *The Star Democrat* (Maryland), September 8, 2015; Eric Horng, "Woman Allegedly Attacked by Group Near U of C Campus with Kids in Car," *ABC 7 News* (Chicago), July 10, 2015; Doyle Murphy, "Cincinnati Bystanders Jeer Unconscious Tourist After Vicious Beating," *New York Daily News*, July 6, 2015; Thomas Tracy, "Man

Hit with Milk Crate, Called 'White Bread' by Group of Black Men in Anti-White Attack on Staten Island," *New York Daily News*, July 4, 2015; Jonathan Grass, "Police Make Arrest in Group Assault at Florence Park," *AL.com* (Alabama), June 16, 2015; Catherine Awasthi, "Assault at 'First Fridays' Under Investigation, Victim Calls Attack a 'Hate Crime'," *WHNT News.com* (Alabama), June 8, 2015; Dave Munday, "911 Calls Describe Terror Caused by Mob Rampage in Charleston," *Post and Courier* (Charleston, South Carolina), April 28, 2015; Phillip Morris, "Cleveland's St. Patrick's Day Assaults in Black and White," *The Plain Dealer* (Cleveland), April 7, 2015; Joel Landau, "St. Louis Man Assaulted on Public Transportation After Declining to Discuss Michael Brown," *New York Daily News*, March 29, 2015; Susan Weich, "Man Beaten on MetroLink Train After Attacker Asks Him About Michael Brown," *St. Louis Post-Dispatch*, March 28, 2015, p. A2; Katie DeLong, "He Thought It Was a Flash Mob: Man Caught up in Attack Outside Kroger Says He Feels Lucky He Wasn't Hurt," *Fox 6 Now* (Memphis), September 8, 2014; Therese Apel, "FBI to Assist in Allegedly Racially-Motivated West Point Beating," *The Clarion-Ledger* (Mississippi), August 27, 2014; "Family Thinks Otterbein Assault May Have Been Hate Crime," *CBS Baltimore*, August 25, 2014; Danielle Schlanger, et al., "Woman Hit in Head with Pellet Gun in Alleged Hate Crime While Walking Through Central Park," *New York Daily News*, August 23, 2014; "White Man Beaten by Mob in Detroit After Hitting Boy with Truck: Was It a Hate Crime?" *CBS Detroit*, April 4, 2014; "Police: Man Punches People in Face, Runs to Getaway Car," *KCCI 8 News.com* (Iowa), February 24, 2014; Ed Gallek, "Mob of Teens Attack Man in Downtown Cleveland," *19 Action News* (Cleveland, Ohio), February 11, 2014; Wayne Crenshaw, "Victim Recounts Snow Day Attack at Warner Robins High; 2 Arrests Made," *The Telegraph* (Macon, Georgia), February 5, 2014; Thomas Tracy, et al., "Wild Bunch: Brooklyn Punks Pummel Couple, Scream out Slurs," *New York Daily News*, October 20, 2013, p. 13; "Father of Teen Charged in Florida School Bus Beating Says Son Is 'Sorry'," *Fox News*, August 13, 2013; Peter Bernard, "3 Teens Charged in Pinellas School Bus Beating," *WFLA.com*, August 8, 2013; Michelle Washington, "A Beating at Church and Brambleton," *The Virginian-Pilot*, May 1, 2012, p. B7; WKRG Staff, "Mobile Police Expect to Make Arrests in the Matthew Owens Beating

Case Today," *WKRG* (Mobile-Pensacola), April 23–24, 2012; Chad Smith, "Gainesville Beating Case Drawing National Attention," *Gainesville Sun*, April 10, 2012; Justin Fenton, "Viewers of Shock Video Shed Light on Baltimore Assault; Tips From Social Media Users Lead Police to Victim, Possible Suspect," *Baltimore Sun*, April 5, 2012, p. 1A; Ray Chandler, "Seneca Police Referring Assault Case to Federal Authorities," *Anderson Independent Mail* (South Carolina), March 28, 2012; Stephanie Farr, "'Geezer' Won't Let Thugs Ruin His Walks," *Philadelphia Daily News*, October 20, 2011, p. 26; "Concealing Black Hate Crimes," *Investor's Business Daily*, August 15, 2011, p. A16; "Walker Calls in the State Patrol; New Rules Require Minors to Be with Adults at Night," *Wisconsin State Journal*, August 6, 2011; Barry Paddock and John Lauinger, "Subway Gang Attack," *New York Daily News*, July 18, 2011, News, p. 3; Meg Jones, "Flynn Calls Looting, Beatings in Riverwest Barbaric," *Milwaukee Journal Sentinel*, July 6, 2011, pp. A1 ff; Joseph A. Slobodzian, "West Philly Man Pleads Guilty to 'Flash Mob' Assault," *Philadelphia Inquirer*, June 21, 2011, p. B1; Mareesa Nicosia, "Four Skidmore College Students Charged in Assault; One Charged with Felony Hate Crime," *The Saratogian*, December 22, 2010; Kristen A. Graham and Jeff Gammage, "Two Immigrant Students Attacked at Bok," *Philadelphia Inquirer*, September 21, 2010, p. B1; Jeff Gammage and Kristen A. Graham, "Feds Find Merit in Asian Students' Claims Against Philly School," *Philadelphia Inquirer*, August 28, 2010, p. A1; Alfred Lubrano, "What's Behind 'Flash Mobs'?" *Philadelphia Inquirer*, March 28, 2010, p. A1; Ian Urbina, "Mobs Are Born as Word Grows by Text Message," *New York Times*, March 25, 2010, p. A1; Kirk Mitchell, "Attacks Change Lives on All Sides," *Denver Post*, December 6, 2009, pp. A1 ff; Alan Gathright, "Black Gangs Vented Hatred for Whites in Downtown Attacks," *The DenverChannel.com*, December 5, 2009; Kirk Mitchell, "Racial Attacks Part of Trend; Gangs Videotape Knockout Punches and Sell the Videos as Entertainment, Experts Say," *Denver Post*, November 22, 2009, p. A1; Samuel G. Freedman, "Students and Teachers Expect a Battle in Their Visits to the Principal's Office," *New York Times*, November 22, 2006, p. B7; Colin Flaherty, *'White Girl Bleed A Lot': The Return of Racial Violence to America and How the Media Ignore It* (Washington: WND Books, 2013).

42. Rasmussen Reports, "More Americans View Blacks as Racist Than Whites, Hispanics," July 3, 2013; Cheryl K. Chumley, "More Americans Say Blacks More Racist Than Whites: Rasmussen Report," *Washington Times* (online), July 4, 2013; Steven Nelson, "Poll Finds Black Americans More Likely to Be Seen as Racist," *U.S. News & World Report* (online), July 3, 2013.

43. James N. Gregory, *The Southern Diaspora: How the Great Migrations of Black and White Southerners Transformed America* (Chapel Hill: University of North Carolina Press, 2005), p. 123; Isabel Wilkerson, *The Warmth of Other Suns: The Epic Story of America's Great Migration* (New York: Random House, 2010), p. 291.

44. Carl Wittke, *The Irish in America* (New York: Russell & Russell, 1970), pp. 101–102; Oscar Handlin, *Boston's Immigrants* (New York: Atheneum, 1970), pp. 169–170; Jay P. Dolan, *The Irish Americans: A History* (New York: Bloomsbury Press, 2008), pp. 118–119; Irving Howe, *World of Our Fathers*, pp. 229–230.

45. See, for example, David Levering Lewis, *When Harlem Was in Vogue* (New York: Penguin Books, 1997), pp. 182–183; Jervis Anderson, *This Was Harlem: A Cultural Portrait, 1900–1950* (New York: Farrar Straus Giroux, 1982), pp. 138–139.

46. Milton & Rose D. Friedman, *Two Lucky People: Memoirs* (Chicago: University of Chicago Press, 1998), p. 48.

47. Jervis Anderson, *This Was Harlem*, p. 344. As a personal note, I happened to work as a delivery boy in a grocery store near the subway station where she would have exited. Although I often worked until about midnight on Saturday nights and walked home past that subway station, I never encountered any problems there, though I weighed no more than about a hundred pounds at the time.

48. Lizette Alvarez, "Out, and Up," *New York Times*, May 31, 2009, Metropolitan section, p. 1.

49. Ibid., p. 6.

50. Walter E. Williams, *Up from The Projects: An Autobiography* (Stanford: Hoover Institution Press, 2010), pp. 6–7.

51. Ibid., p. 7.

52. Robyn Minter Smyers, "High Noon in Public Housing: The Showdown Between Due Process Rights and Good Management Practices in the War on Drugs and Crime," *The Urban Lawyer*, Summer 1998, pp. 573–574.

53. William Julius Wilson, "The Urban Underclass in Advanced Industrial Society," *The New Urban Reality*, edited by Paul E. Peterson (Washington: The Brookings Institution, 1985), p. 137.

54. Theodore Dalrymple, *Life at the Bottom: The Worldview That Makes the Underclass* (Chicago: Ivan R. Dee, 2001), p. 150.

55. Ibid., p. 164.

56. Ibid., p. 159.

57. Ibid., pp. 68–69.

58. Joyce Lee Malcolm, *Guns and Violence: The English Experience* (Cambridge, Massachusetts: Harvard University Press, 2002), p. 168. In the twelve armed robberies in 1954, eight involved weapons that were not real.

59. Ibid., p. 209.

60. Ibid., pp. 90–91, 164–167; James Q. Wilson and Richard J. Herrnstein, *Crime and Human Nature* (New York: Simon and Schuster, 1985), pp. 409–410.

61. Philip Johnston, "The Long Retreat of Order," *The Daily Telegraph* (London), August 10, 2011, p. 19.

62. Joyce Lee Malcolm, "The Soft-on-Crime Roots of British Disorder," *Wall Street Journal*, August 16, 2011, p. A13.

63. See, for example, Sean O'Neill and Fiona Hamilton, "Mobs Rule as Police Surrender Streets," *The Times* (London), August 9, 2011, pp. 1, 5; Martin Beckford, et al., "Carry On Looting," *The Daily Telegraph* (London), August 8, 2011, pp. 1, 2; Philip Johnston, "The Long Retreat of Order," *The Daily Telegraph* (London), August 10, 2011, p. 19; Alistair MacDonald and Guy Chazan, "World News: Britain Tallies Damage and Sets Out Anti-Riot Steps," *Wall Street Journal*, August 12, 2011, p. A6.

64. BBC, "Teenage Girls Give Their View of the London Riots," *ABC Transcripts* (Australia), August 10, 2011.

65. Landon Thomas, Jr. and Ravi Somaiya, "London Riots Put Spotlight on Troubled, Unemployed Youths in Britain," *New York Times*, August 10, 2011, p. A10. Strange as it may seem that a nineteen-year-old would have learned to read only three years earlier, Theodore Dalrymple reported that this was not

uncommon in his book *Life at the Bottom*: "Very few of the sixteen-year-olds whom I meet as patients can read and write with facility; they do not even regard my question as to whether they can and write as in the least surprising or insulting." Theodore Dalrymple, *Life at the Bottom*, p. 69.

66. Theodore Dalrymple, "The Barbarians Inside Britain's Gates," *Wall Street Journal*, August 15, 2011, p. A13.

67. "A New Kind of Ghetto," *The Economist*, November 9, 2013, Special Report on Britain, p. 10.

68. Theodore Dalrymple, *Life at the Bottom*, p. 70.

69. Theodore Dalrymple, "The Barbarians Inside Britain's Gates," *Wall Street Journal*, August 15, 2011, p. A13.

70. Theodore Dalrymple, *Life at the Bottom*, pp. 155–157.

71. Peter Hitchens, *The Abolition of Britain: From Winston Churchill to Princess Diana* (San Francisco: Encounter Books, 2000), Chapter 3.

72. Theodore Dalrymple, *Life at the Bottom*, pp. 155–156.

73. "Hiding in Plain Sight," *The Economist*, August 22, 2015, p. 47.

74. Aneurin Bevan, *In Place of Fear* (London: Quartet Books, 1976), p. 26.

75. To maintain an ability to turn to family or friends for aid in case of misfortunes requires observing some modicum of decency toward them, but to tap the resources of the non-judgmental welfare state has no such requirement. Thus foreign physicians serving in the government-run British Health Service have been surprised to see homeless men picked up off the streets, unconscious and with life-threatening medical problems, later speak abusively to the physicians who had labored to save their lives. Theodore Dalrymple, *Life at the Bottom*, pp. 136–139.

76. "The High Cost of Perpetuating Poverty," *Investor's Business Daily*, June 27, 2012, p. A12.

77. Michael Tanner and Charles Hughes, *The Work Versus Welfare Trade-Off: 2013* (Washington: The Cato Institute, 2013).

78. "Taxing Hard-Up Americans at 95%," *The Economist,* September 7, 2013, p. 30.

79. Ibid., pp. 30, 32.

80. Nicholas Kristof, "When Whites Just Don't Get It, Part 2," *New York Times*, September 7, 2014, Sunday Review section, p. 11.

81. See, for example, the section titled "Unworthy Opponents" in Chapter 8 of my *Intellectuals and Society*, second edition (New York: Basic Books, 2012).

82. Scott Stossel, *Sarge: The Life and Times of Sargent Shriver* (Washington: Smithsonian Books, 2004), pp. 403–406.

83. Donald L. Horowitz, *Ethnic Groups in Conflict* (Berkeley: University of California Press, 1985), p. 180.

84. See, for example, Colin Flaherty, *'White Girl Bleed A Lot'*, 2013 edition, pp. iii, 2, 3, 5, 10, 14, 26, 28, 33, 35, 36, 91, 113, 196–197, 209.

85. Ibid., p. 113.

86. Edward C. Banfield, *The Unheavenly City*, p. 185.

87. Landon Thomas, Jr. and Ravi Somaiya, "London Riots Put Spotlight on Troubled, Unemployed Youths in Britain," *New York Times*, August 10, 2011, p. A10.

88. See, for example, Sarah-Blake Morgan, "Construction Worker Recalls Uptown Charlotte Attack," *WBTV.com* (Charlotte), March 2, 2016; Lisa Rantala, "Marine Corps Veteran Says He Became Target of Hate Crime," *ABC 6/FOX 28* (Columbus, Ohio), February 29, 2016; John Annese, "Cops Release Video of Man Sought in 'Cracka' Racist Attack on Brooklyn Commuter," *New York Daily News* (online), February 11, 2016; Michael Quander, "Man Called 'White Boy' Before Brutal Attack in South Memphis," *WREG.com* (Memphis), January 11, 2016; John P. Wise, "Parental Guidance Required at Mall St. Matthews, Oxmoor," *KMOV.com* (St. Louis), December 30, 2015; Lauren Adams, "Changes Coming to Mall St. Matthews After 'Chaotic Night,'" *WLKY.com* (Kentucky), December 31, 2015; Lynda Cohen, "Atlantic City Man Arrested After Posting Facebook Video of Him Punching Woman," *Press of Atlantic City.com*, October 20, 2015; Angela Price, "3 Charged with Hate Crime over Alleged Attack," *The Star Democrat* (Maryland), September 8, 2015; Eric Horng, "Woman Allegedly Attacked by Group Near U of C Campus with Kids in Car," *ABC 7 News* (Chicago), July 10, 2015; Doyle Murphy, "Cincinnati Bystanders Jeer Unconscious Tourist After Vicious Beating," *New York Daily News*, July 6, 2015; Thomas Tracy, "Man Hit with Milk Crate, Called 'White Bread' by Group of Black Men in Anti-White Attack on Staten Island," *New York Daily News*, July 4, 2015; Michael Chen, "Assault Victim Likely Saw Attacker but Old Head Injury

Prevents Him from Remembering," *KGTV* (San Diego), June 20, 2015; Jonathan Grass, "Police Make Arrest in Group Assault at Florence Park," *AL.com* (Alabama), June 16, 2015; Catherine Awasthi, "Assault at 'First Fridays' Under Investigation, Victim Calls Attack a 'Hate Crime'," *WHNT News.com* (Alabama), June 8, 2015; Dave Munday, "911 Calls Describe Terror Caused by Mob Rampage in Charleston," *Post and Courier* (Charleston, South Carolina), April 28, 2015; Phillip Morris, "Cleveland's St. Patrick's Day Assaults in Black and White," *The Plain Dealer* (Cleveland), April 7, 2015; Joel Landau, "St. Louis Man Assaulted on Public Transportation After Declining to Discuss Michael Brown," *New York Daily News*, March 29, 2015; Susan Weich, "Man Beaten on MetroLink Train After Attacker Asks Him About Michael Brown," *St. Louis Post-Dispatch*, March 28, 2015, p. A2; Katie DeLong, "He Thought It Was a Flash Mob: Man Caught up in Attack Outside Kroger Says He Feels Lucky He Wasn't Hurt," *Fox 6 Now* (Memphis), September 8, 2014; Therese Apel, "FBI to Assist in Allegedly Racially-Motivated West Point Beating," *The Clarion-Ledger* (Mississippi), August 27, 2014; "Family Thinks Otterbein Assault May Have Been Hate Crime," *CBS Baltimore*, August 25, 2014; Danielle Schlanger, et al., "Woman Hit in Head with Pellet Gun in Alleged Hate Crime While Walking Through Central Park," *New York Daily News*, August 23, 2014; "Indiana Man Charged in Shooting Death of Gary Police Officer," *5 NBC Chicago*, July 24, 2014; "Man Charged in Gary Cop Jeffrey Westerfield Killing," *Eyewitness News 7 ABC* (Gary, Indiana), July 24, 2014; Julie Turkewitz and Jeffrey E. Singer, "Family Mourns at Site of a Fatal Beating," *New York Times*, May 13, 2014, p. A14; Mark Morales, "68-Year-Old Man Dies a Day After He Was Beaten in E. Village; Video Captured Assault as Cops Hunt Suspect," *New York Daily News*, May 11, 2014; Paris Achen, "Two Men Held in Rose Village Gun Assault," *The Columbian* (Vancouver, Washington), April 10, 2014; "White Man Beaten by Mob in Detroit After Hitting Boy with Truck: Was It a Hate Crime?" *CBS Detroit*, April 4, 2014; "Police: Man Punches People in Face, Runs to Getaway Car," *KCCI 8 News.com* (Iowa), February 24, 2014; Ed Gallek, "Mob of Teens Attack Man in Downtown Cleveland," *19 Action News* (Cleveland, Ohio), February 11, 2014; Wayne Crenshaw, "Victim Recounts Snow Day Attack at Warner Robins High; 2 Arrests Made," *The*

Telegraph (Macon, Georgia), February 5, 2014; Carlie Kollath Wells, "NOPD Makes Arrest in Connection with French Quarter Beating of Musician," *The Times-Picayune* (New Orleans), January 23, 2014; "Knock It Off," *New York Post*, December 10, 2013, p. 32; Thomas Tracy, et al., "Wild Bunch: Brooklyn Punks Pummel Couple, Scream out Slurs," *New York Daily News*, October 20, 2013, p. 13; Kaitlin Gillespie, "Police Seek Teens in Death of World War II Veteran," *The Spokesman-Review* (Spokane, Washington), August 23, 2013; "Father of Teen Charged in Florida School Bus Beating Says Son Is 'Sorry'," *Fox News*, August 13, 2013; Peter Bernard, "3 Teens Charged in Pinellas School Bus Beating," *WFLA.com*, August 8, 2013; Jennifer Mann, "Man Convicted of Second-Degree Murder in St. Louis 'Knockout Game' Killing," *St. Louis Post-Dispatch*, April 10, 2013; "Sauk Rapids Teen Charged as Adult in One-Punch Killing," *CBS Minnesota*, January 7, 2013; Michelle Pekarsky, "Stone Murder: Metro Squad Will Disband," *Fox 4 News Kansas City*, May 15, 2012; Michelle Washington, "A Beating at Church and Brambleton," *The Virginian-Pilot*, May 1, 2012, p. B7; WKRG Staff, "Mobile Police Expect to Make Arrests in the Matthew Owens Beating Case Today," *WKRG* (Mobile-Pensacola), April 23–24, 2012; Michael Lansu, "Officials: Trayvon Case Cited in Racial Beating," *Chicago Sun-Times*, April 21, 2012, p. 2; Chad Smith, "Gainesville Beating Case Drawing National Attention," *Gainesville Sun*, April 10, 2012; Suzanne Ulbrich, "Father Searching for Answers in Son's Attack," *The Daily News* (Jacksonville, North Carolina), April 7, 2012; Justin Fenton, "Viewers of Shock Video Shed Light on Baltimore Assault; Tips From Social Media Users Lead Police to Victim, Possible Suspect," *Baltimore Sun*, April 5, 2012, p. 1A; Ray Chandler, "Seneca Police Referring Assault Case to Federal Authorities," *Anderson Independent Mail* (South Carolina), March 28, 2012; Stephanie Farr, "'Geezer' Won't Let Thugs Ruin His Walks," *Philadelphia Daily News*, October 20, 2011, p. 26; "Concealing Black Hate Crimes," *Investor's Business Daily*, August 15, 2011, p. A16; "Walker Calls in the State Patrol; New Rules Require Minors to Be with Adults at Night," *Wisconsin State Journal*, August 6, 2011; Barry Paddock and John Lauinger, "Subway Gang Attack," *New York Daily News*, July 18, 2011, News, p. 3; Meg Jones, "Flynn Calls Looting, Beatings in Riverwest Barbaric," *Milwaukee Journal Sentinel*, July 6, 2011, pp. A1 ff; Joseph A. Slobodzian, "West Philly

Man Pleads Guilty to 'Flash Mob' Assault," *Philadelphia Inquirer*, June 21, 2011, p. B1; Mareesa Nicosia, "Four Skidmore College Students Charged in Assault; One Charged with Felony Hate Crime," *The Saratogian*, December 22, 2010; Kristen A. Graham and Jeff Gammage, "Two Immigrant Students Attacked at Bok," *Philadelphia Inquirer*, September 21, 2010, p. B1; Jeff Gammage and Kristen A. Graham, "Feds Find Merit in Asian Students' Claims Against Philly School," *Philadelphia Inquirer*, August 28, 2010, p. A1; Alfred Lubrano, "What's Behind 'Flash Mobs'?" *Philadelphia Inquirer*, March 28, 2010, p. A1; Ian Urbina, "Mobs Are Born as Word Grows by Text Message," *New York Times*, March 25, 2010, p. A1; Kirk Mitchell, "Attacks Change Lives on All Sides," *Denver Post*, December 6, 2009, pp. A1 ff; Alan Gathright, "Black Gangs Vented Hatred for Whites in Downtown Attacks," *The DenverChannel.com*, December 5, 2009; Kirk Mitchell, "Racial Attacks Part of Trend; Gangs Videotape Knockout Punches and Sell the Videos as Entertainment, Experts Say," *Denver Post*, November 22, 2009, p. A1; Samuel G. Freedman, "Students and Teachers Expect a Battle in Their Visits to the Principal's Office," *New York Times*, November 22, 2006, p. B7; Colin Flaherty, *'White Girl Bleed A Lot'*, 2013 edition.

89. Colin Flaherty, *'White Girl Bleed A Lot'*, 2013 edition, pp. 6, 14–15, 77, 83–84, 89, 94, 108–109, 133, 173–174, 178–179, 202, 203, 206.

90. See, for example, Ibid., pp. i, iv, 3, 7–8, 84–85, 88, 95, 112, 192, 220.

91. "Concealing Black Hate Crimes," *Investor's Business Daily*, August 15, 2011, p. A16.

92. See, for example, "Brooklyn Rabbi: Gang of Teens Playing Disturbing Game Of 'Knock Out The Jew'," *CBS New York*, November 12, 2013; Thomas Tracy, "Jews Target of Twisted Street Game," *New York Daily News*, November 13, 2013, p. 45; "Knock It Off," *New York Post*, December 10, 2013, p. 32; Colin Flaherty, *'White Girl Bleed A Lot'*, 2013 edition, pp. 144–145, 151, 330.

93. Colin Flaherty, *'White Girl Bleed A Lot'*, 2013 edition, Chapter 2.

94. See, for example, Norman M. Naimark, *Fires of Hatred: Ethnic Cleansing in Twentieth-Century Europe* (Cambridge, Massachusetts: Harvard University Press, 2001), pp. 117–119; R.M. Douglas, *Orderly and Humane: The Expulsion of the Germans After the Second World War* (New Haven: Yale University Press,

2012), pp. 96–97; Derek Sayer, *The Coasts of Bohemia: A Czech History* (Princeton: Princeton University Press, 1998), p. 243.

95. Howard B. Tolley, Jr., "Rwanda," *Encyclopedia of Human Rights*, edited by David P. Forsythe (Oxford: Oxford University Press, 2009), Volume 4, pp. 383–391.

96. James Bryant Conant, *Slums and Suburbs: A Commentary on Schools in Metropolitan Areas* (New York: McGraw-Hill, 1961), p. 146.

97. See, for example, Donald L. Horowitz, "Racial Violence in the United States," *Ethnic Pluralism and Public Policy: Achieving Equality in the United States and Britain*, edited by Nathan Glazer and Ken Young (Lexington, Massachusetts: Lexington Books, 1983), pp. 188, 190–191; Malcolm McLaughlin, "Ghetto Formation and Armed Resistance in East St. Louis, Illinois," *Journal of American Studies*, Vol. 41, No. 2 (August 2007), pp. 435–467; Stanley B. Norvell and William M. Tuttle, Jr., "Views of a Negro During 'The Red Summer' of 1919," *The Journal of Negro History*, Vol. 51, No. 3 (July 1966), pp. 209–218; Dinesh D'Souza, *The End of Racism: Principles for a Multiracial Society* (New York: The Free Press, 1995), p. 177; David F. Krugler, "A Mob in Uniform: Soldiers and Civilians in Washington's Red Summer, 1919," *Washington History*, Vol. 21 (2009), pp. 48–77; Eric Ledell Smith, "The 1917 Race Riot in Chester, Pennsylvania," *Pennsylvania History: A Journal of Mid-Atlantic Studies*, Vol. 75, No. 2 (Spring 2008), pp. 171–196; Charles Crowe, "Racial Massacre in Atlanta: September 22, 1906," *Journal of Negro History*, Vol. 54, No. 2 (April 1969), pp. 150–173; Richard Maxwell Brown, "Historical Patterns of Violence," *Violence in America*, Vol. 2: *Protest, Rebellion, Reform*, edited by Ted Robert Gurr (Newbury Park, California: Sage Publications, 1989), pp. 43–44; Vincent P. Franklin, "The Philadelphia Race Riot of 1918," *The Philadelphia Magazine of History and Biography*, Vol. 99, No. 3 (July 1975), pp. 336–350; Davison M. Douglas, *Jim Crow Moves North: The Battle over Northern School Segregation, 1865–1954* (New York: Cambridge University Press, 2005), pp. 127–128.

98. Naomi Schaefer Riley, *The New Trail of Tears: How Washington Is Destroying American Indians* (New York: Encounter Books, 2016).

Part V: Conclusions

Epigraph: Alan Greenspan, *The Age of Turbulence: Adventures in a New World* (New York: Penguin Press, 2007), p. 95.

1. P.T. Bauer, *Equality, the Third World and Economic Delusion* (Cambridge, Massachusetts: Harvard University Press, 1981), p. 23.

2. Quoted in Joseph S. Berliner, "The Prospects for Technological Progress," *Soviet Economy in a New Perspective: A Compendium of Papers,* submitted to the Joint Economic Committee of Congress (Washington: Government Printing Office, 1976), p. 437.

3. Daron Acemoglu and James A. Robinson, *Why Nations Fail: The Origins of Power, Prosperity, and Poverty* (New York: Crown Business, 2012), pp. 1–2.

4. H.J. de Blij, et al., *Physical Geography: The Global Environment,* fourth edition (New York: Oxford University Press, 2013), pp. 150–151; Darrel Hess, *McKnight's Physical Geography: A Landscape Appreciation,* eleventh edition (Upper Saddle River, New Jersey: Pearson Education, 2014), pp. 199–200.

5. See, for example, Darrel Hess, *McKnight's Physical Geography,* pp. 199–200; Andrew J. Bach and Larry W. Price, "Mountain Climate," *Mountain Geography: Physical and Human Dimensions,* edited by Martin F. Price, et al (Berkeley: University of California Press, 2013), p. 45.

6. Daron Acemoglu and James A. Robinson, *Why Nations Fail,* p. 428.

7. J.M. Keynes, "Alfred Marshall, 1842–1924," *Memorials of Alfred Marshall,* edited by A.C. Pigou (New York: Kelley & Millman, Inc., 1956), p. 10.

8. Alfred Marshall, "The Present Position of Economics," Ibid., p. 173.

9. Ibid., pp. 162, 174.

10. Ibid., pp. 167, 168, 170.

Chapter 13: Economic Differences

Epigraph: Alan Reynolds, *Income and Wealth* (Westport, Connecticut: Greenwood Press, 2006), p. 22.

1. Barack Obama, *Dreams from My Father: A Story of Race and Inheritance* (New York: Crown Publishers, 2007), p. x.

2. "Class and the American Dream," *New York Times,* May 30, 2005, p. A14.

3. E.J. Dionne, Jr., "Political Stupidity, U.S. Style," *Washington Post*, July 29, 2010, p. A23.

4. Peter Corning, *The Fair Society: The Science of Human Nature and the Pursuit of Social Justice* (Chicago: University of Chicago Press, 2011), p. ix.

5. W. Michael Cox and Richard Alm, "By Our Own Bootstraps: Economic Opportunity & the Dynamics of Income Distribution," *Annual Report 1995*, Federal Reserve Bank of Dallas, p. 8.

6. Ibid.

7. "Movin' On Up," *Wall Street Journal*, November 13, 2007, p. A24; U.S. Department of the Treasury, "Income Mobility in the U.S. from 1996 to 2005," November 13, 2007, p. 9.

8. Niels Veldhuis, et al., "The 'Poor' Are Getting Richer," *Fraser Forum*, January/February 2013, p. 25.

9. Armine Yalnizyan, *The Rise of Canada's Richest 1%* (Ottawa: Canadian Centre for Policy Alternatives, December 2010).

10. Thomas Piketty, *Capital in the Twenty-First Century* (Cambridge, Massachusetts: Harvard University Press, 2014), p. 252.

11. Thomas A. Hirschl and Mark R. Rank, "The Life Course Dynamics of Affluence," *PLoS ONE*, January 28, 2015, p. 5.

12. Ibid.

13. Paul Krugman, "Rich Man's Recovery," *New York Times*, September 13, 2013, p. A25.

14. U.S. Department of the Treasury, "Income Mobility in the U.S. from 1996 to 2005," November 13, 2007, p. 4.

15. Thomas Piketty, *Capital in the Twenty-First Century*, pp. 253, 254.

16. Ibid., p. 278.

17. U.S. Department of the Treasury, "Income Mobility in the U.S. from 1996 to 2005," November 13, 2007, pp. 2, 4.

18. Ibid., p. 7.

19. Ibid., pp. 2, 4.

20. Ibid., pp. 9, 11.

21. Internal Revenue Service, "The 400 Individual Income Tax Returns Reporting the Highest Adjusted Gross Incomes Each Year, 1992–2000," *Statistics of Income Bulletin*, Spring 2003, Publication 1136 (Revised 6–03), p. 7.

22. Devon Pendleton and Jack Witzig, "The World's Richest People Got Poorer This Year," *Bloomberg.com*, December 28, 2015; Devon Pendleton and Jack Witzig, "World's Wealthiest Saw Red Ink," *Montreal Gazette*, January 2, 2016, p. B8.

23. Joseph A. Schumpeter, *History of Economic Analysis* (New York: Oxford University Press, 1954), p. 529.

24. Martin Feldstein, "Piketty's Numbers Don't Add Up," *Wall Street Journal*, May 15, 2014, p. A15; Alan Reynolds, "Why Piketty's Wealth Data Are Worthless," *Wall Street Journal*, July 10, 2014, p. A11.

25. Thomas Piketty, *Capital in the Twenty-First Century*, pp. 473, 507; Robert A. Wilson, "Personal Exemptions and Individual Income Tax Rates, 1913–2002," *Statistics of Income Bulletin*, Spring 2002, p. 219.

26. W. Michael Cox and Richard Alm, *Myths of Rich & Poor: Why We're Better Off Than We Think* (New York: Basic Books, 1999), p. 16.

27. See, for example, Chapter 19 ("Government Finance") in the 5th edition of my *Basic Economics: A Common Sense Guide to the Economy* (New York: Basic Books, 2015) or my monograph *"Trickle Down" Theory and "Tax Cuts for the Rich"* (Stanford: Hoover Institution Press, 2012), pp. 1–5.

28. Adrian Dungan and Michael Parisi, "Individual Income Tax Rates and Shares, 2011," *Statistics of Income Bulletin*, Spring 2014, p. 43.

29. Thomas Piketty, *Capital in the Twenty-First Century*, p. 252.

30. Frank Bruni, *Where You Go Is Not Who You'll Be: An Antidote to the College Admissions Mania* (New York: Grand Central Publishing, 2015), p. 105.

31. "Spare a Dime," a special report on the rich, *The Economist*, April 4, 2009, p. 4; "The March of the 400," *Forbes*, September 30, 2002, p. 80.

32. Robert Arnott, William Bernstein, and Lillian Wu, "The Myth of Dynastic Wealth: The Rich Get Poorer," *Cato Journal*, Fall 2015, pp. 461, 467–468.

33. Ibid., p. 470.

34. Ibid., p. 477.

35. Eugene Robinson, "The Fight-Back Plan," *Washington Post*, September 20, 2011, p. A17.

36. Carmen DeNavas-Walt and Robert W. Cleveland, "Money Income in the United States: 2001," *Current Population Reports*, P60–218 (Washington: U.S. Bureau of the Census, 2002), p. 19.

37. U.S. Census Bureau, "Table HINC–05. Percent Distribution of Households, by Selected Characteristics within Income Quintile and Top 5 Percent in 2010," from the *Current Population Survey*, downloaded on October 28, 2014: https://www.census.gov/hhes/www/cpstables/032011/hhinc/new05_000.htm.

38. François Bourguignon, *The Globalization of Inequality*, translated by Thomas Scott-Railton (Princeton: Princeton University Press, 2015), pp. 136–137.

39. "The World's Billionaires," *Forbes*, March 21, 2016, p. 83.

40. Ibid., pp. 83, 98, 140.

41. Charles Murray, *Human Accomplishment: The Pursuit of Excellence in the Arts and Sciences, 800 B.C. to 1950* (New York: Harper Collins, 2003), p. 298.

42. Ibid., pp. 304, 305.

43. Ibid., p. 98.

44. Ibid., pp. 97–100.

45. James Corrigan, "Woods in the Mood to End His Major Drought," *Daily Telegraph* (London), August 5, 2013, pp. 16–17.

46. Charles Murray, *Human Accomplishment*, p. 102.

47. John Powers, "Kenya's Domination in Marathons Has Raised the Level of Running Excellence, and the Rest of the Field Is Still Having a Hard Time Catching Up," *Boston Globe*, April 12, 2013, p. C2.

48. Joseph White, "A 1st in 52 Years: Co-champs at the Spelling Bee," The Associated Press, May 30, 2014.

49. *The Baseball Encyclopedia*, ninth edition (New York: The Macmillan Company, 1993), p. 34.

50. *The Chronicle of Higher Education: Almanac 2014–2015*, August 22, 2014, p. 45.

51. Ibid.

52. U.S. News & World Report, *America's Best Colleges*, 2010 edition (Washington: U.S. News & World Report, 2009), pp. 137, 140, 191.

53. Mohamed Suffian bin Hashim, "Problems and Issues of Higher Education Development in Malaysia," *Development of Higher Education in Southeast Asia: Problems and Issues*, edited by Yip Yat Hoong (Singapore: Regional Institute of Higher Education and Development, 1973), Table 8, pp. 70–71.

54. Previous lists of statistical disparities in outcomes have appeared in such previous books of mine as *The Vision of the Anointed: Self-Congratulation as a Basis for Social Policy* (New York: Basic Books, 1995), pp. 35–37 and

Intellectuals and Society, second edition (New York: Basic Books, 2012), pp. 116–119. Isolated examples have appeared in *Conquests and Cultures: An International History* (New York: Basic Books, 1998), pp. 125, 210, 217; *Migrations and Cultures: A World View* (New York: Basic Books, 1996), pp. 4, 17, 31, 57, 123, 130, 135, 152, 154, 157, 176, 179, 193, 196, 211, 265, 277, 278, 289, 297, 298, 300, 320, 345–346, 353–354, 355, 358, 366, 372–373.

55. See *The Encyclopedia of Native American Economic History*, edited by Bruce E. Johansen (Westport, Connecticut: Greenwood Press, 1999), pp. 235–236.

56. Thomas A. Hirschl and Mark R. Rank, "The Life Course Dynamics of Affluence," *PLoS ONE,* January 28, 2015, p. 5.

57. Alan Reynolds, *Income and Wealth*, pp. 27–28.

58. Stephen Moore, *Who's the Fairest of Them All? The Truth About Opportunity, Taxes, and Wealth in America* (New York: Encounter Books, 2012), p. 4.

59. John Rawls, *A Theory of Justice* (Cambridge, Massachusetts: Harvard University Press, 1971), pp. 43, 60, 61, 265, 302.

60. Thomas Nagel, "The Meaning of Equality," *Washington University Law Review,* January 1979, Issue 1, *Symposium: The Quest for Equality,* p. 26.

61. Woodrow Wilson, *The New Freedom: A Call for the Emancipation of the Energies of a People* (New York: Doubleday, Page & Company, 1913).

62. Angus Deaton, *The Great Escape: Health, Wealth, and the Origins of Inequality* (Princeton: Princeton University Press, 2013), p. 2.

63. Deepak Lal, *Reviving the Invisible Hand: The Case for Classical Liberalism in the Twenty-First Century* (Princeton: Princeton University Press, 2006), p. 136.

64. Angus Deaton, *The Great Escape*, pp. 267–268.

65. "Here, There and Everywhere," *The Economist,* January 19, 2013, pp. 3, 16, 17 of a special report "Outsourcing and Offshoring."

66. "Your Mine Is Mine," *The Economist,* September 3, 2011, p. 64.

67. Lawrence E. Harrison, *Underdevelopment Is a State of Mind: The Latin American Case* (Cambridge, Massachusetts: The Center for International Affairs, Harvard University, 1985), p. 114.

Chapter 14: Implications and Prospects

Epigraph: Paul Johnson, *The Quotable Paul Johnson: A Topical Compilation of His Wit, Wisdom and Satire*, edited by George J. Marlin, et al (New York: Farrar, Strauss and Giroux, 1994), p. 138.

1. John Rawls, *A Theory of Justice* (Cambridge, Massachusetts: Harvard University Press, 1971), p. 73.

2. Ibid., p. 74.

3. Ibid., pp. 79–80.

4. Thomas Piketty, *The Economics of Inequality*, translated by Arthur Goldhammer (Cambridge, Massachusetts: Harvard University Press, 2015), pp. 1–2.

5. Ibid., p. 1.

6. John Rawls, *A Theory of Justice*, pp. 79–80, 82–83.

7. Herman Kahn, *World Economic Development: 1979 and Beyond* (Boulder, Colorado: Westview Press, 1979), pp. 60–61.

8. "Since about 1950, life expectancy at birth has increased 40 percent or more in many low-income countries. This remarkable achievement has, however, received all too little attention. The people of Western Europe and North America never attained so large an increase in life expectancy in so short a period." Theodore W. Schultz, *Investing in People: The Economics of Population Quality* (Berkeley: University of California Press, 1981), p. 35. This trend continued in later years: "Life expectancy in the typical poor country has risen from forty-eight years to sixty-eight years," according to William Easterly, *The White Man's Burden: Why the West's Efforts to Aid the Rest Have Done So Much Ill and So Little Good* (New York: Penguin Press, 2006), p. 155.

9. John Rawls, *A Theory of Justice*, pp. 4, 302, 303.

10. James M. McPherson, *The Abolitionist Legacy: From Reconstruction to the NAACP* (Princeton: Princeton University Press, 1975), p. 198.

11. Alexis de Tocqueville, *Democracy in America*, edited by J.P. Mayer and Max Lerner (New York: Harper & Row, 1966), p. 485.

12. Edward C. Banfield, *The Moral Basis of a Backward Society* (New York: The Free Press, 1958), pp. 19, 20, 76.

13. Nicholas Eberstadt, *Russia's Peacetime Demographic Crisis: Dimensions, Causes, Implications* (Seattle: National Bureau of Asian Research, 2010), p. 259.

14. Stephan Thernstrom and Abigail Thernstrom, *America in Black and White: One Nation, Indivisible* (New York: Simon and Schuster, 1997), pp. 233–234.

15. *The World Almanac and Book of Facts: 2013* (New York: World Almanac Books, 2013), pp. 748, 770, 771, 796, 806, 818, 821, 832, 839, 846; U.S. Census Bureau, "S0201: Selected Population Profile in the United States, 2013 American Community Survey 1-Year Estimates, downloaded from the Census website on November 10, 2014: http://factfinder2.census.gov/faces/tableservices/jsf/pages/productview.xhtml?pid=ACS_13_1YR_S0201&prodType=table.

16. Rupert B. Vance, *Human Geography of the South: A Study in Regional Resources and Human Adequacy* (Chapel Hill: University of North Carolina Press, 1932), p. 463.

17. Bay Area Economics, *San Francisco Housing DataBook* (Berkeley: Bay Area Economics, 2002); Matt Smith, "Legends in Our Own Minds," *SF Weekly*, January 30, 2002, p. 13.

18. See, for example, Stephan Thernstrom and Abigail Thernstrom, "Reflections on *The Shape of the River*," *UCLA Law Review*, Vol. 46, No. 5 (June 1999), pp. 1588–1590; Richard H. Sander and Stuart Taylor, Jr., *Mismatch: How Affirmative Action Hurts Students It's Intended to Help, and Why Universities Won't Admit It* (New York: Basic Books, 2012), pp. 68, 73, 233–244.

19. Joseph Stiglitz, "Equal Opportunity, Our National Myth," *New York Times*, February 17, 2013, Sunday Review, p. 4.

20. Jason L. Riley, *Please Stop Helping Us: How Liberals Make It Harder for Blacks to Succeed* (New York: Encounter Books, 2014), p. 49.

21. John U. Ogbu, *Black American Students in an Affluent Suburb: A Study of Academic Disengagement* (Mahwah, New Jersey: Lawrence Erlbaum Associates, 2003), pp. 23–31.

22. Daniel Bergner, "Class Warfare," *New York Times Magazine*, September 7, 2014, pp. 63, 66.

23. See, for example, Diana Furchtgott-Roth and Christine Stolba, *Women's Figures: An Illustrated Guide to the Economic Progress of Women in America* (Washington: The A.E.I. Press, 1999), Part II; Thomas Sowell, *Economic Facts and Fallacies*, second edition (New York: Basic Books, 2011), Chapter 3.

24. "The Economic Role of Women," *The Economic Report of the President, 1973* (Washington: U.S. Government Printing Office, 1973), p. 105.

25. For statistical data, see Table 1 in my *Affirmative Action Reconsidered: Was It Necessary in Academia?* (Washington: American Enterprise Institute, 1975), p. 16.

26. Donald Harman Akenson, "Diaspora, the Irish and Irish Nationalism," *The Call of the Homeland: Diaspora Nationalisms, Past and Present*, edited by Allon Gal, et al (Leiden: Brill, 2010), pp. 190–191.

27. Steven L. Pease, *Golden Age of Jewish Achievement* (Sonoma, California: Deucalion, 2009), pp. 48–49.

28. Karyn R. Lacy, *Blue-Chip Black: Race, Class, and Status in the New Black Middle Class* (Berkeley: University of California Press, 2007), pp. 66–68, 77; Mary Pattillo-McCoy, *Black Picket Fences: Privilege and Peril Among the Black Middle Class* (Chicago: University of Chicago Press, 1999), p. 12.

29. Donald R. Snodgrass, *Inequality and Economic Development in Malaysia* (Kuala Lumpur: Oxford University Press, 1980), p. 4.

30. Amy L. Freedman, "The Effect of Government Policy and Institutions on Chinese Overseas Acculturation: The Case of Malaysia," *Modern Asian Studies*, Vol. 35, No. 2 (May 2001), p. 416.

31. Michael Ornstein, *Ethno-Racial Inequality in the City of Toronto: An Analysis of the 1996 Census*, May 2000, p. ii.

32. Charles H. Young and Helen R.Y. Reid, *The Japanese Canadians* (Toronto: University of Toronto Press, 1938), pp. 9–10, 49, 53, 58, 76, 120, 129, 130, 145, 172; Tomoko Makabe, "The Theory of the Split Labor Market: A Comparison of the Japanese Experience in Brazil and Canada," *Social Forces*, Vol. 59, No. 3 (March 1981), p. 807 (note 1).

33. Nicholas Kristof, "The Asian Advantage," *New York Times*, October 11, 2015, Sunday Review, pp. 1, 9.

34. Stanford M. Lyman, *Chinese Americans* (New York: Random House, 1974), p. 133.

35. Jack Chen, *The Chinese of America* (San Francisco: Harper & Row, 1980), Chapters 4–10.

36. Stanford M. Lyman, *Chinese Americans*, p. 92.

37. Betty Lee Sung, *The Story of the Chinese in America* (New York: Collier Books, 1971), Chapter 11.

38. William Petersen, *Japanese Americans: Oppression and Success* (New York: Random House, 1971), pp. 13–14.

39. Terrance J. Reeves and Claudette E. Bennett, "We the People: Asians in the United States," *Census 2000 Special Reports* (Washington: U.S. Bureau of the Census, 2004), p. 12.

40. Betty Lee Sung, *The Story of the Chinese in America*, p. 171.

41. Nicholas Kristof, "The Asian Advantage," *New York Times*, October 11, 2015, Sunday Review, pp. 1, 9.

42. Jean Fetter, *Questions and Admissions: Reflections on 100,000 Admissions Decisions at Stanford* (Stanford: Stanford University Press, 1995), p. 45.

43. Ibid., p. 70.

44. John A.A. Ayoade, "Ethnic Management of the 1979 Nigerian Constitution," *Canadian Review of Studies in Nationalism*, Spring 1987, p. 127.

45. Burton W. Folsom, Jr., *The Myth of the Robber Barons: A New Look at the Rise of Big Business in America*, sixth edition (Herndon, Virginia: Young America's Foundation, 2010), pp. 83–92.

46. Rob Kling, "Information Technologies and the Shifting Balance between Privacy and Social Control," *Computerization and Controversy: Value Conflicts and Social Choices*, second edition, edited by Rob Kling (New York: Academic Press, 1996), p. 617. See also Marvin Cetron and Owen Davies, *Probable Tomorrows: How Science and Technology Will Transform Our Lives in the Next Twenty Years* (New York: St. Martin's Press, 1997), p. x.

47. Richard A. Epstein, *Overdose: How Excessive Government Regulation Stifles Pharmaceutical Innovation* (New Haven: Yale University Press, 2006), p. 15.

Chapter 15: Causation versus Blame

1. David S. Landes, *The Wealth and Poverty of Nations: Why Some Are So Rich and Some So Poor* (New York: W.W. Norton & Company, 1998), pp. 4, 6.

2. Stephan Thernstrom and Abigail Thernstrom, *America in Black and White: One Nation, Indivisible* (New York: Simon & Schuster, 1997), pp. 404, 405.

3. Ibid.

4.   Charles Murray, *Human Accomplishment: The Pursuit of Excellence in the Arts and Sciences, 800 BC to 1950* (New York: HarperCollins, 2003), p. 291; Frederick Law Olmsted, *The Cotton Kingdom: A Traveller's Observations on Cotton and Slavery in the American Slave States* (New York: Alfred A. Knopf, 1953), pp. 366, 396. See also pp. 330, 520, 591 and Arthur M. Schlesinger, "Editor's Introduction," Ibid., pp. liv–lv; Daniel J. Boorstin, *The Americans*, Vol. I: *The Colonial Experience* (New York: Random House, 1958), pp. 302, 303, 304; Arthur Herman, *How the Scots Invented the Modern World: The True Story of How Western Europe's Poorest Nation Created Our World & Everything In It* (New York: Crown Publishers, 2001), p. 20.

5.   Leila Morsy and Richard Rothstein, *Five Social Disadvantages That Depress Student Performance: Why Schools Alone Can't Close Achievement Gaps* (Washington: Economic Policy Institute, 2015), p. 7.

6.   John U. Ogbu, *Black American Students in an Affluent Suburb: A Study of Academic Disengagement* (Mahwah, New Jersey: Lawrence Erlbaum Associates, 2003), Chapters 1, 2.

7.   "A New Kind of Ghetto," *The Economist*, November 9, 2013, Special Report on Britain, p. 10.

8.   David Cole, "Can Our Shameful Prisons Be Reformed?" *New York Review of Books*, November 19, 2009, p. 41.

9.   Sara Rimer and Karen W. Arenson, "Top Colleges Take More Blacks, but Which Ones?" *New York Times*, June 24, 2004, pp. A1, A18.

10. Amy Chua and Jed Rubenfeld, *The Triple Package: How Three Unlikely Traits Explain the Rise and Fall of Cultural Groups in America* (New York: The Penguin Press, 2014), p. 42.

11. "Secret Weapon," *The Economist*, June 20, 2015, "Special Report: Nigeria," p. 8.

12. Amy Chua and Jed Rubenfeld, *The Triple Package*, pp. 43–44; U.S. Census, Table DP03, Selected Economic Characteristics, 2006–2010 American Community Survey Selected Population Tables.

13. Paul Krugman, *The Conscience of a Liberal* (New York: W.W. Norton & Company, 2007), p. 11.

14. William D. Phillips, Jr., *Slavery from Roman Times to the Early Transatlantic Trade* (Minneapolis: University of Minnesota Press, 1985), pp. 34, 59; Martin A. Klein, "Introduction: Modern European Expansion and Traditional

Servitude in Africa and Asia," *Breaking the Chains: Slavery, Bondage, and Emancipation in Modern Africa and Asia*, edited by Martin A. Klein (Madison: University of Wisconsin Press, 1993), p. 15.

15. Ulrich Bonnell Phillips, *American Negro Slavery: A Survey of the Supply, Employment and Control of Negro Labor as Determined by the Plantation Regime* (New York: A. Appleton and Company, 1918), pp. 425–426.

16. Sally C. Pipes, *The Top Ten Myths of American Health Care: A Citizen's Guide* (San Francisco: Pacific Research Institute, 2008), p. 9.

17. A condensed, documented account of this process can be found in the essay, "The Real History of Slavery" in my *Black Rednecks and White Liberals* (San Francisco: Encounter Books, 2005).

18. The years were 1953 through 1959. Editors of Sports Illustrated, *Sports Illustrated Almanac 2015* (New York: Sports Illustrated Books, 2014), pp. 44–45.

19. Ibid., p. 50.

20. "The History of Latinos in America's Pastime Isn't Black and White," *The Game We Love: The Sporting News and 125 Years of Baseball*, 2015, p. 27.

21. Editors of Sports Illustrated, *Sports Illustrated Almanac 2015*, p. 78.

22. *The Baseball Encyclopedia*, ninth edition (New York: The Macmillan Company, 1993), pp. 770, 829, 1034–1035, 1053, 1491.

23. Ibid., pp. 776, 783, 1086, 1090, 1216, 1313, 1315.

24. Ibid., p. 2074; T. Wendel, "Joe McGinnity," The National Baseball Hall of Fame and Museum, *The Hall: A Celebration of Baseball's Greats in Stories and Images, The Complete Roster of Inductees* (New York: Little, Brown and Company, 2014), p. 22.

25. Malcolm Macfarlane, *Bing Crosby: Day by Day* (Lanham, Maryland: The Scarecrow Press, 2001), p. 358.

26. Joel Whitburn, *The Billboard Book of Top 40 Hits*, revised and expanded ninth edition (New York: Billboard Books, 2010), p. 870.

27. Robert G. Barrier, "Only the Game Was Real: The Aesthetics and Significance of Re-created Baseball Broadcasting," *Baseball/Literature/ Culture: Essays, 2006–2007*, edited by Ronald E. Kates and Warren Tormey (Jefferson, North Carolina: McFarland & Company, 2008), pp. 41–42; John E. DiMeglio, "Baseball," *Encyclopedia of Southern Culture*, edited by Charles

Reagan Wilson and William Ferris (Chapel Hill: University of North Carolina Press, 1989), pp. 1210–1211.

28. James S. Gardner, et al., "People in the Mountains," *Mountain Geography: Physical and Human Dimensions,* edited by Martin F. Price, et al (Berkeley: University of California Press, 2013), pp. 288–289.

29. J.R. McNeill, *The Mountains of the Mediterranean World: An Environmental History* (New York: Cambridge University Press, 1992), pp. 223, 225–227.

30. Don Funnell and Romola Parish, *Mountain Environments and Communities* (London: Routledge, 2001), p. 157.

31. Ellen Churchill Semple, *Influences of Geographic Environment* (New York: Henry Holt and Company, 1911), p. 579.

32. Don Funnell and Romola Parish, *Mountain Environments and Communities,* p. 170.

33. T.S. Eliot, "The Cocktail Party," *The Complete Poems and Plays: 1909–1950* (New York: Harcourt, Brace and Company, 1952), p. 348.

34. Robert A. McGuire and Philip R.P. Coelho, *Parasites, Pathogens, and Progress: Diseases and Economic Development* (Cambridge, Massachusetts: MIT Press, 2011), pp. 1–2.

Chapter 16: Goals

1. "To Each According to His Abilities," *The Economist,* June 2, 2001, p. 39.

2. Weiying Zhang, *The Logic of the Market: An Insider's View of Chinese Economic Reform,* translated by Matthew Dale (Washington: Cato Institute, 2015), p. 126.

3. Jeffrey D. Sachs, *Common Wealth: Economics for a Crowded Planet* (New York: Penguin Press, 2008), pp. 162–163.

4. Milton & Rose D. Friedman, *Free to Choose: A Personal Statement* (New York: Harcourt Brace Jovanovich, 1980), p. 147.

5. David S. Landes, *The Wealth and Poverty of Nations: Why Some Are So Rich and Some So Poor* (New York: W.W. Norton & Company, 1998), pp. xvii–xviii.

6. See, for example, Joshua Muravchik, *Heaven on Earth: The Rise and Fall of Socialism* (San Francisco: Encounter Books, 2002).

7. David S. Landes, *The Wealth and Poverty of Nations,* p. 172.

8. Ibid., p. 251.

9. Rondo Cameron, *A Concise Economic History of the World: From Paleolithic Times to the Present* (New York: Oxford University Press, 1989), p. 326.

10. "Going Global," *The Economist*, December 19, 2015, p. 107.

11. Cacilie Rohwedder, "Germans, Czechs Are Hobbled by History as Europe Moves Toward United Future," *Wall Street Journal*, November 25, 1996, p. A15; Ulla Dahlerup, "Sojourn in Sudetenland," *Sudeten Bulletin/Central European Review*, December 1965, pp. 395–403.

12. Manohla Dargis, "Young, White and Male? The Role Is Yours," *New York Times*, August 6, 2015, p. C1.

13. Leon Volovici, *Nationalist Ideology and Antisemitism: The Case of Romanian Intellectuals in the 1930s*, translated by Charles Kormos (Oxford: Pergamon Press, 1991), p. 6.

14. Donald L. Horowitz, *Ethnic Groups in Conflict* (Berkeley: University of California Press, 1985), p. 117.

15. Ibid., p. 118.

16. Mary Fainsod Katzenstein, *Ethnicity and Equality: The Shiv Sena Party and Preferential Policies in Bombay* (Ithaca: Cornell University Press, 1979), pp. 137–138.

17. Donald L. Horowitz, *Ethnic Groups in Conflict*, pp. 117–118.

18. Yash Tandon, *Problems of a Displaced Minority: The New Position of East Africa's Asians* (London: Minority Rights Group, 1973), p. 15; C. Harvey Gardiner, *The Japanese and Peru: 1873–1973* (Albuquerque: University of New Mexico Press, 1975), pp. 67–68; J.F. Normano and Antonello Gerbi, *The Japanese in South America: An Introductory Survey with Special Reference to Peru* (New York: The John Day Company, 1943), pp. 109–110.

19. Wolfgang Benz, *A Concise History of the Third Reich*, translated by Thomas Dunlap (Berkeley: University of California Press, 2006), pp. 30–31.

20. Donald L. Horowitz, *Ethnic Groups in Conflict*, p. 122.

21. Ibid., pp. 113–114.

22. Edward Gibbon, *The Decline and Fall of the Roman Empire* (New York: Modern Library, no date), Volume III, p. 105.

23. See my monograph *"Trickle Down" Theory and "Tax Cuts for the Rich"* (Stanford: Hoover Institution Press, 2012), pp. 1–5.

24. Theodore Caplow, Louis Hicks and Ben J. Wattenberg, *The First Measured Century: An Illustrated Guide to Trends in America, 1900–2000* (Washington: The AEI Press, 2001), p. 99.

25. Stanley Lebergott, *Pursuing Happiness: American Consumers in the Twentieth Century* (Princeton: Princeton University Press, 1993), p. 120.

26. Theodore Caplow, et al., *The First Measured Century*, p. 99.

27. Ibid., p. 135.

28. Stanley Lebergott, *Pursuing Happiness*, p. 130.

29. Stanley Lebergott, *The American Economy: Income, Wealth, and Want* (Princeton: Princeton University Press, 1976), p. 334.

30. Stanley Lebergott, *Pursuing Happiness*, p. 112.

31. Theodore Caplow, et al., *The First Measured Century*, pp. 125, 131.

INDEX

528 Wealth, Poverty and Politics